The Grammar of Status Competition

Advance Praise for *The Grammar of Status Competition*

"This is a path-breaking work for understanding the role of status in international politics. Adopting a critical theoretical approach, the book engages status as a discursive formation central to state legitimation practices. Instead of being something objectively measurable or primarily international in orientation, states are shown to compete—and win—in international status competitions of their own making, with international hierarchies invoked for often largely domestic purposes. The book offers a theoretically sophisticated and powerful reading of the 'grammar of status competitions' and of how the discursive and ambiguous nature of status dynamics in international politics is central to political action and subjectivity."
— **Christopher Browning**, University of Warwick

"In this groundbreaking book, Paul Beaumont demonstrates that much of what we think about how states pursue international status is, at best, incomplete. Departing from the conventional wisdom that status-seeking requires international recognition by others, Beaumont shows that, in fact, states construct and seek status markers themselves, even if no international actor grants this process much attention. Illustrating this highly innovative argument with very diverse, but empirically rich and rigorously researched case studies of the Boer War, Norway's education system, and international nuclear control talks, Beaumont firmly brings domestic politics into the discussion of international status, greatly enriching this scholarship for years to come."
— **Jelena Subotic**, Georgia State University

"In this brilliant and provocative book, Paul Beaumont moves the research agenda on states' status-seeking away from international hierarchies and towards domestic politics. Centering the interpretative agency of domestic actors, Beaumont demonstrates that what may appear as 'international' status-seeking may in fact be spatially demarcated and limited to the imagination of domestic governments and other national actors, with little if any relation to international structures or internationally circulating discourses. A must-read for both IR and comparativist scholars with an interest in better understanding the pervasive quest for international status."
— **Ann E. Towns**, University of Gothenburg

The Grammar of Status Competition

International Hierarchies and Domestic Politics

PAUL DAVID BEAUMONT

OXFORD
UNIVERSITY PRESS

Oxford University Press is a department of the University of Oxford.
It furthers the University's objective of excellence in research, scholarship,
and education by publishing worldwide. Oxford is a registered trade mark of
Oxford University Press in the UK and in certain other countries.

Published in the United States of America by Oxford University Press
198 Madison Avenue, New York, NY 10016, United States of America.

© Oxford University Press 2024

All rights reserved. No part of this publication may be reproduced, stored in
a retrieval system, or transmitted, in any form or by any means, without the
prior permission in writing of Oxford University Press, or as expressly permitted
by law, by license or under terms agreed with the appropriate reprographics
rights organization. Inquiries concerning reproduction outside the scope of the
above should be sent to the Rights Department, Oxford University Press, at the
address above.

You must not circulate this work in any other form
and you must impose this same condition on any acquirer

Library of Congress Cataloging-in-Publication Data
Names: Beaumont, Paul David, author.
Title: The grammar of status competition / Paul David Beaumont.
Description: New York, NY : Oxford University Press, 2024. |
Includes bibliographical references and index.
Identifiers: LCCN 2024013778 | ISBN 9780197771778 (hardback) |
ISBN 9780197771792 (epub)
Subjects: LCSH: Strategic Arms Limitation Talks. |
International relations—Philosophy. | International relations and culture. |
Educational change—Norway. | South African War, 1899–1902.
Classification: LCC JZ1310 .B43 2024 | DDC 327.101—dc23/eng/20240405
LC record available at https://lccn.loc.gov/2024013778

DOI: 10.1093/9780197771808.001.0001

Printed by Integrated Books International, United States of America

Dedicated to Kathleen

Contents

Foreword	ix
Acknowledgments	xiii
Abbreviations	xvii
Introduction: Hierarchies of Our Making	1
1. The Logic of Status Competition	36
2. The Grammar of Status Competition	58
3. Rational Illusions: Britain and the Boer War	82
4. Organizing and Resisting Status Competition: How PISA Shocked Norway	122
5. Symmetry over Strategy: How Status Suckered the Superpowers at SALT	157
Conclusion: Domesticating "International" Status	203
Appendix: Studying Status via Discourse	221
References	233
Index	253

Foreword

Benjamin de Carvalho

Human beings are powerfully motivated by the desire for favorable social status comparisons. As research in a number of disciplines has demonstrated, status—understood as one's recognized position in a social hierarchy—figures centrally in social life. Long downplayed in international relations (IR), status-seeking now also stands at the center of a large and growing research program, as *The Grammar of Status Competition* bears witness to.

However, this has not always been so. While we often encounter the contention that the study of polities' status concerns can be traced back to Thucydides, such a sensitivity to status concerns is something quite different from the research agenda which has emerged over the past two decades or so. It could also be argued that while the literature on status in IR is often said to date back to the great classics of modern political theory, I think such claims often obscure more than they are helpful. However, they do serve to help legitimize the status of status as one of the key, perennial, aspirations of states by conferring upon status a status equal to the conventional stuff of high politics: the relentless pursuit of security and the ceaseless appetite for wealth. While status may indeed be a perennial concern to every human community, as it is to the human (social) condition, in terms of making sense of status, what Beaumont calls the recent "waves of status research" remain unparalleled in IR, as do the advances we have made in understanding how status affects the policies of states. Yet a lot remains to be made sense of. How do status concerns affect the international (state) system and its different modes of stratification is one issue that certainly needs further poking, as does the way states' status concerns relate to the people who make up these states—the so-called domestic level. But as with any theoretical advances in the discipline, there is a danger of becoming tired of poking around in the same agenda and that the research innovations move on to another domain without the full implications of the status agenda being known to us.

X FOREWORD

The Grammar of Status Competition is a serious antidote to this. Not only does Paul make sure we keep to our path, but he does so by offering key advances that have long been called for in terms of making sense of states' status-seeking in relation to their domestic constituencies. Paul's point is as remarkable as it is simple, and I can still remember the first time we spoke about it. "Ben, states can both construct status and recognize it at the same time!" Paul erupted during one of our many meetings. Indeed, while human beings are profoundly social, and therefore prone to care more about the other's *regard* than their own self-esteem, states are also profoundly self-sufficient, to the point where speaking to oneself and holding oneself in high esteem can be sufficient. Moving away from the charge that status concerns are irrational to states, Paul's solution to making sense of the prevalence of status concerns in spite of their perceived irrationality is illuminating how competing for "international" status serves domestic functions quite regardless of the international status dividends. As he states in the introduction to this book, "it is possible for states to construct, compete in, and win status competitions of their own making." Doing so also contributes to further problematizing the assumptions about the state as a unitary actor which have both helped and hindered much of the early research on status.

In many ways my job as a foreword writer could be done here. The book is a fantastic achievement and, in my humble and unbiased opinion, a decisive intervention in the debate on status in IR. And while my writings on status may have been the primary reason Paul honored me by asking me to write this foreword, another reason will probably have been my long-term acquaintance with his work as well as our friendship, to which I will turn now.

In the Norwegian university tradition, one of the highlights of any PhD defense is when the supervisor gives their appreciative speech at the doctoral banquet following any successful defense. Norway being the type of country where people have lived a stone's throw away from their closest neighbor since time immemorial, and usually only met for a few annual festivities, emotion-laden words of approval to each other are not part of our *quotidien* but reserved for these festive orchestrated occasions. Tongue in cheek, we could say that to most Norwegian doctoral students, such a speech is probably the first approbation they receive from their guide. And although I like to think that I was kinder and warmer than that to Paul, a COVID-19 online defense deprived us both of the post-viva festivities, and thus also Dr. Beaumont of

FOREWORD xi

his big chance to receive a public, official, and overly emotional approbation from his supervisor.

So, in accepting the honor of writing this foreword, I feel it expected of me to stay true to this Germano-Norwegian tradition and deliver on what the pandemic took away from Paul, while at the same time straying from it and indulging in a bit of a roast in my contextualization of the extraordinary endeavor this book represents.

Now a wonderful colleague, I have known Paul for over a decade, ever since he first started his graduate studies and submitted his first (pretty damning) book review of Risse, Ropp, and Sikkink's *The Power of Human Rights* with the punchline "But states are not humans and traffic lights are not human rights." Our common trajectory has been quite an adventure, which in the end has been at least as rewarding to me if not more than it has been to him. To be fair, and in order not to fall into the trap of being overly laudable here, it is certainly true that not all parts of the journey were equally rewarding. I for one have learned more than I ever cared to know about the United Kingdom's nuclear weapon's program, Trident (the subject of Paul's master's dissertation and first book)—a knowledge I would gladly have kept at the level I had from *Yes Minister*:

SIR HUMPHREY: With Trident we could obliterate the whole of Eastern Europe.

JIM HACKER: I don't want to obliterate the whole of Eastern Europe.

Which, as it happens, also perhaps nicely summarizes Paul's early academic interests. One of my academic heroes, Gianfranco Poggi, once started a lecture by stating that "there are two ways of learning about politics. One is reading Max Weber. The other is watching *Yes Minister*." All in all, though, it has to be said that it has been a huge intellectual and social pleasure to be able to accompany Paul on his academic trajectory, and the results never cease to impress me.

But, again, I ramble . . . It is said that Winston Churchill once wrote the following:

Writing a book is an adventure. To begin with it is a toy and an amusement. Then it becomes a mistress, then it becomes a master, then it becomes a tyrant. The last phase is that just as you are about to be reconciled to your servitude, you kill the monster and fling him to the public.

xii FOREWORD

This has never been truer of any writing process, although Churchill's quote says little about the quality of the work flung to the audience. In this case, let me end by saying that I am proud beyond words to write this short *vignette* and I hope these few words have done justice to an endeavor and a book which by any measure is a huge accomplishment!

Norwegian Institute of International Affairs
Oslo

Acknowledgments

This book benefited from the generosity and insight from numerous people, so many that I will almost certainly neglect to mention some here. Where to begin is a difficult question, but this book's genesis can be traced to those teaching the IR program at the Norwegian University of Life Sciences (NMBU), where I did my master's and PhD. Established to offer a much needed counterpoint to the methodological conservatism of Oslo's political science department, the IR program was entering its third year when I arrived as a mature student back in 2012. The program was animated by the relentless energy and open-door policy of Stig Jarle Hansen, who headed and held together the IR program of 50 students with just 2.6 full-time professors. The theoretical pluralism that would prove formative for my research and this book was baked into the IR theory course design. Halvard Leira and my later master's thesis and PhD supervisor, Benjamin de Carvalho, brought IR theory to life with a double act that was part Socratic dialogue, part inside-baseball romp through IR past and present. One that opened with the history, philosophy, and sociology of IR theory—the myths that IR still teaches us (de Carvalho, Leira, and Hobson 2011)—and dedicated as much time to poststructuralism as it did to realism. The exam would include the option to respond to the prompt. "War. Discuss."

While I initially recoiled from the postmodernist sirens, with the help of Ben and my peers John Todd and Anders Bjørkheim, I would eventually embrace the Copenhagen School in my master's thesis that formed the basis of my first book (Beaumont 2021). In short, as I was trying to make sense of the United Kingdom's nuclear storytelling, I realized I needed an approach that took language to be ontologically and thus politically significant as a meaning-*producing* force. At the time, I wrote an email to Lene Hansen (2006) thanking her for her writing *Security as Practice* and thereby explaining poststructuralist discourse analysis in a way I could understand and put into practice. But in retrospect, it was her work together with the openness to discourse analysis and the rigor with which it was taught at NMBU that I am convinced proved crucial to my career and ultimately this book.

xiv ACKNOWLEDGMENTS

It was while I was beginning my master's thesis at NMBU that I happened to move into a shared student house with Pål Røren. Sometimes you just get lucky, and I got lucky with Pål: not only did he become my long-term co-author, but even better, my good (and bad) idea detector, last-minute proofreader, mock-job-interviewer, and much more besides. Every aspiring academic needs a Pål in their lives. It was also Pål who introduced me to status research, and thus downstream led me to declare—somewhat absurdly—in my PhD research proposal that I would strive to do for status research what securitization did for security studies. Remarkably that plan remained intact during my PhD and, following the anonymous reviewers' (constructive and generous) advice, became even more central in this book.

It is a cliché that books often tell you more about the context within which they were written than the phenomenon they would explain. I hope that is not too true for this work, but it is probably not a coincidence that the core of this argument was forged in a period punctuated by Brexit, the election of Trump, and the subsequent coining of the term "posttruth politics" (see Tallis 2016). The observation that great swaths of U.S. and British politics seemed not only to disagree but to operate using radically different understandings of reality (Beaumont 2019a) surely made the thesis of this book more intuitively plausible, evident, and salient: that the international status hierarchies to which domestic actors refer and respond may be as much a product of their parochial discourse as they are reflections of international "collective beliefs." Moreover, governments' and states' success in their status quests may not depend upon international recognition as much as whether it satisfies domestic audiences. Thus, I should acknowledge, if not thank, the Brexiters and Trump for rendering this quality of "international" status unusually visible during the genesis of my PhD.

I am in debt to a host of scholars whose generous and critical engagement helped sharpen the argument and who were instrumental in bringing it to the press. First and foremost my two long-suffering PhD supervisors constituted a dream team. Benjamin de Carvalho played the reviewer 1 role: a source of optimism amid my darker moments and a reliable source of inspiration and reading recommendations. Operating as my personal reviewer 2, Kirsti Stuvøy provided the necessary curb on Ben's enthusiasm, asking difficult questions at the right times and helping me clarify the fuzz and streamline the tangential. Meanwhile Ayse Zarakol, Brent Steele, Katharina Glaab, Halvard Leira, Stig Jarle Hansen, and Ann Towns were tasked with reviewing earlier versions of the manuscript at key points in the process; each undertook this task with characteristic verve and insight. The PhD that formed the basis of this book would then be cross-examined by Bill Wohlforth and Rebecca Adler Nissen, whose feedback and encouragement would catalyze the transformation of the PhD into the book you are reading now.

Following my PhD, I had the good fortune to become a senior researcher at the Norwegian Institute of International Affairs (NUPI). NUPI has supported this book project from the moment I arrived there in 2020. I have been blessed with inspiring and motivating Principal Investigators (Elana Wilson Rowe, Cedric de Coning, Julie Wilhelmson, and Jon Harald Sande Lie) as well as intellectual, financial, and emotional support from my research group leaders (Kristin Fjaestad and Morten Anderson) and NUPI's research director (Ole Jacob Sending). Taken together, NUPI has provided the scholarly milieu and resources for making this book a timely reality: not only providing me with dedicated months ring-fenced for the project but also organizing a book workshop where the brilliant Chris Browning and Anders Wivel could help me ready the manuscript for review. A special mention should go to my research group, GOaD, who in the run-up to my final submission spent days hotly debating potential titles for the book on our group chat, even harnessing AI for the purposes. (AI skeptics will be pleased to learn that ChatGPT has some way to go before it can replace the human hive mind. Its suggestion was not exactly snappy: "Status Games in the International Hierarchy: Unraveling Useful Illusions and Domestic Politics in Status Competition.")

Beyond NUPI and NMBU, the book's core arguments have been formed and fine-tuned following critical engagement from dozens of others at workshops, conferences, and seminars. Crucial here was Adam Lerner, my "book buddy." We exchanged feedback on our book manuscripts early in 2021—his astute comments and thorough reading were invaluable for kickstarting my process of revising my PhD into a book. For the record, I definitely got the better end of the bargain, as his manuscript (Lerner 2022) was already in award-winning shape; at best he perhaps just needed someone to confirm it. Likewise, I am indebted to the generosity of spirit and wisdom of Nick Onuf, who read early work that would prove foundational for the book and gave extensive constructive and critical feedback on the full book manuscript too. A number of others deserve special mention for their critical engagement with my ideas and/or for generally facilitating its formation in one way or another: Kristin Haugevik, Øyvind Svendsen, Marina Duque, Joakim Brattvoll, Felix Anderl, Lucas de Oliveira Paes, Minda Holm, Cristiana

xvi ACKNOWLEDGMENTS

Maglia, Steven Ward, Audrey Alejandro, Bjørnar Sverdrup-Thygeson, Tim Richardson, Julia Rone, Patrick Thadeus Jackson, Fabricio Chagas-Bastos, Rolf Hansen, Wrenn Yennie Lindgren, Alex Yu-Ting Lin, Ellen Stenslie, Joshua Freedman, Inanna Hamati-Ataya, Andreas Gofas, Shai Divon, Berit Bliesemann de Guevara, Ana Flamind, Barbara Gruber, Anahita Arian, Daniela Morgen, Jason Sharman, Adrian Rogstad, Srdjan Vucetic, Kostas Zivas, Sophia Marie, Rob Gruijters, Olga Löblová, Neil Davey, Ben Tallis, Andy White, and David Hughes.

Last but certainly not least, I want to thank my wife. It is not easy birthing and raising two kids at the best of times, and the job is not made easier when your partner is working on a book manuscript. I am thankful you stuck with me and (more or less) patiently tolerated the occasions when my mind was on the book when it should have been on our family.

Funding

This book benefited from funding from the Norwegian Research Council project DEVINT (315356).

Abbreviations

ABM	antiballistic missile
ALCM	air-launched cruise missile
CPI	country performance indicator
EU	European Union
FRUS	*Foreign Relations of the United States*
ICBM	intercontinental ballistic missiles
IR	international relations (the discipline)
JCS	Joint Chiefs of Staff
MAD	mutually assured destruction
MIRV	multiple independent reentry vehicle
MP	member of Parliament
NATO	North Atlantic Treaty Organization
NGO	nongovernmental organization
Nimby	Not in my back yard(er)
NPT	Non-Proliferation Treaty
NSC	U.S. National Security Council
OECD	Organisation for Economic Co-operation and Development
PISA	Programme for International Student Assessment
SALT	Strategic Arms Limitation Talks
SIT	social identity theory
SLBM	submarine-launched ballistic missile
TIS	theories of international status

Introduction

Hierarchies of Our Making

At the Strategic Arms Limitation Talks (SALT; 1969–1979), President Nixon and his team were negotiating to curtail the nuclear arms race between the superpowers that threatened the survival of both the superpowers and the planet's capacity to support human civilization. Yet despite the high stakes, the backstage discussions of the U.S. negotiating strategy belied a preoccupation with how international and especially domestic audiences would understand the outcome of the treaty, quite besides whether it would serve its intended purpose. As Nixon complained to his deputy assistant for national security affairs in the concluding stages of SALT I, "[E]verybody is going to be watching the darn thing. *Who won? Who lost?* . . . Did we get, you know, suckered here by these people and the rest?" (my emphasis).[1] Indeed, avoiding *looking* like the sucker was at least as important as avoiding getting suckered, as President Nixon explained, not only did the US have to worry about getting a deal "that is sound" but "that about half of this battle—maybe a little more than half—it's got to appear that way. It's got to appear that way."[2] Nixon's obsession with appearing to win—or at least appearing to avoid defeat—during SALT may come as a surprise to traditionalists within the field of international relations (IR), who assume that high politics is the domain of hard-headed strategic analysis. However, it does align with a burgeoning body of research that documented how concerns about international status drive a broad array of foreign policymaking.

Indeed, this book contributes to the recent waves of status research that have swelled the field of IR over the course of the past two decades.[3] Stripped

---

[1] Conversation among President Nixon, the Chief of the Delegation to the Strategic Arms Limitation Talks (Smith), and the President's Deputy Assistant for National Security Affairs (Haig), *FRUS 1969–1976*, vol. 32, p. 721.

[2] Conversation among President Nixon, the Chief of the Delegation to the Strategic Arms Limitation Talks (Smith), and the President's Deputy Assistant for National Security Affairs (Haig), Washington, March 21, 1972, *FRUS 1969–1976*, vol. 32, p. 723.

[3] Key works include but are not limited to Larson and Shevchenko (2003, 2010, 2019); Paul, Larson, and Wohlforth (2014); Wohlforth (2009); Renshon (2016, 2017); Stolte (2015); Ward (2013, 2017a,

---

The Grammar of Status Competition. Paul David Beaumont, Oxford University Press. © Oxford University Press 2024.
DOI: 10.1093/9780197771808.003.0001

2 THE GRAMMAR OF STATUS COMPETITION

to its core, this research agenda has set about substantiating the claim that states often undertake activities to improve their social status in international hierarchies and avoid activities that threaten their position. Here, status is conventionally defined as "collective beliefs about a given state's *ranking* on valued attributes" (Larson, Paul, and Wohlforth 2014, p. 7). Simplifying, these collective beliefs are theorized as a social structure to which states *respond*, given their position and/or the nature of the hierarchy.[4] The usual methodological procedure then involves demonstrating that foreign policies that appear irrational from conventional approaches become tractable if we assume a motivation for international status (rather than wealth or security). Variations on this operation have succeeded in providing compelling and sophisticated explanations for war-waging (e.g., Ward 2017b), arms-racing (Murray 2018), as well as humanitarian aid (de Carvalho and Neumann 2015b), big science projects (Gilady 2018), and even Brexiting (Beaumont 2017). Moreover, status research has shed new light on the behavior of great powers, small powers, and rising powers across a range of historical periods. In short order, this research agenda has documented how states of all sorts often spend considerable time, energy, and even blood and treasure trying to impress their peers on the world stage.

There is a hitch, however. While status scholars have proven highly adept at cataloguing instances of status-seeking, they have been less adept at showing how status-seeking has led to higher status (Macdonald and Parent 2021, pp. 367–8). Instead, research that has addressed the question of whether status-seeking works makes sombre reading for status seekers. It strongly suggests the quest for status recognition in international society is usually grueling and often unfair (see Naylor 2018; Ward 2013; Pouliot 2014; Zarakol 2010a). History stacks the deck in favor of early entrants to

---

2017b); Dafoe, Renshon, and Huth (2014); Duque (2018); De Carvalho and Neumann (2015b); Wohlforth, de Carvalho, Neumann, and Leira (2017); Murray (2010, 2018); Clunan (2009, 2014); Freedman (2016, 2020); Gilady (2017, 2018); Wolf (2011, 2019); Subotic and Vucetic (2019); Pu (2019); Deng (2008); Naylor (2018, 2022); Krickovic and Chang (2020); Barnhart (2016, 2020); Onea (2014); Beaumont (2017a); Mälksoo (2021); Røren (2019, 2020, 2023); Yanik and Subotic (2021); Schulz, (2017).

[4] Mattern and Zarakol (2016, p. 637) call this "the logic of positionality." By far the two largest and longest running research agendas—Status Discrepancy Theory (Galtung 1964; Volgy and Mayhall 1995; Volgy et al. 2011, 2014; Renshon 2016, 2017), and Larson and Shevchenko's translation of Social Identity Theory (2003, 2010, 2014; Larson 2019)—both theorize the international status hierarchy as a structure to which states, conceived of as singular actors, respond. Also influential is Wohlforth (2009), who theorizes how variance in overall structure (polarity) affects prevalence of status competition.

INTRODUCTION   3

international society, which having established the rules of the game on their terms, can move the goalposts, and generally gatekeep with little justice or consistency. Even model members of international society can expect a long slog before they acquire higher status (Beaumont and Røren 2020). Even worse for status seekers, recent work suggests that while status-seeking is ubiquitous in world politics,[5] the quest is theoretically prone to prove futile (Mercer 2017). This argument runs that because status is relative, other states have built in incentives to discount good performance, hold back recognition, and thus preserve their own status position. According to Mercer (2017, p. 168), alleged gains from seeking status are psychological illusions, and thus policymakers should cease trying to "chase what you cannot catch."

Ultimately, these findings paint a depressing picture for status seekers but also present a puzzle: Why is status-seeking so prevalent in international relations when the rewards are so ephemeral and perhaps illusionary? Mercer's solution is that status-seeking is in fact an irrational pastime that states will eventually learn to give up. Here, I seek to provide an alternative answer that does not require governments past and present to have been fools. Moreover, my theoretical solution opens up an important new vector for studying the influence of status on world politics: investigating "international" status as a domestic practice, one that can (de)legitimate both domestic and foreign policies regardless of whether international recognition is forthcoming.[6]

Expressed at its boldest, this book contends that it is possible for states to construct, compete in, and win status competitions of their own making. Citizens can take pride and governments can generate legitimacy from topping a "status" hierarchy without international audiences being party to the hierarchy in question.[7] Put more humbly, I suggest that states have varying degrees of leeway to *develop* and *maintain* competitive hierarchical constructions of the world that are not actively shared or recognized by international audiences yet remain salient and have political effects domestically. As a result, governments can enjoy benefits of status-seeking in terms of legitimacy, without being beholden to international recognition.

---

[5] While there is disagreement about just about everything else, a growing consensus among IR scholars exists that states and leaders are often obsessed with status and that status matters a great deal in world politics (Dafoe, Renshon, and Huth 2014).

[6] I have put *international* in quotation marks here because this book concerns domestically produced *representations* of international hierarchy and international status.

[7] This theoretical possibility is unlikely to be realized in practice, though North Korean citizens may come pretty close.

4 THE GRAMMAR OF STATUS COMPETITION

This has been overlooked, I will argue, because prior works have tended to bracket the domestic audience and thus overstate the degree of intersubjective agreement about international status and understate the degree of interpretative agency located within domestic discourses. Moreover, if this were the case, it would provide a theoretically informed answer for how states could "compete" for positional status without its manifesting in a zero-sum game. It would also help explain why states undertake what look like wasteful status quests, despite international recognition being so difficult to come by.

If this sounds outlandish, consider Benedict Anderson's (1991) famous claim that the nation is an imagined community comprised of the stories that people tell about their collective self. Crucially, these narratives need not be empirically accurate nor accepted and recognized by other imagined communities for them to inform, inspire, and legitimate collective action on behalf of that community. Indeed, unlike humans, states contain people and social groups that can provide *both* a source for narratives *and* sites of recognition for those same narratives. For instance, several countries lay claim to an exceptionalism that would not travel far beyond the members of their community, yet these representations of the nation's *position*—exceptional compared to the unexceptionals—are often intimately imbricated in these countries' domestic politics of legitimation.[8] While Anderson does not mention it, it is a short jump from being able to imagine one's community progressing through time and space to imagining communities competing in a hierarchy.[9] How we can identify and study systematically these imagined "international" hierarchies, as they become manifested and contested in domestic discourse, together with how they affect political processes, is the theoretical contribution of this book. The next section reviews the extant status literature to develop the theoretical warrant for this approach by explaining how I build upon but also depart from prior works, especially those that have theorized how domestic processes inform international status-seeking.

---

[8] Perhaps the most well-known are the United States, Russia, China, and Israel. Yet if one looks closely enough, most countries' national narrative contains elements of exceptionalism. See Restad (2014) for a compelling illustration of why narratives of exceptionalism matter in U.S. politics.

[9] These national narratives depend upon the "idea of a sociological organism moving calendrically through homogeneous, empty time" and thus allow it to be "conceived as a solid community moving steadily down (or up) history" (Anderson 1991, p. 26).

The Trouble with Structural Theories of International Status

While status research in IR has only gathered and sustained momentum over the past two decades, it has a long and strong pedigree in IR. Classic thinkers such as Thucydides, Hobbes, and Machiavelli all recognized status, or close synonyms, as an important driver of "man," while Hans Morgenthau and Robert Gilpin considered prestige to be integral to great power politics (see de Carvalho and Neumann 2015a, p. 2).[10] This intellectual heritage has been buttressed by social psychology, evolutionary biology, neuroscience, and economics research that demonstrates that individuals often forgo prosperity and even security to pursue higher social status for them and their group (Paul, Larson, and Wohlforth 2014). Building upon these foundations, what I call the "first wave" of IR status research[11] has primarily theorized how the international hierarchy and a state's position within it encourage or trigger various types of status-seeking behaviors that otherwise appear irrational (Mattern and Zarakol 2016, pp. 639–641). Challenging the mainstream rationalist theories of IR, first-wave status research has proven exceptionally successful in establishing status as a significant driver of international politics across time and space.

Yet as strong as IR status research's micro-foundations may be, translating theories designed for either humans or groups that operate within a domestic society onto states within international society presents tricky theoretical and methodological challenges (Wohlforth 2009, pp. 34–38). The difficulty is most apparent if we treat status-seeking as a process rather than a discrete response to structure. Stripping it down to its most basic form (whether individual, group, or state), status-seeking can be reduced to a simple continuous process:

1. An actor assesses their status in a hierarchy of other actors.
2. The actor responds to their status position by seeking status.
3. Upon undertaking the status-seeking activity, the actor receives recognition of their new status, and the process begins afresh.

---

[10] The status discrepancy research agenda inspired by Jonas Galtung (1962) burned only briefly in the early 1970s (Wallace 1972, 1973; East 1972). However, this approach has been rekindled—with some success—recently by Volgy and colleagues (2011, 2014) and Renshon (2016, 2017).

[11] By "first wave" we do not mean building from ex nihilo; however, I would argue that the status research that took off in IR in the 2000s is the first sustained collective effort that has had and will have a permanent impact on the field of IR.

6 THE GRAMMAR OF STATUS COMPETITION

First-wave status research has proven extremely successful at empirically documenting stage 2 in the process, which is usually the dependent variable.[12] Such is IR's predilection that the earliest status theories concentrated on explaining great power war as a type of status-seeking: as an attempt to overthrow the international hierarchy itself and remake the rules granting them more favorable status and institutional privileges (e.g., Gilpin 1983); a rational strategy, whereby war is a sensible response to the international hierarchy which systematically rewards war-wagers with more recognition (e.g., Renshon 2016, 2017); the bubbling up of frustration born from international society's lack of recognition that leads to states lashing out (e.g., Volgy et al. 2011, 2014; see also Murray 2018). Beyond war, status research has expanded the range of stage 2 outcomes to different types of state and other status-seeking policies. For instance, some suggest small states seek status by being the best at doing good (Wohlforth et al. 2017; de Caravalho and Neumann 2014; Røren 2019). Stage 2 also encompasses attempts to *reform* the rules of the hierarchy. IR's translation of social identity theory (SIT; Tajifel and Turner 1979) theorizes how states dissatisfied with their status may attempt to redefine a quality in a positive manner such that international society is persuaded to grant the actor higher status (Larson and Shevchenko 2003, 2010, 2014, 2019). Thus, social creativity should be understood as an attempt at revisionism but without violence. Here socially creative states wish to reform the rules, but they know what the rules are—and thus where they stand—in the first place. At this point, stage 2 enjoys firm empirical support (Ward 2017b, p. 38; Wohlforth 2019, p. 2): once IR scholars began looking, they spotted status-seeking everywhere.

Yet, within the first wave of status research, stages 1 and 3 are seldom *empirically* investigated, but are glossed over in both theory and analysis.[13] Rather than investigating how actors actually *assess* their status, IR scholars have tended to make that assessment on their behalf (Mercer 2017, p. 138; see also Wolf 2019), and set about theorizing and operationalizing how various sorts of international hierarchy produce different types of stage 2 outcome.[14]

---

[12] Though not always: see Duque (2018); Røren and Beaumont (2019); Renshon (2016); Buarque (2022).

[13] This is not true of status discrepancy scholarship, however; the proxies that are used to measure recognition—counting and ranking the number of diplomatic embassies a state receives—are at best crude (Røren and Beaumont 2019, pp. 5–6).

[14] Notably, Renshon explicitly backs up this assumption that states know their status by citing research that people who interact have a (surprisingly) good grasp of their in-group's status. Renshon uses this to underpin his assumption that leaders of states understand where their state stands in the international status hierarchy (Renshon 2017, pp. 50–51). This book's argument does not directly

INTRODUCTION 7

For Larson and Shevchenko (2003, 2010, 2014, 2019), it is the legitimacy and permeability of the international hierarchy that matters. Wohlforth (2009) theorizes how variance in polarity affects status competition; status discrepancy research theorizes how differences between level of recognition and "objective" status attributes produce different responses (Volgy et al. 2011, 2014; Renshon 2016, 2017). What all these approaches share is that there is such a thing as "collective beliefs about a given state's *ranking* on valued attributes" (Larson, Paul, and Wohlforth 2014, p. 7) and that states thus know their status in the international hierarchy, even if they may consider it unfair and wish to revise it. Indeed, as Mercer (2017, p. 138) notes, "traditional" (I would prefer "first-wave") status theories assume that "actors and observers will agree on what constitutes prestige, and they will update their beliefs about prestige accordingly. A state might believe that other states underestimate its prestige, but everyone knows who has how much prestige." Thus, although logically prior to any status-seeking strategy (stage 2 outcome), states' ability to assess their own status—at stages 1 and 3—has mostly been treated as unproblematic.[15]

This background assumption provides the premise and the promise of a truly structural theory of international status-seeking, one where "international" or factors external to a given state can be used as an independent variable. If states did share a common understanding of the international status hierarchy, then if scholars could just get a sound enough theory of how states respond to variation in that hierarchy, they could explain and predict when particular types of status-seeking will obtain. Moreover, this assumption underpins a crucial methodological shortcut for studying status: because every state is presumed to understand its position in a given international

---

contradict Renshon because it concerns discursive theories about international status within domestic politics rather than individual leaders' comprehension of their state's international status. It would be quite possible and even likely that a leader's private view and public expressions about their state's international status diverge.

[15] There are some partial exceptions among those I just mentioned. First, Wohlforth (2009) theorizes how ambiguity about status prompts status competition. Yet Wohlforth's ambiguity concerns only ambiguity produced by states ranking above one another in different valued attributes selected by Wohlforth. Thus, Wohlforth has already determined that states agree upon what those three key dimensions of status are and *how* these various attributes should be counted and ranked. Meanwhile, Gilpin's (1983) classic work notes that status is "imponderable," but he is referring mainly to reputation for power and the implication that he draws from this is that it can be clarified only via war. In contrast, my concern with status's ambiguity emphasizes its "productive" effects, that is, how it enables multiple divergent status theories to coexist at the same time and the political agency this generates for domestic actors to theorize status to suit their interests.

8   THE GRAMMAR OF STATUS COMPETITION

status hierarchy, there is no need to empirically investigate (or theorize) how different states perceive the very nature of the hierarchy itself. Thus, rather than empirically investigating how individual states *assess* their status, first-wave status scholarship assumes it on their behalf with the goal of explaining their *response* to their position in preexisting and well-understood international hierarchies (see Zarakol 2017, p. 12).

Yet, at the same time as positing the existence of some kind of international social structure to which all states have access, the same scholars also insist status is perceptual, contextual, and intersubjective (Paul, Larson, and Wohlforth 2014). Thus, to posit an (international) structural theory of status demands that states agree upon the "valued attributes" *and* interpret other states' collective beliefs about those attributes accurately enough to gauge their position. This assumption is rendered potentially plausible—leaving the structural aspirations of status theories intact—via simplifying assumptions about who or what does the assessing: realism-inspired models treat the state as unitary (e.g., Khong 2019); SIT-based approaches (tacitly) anthropomorphize the state;[16] some theorize that *the leader* experiences and acts upon status concerns (e.g., Renshon 2017, pp. 41–42; Dafoe and Caughey 2016); others "zoom in" on diplomats' field of practice (e.g., Pouliot 2014, 2016; Røren 2019).[17] While all four approaches imply quite different explanations of status-seeking, they all address the challenge of intersubjective agreement about status by abstracting away or bypassing any disagreement *within the domestic politics* about either stage 1 or 3 in the status-seeking process outlined above. While there is nothing a priori wrong with simplifying assumptions, and it would be certainly useful if we could study status without getting our hands dirty with the domestic, it does beg the question: To what extent does excluding domestic audiences, actors, and processes from theories of international status matter?

Domesticating International Status.

This book argues that it matters a lot. In fact, I argue that the solution to the puzzle outlined above—why states seek status with such vigor when the

---

[16] Or at least the many works that use Larson and Shevchenko's translation of SIT. Ward (2017a, 2019) explicitly brings the individual level back. I will discuss this research below.

[17] Pouliot's (2014, 2016) approach is less a simplifying assumption than a different level of analysis. However, it is relevant here because it can be understood as a means—very effective on its own terms—of overcoming the methodological problem presented by trying to investigate "international" status.

INTRODUCTION 9

rewards seem so ephemeral—is located in status scholars' underapprecia-tion of the double interpretative role of domestic actors in stage 1 and stage 3. Contests within domestic discourse shape a state's own understanding of what its international status is prior to any status-related policy outcome *and* again in the evaluation of that strategy.[18] Crucially, as I will show in the chapters that follow, domestic actors do not necessarily agree about what status *is* and thus their state's status, let alone whether their perception of status aligns with that of international audiences. Indeed, bringing in the do-mestic and investigating status-seeking as a *process* can both solve the puzzle and underpin a new framework for analyzing the domestic production and contestation of "international" status and how these processes affect policy outcomes. In so doing, I build upon the growing body of what I call "second-wave" status research, in which scholars have begun to illuminate the ana-lytical cost of treating the state as unitary and assuming that states share and respond to a common understanding of international hierarchies.

Indeed, the success of the "first wave" has generated a second wave of status research that has begun to develop, nuance, and often question the pi-oneering works of the first wave. The defining feature of this second wave is that, rather than using conventional rational theories as a foil and showing how status concerns explain outcome, they take for granted that status matters but challenge the first-wave status theories theoretically and/or methodologically to develop and refine our understanding of international status dynamics.[19] This book picks up and builds upon one of the most prom-ising areas of the second wave of status research: research that problematizes and theorizes how domestic political processes enable status-seeking and/or respond to international status dynamics. These works take issue with the first wave's tendency to treat states as unitary actors (Pu 2019; Ward 2017a, 2017b, 2022; Powers and Renshon 2023), thereby eliding domestic politics and thus the complexity it generates for aspiring theorists of status-seeking in world politics.

---

[18] As I alluded to earlier and explain in more depth in chapter 2, this does not imply status is sub-jective: the people within a group (in this case, the state) are still subjects, and their discussions of their own status are still intersubjective. Thus, they are still limited by the intersubjective structures—discourses—to which they and their audience are party to.

[19] For instance, the debate that has ensued around how to measure, conceptualize, and assess status recognition to be a paradigmatic example of second-wave status research (Mercer 2017; Duque 2018; Ward 2020; Røren and Beaumont 2019; Røren 2023). Here, the limitations of using embassies as a global proxy for status recognition have been rendered explicit and prompted more careful use of these data and inspired the development of new methods for assessing status recognition (Buarque 2023, 2022, 2019).

More Than Vanity: Status and Legitimacy

Recent works have shown how treating the state as unitary occludes a crucial mechanism encouraging governments to seek status: to bolster domestic legitimacy. Indeed, without paying attention to domestic legitimacy one could easily reach Jonathon Mercer's (2017, p. 168) conclusion that scholars must resort to using "vanity to explain prestige policies." Yet, unpacking the state, Steven Ward (2017b, pp. 37–38) develops a more satisfying mechanism (see also Powers and Renshon 2023). Critiquing IR's popular translation of SIT,[20] Ward (2017a) draws attention to the original, which suggests individuals may disidentify with the in-group if they cannot make positive status comparisons with outgroups. Indeed, as the pioneers of SIT in social psychology Tajfel and Turner (1979, p. 44) note, where possible, "low status may tend, in conditions of unsatisfactory social identity, to promote the widespread adoption of individual mobility strategies." This is bad news for a low-status social *group*:

> Insofar as individual mobility implies disidentifaction [it can] create obstacles to mobilizing group members for collective action over their common interests. Thus the low morale that follows from negative social identity can set in motion disintegrative processes. (Tajfel and Turner 1978, p. 44)

It should be apparent why this would immediately be relevant to states. Put simply, mobilizing citizens for collective action over their common interests is a pretty good definition of the state's purpose, not least during war (see Sambanis, Skaperdas, and Wohlforth 2015, p. 280). Ignoring this would be justifiable if people had no option but to identify with the state (as most status research tacitly tends to presume), but given the existence of secessionist movements in many if not most states, this is not something a "rational" state can afford to ignore.[21] But beyond maintaining self-esteem, citizens may value international status for realist reasons, or perhaps they may merely see rank in a particular

---

[20] This theory was pioneered by Larson and Shevchenko (2003, 2010, 2014, 2019), who rework the original social psychology SIT for studying international politics. Whereas in the original SIT, one of the status-seeking strategies involves individuals leaving their group, in the translation all strategies become group strategies. This cuts off both analytical possibilities of studying the effects of status-seeking at the domestic level (Ward 2017a, 2019).

[21] But even if secessionist movements are not plausible, they may lead to an individual identifying more strongly with other group identities available: religious, supranational (e.g., EU), family or clan (etc).

activity as a good measure of their government's competence. Regardless of the precise reason, if citizens value international status, then seeking it becomes a matter of domestic legitimacy,[22] and status-seeking a prudent part of statecraft rather than mere "vanity" (e.g., Mercer 2017). This implies that international status can and does become implicated in domestic political debates about the legitimacy of the government and can be understood as a "political resource that influences domestic contests over foreign policy" (Ward 2017b, p. 4). Certainly, given that status-seeking is usually costly and wasteful, it would appear unlikely that even vain leaders would pursue status at the risk of losing support;[23] it seems far more likely that where possible they will strategically use status-seeking to satiate the status concerns of their electorate.

Ultimately, as MacDonald and Parent's (2021, p. 375) recent review of status research notes, tying status-seeking to the need to please domestic groups "is compelling because it provides a plausible political account of how status concerns can shape the policy process." Indeed, my approach here takes from Ward the notion that international status can become an important political resource for (de)legitimation of a government and its policies, and that we can thus study how international status informs policy outcomes via domestic debates (see also Clunan 2009).[24] However, I depart quite radically from Ward's "second image reversed" approach, which suggests that acts of international recognition or denial are crucial for influencing a state's status strategy (Clunan 2019, p. 27).

Individual versus Group Identity Formation

Indeed, although Ward is critical of status theories that anthropomorphize the state, in maintaining the primacy of *international* recognition (or lack

---

[22] Ward (2013, 2017b), Sambanis, Skaperdas, and Wohlforth (2015), Clunan (2008), and Pu (2019) are also relevant.

[23] Using survey experiments, Powers and Renshon (2023, p. 17) have identified an "unambiguous" relationship between unfavorable foreign policy events, increased status concerns, and presidential disapproval.

[24] My approach shares similarities with Ann Clunan's (2009), which also theorizes and illustrates how anthropomorphizing the state occludes from view potentially important domestic contestation over what status-seeking strategy a state should pursue. She shows how status strategies not only are formed in response to the international hierarchy but must prove consonant with domestic elites' conception of their state's historic role. I follow Clunan in granting the domestic discourse (and thus history) an independent role in explaining status-seeking activities. However, while Clunan theorizes how elites contest a particular status strategy, she does not problematize how those elites may contest what status is or what status the state has in the first place.

12   THE GRAMMAR OF STATUS COMPETITION

thereof) in his theory, Ward reproduces a widespread[25] yet dubious assumption that collective identity or status formation works the same way as individual identity or status formation (e.g., Ringmar 1996; Murray 2018). To be sure, at the individual level, short of insanity, humans cannot claim a status or identity that at least some of their peers do not recognize: one cannot go around for very long believing they are a great stand-up comedian without people laughing. Yet, this requirement for recognition from others cannot just be scaled up to groups (Abizadeh 2005, pp. 56–58). In short, when scholars translate individual theories of identity formation onto collectives, they overlook how "the sources of recognition and dialogue required in the formation of a collective identity need not be humans excluded from membership" of the community in question (Abizadeh 2005, p. 58). In other words, because collective identities are shared by individual *people*, the processes of self-construction and mutual recognition of collective identities can take place discursively among members *within* that *same* group. Or for that matter, recognition could come from dissimilar entities that are neither states nor individuals within the group. In the IR context, this might be IOs, NGOs, or even transnational terrorist groups: any individual or group that can communicate can plausibly contribute to identity recognition.[26] This is no less intersubjective because it involves members of the same group and is thus quite different from the stand-up comedian who *subjectively* convinces themselves they are funny. Following Abizedah (2005), then, it becomes theoretically possible that while sane individuals cannot recognize their own status, states have plenty of humans and other internal actors that can recognize and reproduce salient representations of its international status, that the state can act upon, without requiring the other states' recognition to bring it into being. While practices of recognition from similar collectives is likely to influence the identity or status narratives shared by an in-group, we need not assume they are determinative (contra, e.g., Murray 2018, pp. 6–7).

[25] While status scholars disagree about many aspects of status-seeking, it is largely taken for granted that for state status-seeking to be successful—and thus generate the gains potentially available for status-seeking—it requires that states achieve internationally *recognized* status. Indeed, this assumption is found in de Carvalho and Neumann's (2015a, p. 16). Weberian-inspired approach and Michelle Murray's (2018, p. 6) insightful symbolic interactionist theory of status, and it holds for Larson and Shevchenko's pathbreaking SIT-inspired theory of status-seeking. According to Larson and Shevchenko, "[t]o be successful" a status-seeking strategy (mobility, creativity, competition), "requires that the higher-status group *accept* and *recognize* the aspiring group's improved position" (2014, p. 41, my emphasis).

[26] It is also worth noting that recognition in the distant past can remain salient to a collective's understanding of its position in the world: as Alexis de Tocqueville's writings on America illustrate, a statement of recognition can be milked centuries later (Hughes 2015).

Further, although the conventional assumption in SIT-based IR status literature is that external recognition determines the success of a status strategy, it does not find support in SIT proper.[27] The original SIT suggests that "social creativity" strategies require only that individuals can find socially valuable attributes to make positive *comparisons* possible for people who identify with a particular social identity (Tajfel and Turner, 1979, pp. 40–43). Although it is desirable that the out-group recognize these qualities and improve its "real" status position, it is not *necessary* to generating self-esteem and pride from those intergroup comparisons. To take a paradigmatic example of social creativity, the "Black is beautiful" movement in the 1960s did not depend upon recognition from Whites to improve the self-esteem of the ingroup, even if this may have been the eventual goal. Indeed, as Tajfel and Turner make clear, pursuing social creativity, group members "may seek positive distinctiveness for the in-group by redefining or altering the elements of the comparative situation. *This need not involve any change in the groups actual social position*" (Tajfel and Turner 1979, p. 43, my emphasis). Crucially, then, social creativity does *not* require the *out*-group to agree on the comparative dimensions of social value (p. 40). Hence, as Ann Clunan (2019, p. 17) notes in her review of Ward (2017b), "social creativity strategies can actually improve the self-esteem of low-status groups even when their social position remains the same."

Collectively, this short discussion demands the domestic audience be taken into account. As a growing number of second-wave works demonstrate, the domestic audience provides a crucial reason for seeking status in the first place: state legitimacy. Thus, any government with citizens who value their state's status has some incentive to seek to maintain and improve it or at least avoid decline. Second, contra the conventional wisdom in both first- and second-wave status research, I argue that domestic actors can serve as independent sources of recognition for their own status-seeking activities, and thus international recognition need not be crucial to whether a status-seeking strategy is a success. If this reasoning is correct and the domestic actors take on a significant role in both incentivizing status-seeking and potentially operating as an independent audience of recognition, then it would have the downstream consequence of putting severe pressure upon the assumption that states share and act upon common understandings of

---

[27] It is also relevant, given its salience in IR status works (e.g., Gilady 2018), that in Thorstein Veblen's seminal *Theory of the Leisure Class* (1899) the locus of status competition is "invidious comparisons" rather than recognition.

14 THE GRAMMAR OF STATUS COMPETITION

international status hierarchies. If individual leaders and diplomats might be expected to have a sense of their state's international place, it seems more doubtful that the average citizen will. Although it may seem fairly obvious, it is worth spelling out exactly why agreement over the "valued attributes" that are said to constitute international status hierarchies seem unlikely to obtain within domestic politics and across states.

Obstacles to Agreement about International Status Hierarches

First, it requires considerably more discursive labor for a social hierarchy among groups to become agreed upon than among individual people. To understand why this is so it is useful to lean on Vincent Pouliot's sociological explanation of how hierarchies emerge. Pouliot (2014) argues that status hierarchies and status concerns are a function of sociality itself. In short, because people are born into societies in which comparisons with those around them are unavoidable, status hierarchies quickly emerge through practice. Pouliot (2014, 2016) uses this rationale to "zoom in" on the endogenously produced hierarchies that structure diplomats' field of practice. I concur with Pouliot's point that socially meaningful hierarchies emerge, change, and are sustained by (discursive) practice.[28] However, states are clearly not social in the way people are. Unlike a community of humans, comparisons between states—that are a necessary condition for status competition—need considerable social and technological labor in order for just *comparison* to become possible in the first place. In short, comparisons are possible only once they are conceived of and the technology for measuring and comparing becomes available and legitimated. Given that global comparisons are a logical prerequisite to making even a crude social hierarchy within which one can have a status (Onuf 1989, pp. 264–267), status hierarchies among states emerge in a quite different manner than among people.[29]

---

[28] I do not accept the common distinction between "discourse" and "practice": the linguistic emphasis of discourse analysts is a methodological choice of how to get at meaning, not a rejection of the meaning-producing quality of "material" practices. Indeed, as I discuss in chapter 2, properly understood, saying *is* doing in discourse analysis. Indeed, my notion of discourse is derived from Foucault, whose empirical work emphasizes meaning-producing material practices as well as linguistic practices. See also Epstein (2015).

[29] Moreover, while individuals within a domestic society receive constant feedback about their group's social status, the individuals do not receive the same kind of feedback regarding their country's status. Instead—besides diplomats and leaders—citizens will generally encounter other people from other nationalities in contexts providing them with advantages over other groups.

INTRODUCTION 15

Moreover, beyond the sheer difficulty in making comparisons between states, international society lacks a referee—or in Pouliot's terminology, "symbolic hegemon"—to set and enforce the rules of the status hierarchy. Absent a referee, agreed-upon rules of the game, and a formalized system of recognition—as one finds in the Olympics—citizens have considerable interpretative leeway to interpret their state's status position in a manner that diverges from their international and indeed their domestic peers. Indeed, status researchers' "valued attributes" do not reveal themselves to the observer ready-ranked. Just as a Louis Vuitton bag can mark its owner as stylish or stupid depending on the social context, so too can a nuclear weapon symbolize greatpowerdom but also pariah status (Beaumont 2021; Røren 2023). This intersubjective agreement upon the rules of hierarchy—for instance, how to value nuclear weapons—is a precondition to knowing one's status position in a given context. This matters because to know *how* to compete for status, one must know and agree to follow the rules of the competition; otherwise, to borrow a phrase, one may end up castling with a queen.

Indeed, some second-wave works have directly cast doubt upon the plausibility of the assumption of interstate agreement about status. As Joshua Freedman (2016) has convincingly argued, states may hold different "ontologies" of status recognition, which helps explain how China's status dissatisfaction and status-seeking can be squared with its ostensibly high status in international society (see Røren and Beaumont 2019). If Freedman theorizes how *states* can disagree about the international status hierarchy, Jonathan Mercer (2017) goes one further: he uses Britain's decision to wage the Second Boer War to demonstrate how various groups *within the same country* can hold rival conceptions of the state's status.[30] While Mercer suggests the variance stems from "feelings," I will argue shortly that such divergences are better understood as the result of rival *theories of international status*.

Taken together then, these works and this discussion provide the warrant for a framework that treats international status as crucial for domestic legitimation and also grants domestic groups' interpretative agency to actively

---

[30] Relatedly, Ward (2023) highlights how partisan affiliation strongly shapes American citizens' assessments of the United States' relative position in the world. It is also worth noting that although their experiments manage to isolate the effect of negative status events upon leadership approval, Powers and Renshon (2023, pp. 24–25) conclude that "in the real world" such events are discursively mediated (open to "reframing") and that different publics (domestic and international) will likely vary in how they value and assess the status implications.

16 THE GRAMMAR OF STATUS COMPETITION

produce and contest among themselves, and to some extent recognize their own conceptions of their state's status in the world. Indeed, the lack of agreed-upon rules need not stop states from acting *as if* they are in a status competition. Instead, the absence of a "symbolic hegemon" implies that they may make sense of their performance in terms of a hierarchy of their own construction. For instance, one frequently hears that most drivers consider themselves above average. While this factoid is usually used as an example of human hubris, it can be reconciled quite logically if we consider that people may define "good driver" differently. Some may value the ability to avoid accidents; others may value the ability to do hand-break turns. Put simply, without an agreed-upon standard, it is possible for every driver not just *to think* they are above average but *to be* above average according to their own criteria. As later chapters will seek to highlight, states can understand, act upon, and "compete" in status hierarchies of their own making too.

Studying *Theories* of International Status

Instead of theorizing and trying to ascertain and operationalize international status hierarchies as they really exist, as most first- and second-wave scholarship does, I propose studying the *theorizing about status* that people, groups, and governments undertake and act upon. Indeed, as Mariysia Zalewski (1996, p. 347) long ago noted, "theorists" do not have a monopoly on theorizing: "theorising is a way of life, a form of life, something we all do, every day, all the time," from how to make the perfect cup of tea to figuring out how to beat the traffic. Thus, "if one believes that theory is everyday practice then theorists are global actors and global actors are theorists" (p. 348). To use an example from one of my cases (chapter 5), in a National Security Council meeting about SALT, the idea of developing a mobile land-based nuclear weapons force was ruled out by President Ford, who said, "Everybody wants it in somebody else's backyard. . . . I predict [Congress] would be 10 to 1 or more against it."[31] In short, Ford theorized and acted upon the assumption that Nimbies[32] in Congress would reject it. It did not require the theory to be tested or necessarily accurate for it to be acted upon. Similarly,

---

[31] Minutes of a Meeting of the National Security Council Washington, September 17, 1975.
[32] Nimbies are people who are not necessarily against something being done but would rather it "Not [be] in my back yard."

chapter 3 analyzes how the British government legitimated going to war with the Boer by theorizing what *would* happen to their status if they did not. Again, the theory was not tested, but as I will argue, it was nonetheless fundamental for legitimating the war. However, I also mean theorizing in a constitutive sense: any representation of an international hierarchy—whether in military power or quality of democracy—requires an "ontological theory" of *what is* power or *what is* democracy (Guzzini 2013, p. 534). This sort of representation of a hierarchy is also a type of theorizing because it necessarily requires *selecting* what counts as power or democracy (etc.). With these understandings of theorizing in mind, I will investigate (in chapters 5, 6, and 7) how different groups within states produce rival theories of international status (TIS), and whether and how these theories legitimate their preferred strategy for how to proceed (while delegitimizing others).[33]

The key difference between a TIS approach and the overwhelming majority of prior status research is that it involves inductively exploring how actors themselves define and contest the status hierarchy rather than assessing it on their behalf prior to analysis. While such actor-defined ontologies, as opposed to scholarly defined ontologies (Jackson 2010; Bettiza 2014), have been little used in status research,[34] this approach has been put to good use by constructivists working on sovereignty (e.g., Adler-Nissen and Gammeltoft-Hansen, 2008), civilization (Bettiza 2014), or the international order (Kustermans, de Carvalho, and Beaumont 2023). Here, rather than imposing a coherent meaning upon their object of analysis (e.g., the status hierarchy), they explore how these concepts are "wielded, contested, and adapted in practice, and with what consequence in specific political contexts" (Kustermans, de Carvalho, and Beaumont 2023, p. 10). In this way, these approaches treat the contestation around their object of inquiry as an empirical puzzle rather than an epistemological problem. While constructivism provides several plausible alternative ways of conceiving of the unreliable link between real status and actors' descriptions—notably narratives, representations, framings—the concept of theorizing embraces the uncertainty, creativity, and agency involved in assessing status that has hitherto been considered a problem by most prior status research.

---

[33] Together with Katharina Glaab (Beaumont and Glaab 2023), I have recently used this notion of theorizing to understand how migrants navigate the hierarchies constituting the EU's visa regime.

[34] A recent exception to this rule is Røren's (2023) pathbreaking analysis of how different status orders responded to Russia's annexation of Crimea.

18   THE GRAMMAR OF STATUS COMPETITION

Perhaps paradoxically, switching from investigating "real" status hierarchies to investigating people's theories about those hierarchies puts us on firmer methodological footing. In practice, studying collective beliefs and motivations requires developing proxies for unobservable beliefs and trying to infer what is going on within people's minds. In short, it leaves status research in the realm of metaphysics. In contrast, studying theories of international status and how they legitimate particular activities involves studying observable phenomena: *discourse*.[35] Indeed, what governments actually act upon and *legitimate* their actions in response to are discursive theories of their state's status position.[36] Crucially, if we assume people or groups have some agency to reinterpret their state's international status, then these theories of status need not have a *necessary* relationship to the "collective beliefs" of other members of international society.[37] This opens up for studying status in the manner thick constructivists study the discursive battles over framing that make up the everyday politics of legitimation (Adler-Nissen and Gammeltoft-Hansen 2008, p. 7; Krebs and Jackson 2007, p. 38). To be sure, "external" goings on and practices of recognition in international affairs likely influence these framing contests, but we need not analytically privilege them a priori (Buzan et al. 1998, p. 38; Hansen 2006). However, changing the locus of analysis of status from international collective beliefs about status to discursive theories of international status requires a radical gestalt switch and thus some careful conceptual labor.

Narrowing Down: Theories of Status Competition

So far I have painted in broad strokes the state of the field and suggested studying how theories of international status hierarchies inform government policy. This section further narrows down and differentiates my

---

[35] Chapter 4 will elaborate the specific theoretical meaning of discourse (productive, social, political, and always somewhat "unstable"), but in short it can be defined as the pattern of representation through which humans give meaning to and make sense of their world(s) (see Campbell 1992; Hansen 2006; Neumann 1996; Diez 1999).

[36] I have emphasized the "re" because, as Neumann (2008) notes, no presentation of the world in language is ever immaculately conceived; it always recursively depends upon prior representations.

[37] To theorize an *international* status hierarchy as a social structure requires ascertaining what attributes are valued and by whom. Therefore, the theoretical and methodological challenge to scholars becomes to theorize what attributes are commonly valued and to ascertain international society's "collective beliefs" about those attributes. Only once this procedure is undertaken can the analyst plausibly explain a state's response to the social hierarchy.

object of analysis—status *competition*—from other kinds of status-seeking and discusses why my definition offers major advantages for empirically exploring the substance of international hierarchies, their contestation and change over time, and their political consequences.

Indeed, this book investigates theories of *status competition* rather than status-seeking per se. Previously I used "status-seeking" to refer to any activity that involves striving to improve or maintain an actor's position in a hierarchy. This captures three types of activity, of which status *competition* is only one:

1. Seeking membership into a club with absolute standards.
2. Competing for position in relative hierarchy of rank.
3. Attempting to reform either violently or peacefully the rules of club or rank hierarchy.

This definition of status-seeking while broad, immediately rules out emotional spasms of frustration born from status denial (e.g., Volgy et al. 2014; cf. Renshon 2017). Here, seeking status is rational in the broad sense: the means must be plausibly connected to the goal of achieving higher status (Onuf 1989, pp. 259–263; Renshon 2017).[38]

To narrow down further, I do *not* consider status competition to include attempting to reform the rules of a status club or rank hierarchy—usually known as social creativity or revisionism in prior IR status work. The crucial difference here is that while reforming or overturning the rules is necessarily radical with regard to contesting the existing hierarchy, the other two strategies are rule-governed status quo strategies: applying for club membership and competing in a rank hierarchy both reproduce the rules of the hierarchy (Ward 2017b, p. 49; Naylor 2018, p. 63). Regardless of whether they are undertaken in an affable or an aggressive manner, competing for position in a ranking reaffirms the rules: building battleships might threaten one's rival, but it reproduces the value placed upon battleships in the same way competing on overseas aid reproduces the hierarchy of aid-giving. Meanwhile, applying to enter the EU by meeting its democratic standards reproduces and legitimates those standards, akin to how striving to enter the nuclear club reproduces the salience of the nuclear club.

---

[38] To be clear, status-seeking need not be rational in the sense it is conventionally used in IR: seeking-status need not make the actor more secure or richer.

20 THE GRAMMAR OF STATUS COMPETITION

This begs the question: How can we distinguish between seeking membership in a club and seeking to rise in a ranking? This is crucial to get clear because prior works often "lump" the two together despite their "essential differences" (MacDonald and Parent 2021, p. 366). The following chapter will discuss this question in more depth, but in short, rankings and clubs can be distinguished by the relationships they produce between actors. Indeed, a club hierarchy produces a gatekeeper-applicant relationship, while a ranking hierarchy produces a relationship of rivals competing in the same game. Following Onuf (1989, p. 267), logically one can *only* compete in a ranking hierarchy by first assessing one's relative position to rivals, which necessarily requires rules of comparison. In contrast, *in the ideal*, when entering a club defined by absolute standards (e.g., joining the nuclear club), status seekers are not engaged in a relative competition with either other applicants or existing members (see also Towns and Rumelili 2017; McDonald and Persons 2021, p. 9). Instead, whether they manage to join depends upon their individual actions and whether they meet the absolute standard. As such, when seeking to join a status club, the actor can ignore the "performance" of its significant others. This discussion of status competition puts me in the same ballpark as prior theories of status competition but places new emphasis on the rule-governed nature of status competition and avoids conflating status competition with a substantive type of activity or one associated with a positive or negative valence.

This latter difference is crucial because while prior work tends to acknowledge the idea that states could theoretically compete for status in anything, they tend to move quickly onto defining status competition in international relations as aggressive and/or militaristic prior to analysis. The clearest example is also the status theory in widest use: Larson and Shevchenko's translation of SIT. Larson and Shevchenko (2010, p. 73) define social competition as a status-seeking strategy that "aims to equal or outdo the dominant group in the area on which its claim to superior status rests. In international relations, where status is in large part based on military and economic power," the "[i]ndicators include arms racing, rivalry over spheres of influence, military demonstrations aimed at one-upmanship, or military intervention against a smaller power." Notwithstanding that this definition collapses into one of their other types of status-seeking (emulation) (Ward 2017a, p. 6), by tying status competition to a concrete activity, it tacitly reifies the rules of international competition. While others ground their explanation more specifically in the historical context of great power rivalry (Wohlforth 2009;

Barnhart 2016), these works still define the substance of status competition prior to analysis. For Wohlforth (2009, pp. 40–41) the indicators of status competition are frequency of conflict; for Barnhardt (2016, p. 386) status competition is indicated by "competitive practices such as the development of advanced weaponry, competition over spheres of influence or influence within international organizations, or, as demonstrated here, the acquisition of vast amounts of territory." In short, these scholars have produced theories of status competition among great powers *given* the existing prevailing rules of great power hierarchy.[39]

What each of these works glosses over and thus assumes is that states already agree upon how to compete for status: the rules of the game. For instance, by suggesting that status competition involves arms racing, the analyst has already presumed agreement among states that more arms warrant higher status and how to evaluate the race. In other words, the outcome that is said to indicate status competition is tied to a specific understanding of the rules of the international status hierarchy. This is problematic for two reasons. First, it overlooks how alternative metrics of status coexist at the same time. For instance, depending upon the context, the same nuclear weapons can function as stigma or status symbol. Thus, as Macdonald and Parent (2021, p. 7) point out, ignoring alternative ways to assess international hierarchies elides several important questions:

> Do valued attributes refer primarily to the impressive means states possess or to the virtuous ends they pursue? Who decides which attributes are prized and how? Should we treat standing as a universal metric or disaggregate it into one's standing in a particular issue area, institutional context, or geographic region?

Moreover, and equally important, if the indicator of status competition is tied to a *substantive* notion of the international hierarchy, there is no way of analyzing any changes in the rules of the game or status competitions that do not conform to the analyst's a priori assessment of the international hierarchy. Taken together, defining the substance of the status hierarchy a priori leads scholars to overstate both the degree of agreement around the status

---

[39] Pouliot (2014, p. 192) (again) is the exception; however, his use of the term "status competition" suffers from the opposite problem. Pouliot treats contesting the rules of the game as status competition. Yet this seems to stretch the notion of competition too far; it would mean we have no way of distinguishing between people running in a race and people arguing about the rules of the race.

22 THE GRAMMAR OF STATUS COMPETITION

hierarchy (by overlooking alternatives in circulation) and its stability (by overlooking contestation and change in the hierarchy).

There is, of course, a good reason why prior works define status competition by the substance of the hierarchy: it allows them to develop clear indicators for when status competition obtains, for instance, a decision to arms-race, even when it runs against a state's security interests. Lacking a substantive notion of the status hierarchy, we would run the risk of seeing status competition everywhere and thus explain everything yet nothing. This challenge is only exacerbated by the tendency for policymakers to use fuzzy and overlapping vocabulary to describe their activities. While it is quite possible to analytically distinguish between reputation, prestige, standing, honor (etc.) in the abstract (Dafoe, Renshon, and Huth 2014), policymakers rarely use these terms as scholars define them. Meanwhile, in many countries explicit use of status to justify a policy is taboo (Gilady 2018, p. 24). Taken together, these issues generate two theoretical-cum-methodological conundrums that my TIS framework must solve:

1. How can we identify and differentiate status competition from other types of state action *without* defining the rules of the status hierarchy prior to analysis?
2. How can we study status competition systematically but also remain sensitive to changes in the rules of a status hierarchy?

In order to tackle these riddles, the book develops a Copenhagen School–inspired theoretical framework to problematize and investigate actor-defined *theories* of international hierarchies and their effects.[40] Indeed, similar how to Lene Hansen (2006) developed a metalinguistic framework for investigating systematically how national identity informs foreign policy without reifying identity, or how Ole Waever's securitization framework (Waever 1995; Buzan et al. 1998) identifies threats by virtue of their "grammar" rather than by their substantive referent, this book strives to do the same for status competition.

Indeed, the status riddle closely resembles that which plagued security studies at the turn of the 1990s, which securitization theory went a long way toward solving: how to define and measure threats and thus theorize how

---

[40] In short, the Copenhagen School developed various analytical frameworks for studying discourse and its effects in international relations (e.g., Buzan et al. 1998; Hansen 2006). See Van Munster (2007) for a critical discussion.

states respond to them. The conundrum turned around the observation that even if security scholars might agree about what objectively constituted a security threat, states' threat perceptions in practice vary enormously. Thus, security scholars' attempts at general theorizing of security policy appeared esoteric and at times only tangential to what states actually act upon. Buzan and colleagues' (1998) seminal intervention in this debate called for security scholars to spend less time speculating on the reality of threats and instead systematically study how threats become successfully framed as threats within a given community and the political consequences of these processes.[41] Similarly, rather than trying to accurately gauge international status, scholars can study the discursive processes through which a state activity becomes constructed as a status competition and how and with what consequences their theory of status changes or becomes contested as a policy proceeds. The key move required to develop such a framework is a rigorous discursive metatheory of status competition—a grammar—that differs substantively from alternative discursive framings and logics. The next section will outline how this book sets about meeting this challenge.

The Logic and Grammar of Status Competition

Both lay people and scholars will be immediately familiar with and capable of recognizing the Olympic Games as an instance of international status competition. To be sure, prior status works might not consider the Olympics an especially important status competition for states, but they would accept that it can be conceptualized and analyzed as one.[42] What is theoretically interesting about the Olympics vis-à-vis other international activities that are often treated as status competitions (e.g., arms-racing) is not its political significance but the high degree of institutionalization. Indeed, unlike other international status competitions, the Olympics is *designed* to be a status competition among states. We can therefore reasonably expect that the theoretically important aspects of status competition are visible and amenable to abstraction and illustration.

---

[41] See Wilhelmsen (2017) for a thorough explication of the discursive version of securitization theory that most closely resembles my approach here.

[42] Indeed, some IR scholars have empirically investigated state status-seeking via the Olympics (Rhamey and Early 2013).

24 THE GRAMMAR OF STATUS COMPETITION

Indeed, using the Olympic games to model the crucial sociological aspects of an international status competition, chapter 1 develops an ideal-typical account of status competition. In short, the chapter argues that status competitions require competitors to share the same understanding of the rules of the game, have near perfect information about one another's performance, and share a common understanding of what constitutes winning. Crucially, one cannot define good performance or success without *ongoing* reference to the relative performance of the others involved in the competition. Therefore, to compete for higher status requires formulating a dynamic strategy based upon the activities of the others in the hierarchy. However, as the Olympics illustrate, it is not the activity itself—running, sailing, or arms-racing—that tells one how to compete; it is the specifics of the rules defining the competition that enables a distinct *processual-relational* competition to unfold among participants. If the competitors in any Olympic event did not share a common understanding of those rules, then a relational logic may well inform the players' actions, but it would be impossible to agree upon who led and who lagged, and meanwhile disagreement about who won and who lost would be endemic. It bears emphasis that status competition thus defined does not require an actor to be motivated by status; players may compete for a multitude of reasons. Nor does not it require an analyst to define (and thus reify) status attributes prior to analysis; it is the processional relational logic that defines the status competition, not the activity animating the game.[43]

Notably, although defining status competition as rule-governed is broadly consistent with prior work on status competition, rules are seldom emphasized in either the definition or the analysis.[44] The main advantage of foregrounding rules is that it enables the analyst to problematize stage 1 and stage 3 in the status-seeking process outlined above: how domestic actors interpret the status hierarchy prior to, during, and after a government's status-seeking activity. Finally, the ideal type also allows the analyst to

---

[43] For an in-depth discussion of processual-relational approaches and their implications for research, see Jackson and Nexon (1999) and chapters 1 and 2.

[44] Notable exceptions include Onuf (1989) and Towns (2010), which will both be drawn upon in the following chapters. It is also important to note that even those that seek to use status competition to explain war often tacitly imply common rules. For instance, Renshon (2017) argues that "fighting for status" is rational because international society systematically rewards war-wagers with more recognition. Implicit in this model is that members of international society understand that waging war will generate recognition: fighting for status from this perspective is not a strategy to smash the hierarchy, it is a conservative strategy encouraged by the very rules of the hierarchy. Indeed, rules need not be either "liberal" or "good" to be rules.

differentiate—according to their respective relational logics—status competition from other types of status-seeking (e.g., striving to join a status club) as well as distinguish it from the logic of appropriateness and securitization. This is crucial to avoid the trouble of overdetermination noted to be a problem with prior qualitative status studies (McDonald and Persons 2021, p. 11).

Critics might object at this point that by insisting upon shared rules, I have defined international status competition out of existence. However, this would miss the methodological purpose of ideal types (Jackson 2010, p. 166). For instance, the rational actor model (an ideal type) is useful precisely because it draws to our attention to the ways that humans and groups *diverge* from rational behavior. For instance, when psychologists wish to identify perception biases, they use a rational-actor baseline to compare against reality. Similarly, although several factors inhibit the ideal international status competition from being realized (e.g., ambiguity around the rules), this does not foreclose the *logic* of status competition from informing government policy. Instead, the difficulty of reaching agreement over the rules of the game and the possibility of self-recognition mean that domestic actors can frame a policy and act *as if* they are in a status competition—*a processual-relational, rule-governed competition for relative position*—even if the other players do not agree to the same rules or are not even paying attention. Indeed, in the empirical inquiries (chapters 3–5) that follow, the fact that the states in question do not compete in pure rule-governed competitions for position in which no other logics operate, or where there is no disagreement over the rules, is not a problem for my analysis but a deliberate consequence of my research design. It is these disagreements and their consequences that I wish to draw attention to. Ultimately, it is the prevalence of states conducting activities that *resemble* competitions for status—in which the logic is visible—that I would argue explains why status-seeking appears so widespread in international affairs even if "international" hierarchies are often ambiguous and contested.

If chapter 1 defines the logic of status competition in the abstract, chapter 2 develops a framework I call the *grammar of status competition* to make sense of how it manifests in domestic politics and for studying its political effects. Here, I leverage the previous chapter's elaboration of processual-relational logic to argue that three types of representation invoke and embody the logic of status competition, and simultaneously define the rules of a hierarchy: (1) competitive comparisons and superlatives,

26 THE GRAMMAR OF STATUS COMPETITION

(2) competitive positional identity constructions,[45] and (3) sports metaphors. When any one of these "grammatical units" is invoked, they are in that instant theorizing and instantiating a status hierarchy, defining the rules of the game and thus implying and legitimating how to compete. For instance, when the U.K. government claimed to be a "leader of nuclear disarmament" prior to acquiring a new nuclear weapons system, it simultaneously defined the rules and invoked a competitive disarmament hierarchy within which some countries are leading and others are lagging. Although the United Kingdom's theorization of the disarmament hierarchy received little international recognition (beyond derision), it nonetheless helped legitimate its new nuclear weapons system to the antinuclearists among its domestic supporters (Beaumont 2021). Indeed, as I will demonstrate in the coming chapters, even if the ideal of a status competition is seldom realized, the logic of status competition can still inform political practice as a mode of legitimation.

Moreover, the "grammar of status" heuristic can enable the analyst to identify competing theories of the international status and how they emerge, are contested, and perhaps solidify across time, even when the word "status" or "hierarchy" is not mentioned.[46] Unlike prior works, this technique allows me to identify whether and how the rules of the hierarchy changed during the policy process. It will also enable investigating how political opponents challenge governments' theories of international status and potentially undermine their ability to legitimate competing for status. Conversely, it enables the study of how domestic opposition groups may successfully mobilize the grammar of status competition and impel the government to compete. To be clear, while I would argue that whenever the grammar of status is uttered it invokes a competitive status hierarchy and implies how to compete, whether and how such representations inform political outcomes require empirical analysis.

Thus, if the ideal type developed in chapter 1 tweaks the prevailing conceptions of status competition, chapter 2 draws upon "thick

---

[45] All identities are in some sense positional, but as chapter 1 elaborates, positional identities can be differentiated according to whether the position is constituted by fixed criteria or changeable, and whether the hierarchy involves a club or a rank. These different combinations produce different the relations with the other. Only one type—competitive positional identities—invokes status competition (chapter 2).

[46] This helps address the issue that among many countries it is inappropriate to explicitly use "status" as a rationale (Sagan 1997).

constructivist" research to depart quite radically from extant status works.[47] Three moves are central: I replace *motivation* with *legitimation* as the locus of status-related political action, and I replace collective *beliefs* about position in social hierarchy with *theories* of international hierarchies. Finally, language here is treated as *productive* rather than (imperfectly) reflective of reality. Taken together, this means that instead of studying how states respond to their "real" international status position via various proxies, the researcher can analyze how discursively observable theories of status competition legitimize and delegitimize particular courses of action. From this perspective, like stories that constitute our national identity, whether or not they are true or accurate is by the by; what matters is whether and how they inform and legitimate political practice. If previous research has given analytical priority to *international* beliefs and practices of recognition, this approach trains our gaze upon the interpretative agency that governments and citizens may possess to construct and act upon their own hierarchical orderings of the world without international recognition being determinative.

To be clear, although the book contends that international recognition does not determine whether a particular status theory sinks or swims in domestic politics, this does not mean anything goes. Instead, domestic actors' hierarchical orderings of the world are structured by preexisting discursive resources available in the policy context within which a government operates (chapter 2; see Diez 1999; Hansen 2006). Put differently, even if skeptics are correct and status is an illusion, if a status *theory* is widely shared among the electorate, then a government *will still need to* legitimate its policies in a way that does not puncture that illusion. For instance, all American presidents need to square their policy agenda with America's alleged exceptionalism (Restad 2014). Whether or not America is indeed exceptional is irrelevant to whether this theory of American status is influential or durable. Meanwhile, beyond grand narratives, particular policy fields can become structured by the prior stories that have been told about the country's status. For instance, as chapter 5 documents, the dominant status theory around Norwegian

---

[47] Vincent Pouliot's (2014, 2016) work is the exception here. I will explain how my work departs from his in more detail in chapters 1 and 2. But in short, he solves the problem of knowing one's status by zooming in on diplomats, who interact on a regular basis and thus can plausibly be expected to know their status in the way that individual humans in a society normally do not. States, however, are not humans, and the citizens of international society do not interact in the same way with foreign citizens, and thus they cannot be expected to get a sense of the game (habitus) in the manner that diplomats do.

schools during the 1990s was that they offered the best education in the world. Thus, when Norway finished mid-table on international education rankings in 2001, the government and opposition needed to reconcile this new information with their previous status theory, which in turn limited the available policy responses. Indeed, as Macdonald and Parent (2021, p. 11) argue, status researchers have been too quick to assume "status talk" refers to international hierarchies rather than constituting "rhetorical *necessities*" intended to "mobilise domestic support." While the authors intend this as a critique of status scholarship, it also implies the fruitfulness of the approach undertaken here: studying empirically the domestically produced theories of international status that become *necessary* or at least beneficial for domestic actors to mobilize in policy debates.

At the same time, this approach does not treat the domestic discourse as hermetically sealed from external events or criticism. Rather, I only assume that actors always have *some* agency to reinterpret (or perhaps discount or ignore) inconvenient events or facts that would appear to undermine their preferred status theory (see Hansen 2006, pp. 32–33). Indeed, as misrecognition theorists point out, "the reflection in the 'international mirror' will always disappoint," and thus states must find ways to reconcile the inevitable "gap" that emerges between "domestic discourses of the national Self and the way in which Others understand and represent this Self" (Adler Nissen Tsinovoi 2019, p. 5). However, if the international and domestic critics seem likely to hold up a black mirror, governments have strong incentives to develop a rose-tinted one. Indeed, the central argument of this book is that the essential ambiguity and unknowability of international status provides an unusual flexibility for governments and oppositions to generate rival, contradictory, but also plausible theories of their state's status in the world.[48] It follows that rather than beginning analysis from guestimates about real status hierarchies, we can study the battle among these status theories as it unfolds within domestic politics. Afterall, as Macdonald and Parent (2021, p. 11) suggest, it may often be these "rhetorical necessities" that do the "causal work" rather than quasi-mystical international status hierarchies themselves.

---

[48] See Rumelili and Towns (2022) for a related argument about how the abundance of country performance indicators generates status ambiguity that enables governments to pick and choose which ranking they pay attention to and emphasize.

The Empirical Payoff

All this theorizing ain't worth a dime if it cannot provide useful insights into world politics. Therefore, each empirical chapter utilizes my framework to address significant puzzles in IR. Each chapter follows a systematic procedure: guided by the grammar of status, they all conduct longitudinal analyses of domestic political discourse and pay special attention to whether and how theories of international status were used to legitimate (or not) the policies in question.[49] Such longitudinal analyses, when paired with my grammar-of-status lens, allowed me to detect how these theories often changed through the different stages of the policymaking *process* in ways that proved crucial for understanding the size, shape, and timing of the policy outcomes.[50]

To begin, chapter 3 addresses directly the "status skeptics" puzzle of why states exert resources competing for international status when international recognition is seldom forthcoming and the gains from status are seemingly so ephemeral (Macdonald and Parent 2021, p. 12; Mercer 2017; Glaser 2018). Specifically, the chapter addresses the challenge set by a leading status skeptic, Jonathon Mercer (2017), by providing an alternative explanation for the same Boer War case that he used to contend that status is a psychological illusion that states will eventually learn to cease chasing. Tracing the British discourse across three episodes prior to and during the Boer War (1899–1902), the chapter shows how government first theorized the war as necessary to preserve Britain's status as a great power and avoid humiliation at the hands of a tiny foe. However, with the help of the press over the course of the war, and despite Britain's embarrassing struggles on the battlefield, the government and pro-war press retheorized the rules of competition and the worthiness of their enemy, such that it became possible to present victory on the battlefield as a boon to Britain's status. This new status theory underpinned the wild celebrations that ensued and saw a new word for euphoric to enter the dictionary. This occurred even though, as Mercer (2017)

---

[49] See the appendix for methodology, method, and discussion of primary sources.

[50] To be clear, I am not setting out to pose status as a rival, all-or-nothing explanation. Status—by definition—can never be the sole explanation for anything: all status-granting activities must have a "primary utility" as well as symbolic utility (Gilady 2018). For instance, even a Ferrari gets a person from A to B. The decision to buy *a* car may have little to do with status, but the decision to buy a *red, super* car, does. Similarly, most government activities—like education, healthcare, or security policy—are broadly driven by conventional concerns for maximizing public utility in those fields. However, exactly when, why, and how particular policies came to take the form they did may depend upon reference to, and legitimation via, theories of international status.

30 THE GRAMMAR OF STATUS COMPETITION

has demonstrated, international audiences remained obviously unimpressed by Britain's success. Indeed, when the domestic audience and the landslide election that followed the war are taken into account, the skeptics' puzzle dissolves. From the government's perspective, despite the huge economic cost and lack of international recognition, the Boer War helped legitimate the government and secure a second term in office. Hence, the governments status theory may well have been an illusion, but it was a rather useful one. Rather than a collective *psychological* illusion that duped Britain then, I argue that Mercer's illusion is more accurately described as a *sociological* construction the government had considerable interest in fostering and maintaining. Further, a close study of the unfolding meaning of the war in domestic politics shows how the flattering status theory used by the government to celebrate triumph did not pop up out of the emotions at victory, as Mercer claimed, but had been developed in the months preceding victory.

There was, however, a limit to the government's agency to retheorize the war in a favorable manner. Following the election, when the war transformed into a counterinsurgency effort, the government ran afoul of its own gendered and racialized civilizational theory of Britain's moral status and superiority. Domestic critics wielded gendered and racial civilizational norms to delegitimize the use of concentration camps and destabilize the government's claim that the war was a performance befitting a great power. Indeed, akin to how if one castles with a queen one cannot be said to be playing chess, so it was that once Britain began to use "methods of barbarism" the war became difficult to present as a rule-governed competition they could take any pride in winning. Hence when Britain finally triumphed it would elicit little joy but instead initiated a period of recriminations. By paying heed to the discursive context, the TIS approach illuminates how the domestic theories of the status value of the war were bound up with racialized and gendered discourses in circulation at the time. As such, the case highlights how my grammar-of-status framework can help address status research's gender and racial blind spots.

Chapter 4 tackles the question of how international organizations can exert influence even when lacking legal authority and any carrots or sticks. Using Norway's response to the OECD's Programme for International Student Assessment (PISA) ranking as a case, the chapter argues that international rankings operate as "status Esperanto" that allow "foreign" theories of status hierarchies to bypass the obstacles that I argue usually hinder international agreement about the rules of international status competitions. In this way, rankings provide discursive resources to domestic actors that can enable them to legitimize policy reforms that would otherwise face more domestic opposition. Indeed, the chapter suggests that the raft of education reforms Norway carried out in the 2000s would not have taken place at the time they did, in the form they did, without PISA's construction and circulation of a specific theory of the international education hierarchy. However, tracing 19 years of the education policy discourse highlights a more critical "reactivity," hitherto overlooked by prior international rankings and status research. The process of competing in the PISA rankings led a growing number of domestic groups to question the rules of the game and develop rival theories of educational status that have now spread to mainstream politics. This emergent resistance to the competition, I argue, has undermined the potential for PISA to legitimate future policy reforms and highlights the theoretical importance—for critical rankings researchers—of treating an international ranking's influence as a discursively mediated process that is always susceptible to resistance and contestation from below.

Finally, chapter 7 seeks to shed light on why SALT proved so difficult and underwhelming. As such, this chapter speaks to what remains the most significant and long-standing puzzle in (traditional) security studies (Kroenig 2018; Green 2020): Why did the "superpowers" continue to arms-race even when a second-strike capability was assured? To make this puzzle tractable, the chapter zooms in on SALT I and II, which took place between 1970 and 1979. For several pro-nuclear realists, nuclear arms control should have been straightforward, given the declining utility of each extra weapon (e.g., Glaser 1994; Waltz 1981). By tracing the official top-level security discourse via recently declassified archives, the chapter shows the negotiating positions the United States took were primarily legitimated by theories of how domestic and international audiences would respond, rather than what was deemed necessary to deter the Soviets. Moreover, the chapter shows how the specific theory for evaluating the status value of the U.S. negotiation position(s) was contested through the process of SALT I, and only solidified several years into SALT II. Indeed, the eventual theory of status that was settled upon was a downstream consequence of the domestic debate that followed SALT I. In this way, domestic rules defining international status solidified and crystallized during the process of SALT II, structuring the U.S. negotiating position, slowing down negotiations, and limiting the ability of the United States to pursue other strategic objectives (both hawkish and dovish). Ultimately, the chapter argues that the difficulty of Cold War nuclear arms

32　THE GRAMMAR OF STATUS COMPETITION

control is better understood as the result of a (domestically produced) international status competition rather than a security dilemma.

To conclude, I elaborate how studying the effects of *theories of* international status instead of international status opens up a new research agenda that significantly expands the range of policies and practices that an international status lens can be used to account for. For instance, one blind spot I identify here is the *rationalist baseline bias* in IR status research. In short, if we deduce status's effects by showing the outcome to be irrational by other theories, we overlook how status can also be crucial for legitimating seemingly rational policies. Meanwhile, the conclusion elaborates how treating status as a discursive phenomenon provides a practical means of empirically tracing the geographical and temporal emergence, spread, and potential withering of specific theories of status, as well as their political consequences. Relatedly, I discuss how my TIS framework can illuminate how domestic groups can resist and undermine a state's attempts to compete for international status and thus help states avoid zero-sum status competitions. A red thread throughout the cases is that ambiguity (lack of agreement around the rules) around international hierarchies varies, and this has consequences for whether and how states can compete for status. Indeed, the cases provide provisional evidence that ambiguity around international hierarchies is productive of rival theories of status, and this can mitigate the zero-status competitions of which prior status research warns, while agreement around the rules of the status hierarchy facilitates governments' ability to legitimate competing. Thus, the conclusion suggests that, contra conventional wisdom, ambiguity around social status may be a social good that governments and citizens would be wise to cherish and protect.

A Note on Methods

An extensive critical discussion of the methods and methodology underpinning this book's empirical analysis can be found in the appendix. However, it is useful to outline here the evidentiary basis for the empirical analysis and the logic underpinning the case selection. As noted, each chapter conducts a systematic longitudinal discourse analysis that traces how specific theories of status were used to legitimate or delegitimate specific policies and whether and how the theories changed, became contested, and/or became solidified within domestic politics. Although the cases are very different and required different text selection strategies (see appendix), each analysis involved a common procedure: first exploring *whether* theories of status were used in the policy debate and mapping their use over time, before assessing to what extent and how they were significant for the legitimation of the policy at different steps in the process. This latter step required taking seriously alternative explanations and justifications for the same policy and remaining open to the possibility that a given status theory was merely window-dressing. Hence, each case study responds to the counterfactual question: Could one imagine the policy taking place in the way it did without a specific theory of status? In this way, my methodology (again) mirrors securitization theory, whereby the researcher examines whether a securitization process was sufficient to enable a government to break the "normal rules of politics." Rather than breaking the normal rules of politics, however, the "threshold" for identifying whether a theory of status has decisively informed a policy outcome is whether the substance and/or timing of a policy outcome is inexplicable otherwise. Within this process of mapping modes of legitimation in a policy debate and analyzing whether they were consequential, it also becomes possible to trace whether and how a given theory of status was contested or changed, and whether and how such rival theories of status were implicated in policy outcome.

Regarding case selection, each case performs two interconnected but distinct purposes. First, each can stand alone as an empirical analysis that showcases how my TIS framework can shed light on major issues and theoretical puzzles in international relations scholarship: why states seek status when the gains appear so ephemeral (chapter 3); how international indicators exert influence over states when lacking carrots or sticks (chapter 4); and why nuclear arms control among the superpowers proved so difficult even when mutual destruction was assured (chapter 5). However, taken together the cases serve a larger collective methodological and theoretical purpose: Norwegian education reform, arms control negotiations, and the Boer War constitute deliberately different cases that seek to illustrate the broad usefulness and potential transferability of my theoretical framework. To be clear, this approach should not be conflated with Mill's method of agreement, whereby the goal is to find a common factor that accounts for a similar outcome in very different cases (Jackson 2010, p. 70). Instead, by undertaking three very different cases, I intend to suggest that the TIS framework—using ideal typification of status competition in conjunction with the grammar of status—could be used to produce systematic empirical insights into a broad

34   THE GRAMMAR OF STATUS COMPETITION

range of foreign and domestic policies undertaken by very different states.[51] Crucially, rather than generalizability, interpretivist scholarship like mine aims for "transferability" (Lincoln and Guba 1985, cited in Schwartz-Shea 2015, p. 142): to provide sufficient explanation and description such that other researchers can assess whether the framework is *transferable* to another setting. My hope is that future scholars will explore the potential of this approach in the manner that securitization theory has been fruitfully applied to an ever-expanding range of cases. Here, each case added does not accumulate into a law of securitization; rather it adds to our confidence that securitization is a useful analytical framework that can produce important insights into a range of issues.

It is nonetheless possible to outline some broad-scope conditions for when it could prove useful to apply the framework developed here. Indeed, a powerful ideal type has a "scope and relevance" that "supersede a particular situation or instance" (Balzacq 2015, p. 105). To understand how my framework might apply elsewhere we should briefly recount how it was formed. Ideal types are developed "inductively from the 'extensive study of relevant materials'" (Nicholas Timasheff 1957, p. 178, cited in Balzacq 2015, p. 105). The scope of these "relevant materials" should therefore give an indication to the scope of the possible applications of my ideal type. For this research, this involved extensive study of my cases presented here, but also a close reading of the extant status literature and the close practical involvement required to write several article-length research papers wherein I analyzed status hierarchies in very different contexts, using different status theories and methods.[52] Given the scope of "relevant materials," I would suggest that my grammar-of-status framework could be applicable to international relations insofar as a country has a population who understands themselves as a collective situated among similar collectives. Thus, if a population begins to understand themselves as part of an "imagined community" (Anderson

---

[51] For a detailed explication of the philosophy of science warrant for this approach to social scientific research, see Jackson (2010). See also Schwartz-Shea and Yanow (2015) for several chapters explaining and illustrating the systematicism in interpretative research methods, as well as Beaumont and de Coning (2022) for an in-depth discussion of the costs were social science to limit itself to one mode of inference.

[52] Including but not limited to SIT-inspired work on Brexit (Beaumont 2017) status discrepancy–inspired work on Brazil (Beaumont and Røren 2020) and the BRICS (Røren and Beaumont 2019), ontological security–inspired work on the unrecognized peoples' quest for state status (Beaumont and Røren 2019), new hierarchies studies–inspired work on Caspian Sea ecosystem cooperation (Beaumont and Wilson Rowe 2023), and feminist-inspired work into everyday migration hierarchies (Beaumont and Glaab 2023),

1991) moving through time and space, then the grammar of status competition would become "empirically possible."

However, narrowing down, the types of activity that can become constituted as a status competition (via the grammar of status) are also historically conditioned: they require both the social capability to conceive of criteria by which to make a comparison, and the technical capacity to do so (Beaumont 2017b, p. 7). For instance, it would be virtually impossible for people in the 18th century to conceive of a status competition in gender equality. Indeed, it is only the invention of gender equality as an category of practice that has made it possible for states to compete for international status in gender equality (see Towns 2010). Finally, my grammar-of-status framework seems likely to be most useful and insightful in places and policy domains where governments are under significant pressure to legitimate their actions to the domestic population, and more likely to provide interesting insights where the rules of the international status hierarchies are ambiguous and/or contested.

If these scope conditions appear hopelessly vast, it is worth recalling that they are considerably narrower than evolutionary-psychological theories that posit status motivation as a universal driver of human behavior. Ultimately, the extent to which my approach has broader usefulness will be discovered only by further empirical inquiry.

1

The Logic of Status Competition

Now, here, you see, it takes all the running you can do,
to keep in the same place. If you want to get somewhere else,
you must run at least twice as fast as that!
—The Red Queen, in Lewis Carroll's *Through the
Looking Glass* (1871)

Introduction

Every four years between 776 BCE[1] and 200 BCE, citizens representing Greek city-states would converge upon Olympia in the Greek city-state of Elis to compete in the Panhellenic Games. It was not uncommon for city-states be at war with one another during the events. However, their military differences seldom[2] stopped them from sending their best men (it was always men) to compete in rule-governed tests of strength, courage, and above all masculinity. The games evolved over time, but their mainstay involved the *stadion* (600-meter sprint), wrestling, boxing, chariot racing, and horse racing. The events embodied the primary skills prized in Greek city-states: those needed for hunting and warfare. The games were thus an opportunity for cities to display the "excellence" of their citizens, fostering civic pride, not to mention offering a useful distraction from any social-economic unrest among their citizenship. The city-states were not ignorant of the political benefits, sponsoring gymnasiums and rewarding Olympic champions handsomely. Like the Olympics today, the competitors could expect to be cheered on by thousands of partisan supporters in attendance and welcomed home as heroes should they return victorious. Indeed, the tendency for citizens to live

---

[1] Though the precise date is disputed among historians (Faulkner 2012).
[2] Sparta were once banned from the games and subsequently fought a war to gain readmittance; however, they were not banned from the games *because* of an ongoing war Faulkner (2012).

The Grammar of Status Competition. Paul David Beaumont, Oxford University Press. © Oxford University Press 2024.
DOI: 10.1093/9780197771808.003.0002

vicariously via the successes of other members of their group is certainly not only a modern phenomenon (Browning, Joenniemi, and Steele 2021).

This chapter uses the Olympic games to develop and illustrate an ideal-typical sociological account of international status competition and the specific logic it embodies. By "sociological" I mean defining status competition by its intersubjective features without recourse to psychological processes: motivations or beliefs. As I noted in the introduction, the Olympics are unusually useful for this purpose not because they are an important international status competition but because, unlike almost all other international phenomena commonly treated as status competitions, they are *self-consciously designed* to be an international status competition. Thus, the key features of status competitions should prove visible and amenable to abstraction. Moreover, the global nature of the Olympics means that I can assume readers will already be familiar with the examples and therefore they will prove less controversial and require less explanation than imperfect examples of status competition from international relations proper.

Drawing on prior research and by specifying an ideal type of status competition and its distinct logic, this chapter undertakes several crucial conceptual functions that underpin the rest of the book. First, status competition has a general, fuzzy meaning in both layperson's language and academia.[3] Sometimes status competition is used to refer to *any* activity aimed at improving an actor's social position, whether acquiring status symbols, striving to enter a club, besting a rival, or contesting the rules of a hierarchy (see introduction). Worse, as McDonald and Parent (2021, p. 366) lament, status research often relies upon "hybrid solutions" that sidestep "essential

---

[3] Two other concepts bear close resemblance to status that are worth a footnote: prestige and standing. Indeed, prestige is often explicitly treated as an analytical synonym, or at least near enough. I am inclined to agree that when hierarchies of prestige are defined as inherently positional, social, and not tied to any particular quality, there is little need to differentiate (e.g., Mercer 2017). However, there is a narrower analytical use that retains popularity among realist-orientated status scholars: Gilpin's (1983) definition of prestige as "reputation for power." This is obviously unhelpful for me because (a) reputation is not relative and positional in the same sense as status in a status competition, and (b) my definition means one can have status in any social activity, including those unconnected to "power" in Gilpin's realpolitik sense. The difference between standing and status is even more fine-grained and almost boils down to semantic ease: standing is always positional like status, refers to a social hierarchy like status, and indeed almost always implies a status. However, status implies a particular identity that goes with the standing in some activity. One can *be* a social status— for example, a great power—but one can only *have* a high standing. This is also true for status versus prestige: if one has a prestigious position, that position *is* normally a social status. Ultimately, the analytical differences between standing, status, and prestige would not make a great deal of difference to the analysis except that it would likely prove harder to read and less intuitive. Thus, to be clear, while I hold that it is crucial that reputation and status not be conflated analytically, my positive selection of status over prestige and standing has more to do with pragmatic reasons and aesthetic preference.

differences" between types of status-seeking even though what "kind of status states are preoccupied with matters a great deal."[4] This chapter ensures that this book emphatically does not fall into this trap: it develops a typology of status that systematically distinguishes between types of status dynamic: status *competition*, status *application*, and status *domination*. While other typologies of status exist in IR, the key innovation and value added of my approach is that it defines status dynamics by their processual-relational logic rather than by either the motivation or the substance of the behavior. This typology thus lays the groundwork for solving one of the methodological riddles of the introduction: How can we identify and differentiate status competition from other types of state action without defining the substance of the status hierarchy prior to analysis? Moreover, defining status competition sociologically rather than psychologically avoids setting up an unhelpful and unobservable distinction between status and "material" motivations.

This procedure delivers an ideal-typical definition of status competition as *a rule-governed competition for position whereby the relative performance of competitors is easily identifiable by virtue of the shared understanding of the rules of the game*. While broadly consistent with extant status research, the advantage of my ideal type is that it gives new but due emphasis to the *rule-governed* nature of status competition and the specific processual-relational logic of action it produces (see below).[5] It is useful to emphasize again that because ideal types are deliberate accentuations of reality, it is nonsensical to "test" them against that empirical reality (Jackson 2010, p. 166) Instead, the ideal type disciplines the researcher by calling attention to particular aspects of concrete phenomena (while deliberately backgrounding others) that can be more or less *useful* to helping a researcher apprehend happenings in a given case (p. 166). By their very nature ideal types are seldom found in their pure form; it is up to the researcher to adduce additional factors—hopefully theoretically interesting ones—that *interplay* (or not) with the modeled dynamic in order to generate a plausible case-specific explanation that adequately accounts for events (Jackson 2010, p. 170). Indeed, in the empirical chapters that follow, the fact that the states in question do not compete in

---

[4] Parent and McDonald (2021) review four recent major monographs: Renshon (2017), Murray (2018), Ward (2017), and Larson and Shevchenko (2019). However, the context of the critique suggests they have in mind status research in general.

[5] All the works cited make reference to status being positional and/or based upon rank in valued attributes. Thus, even if they seldom state it explicitly, they necessarily imply rules (broadly understood as principles of comparison, not necessarily rules backed with authority).

perfectly rule-governed competitions for position in which no other logics operate is not a problem for my analysis but *a deliberate consequence of my research design*. Indeed, it is precisely the divergence in the rules of the competition and the consequences that I wish to investigate.

The chapter proceeds in three moves. I begin by clarifying why the dominant—and seemingly quite similar SIT typology of status-seeking (Larson and Shevchenko 2003, 2010, 2019)—cannot just be repurposed for my analysis. Then I set about defining status dynamics sociologically, that is, from the social structures that give rise to different types of status-seeking. Building on prior research, I elaborate the specific processual-relational logic embodied by status competition and the relationship between players it produces. I then parse from prior works three analytically distinct mechanisms that can push an actor to engage in a status competition: *prizes*, *pride*, and *pleasing the group*. I show how the first and the last push a state to compete for status yet do not require status to be the motivation. I contend that these mechanisms taken together provide sufficient grounds to use the ideal of status competition as a baseline for analysis from which reality departs, rather than using conventional security or economic models as the default.

From Social-Psychological to Sociological: Foregrounding Rules and Process

Before I develop my typology of status dynamics, this section elaborates the value it adds to prior conceptions of status competition already in circulation. Status research in IR already has an existing typology based upon SIT (Larson and Shevchenko 2003, 2010, 2014, 2019)—in widespread use[6]—that specifies different ideal-typical status-seeking strategies, including one called "social competition." Moreover, Larson and Shevchenko's concept of social competition may at first blush seem somewhat similar to mine, and without clarification there is a risk a reader may consider my rendering of status competition redundant. Finally, it is useful to differentiate because their work is paradigmatic of first-wave research: it aims to establish the importance of

---

[6] As Ward (2017, p. 2) notes, "No other [IR status] framework has as much influence." Indeed, Larson and Shevchenko's pioneering articles in *International Security* (2010) and *International Organisation* (2003) have over 700 Google Scholar citations and have provided the theoretical basis for a host of other major status works.

40 THE GRAMMAR OF STATUS COMPETITION

status as universal motivation to rival conventional interests;[7] it treats the international hierarchy as a well-understood structure to which states respond; and it downplays the significance of domestic audiences in theory and analysis. Thus, explaining how and why my conceptualization of status competition departs from theirs is useful for understanding the contribution of my TIS approach to status research more broadly.

Larson and Shevchenko's (2003, 2010, 2014, 2019) pioneering work provides a useful typology for identifying international status-seeking strategies. Drawing from social psychology, the basic assumption of the theory is that individuals' desire for positive intergroup comparisons manifests in status-seeking activities at the state level. To theorize how this internal impulse is manifested in international politics, Larson and Shevchenko ostensibly directly transpose Tajfel and Turner's (1979) typology of status-seeking strategies:

> The lower-status group may seek to imitate the higher-status group (social mobility), defeat the other group (social competition), or find new value dimensions in which it is superior (social creativity). Similarly, states may emulate more advanced states, compete to outdo the dominant state, or identify alternative values. (Larson and Shevchenko 2014, p. 38)

They go on to theorize environmental factors that would lead to one or another strategy: legitimacy, stability, and the permeability of the status hierarchy.

As intuitive as this sounds, this IR translation of social psychology suffers from considerable analytical shortcomings (Ward 2017). As the introductory chapter noted, by turning individual mobility into a group strategy, Larson and Shevchenko's rendering of SIT occludes a crucial rationale for status-seeking: pleasing the in-group lest they decide to disidentify or leave (see introduction). However, this move also has a second conceptual cost. By turning mobility into a collective strategy, Larson and Shevchenko blur the conceptual distinction between mobility and competition (Ward 2017). The problems this causes become clear in their use of examples to illustrate their types. They use NATO and the EU expansion as examples of social mobility by new members, and Imperial Britain and Wilhelmine Germany's

---

[7] Here Larson and Shevchenko's SIT framework has a proven track record of showing that status concerns matter for foreign policy—against the once conventional wisdom in mainstream IR.

arms-racing and war as their example of social competition. However, by seeking a "place in the sun" and trying to surpass Britain's navy, it seems clear that Germany was "emulating the values and behaviours" of its rival as well as seeking to outdo them. As Ward (2017, p. 6) notes, "All that remains to separate the two [types] is the arbitrary distinction between the pursuit of status markers that are militarily or economically significant and those that are not." Thus, within Larson and Shevchenko's typology emulation and competition collapse into one another; meanwhile their concept of social competition makes an a priori commitment to the substance of international status competition prior to analysis.

In addition, Larson and Shevchenko's status-seeking strategies are explicitly tied to status as a motivation. This is not a problem for their research design: investigating activities in world politics that seem better accounted for by status motivation than security or economic motivations. However, tying status competition to a distinct motivation also occludes fruitful inquiries into *how* states seek to "outdo" one another in international status hierarchies for reasons not *necessarily* related to status motivations. Indeed, this chapter contends that there is value in investigating status competition as a sociological phenomenon defined by its social characteristics rather than the inner psychological motivations that may *sometimes* give rise to it. Unmooring status competition from any one motivation thus provides a means of escaping the infamously difficult task of trying to discern motivations (Wittgenstein 1958). However, it also sets a challenge: how to produce insights about status competition without juxtaposing my explanation with conventional explanations based upon security and wealth.

To undertake this task, the following section foregrounds what Larson and Shevchenko and other social-psychology-inspired scholars have hitherto left tacit in their frameworks: rules of the game. Put simply, before one can plausibly "outdo" a rival, one must first understand what activity to outdo the rival in and what would count as having outdone that rival. Status competitions require rules; otherwise status-seeking would be akin to playing the lottery. Hence, Steven Ward (2017, p. 4) has called for further theoretical work along precisely these lines, noting, "Status markers are social constructs, and explaining their origins and evolution—why, for instance, empire was once valued as a marker of high standing but is no longer—requires going beyond the world of social psychology." In other words, Ward calls for further research into how changes in the rules structure states' status-seeking. To be sure, prior status research—Larson and Shevchenko included—is not oblivious to the rule-governed nature of status competition, but it is tacit rather than explicit. One result of this thin theorization of rules of status competition is that scholars end up defining the indicators of status competition in terms of the very rules of the game they are analyzing. For instance, defining suboptimal arms-racing as an indicator of status competition implies that arms have already been agreed upon as a status symbol. This, as I noted in the introduction, precludes investigating change in or contestation of the rules.

The following section picks up on Ward's call to foreground these *processes* of social construction that SIT-based scholarship brackets. In particular, I take inspiration from sociology-inspired scholarship to foreground the role that rules play in defining status hierarchies and the type of status dynamic different rules produce (Onuf 1989; Towns 2010; Towns and Rumelili 2017; Naylor 2018). This enables me to distinguish status competition from other status dynamics and, crucially, abstract a distinct processual-relational logic of status competition that can be discerned without reference to motivations and/or defining the substance of the hierarchy prior to analysis. Ultimately, by foregrounding rules in my ideal type of status competition, I lay the groundwork for problematizing those rules in the analyses (chapters 3, 4 and 5).

Developing an Ideal Type of Status Competition

This section sets out to conceptually distinguish between status dynamics by virtue of the rules of the status hierarchies that give rise to them. We should begin with a meat-and-potato definition of "status." At its simplest, status is a position in a social hierarchy that is based upon a quality, attribute, or activity. For one person or group to have high status requires that another have low status, and there is an audience to recognize these positions, whether it be other members of the hierarchy or a third party. To be clear, status always implies hierarchy of actually existing positions of superiority and inferiority. This sets status apart from reputation and identity. Everybody in a village can conceivably have a reputation as a reliable debtor and the identity of an "upstanding citizen." These could rely upon the discursive imagination of what would generate a bad reputation or what it would mean to be a citizen in poor standing. For instance, the EU's Self relies partly on an Other from its past (Diez 2004); meanwhile every state

THE LOGIC OF STATUS COMPETITION   43

could have the identity of democracy with its meaning generated in reference to history (Hansen 2006).[8] However, once one starts ranking reputation as better or worse, or ordering identity into positions, one has a status hierarchy.

Status hierarchies require shared "rules" that define the criteria by which status positions are attributed (see also Towns 2010; Towns and Rumelili 2017). For instance, the status hierarchy of the 100-meter sprint is determined by the simple rule that the winner is she who can run the fastest over 100 meters, starting from when the starting gun goes off. It is not, for instance, decided by who reaches the fastest speed during the race. Similarly, during the early 20th century, possessing battleships became a relatively accepted measure of "world power," while having the most battleships granted their possessor the status of leading world power (Murray 2010, p. 665). It is important to note that such status hierarchies do not *require* authority in the legal/rational sense to become meaningful. To be sure, authority can help organize a status hierarchy, but it is not necessary for status hierarchies to emerge. This sort of informal "broad" hierarchy—patterns of inequality in material or symbolic resources—can cut against and across "narrow" hierarchical relations of formal authority (Mattern and Zarakol 2016, p. 630). For instance, in the schoolyard status hierarchies often develop that run counter to the wishes of the school authorities: seldom do the hardest-working or academically successful get the highest social status.[9] They are *rule-governed* in the sense that to define a better or worse, high or low position requires a principle of comparison (Onuf 1989, p. 267); it need not require formal authority to back it up. In this sense, status hierarchies are perfectly compatible with anarchy understood as the absence of formal authority (McConaughey, Musgrave, and Nexon 2018, pp. 186–187).

At this point, a reader might reasonably suggest that I am in danger of defining all social life as implicated in status hierarchies, thus rendering the concept less than helpful. We can escape banality (the observation that societies are always hierarchical and every activity is a kind of status-seeking) in at least three ways. First, one can investigate variance in individuals' or groups' concern for status (e.g., Renshon 2016, 2017). One can historicize status as the empirical chapters of this book does: asking how particular

---

[8] In practice, it is almost certain that a good reputation and an upstanding citizen would be defined in such a way that real and existing members of the community did not meet the criteria. However, here we would quickly get into some kind of status hierarchy.

[9] At least not at my high school.

hierarchies emerged, changed, and dwindled across time (e.g., Towns 2010, 2012;chapters 3–5). However, here, I will focus on differentiating between *types* of status hierarchies and the types of *relations* and *processes* that they engender. This is necessary because, as Ayşe Zarakol (2017, p. 12) points out, most status research tends to focus on investigating states' responses to their position in preexisting hierarchies and suggests "[w]hat is lacking from this body of work is a more direct engagement with the concept of hierarchy itself" (see also McDonald and Parent 2021). Addressing this issue conceptually, the next section will draw on extant work and develop a new typology that remains in the same etymological ballpark as prior IR status research, but draw out essential features hitherto downplayed or undertheorized: status competition's rule-governed nature and the specific processual-relational dynamic status competitions embody. In the process, I develop a sociological ideal type of status *competition* and logically differentiate it from other types of status-seeking.

Fixed and Changeable Criteria

The first step toward defining status competition is to divide status hierarchies according to whether the criteria upon which they are based are changeable or fixed. It is not difficult to find instances of fixed status hierarchies in history and indeed the present day. The Indian caste system is paradigmatic of a status hierarchy that is based upon fixed criteria, "ascribed" by the rules of society (Linton 1936). Within some cultures, age defines one's place in a society, and as such while one gradually does move up the hierarchy it is independent of one's will. Crucially for our purposes, there is no meaningful way in which status *competition*—rule-guided efforts to move up a social hierarchy—can obtain in such a social arrangement. To be sure, members can contest the hierarchy and strive to overturn it, but they cannot *compete* for status position. In international society, the neo-Darwinian racist hierarchies that underlay slavery and imperialism come closest to the ideal of fixed-ascribed status hierarchies.

Conversely, the EU's membership criteria and the OECD's PISA education rankings come close to constituting the ideal of *achieved* status hierarchies. Here status is attributed according to what an individual or group do or acquire. Actually existing international institutional arrangements often embody a mix of both fixed and changeable criteria: the EU requires prospective

THE LOGIC OF STATUS COMPETITION   45

members to be "European"[10] *and* to meet certain criteria for admittance (democratic and economic norms). The great power club once admitted only Western states (fixed) that had *achieved* relatively high levels of material power.

While status-seeking research in IR implicitly focuses on *achieved* status hierarchies, making this distinction allows us to understand how achieved hierarchies are often nested within fixed hierarchies but analytically distinct from them. It thus allows us to avoid conflating logically and substantively different status dynamics: contesting imperial hierarchies with striving to meet criteria for entering the EU. Moreover, and crucially for my purposes, it allows us to see that striving to improve one's position in a fixed hierarchy is logically impossible without contesting the rules. Here, following the rules can lead to only one type of status dynamic: perpetual domination. In other words, the relations of super- and subordination will remain for as long as the rules of the game are not challenged.

Status Clubs and Rankings

The next distinction is between status clubs and status ranking. To draw as sharp a conceptual line between these two types as possible, I will distill them to their simplest and most extreme form. At its simplest, to enter a status club requires an entrant to meet an absolute standard and creates a simple hierarchy of in-group and out-group: those that can meet the standard and those that do not (traditional/modern; nuclear/nonnuclear; democratic/autocratic).[11] Esteem from membership of clubs is generated by difficulty, scarcity, and exclusivity (Gilady 2018; Paikowsky 2017): as more join the group, membership becomes less exclusive, and thus the number of rivals to whom members can seem superior dwindles. (Paul, Larson, and Wohlforth [2014] call this "dilution.") Related, but distinct, *ranking* hierarchies turn these standards into a continuum in which everyone's performance generates a position that is relative to others. No longer is one democratic or not; one can have better or worse democracy and even have the best democracy. Because

---

[10] Though the extent to which this is fixed must come with an asterix; see Neumann (2003) and Rumelili (2004) on the politics and malleability of what counts as "Europe."

[11] In theory at least, in practice it will depend upon how others interpret the standard, which in IR is seldom consistent and certainly not immutable. On shifting the goalposts, see Zarakol (2010) and Naylor (2018); on the evolving definition of democracy, see Oren (1995).

only one can rank top, relative rankings automatically guarantee and generate scarcity and exclusivity and facilitate and encourage relative competition: because one cannot improve position without at least one rival moving down (see Towns and Rumelili 2017 for a related discussion).

Joining a Club

The usual way to leverage this difference is to note how status groups operate like "club goods," which mitigate the zero-sum competition for status position in a ranking (e.g., Paul, Larson, and Wohlforth 2014). Though each new member reduces the exclusivity of the group, new members do not push out the old members so long as they continue to meet the absolute standard. Thus, existing members may try to block new members (e.g., the nuclear club), but they are not directly competing for position with aspiring members (though they may do once they have joined the group). What is lost in this discussion is that seeking to gain access to a status club with absolute standards does not only mitigate competition; the dynamic it produces *does not* constitute a relational competition between in-group and out-group *at all*. To be sure, there is a hierarchical relationship between aspiring members and members. If the club is desirable, it may imply the members wield power (symbolic or material) over aspiring members. However, because absolute standards are independent from a rival's performance, the relationship between members and nonmembers is one of *gatekeeper and applicant* or perhaps *teacher and student*. Thus, when club hierarchies have absolute standards as a rule of entry, it does *not* make members and nonmembers *rivals* like those competing for position in ranking hierarchy. Moreover, such a hierarchy does not imply a potentially endless *process* of competition: once one has met an absolute standard or entered a club one can theoretically cease one's status-seeking.

Some caveats and clarifications are in order here. It is crucial to distinguish between the everyday understandings of status clubs and a conceptually useful definition that can be distinguished from rankings. Lots of existing status clubs are derived from *rank* in a given metric (see Naylor 2018).[12] For instance, the realist description of the great power status (club) is one based

---

[12] Naylor (2018) provides an insightful historical analysis of how the rules governing in-group membership in international society's more exclusive institutions—or status clubs—have structured state behavior over time.

upon relative power position; aspiring members and members are in direct competition with one another for position. Indeed, when club membership is based upon ranking in an achieved hierarchy and the club membership is permeable, then *ceteris paribus* it will produce the same dynamic as a status hierarchy based upon rank. As such, in a club based on rank, the *dynamic process* that unfolds between members and applicants is analytically identical to those that unfold between states fighting for position in a ranking.[13] Thus, it would be redundant or at least confusing to use this everyday understanding of clubs.

Status Competitions

Drawing this all together and excluding fixed hierarchies and club hierarchies, we arrive at the type of hierarchy that engenders and makes possible *status competition*. Status competition requires the hierarchy's criteria to involve attributes that can be changed via the agency of the members of the hierarchy. To be a competition rather than a club there must be different *relative* positions within the hierarchy: one can move up only if another moves down (in its ideal form). The visual abstraction of a status competition is the construction of an ordinal ranking whereby competitors are ordered according to their relative performance in a given metric (Onuf 1989, p. 267). Crucially, unlike status applicant–gatekeeper relations or relations of domination, members of the hierarchy have the *relationship of rivals*: they cannot know their status without reference to the relative performance of the others involved in the competition. Moreover, in the ideal, all the players involved understand and accept the rules and have perfect information about the game. Thus, there is no ambiguity about who has the status of winner or leader nor ambiguity over which suffers the ignominy of losing or lagging behind. With status competition distinguished from other types of status dynamic, the next section turns to the specific relational process that status competition embodies.

---

[13] Where the line is drawn in practice, and whether status clubs are institutionalized, is not irrelevant. By virtue of defining the terms of entry, they can standardize the competition, while their exclusive meetings may engender feelings of inclusion and pride in their members, and feelings of exclusion and jealousy in outsiders. These social privileges/punishments associated with status competitions and clubs will be addressed in the next section. They can affect the intensity of competition but not the positional dynamic itself.

48 THE GRAMMAR OF STATUS COMPETITION

	Inherent Status	Achieved Status
Status Club	Status Domination	Status Application
Ranking Hierarchy		Status Competition

Figure 1.1 Typology of Status Hierarchies and Status Relations

The Processual-Relational Implications of Status Competition

Understood in this manner, status competitions engender a peculiar dynamic process that is recognizably different from other types of goal-oriented action. Status competitions are relational for everyone (because every move up or down a ranking has ripple effects), and position cannot be determined without comparison. Critically, when there is more than one other, if an actor takes on losses in order to make the rival have even less (in contrast to a zero-sum game), they risk moving down the rankings (even if they best that specific rival). Indeed, sprinters in a race do not rugby-tackle their opponents; it would be self-defeating. Similarly, the superpowers did not use their nuclear weapons to "win" the arms race. Even if they might have had the last nuclear weapon standing, they would have blown each other to the bottom of the global rankings. Additionally, because one's performance is always relative to others', there is no necessary limit on the *process* of competition. Such a process in the extreme may end up resembling Lewis Carroll's Queen's Race, in which "it takes all the running you can do, to keep in the same place." This stands in stark contrast to absolute standards defining status clubs, where one need not pay attention to one's rivals to meet the standard (see Towns and Rumelili 2017), and fixed hierarchies where only contesting the rules can avoid perpetual domination. Moreover, while relative rankings are always relational, competitors are not related in the same way. When an actor placed low in the rankings moves up to the middle it affects all the others below, who will experience a ripple effect upon their position. However, those placed above it will not feel the ripple. All this implies that actors engaged in status competition will pay closer attention to the performance of those near them in the hierarchy (see also Frank 1985; Renshon 2017; Røren 2019).

The Olympics illustrates how status competitions generate a specific processual-relational dynamic among the "players." A sailing competition is particularly apt for putting into focus the rule-governed, processual-relational dynamic. A competitor in an Olympic sailing race has a position in the ranking, but she also has a socially significant status that changes as the competition proceeds. While the participants begin equal, the process of racing soon generates a socially consequential status hierarchy. The first-place participant gets recognized as having the status of "winner" of the first race and the status of "leader" going into the next. The second-place contestant becomes "the challenger," and depending on the scoring system the rest of the competitors might be identified as "laggards." The rules of the competition stipulate that players accumulate points that carry over into the next race. These points define position and statuses that emerge and change as the races proceed. Usually, by the latter races the behavior of the sailors seems odd because the leader in the final round ceases trying to win the race itself and sacrifices winning that round to block off the challenger. In short, the mutual understanding of the rules grants the sailors an awareness of their respective status as the game proceeds, which in turn informs their behavior to one another. This is contra the usual rationalist conceptualization of interaction whereby "players" compete in "context free games" in which they "enter with preferences formed and leave with identities unchanged" (McCourt 2014, p. 42). Within sailing competitions the processual-relational dynamic is especially apparent; however, other Olympic events—which all share the generic conception of status competition outlined above—also embody it.

Indeed, very different Olympic events share this processual-relational logic even if the precise form it takes differs. For instance, long-distance road cycling races tend to follow a pattern whereby a large number of competitors deliberately flock together to enjoy the benefits of sitting in the slipstream of the others, thereby saving energy. They quite deliberately cooperate by taking turns to lead the peloton to equalize the advantages to all. However, while this cooperation carries on throughout, it is still a competition. Throughout

50   THE GRAMMAR OF STATUS COMPETITION

the race, competitors will seek to break away from the group, which will usually prompt the peloton to up the pace and attempt to run down the leaders. Of particular interest to us here is that the speed at which the peloton moves is a relational consequence—or ripple effect—of the timing of one competitor's decision to try to break away. This cannot be predicted a priori by any one rider, nor by assessing each rider's physical qualities. Elsewhere, the 100-meter sprint arguably has the least pronounced processual-relational dynamic, but nonetheless even here we find that upon realizing they are winning the race, a sprinter may ease up toward the finish and may raise their hands in the air in celebration before crossing the line.

These very different events nonetheless share a processual-relational logic that can shape the behavior and strategies of participants. It is not the activity itself—such as running or sailing—that tells one how to compete: it is the specifics of the rules defining the competition that enables processual-relational competition to unfold among participants. Crucially, if the competitors in any of these events did not share a common understanding of those rules, a relational logic may well inform the players' actions, but it would be impossible to agree upon who led and who lagged; meanwhile disagreement about who won and who lost would be endemic. Ultimately, these examples illustrate the importance of rules to status competition and thus why—unlike prior research—I place such emphasis on them in my definition of status competition as *a rule-governed competition for position whereby relative performance is easily identifiable by virtue of the shared understanding of those rules.*

Back to International Relations

In the context of government policymaking, we can recognize the processual-relational logic of status competition when relative position in an international hierarchy affects the size, form, and timing of the particular policies a state pursues.[14] While international politics is messier than the Olympics, this processual-relational logic of status competition is often visible. For instance, as Nicholas Onuf (1989, p. 283) has pointed out in *World*

---

[14] Although my empirical focus is on international status competition among states, this logic can theoretically inform any activity undertaken by individuals or groups that can conceive of themselves in a rank-ordered hierarchy.

of Our Making, the Cold War "superpower" competition resembled such a dynamic, whereby their status competition produced a "climate of contest and spectacle—an unending tournament, rounds of play in many arenas, all of us a captive audience." What makes this processual rather than just embodying the "logic of positionality" (Mattern and Zarakol 2016, p. 637) is that a policy that targeted higher status in a given ranking would need to be *continuously* informed by consideration of how that policy would improve or downgrade their position in the ranking. Indeed, when treated as a process that unfolds rather than a one-off strategy prompted by position, we can see how status competitions engender change as a series of "reverberations along a web of interdependencies" (Jackson and Nexon 1999, p. 299). Defining international status competition as a dynamic process—rather than a discrete outcome—thus opens up for analysis of how changes in relative position *or* changes in the rules affect the behaviors of players/states.

As I illustrated with the Olympics events, the *processual-relational logic* of status competitions is not limited to any specific referent: it can theoretically emerge in any public activity, whether consumption patterns or norm adherence. It makes no difference whether a state is competing in "material" hierarchies (e.g., tanks, GDP, battleship tonnage) or moral competition over human rights records (see Matter and Zarakol 2016, p. 638). If one wishes to establish oneself as the greatest of "great powers," one may well need to invest in more battleships or aircraft carriers than a rival, even if the military's analysis suggested submarines offered better bang for the buck (see Gilady 2018, pp. 59–60; see also Murray 2010, 2018). Similarly, if accepting many refugees became the barometer of status as a "good power," a state would need to know how many refugees its rivals took to know how to compete. Here, it is not reference to the law or economic cost-benefit analysis that shapes the specific size and shape of the policy, but comparison to specific peers' policies over time. Indeed, while liberal-inflected norms scholarship (e.g., Finnemore and Sikkink 1998) tends to assume an individualist relationship to the norm determines appropriate behavior (one either follows it or not; see Sending 2002), international society's expanding array of governance ranking practices (Broome, Homolar, and Kranke 2018) highlights how norms can be performed well or badly and actors can be ranked accordingly (Towns and Rumelili 2017).[15] If those ranked decide to compete for position, then

---

[15] Since the 1990s, the number of country performance indicators has grown almost exponentially: quadrupling in the 1990s and tripling over the next 15 years (Kelley and Simmons 2019).

52 THE GRAMMAR OF STATUS COMPETITION

this process embodies the logic of status competition rather than the logic of appropriateness (see chapter 4). However, as noted, these activities and attributes do not come already ranked and valued. Similar to how whether a running race is 100 meters or 10,000 meters will affect the strategy and favor certain players, so too does the substance of the rules ranking military power or democracy favor certain countries over others in any competition.[16]

So far I have elaborated the rule-governed nature of status competition and the specific processual-relational logic that it produces. We now turn to the question I have hitherto avoided: *Why* would states and citizens be moved to compete in state status competitions? I have deliberately separated the relational logic of status competition from the reasons why one might compete in a status competition in order to unmoor status competition from its connection to motivation and any substantive type of behavior. This is crucial because in the following chapter I will develop a framework for identifying how the logic of status competition manifests in practice without requiring the analyst to attempt to infer motivations.

Why Compete in a Status Competition?

In the popular imagination, athletes in the Ancient Greek Olympics are often presumed to compete for glory and honor. This was certainly a big part of the story. The athletes who took part were concerned with displaying "excellence" in the valued attributes that Hellenic society held in high esteem: manly beauty, courage, staying power in battle (Faulkner 2012). The prizes reflected this concern for signaling social status: gold, silver, and ivory ornaments and elaborate embroideries—in other words, "phenomenal prestige goods, designed not for use but for display and donation" (p. 385). However, motivation could not be reduced to status and prestige alone. Winners' "star status" at the Ancient Olympics ensured they could expect invitations to the numerous financially incentivized games that took place in other cities all year round. Meanwhile, because Olympic success generated prestige for the city and joy to its citizens, Olympians were rewarded handsomely by their hometown should they return home victorious. As we shall

---

[16] As Lilach Gilady (2018) has convincingly argued big, expensive, visible boats (battleships and lately aircraft carriers) have consistently been demanded at higher levels than submarines because of their symbolic value.

THE LOGIC OF STATUS COMPETITION   53

see, the status competitions of international politics reflect a similar mix of incentives. Indeed, the IR status literature provides three solid answers to this question that mirror the Olympics: prizes, pride, and pleasing the in-group.

The *prizes* for status competitions consist of the rewards that others bestow upon a state for achieving recognized status on a given hierarchy. Crucially, the rewards for ranking high on a status hierarchy are *independent* from whether the government and population are ethically, analytically, or emotionally invested in the criteria of the hierarchy and their position within it. For instance, realists have posited that ranking high on whatever counts for military power may provide the prize of deterrence and deference, and perhaps a seat at important tables (e.g., Gilpin 1983). It does not matter whether the state or its population considers the power hierarchy just or accurate; if they value the prizes, they may well still compete (Beaumont and Towns 2021). However, other rankings also provide prizes. Scoring high on the World Bank's Ease of Doing Business index encourages external investment, *regardless* of whether business is actually easier,[17] or whether the country agrees with the measure of easy business. Similarly, Transparency International's ranking of perception of corruption is (rightly) contested in terms of validity (De Maria 2008), yet because it is tied to development aid and indeed credit ratings, avoiding a low score is instrumentally valuable to states (Bruner and Abdelal 2005, pp. 199–200). However, the prizes that incentivize states need not only be economic and security based (though these are in many cases the easiest to observe). A leader and citizenry might enjoy the international praise and back-patting they can expect from topping the list of aid donors; similarly states might place a value on avoiding the international opprobrium that may follow from finishing low (Johnston 2001, p. 500). In short, a state might compete for the prizes associated with a status competition that the leader, government, or citizens take *no pride* in winning.

Quite distinct from the prizes bestowed upon winners is the *pride or* "intrinsic" rewards for competing in a status competition. As Ringmar (1996, p. 3) notes, "people do not generally engage in them [competitions] because of what they can win, but instead because of who or what the game allows them to be." SIT-based accounts reach the same conclusion but from different roots, claiming that people generate pride and self-esteem (and risk shame) based upon intergroup *comparisons* vis-à-vis significant Others. One way a

---

[17] See Schueth (2015) on how Georgia managed to move up the Ease of Doing Business rankings by 82 places (record), while staying in more or less the same position on the World Economic Forum's annual Global Competitiveness Index.

54   THE GRAMMAR OF STATUS COMPETITION

group can achieve this is to compete to improve "the relative positions of the in-group" vis-à-vis "the out-group on salient dimensions" (Tajfel and Turner 1979, p. 44). In the field of IR this underwrites approaches that treat the state like a human (Larson and Shevchenko 2003, 2010, 2019) and approaches that specify that leaders are likely to invest their self-esteem in the state's status (e.g., Renshon 2016, 2017). Although recognition could be conceived of as a reward, and thus a prize, for a competitor to rest their esteem upon a competition requires they consider its rules legitimate and value the game. If players compete in a game they do not value, neither playing the game nor winning it can generate self-esteem or shame. From this perspective, if one adds this social dimension to game theory, it may not be the material loss of being the sucker that matters, but the fear of being *seen as the sucker*.

The third reason for *a state* to compete in a status competition can be termed *pleasing the group*. Similar to how the Greek city-state may subsidize its potential athletes in the hope of fostering civic pride, so the leaders may compete for status for their group in order to generate solidarity and pride among the group's members (Ward 2013, 2017). In international relations this becomes especially visible when leaders or the opposition deliberately stoke nationalism (encouraging rallying around the flag) for political gain. While this third mechanism depends upon the second—in that it requires group members to rest their self-esteem upon and act to improve or maintain social position—it is analytically separate in an important regard. The leader or members of the government need not themselves be invested in the status competition but only understand that their citizens are, and thus that their legitimacy, popularity, and, to some extent, authority rest upon it. Indeed, as the pioneers of SIT in social psychology Tajfel and Turner (1979, p. 44) note, where possible, "low status may tend, in conditions of unsatisfactory social identity, to promote the widespread adoption of individual mobility strategies": leaving the social group. Even if leaving is not an option, if membership does not allow the individual to make positive comparisons, they may disidentify with the group and prove less willing to make sacrifices on its behalf (Tajifel and Turner 1978; see also Ward 2022). As a result, leaders face strong incentives to help their citizens make positive competitive comparisons with other states. Indeed, as Ned Lebow (2010, p. 63) has argued, if we can recognize that leaders face incentives to quench the material appetites of their populations, then if people—especially nationalists—invest their self-esteem in their state's status, leaders and governments have good reason to take this into account too (see also Ward 2017a, pp. 37–38). Yet, this mechanism need not be strictly

THE LOGIC OF STATUS COMPETITION   55

tied to pride and esteem of the citizens; as chapter 4 shows, citizens may consider just relative international ranking and status in a given activity to be an appropriate measure of their government's performance.

Thus, there are at least three mechanisms that may incentivize competing in a status competition and two (prizes and group-pleasing) that do not require the government to intrinsically care about the status competition. Moreover, it is quite possible for different members of a group (or citizens of the state) to care about the status competition for different reasons. For instance, some members of a group may wish to compete in a nuclear arms race because they consider it essential for deterrence; others may take pride in besting the rival group. Given that this book aims to investigate how activities become discursively constituted as status competitions, how the rules are formed and contested, and with what consequence for legitimating policy, I can remain ambivalent about exactly how much causal weight each mechanism accounts for, even if it were possible to assess.[18]

Instead of trying to disentangle these mechanisms in analysis, I will use them as a warrant for flipping the usual methodological MO of status research. Instead of using a rational economic or security-maximizing model as the baseline and treating status as residual, I assume that *ceteris paribus* states have several social mechanisms pushing them to compete for status, and as such the logic of status competition should be widespread in international relations.[19] I therefore use status competition as a baseline and

[18] We might also add fourth mechanisms for competing that is complementary to this list: ontological security research (Steele 2008; Zarakol 2010; Subotic 2016; Browning and Joenniemi 2017) theorizes and empirically shows how individuals and collectives place an independent value upon maintaining stable narratives of the self, and this encourages actors to persist with routines and practices that cut against conventional interests. While such narratives need not involve competing for status, it is possible and even likely that states and citizens that have a long history of competing for status in a particular hierarchy by particular rules may prioritize continuing to compete in this manner in order to avoid ontological insecurity that changing their behavior could bring about. See Browning, Joenniemi, and Steele (2021) and Beaumont and Røren (2018) on how ontological security and status theories can complement one another. I have largely eschewed combining these theories here in order to avoid complicating an already theoretically complex work.

[19] Although I emphasize here the positive reasons why status competition can be used as a baseline, it is possible to make the negative case against assuming that wealth maximization and especially security should be the default assumption. For instance, given so few states these days get "selected out" in the manner neorealists suggest "anarchy" enables and encourages, states have a great deal of leeway to pursue other goals. Powerful states in particular can pursue extremely inefficient security policies before their territorial integrity is threatened (see Kirshner 2015, p. 160). It is for this reason that I do not find the common claim that security policy is a "hard case" for status very compelling. In fact, given the close historical association of war and military capabilities with great power status, I would be amazed if status dynamics did not emerge in security affairs. Indeed, we now have numerous works documenting precisely this (e.g., Gilady 2018; Pu and Schweller 2014; Renshon 2017, to name just a few).

conduct case-specific analyses that explore how manifestations of status competition within international politics *departs* from the ideal (Jackson 2010; see chapters 1 and 2). This strategy allows each case study to go beyond showing *that* status mattered and to identify *how* status mattered in ways underappreciated by existing status scholarship. In particular, as I argued in the introduction, there are good reasons to expect that different groups within the state will not agree on the rules of the status hierarchy and that these rules may not prove stable as any given status competition unfolds. Instead, I expect that the international hierarchies to which domestic actors refer will often be contestable, and this ambiguity will likely prove productive of rival, contradictory, and perhaps evolving theories of a state's status. My approach is thus geared toward identifying how the contestation and change in those rules affected policy processes and outcomes, as well as identifying other case-specific factors that may have inhibited the ideal of status competition from being realized.

Toward the Grammar of Status Competition

This chapter has laid the groundwork for developing a theoretical framework capable of identifying the logic of status competition as it manifests in discourse. I argued that because prior work has tended to define status competition in terms of the substance of the international hierarchy and generally understated the rule-governed nature of status competition, I had to go back to the drawing board. First, in my account, the ideal of status competition is possible only in rank-ordered hierarchy based upon changeable metrics of performance. This type of hierarchy produces the *relationship* of rivals rather than (a) club hierarchies which produce the relationship of student-teacher or gatekeeper-applicant or (b) a fixed hierarchy of superiority/inferiority, such as a caste system. Second, given that all rankings require rules to define good and bad performance, I argued that an ideal-typical status competition requires intersubjective agreement over those rules, lest competitors find themselves playing different games. Third, I argued that competing in rank-ordered hierarchy produces a specific processual-relational dynamic whereby ascertaining performance requires continuous comparison to others. This sets status apart from individualistic logics such as wealth maximization or abstract rule-following. Finally, I argued that there are solid reasons why a state might compete in status competition and there is no a priori need to define status competition in terms of motivation for status. However, I suggested that these mechanisms taken together are sufficient to use the ideal of status competition as a baseline for analysis instead of conventional approaches that give analytical priority to wealth or security.

Although several factors inhibit the ideal international status competition from being realized (see introduction), I contend that this does not foreclose the logic of status competition from informing government policy. Instead, the difficulty of reaching agreement over the rules of the game and the possibility of self-recognition mean that domestic actors can frame a policy and act *as if* they are in a status competition—*a processual-relational, rule-governed competition for relative position*—even if the other players do not share the same rules or are not even paying attention. It is the prevalence of states conducting activities that *resemble* competitions for status—in which the logic is visible—that explains why status-seeking appears so widespread in international affairs even if "international" hierarchies are often ambiguous and contested. Thus, before turning to the cases, the next chapter develops what I call "the grammar of status," which lays out a toolkit for recognizing the logic of status competition as it is deployed in political discourse. This heuristic device allows systematic empirical investigation into whether and how rival theories of international status hierarchies are used to (de)legitimate government policies.

2

The Grammar of Status Competition

You don't need to eat so quickly! It's not a competition.
—*Cambridge Dictionary*'s example sentence
for "competition"

Introduction

To illuminate how the logic of status competition can manifest in practice without the ideal being realized, I will begin with a brief vignette. When I was an English teacher,[1] I would routinely put my students into pairs and encourage them to practice speaking by giving them a series of open-ended questions to discuss. The point of the activity was to "maximize student talk time" and give them an opportunity to practice the new language they were learning. Although practice for its own sake was the stated goal, usually at least one pair of students would race through the questions and proudly declare that they were "finished!" in one-fifth of the time allocated. At which point, I would typically exclaim, "It's not a competition! There are no prizes for coming first." Most people will be familiar with this refrain for when a person treats an activity like a competition when it is not intended as such. The fact that the *Cambridge Dictionary* lists it among the example sentences for explaining the meaning of competition would indicate this is not an uncommon situation. Its prevalence might seem to illustrate evolutionary biologists' claim that humans are "hard-wired" to compete for position (Paul, Larson, and Wohlforth 2014, p. 18). Yet even if we are born with the urge to compete, this urge does not tell us *how* to compete in a given context. Hence, this example also illustrates humans' remarkable ability to *conceptualize* nearly any activity as a relative competition

---

[1] Between 2005 and 2011, I was an English teacher in Poland, Czech Republic, Japan, the United Kingdom, Argentina, and Norway.

The Grammar of Status Competition. Paul David Beaumont, Oxford University Press. © Oxford University Press 2024.
DOI: 10.1093/9780197771808.003.0003

THE GRAMMAR OF STATUS COMPETITION   59

for position, a race for first place.[2] Without prompting, the students had conceived of their own rules and imposed them upon the activity—answer all the questions in the shortest time possible—and set about racing to "victory."[3] The students may even have felt pride in their "status" as the winner. In short, the students theorized, competed, and won a competition of their own making. It did not require anybody else to share the same rules of the game for those rules to shape the students' decision to answer the questions as quickly as possible.

The point of this vignette is to illustrate how the logic of status competition can obtain and explain human behavior, even when nobody else is playing the same game. I argue that analogous "imaginary competitions" can operate and inform government policy. However, unlike our students, states (or more precisely, governments) must justify their actions to public audiences and consequently leave behind a textual trail.[4] As such, rather than striving to infer motivation from actions, the analyst can study patterns of legitimation via discourse.[5]

The rest of this chapter is dedicated to explicating how (1) the logic of status competition can be conceived as a mode of discursive legitimation and (2) how we can recognize it. To this second end, I elaborate what I call the "Grammar of Status Competition": a metalinguistic means of recognizing the logic of status competition as it manifests in language without "status" needing to be uttered as a rationale. Here, I leverage the processual-relational logic outlined in the previous chapter to develop a lens for identifying theories of status competition as they manifest in discourse, as well as their political effects. Crucially, by focusing on what speaking status *does* and the *effects* it *has* in practice, we can study status and its effects without assuming (and reifying) the rules of an international social hierarchy or trying to infer motivations. To get there, I must begin by spelling out the theory of discourse that underpins this framework.

---

[2] As Onuf (1989, pp. 266–270) notes, ascertaining the evaluation rules of a ranking is logically prior to any efforts to compete for position.

[3] If the urge to compete might be hardwired at birth to some extent, the notion of how to compete must surely be social. I would suggest that students' prior experience of competing in other activities led them to assume that speed was the crucial criterion.

[4] While the student could construct the rules of his imaginary competition and decide to compete without justification, most modern governments must legitimate policy decisions to their citizenry.

[5] See Jackson (2006), Krebs (2015), and Hanson (2006) for seminal research that centers on processes of legitimation.

60 THE GRAMMAR OF STATUS COMPETITION

Status as Legitimation

States are extremely talkative. This is because the people and the bureaucracies that perform a state's activities must continuously justify their activities undertaken in the name of the state. As Ronald Krebs (2015, p. 14) notes, "legitimation—the articulation before key publics of publicly acceptable reasons for concrete actions and policy positions—is typically an imperative, not a mere nicety, of politics, both domestic and foreign." To be sure, Krebs notes, most of a state's day-to-day activities do not come under much public scrutiny; however, "in large-scale, bureaucratic nation-states, policies must be, at least, capable of public legitimation" (p. 14). Yet, given that most policies are ongoing, legitimation is rarely a one-off action, but instead is a continuous process (Jackson 2006, p. 16). Consequently, states produce an ongoing supply of textual representations of the social world within which they operate (also see Hanson 2006, chs. 2–3). Here, legitimation via these texts enjoys "a 'prosthetic' character: simultaneously revealing and producing the world under investigation" (Jackson 2006, p. 16, n. 7). I will turn to the assumptions that underpin this understanding of texts shortly. For now, it suffices to note that this implies that state bureaucracies leave behind substantial evidence of their legitimation of policies, which the analyst can use as primary data.[6] Thus, one methodological implication is that we can study policy legitimation by tracing these texts.

However, if states had perfect flexibility to legitimate anything they pleased by whatever means they preferred, studying legitimation would not provide any analytical purchase upon state actions. But most governments do not have such flexibility: not all potential activities can be legitimated, and not all logics of legitimation work for a given policy. Instead, the range of reasons that could be used to legitimate a given policy is bound—prestructured—by the social context within which governments operate (Hansen 2006; Jackson 2006; Krebbs 2015). At a minimum, a government cannot legitimate a policy in reference to something that the audience does not understand.[7] Second, and crucially, the reason given must resonate with its audience. For instance,

---

[6] To be clear, to study legitimation is to study what reasons worked in a concrete social context to render the particular course of action legitimate, *not* how well it fits with some objective abstract notion of legitimacy or how accurately it depicts reality (Jackson 2006, pp. 16–19).

[7] In poststructuralist language, this is called intertextuality: the need to refer to some idea already in circulation in order for it to be intelligible (see Hansen 2006, p. 7). Lest this sound banal, tracing the conditions of possibility for the sayable and thus thinkable is a basic premise of the genealogical method (see Vucetic 2011b).

if the leader of a secular country attempted to use a religious text to legitimate a policy, it would be unlikely to succeed, even if the audience were familiar with the religious text. Conversely, the leader of a religious country may struggle to legitimate a policy if they do not relate it to scriptures. Although the discursive resources available to a government limit the scope of legitimate action, they are not determinative (Diez 1999, p. 611). Actors have agency to improvise, alter, and combine in imaginative new ways the intersubjective materials at their disposal to render a policy legitimate (Jackson 2006, pp. 27–29, 39–41; see also Ringmar 2012, p. 18). This notion of improvisation and adaption allows a degree of agency to frame the world in different ways that do not depend entirely either on the essence of the world or the social structure within which an actor operates (Jackson 2006, pp. 15–16, 25–26; Hansen 2006, p. 7). In the process, individual acts of representation and legitimation contribute to the social resources available to future legitimation efforts.

A crucial ontological and methodological implication flows from this way of understanding legitimation: legitimation has no necessary relationship to motivation. Indeed, one result of treating the state as a human or unitary—as first-wave status research does—is that status tends to be understood as an internal motivation rather than a mode of legitimation. This has the downstream methodological consequence of treating words uttered by states mainly as a means of inferring motivation rather than as ontologically significant in terms of legitimating the action they explain. Lest this appear merely a semantic alteration, it is useful to juxtapose my assumptions about language with the conventional neorealist attitude to words spoken by governments: "talk is cheap" (e.g., Mearsheimer 2010, p. 383). The argument runs as follows: given governments' opportunity and incentives to lie, instead of listening to what they say, analysts should focus on what they do. Simplifying, the result is that neorealist-inspired scholarship produces theories that assume states' motivations—whether it be security, wealth, or, latterly, status—and then develop hypotheses about what sort of outcomes such a motivation would produce given x, y, z objective conditions. Whether the policy outcome matches the theoretical expectation matters; the social processes that take place in between the input and the output are at best only epistemologically useful as a proxy to ascertain motivation, or at worst mere noise that can be safely ignored (see also Ringmar 1996, p. 35).

In contrast, scholars assuming that states/governments must always legitimate their actions in reference to some sort of limiting social structure can

62 THE GRAMMAR OF STATUS COMPETITION

remain ambivalent about motivations.[8] Without pondering motivation at all, securitization scholars investigate how threats become threats via securitization processes (Buzan et al. 1998). When investigating the securitization of migration in the EU (e.g., Huysmans 2000), it is neither here nor there for the securitization scholar whether the securitizing actors *believe* the migrants are a threat to national security or are *motivated* by security. The question is whether the securitization move was sufficient to legitimate breaking "the normal rules of politics" (Buzan et al. 1998, p. 32). Similarly, investigating how status was implicated in the public legitimation of policies can generate analytical purchase on outcomes without recourse to speculating about motivations or assuming them.

A second analytical advantage of treating legitimation as a locus of status-related political action rather than motivation is that this opens up for studying cases in which status may have been implicated in legitimation processes, but because the outcome seems "rational" it is overlooked. This is because the conventional methodological procedure of first-wave status research takes security or wealth as a baseline interest and uses status as an explanation for policies that deviate from this expectation (e.g., Gilady 2018, p. 30; de Caravalho and Neumann 2014, p. 15; Larson and Shevchenko 2019, p. 15; Murray 2010, p. 658).[9] Although this residual has been shown to be far larger than hitherto believed, it does not exhaust the ways that status can influence outcomes (Yu-Ting Lin 2023). It is quite possible that policies that make sense from a materialist-rationalist theoretical perspective were in fact legitimated in reference to status hierarchies and may not have been possible otherwise. For instance, chapter 4 explores how Norway undertook a series of education reforms in the 2000s that were constructed as necessary and urgent because Norway had finished only mid-table on the PISA international education rankings. Reforming education with the goal of improving education performance is standard practice for states seeking to maximize public utility, and as such would not ordinarily capture status scholars' attention. Yet, through tracing the processes of legitimation in the public discourse, it is clear that representations of Norway's international status in education were crucial to understanding the timing of the policy and the shape it took, and

---

[8] Following Wittgenstein (1958), scholars who study legitimation tend to be skeptical that the researcher can access motivations (or beliefs; see Jackson 2006; Hansen 2006).

[9] As a result, a great deal of status research resembles—and shares the weaknesses of—"thin constructivist" research that strives to show how ideas and beliefs can account for leftover variance once rational interests have been taken into account. For a critical discussion, see Laffey and Weldes (1997).

THE GRAMMAR OF STATUS COMPETITION   63

likely were necessary for the policy to be undertaken at all. Ultimately, first-wave status research has given us strong reason to believe status matters, but the methodological convention of assuming a materialist-rationalist baseline risks drastically understating the extent to which representations of international status have affected policy outcomes.

However, to analyze patterns of legitimation requires us to treat language and texts as ontologically significant in international relations. The following section thus outlines the assumptions about language, texts, and discourses that underpin this approach, before turning to how these assumptions inform my framework for studying international status competition as a discursive practice.

The Productivity of Language and the Politics of Meaning Production

To investigate legitimation via texts requires conceiving of language as *productive* rather than merely (imperfectly) reflective of reality. This way of conceiving of language, widely used by discourse analysts, has a strong pedigree and has become established within IR at least since the 1990s.[10] However, it has some crucial ontological and methodological implications for studying international status that are not self-evident, and thus require elaborating.[11] First, following speech act theorists, I treat speaking, writing, and texts as acts in and of themselves: "[I]n saying something we do something" (Austin 1975, p. 94). When the bride and groom say "I do" at their wedding, it does more than describe an external reality, just as signing a treaty has effects beyond the scribbles on the paper (Diez 1999). Further, I assume that actors' words are simultaneously implicated in both describing the world *and* legitimating the response to that world (see Jackson 2006, p. 16, n. 7). For instance, when one describes a person as a terrorist, it has legitimizing and delegitimizing effects: it can serve as a justification for striving to capture the

---

[10] Stretching at least from Nietzsche through Wittgenstein, from speech act theorists to Foucault and Derrida. There are major differences between these theories of language, but they all share rejection of the correspondence principle and the notion of language as merely a "conduit" (Fierke 2002; also see Diez 1999; Milliken 1999; Epstein 2013). For classic "empirical" analyses in this genre in IR, see Campbell (1992), Neumann (1999), Crawford (2002), Leira (2019).

[11] It also remains controversial and not infrequently misunderstood in mainstream circles of political science. The notion that meaning is produced in practice rather than a function of external reality is often conflated with idealism and the denial of reality. See Hansen (2006, pp. 19–20) for a robust defense of this position against the accusations of idealism.

64 THE GRAMMAR OF STATUS COMPETITION

person (We must go get 'em!), while simultaneously delegitimizing inaction (We cannot let the terrorist escape!). Similarly, representations of a social hierarchy of actors may serve to legitimate action undertaken to move up (We are losing the race; we must do better!). Treating *speaking as doing* in this way implies that descriptions of the world also justify a response to it, and texts are transformed from (dubious) proxies for inferring motivation or beliefs into ontologically significant actions in themselves and a political, meaning-producing force in their own right.[12]

Indeed, this book assumes that language can never provide a neutral vehicle of comprehension and thus legitimation. Contra philosophical realists, a discursive approach assumes the social world contains no inevitable, natural, or prediscursive facts, only an evolving stock of context-bound, shared meanings that should be understood as an ongoing feat of human construction (Doty 1996). Lest this sound like metababble, the meaning of a humble dog can serve to illustrate what this discursive theory of meaning construction implies for analysis. Nothing about the physical qualities of a dog allow the observer to infer in advance whether the dog is lucky enough to live as a pet or or end up getting eaten as food.[13] Instead, the dog's meaning depends upon the representational practices of the social context within which it exists. Borrowing Foucault's (1980, p. 131) metaphor, humans' meaning-production practices resemble a *"regime* of truth"; the regime may *appear* fixed, but zoom in, and it is *necessarily* always temporally and spatially bounded and depends upon many people's disparate and diverse micropractices, not unlike a political regime. For instance, each person who pats a dog or talks about dogs as pets is implicated in the reproduction of the meaning of dogs as pets. While the meaning of an object—dog, husband, or terrorist—may appear so stable it becomes taken for granted, for a discourse analyst this stability in meaning is an illusion brought about by constant discursive labor (see Neumann 1999, pp. 35–36). In this way humans "systematically form the objects of which they speak" (Foucault 1972, p. 54), and

---

[12] For positivists, in contrast, meaning is given by the object being described, and thus language's role is to reflect reality to the best possible extent and can therefore be judged by how well it "fits" with that external phenomenon. This notion of language leads to scholars striving toward better definitions of objects (Fierke 2002). In contrast, if one treats language as productive and political, it makes no sense to inquire how well a word fits with an external reality, but it does enable inquiring into how selecting one mode of representation over another has political consequences (Campbell 1992).

[13] I have found that when lecturing on poststructuralism, using the mundane example of a dog helps students concentrate on the theory of discourse rather than on the politics of the referent.

THE GRAMMAR OF STATUS COMPETITION 65

language becomes not just a means of apprehension but a "reality producing force" (Shapiro 2012, p. 21).

Consequently, because the meaning of any given thing is assumed to depend upon ongoing practice and bounded by the spatial and temporal limits of discursive practices, such an approach also opens up for exploring critical questions of resistance and change. If people cease talking about and treating dogs as pets, it will open up space for rival discourses to imbue the local dogs with alternative meaning—perhaps these pets will become constituted as vermin, and instead of patting dogs, people will begin shooting them. Similarly, if one steps outside the spatial limits of Britain's pet regime of truth, we may happen upon dog meat.[14] As the metaphor of the regime captures, these processes of meaning production are not "politically innocent" (Diez 1999, p. 599). For instance, it matters very much for the dog if her local humans represent her as a food or a pet. Similarly, it matters very much whether a person is constituted as a terrorist or a freedom fighter. Consequently, it becomes fruitful for the critical scholar to investigate "the manifest political consequences of adopting one mode of representation over another" (Campbell 1992, p. 7)—in this book, the consequences of adopting one theory of international status over another.

To be clear, treating language as a productive force does not imply that humans are at liberty to create meaning out of nowhere. Rather, each utterance is recursive in that it must refer back to the pattern of representational practices—the discourse—in which people are embedded.[15] In other words, each utterance depends for intelligibility upon prior representational practices, but also in a small way reproduces, replenishes, and may well modify the discourse from where it emerged. Discursive practices can thus be thought of as "linguistic structurationalism" (Diez 1999, p. 603). It is with this process in mind that in the analysis chapters I will often refer to the words published in newspapers, uttered by politicians, and written in academic research as "*representations*"—because they both present reality anew and also re-present that reality (Neumann 2008a, p. 61). It is this discursive context that governments must refer to (and reproduce) when legitimating a policy. The upshot is that for governments the prevailing discourses limit (but do not determine) and enable (but do not "cause," in the Humean sense) the possible justifications available to enact policy (Diez 1999, p. 611).

---

[14] At the time of writing, Nigeria, China, and Vietnam permit eating dog.
[15] The exception to this proves the rule: the gibberish spoken by a madman or a religious person speaking in tongues would count as nonrecursive discourse (at least not one amenable to analysis).

66 THE GRAMMAR OF STATUS COMPETITION

Methodologically, then, texts become primary data that can be treated as both (1) a productive force that has political effects and (2) a window into a broader pattern of meaning that was sayable and intelligible in the context within which it was uttered. This implies that the analyst can trace how particular meanings emerge, are contested, become sedimented, and/or wither over time and space, and can assess the political consequences. In the case of this book: how discursively (re)produced theories of international status hierarchies inform (or not) policy outcomes.

International Hierarchies as Domestic Discourse

With these understandings of legitimation and discourse in hand, we are now in a better position to elaborate the *grammar of status competition*: how the logic of "international" status competition becomes visible and consequential in domestic discourse. As I elaborated above, the main, and indeed major difference between the grammar of status I will present and the extant status literature in IR—both first and most second wave—is that I conceive of language as *productive* of the object rather than reflective. Akin to how a successful securitizing move can be understood to *produce* a threat, I argue that when an actor mobilizes the grammar of status, they produce a social hierarchy, designating (potentially) socially valuable status positions. Such an approach allows us to zoom in and analyze how people are implicated in (re)producing—via discursive practice—the hierarchies within which they understand themselves to exist. The point here is to focus on how actors *re*-present or theorize their state's position and how they act upon that understanding. From this perspective, when a leader gives a speech comparing their state and another, they are—in that moment—(re)producing a hierarchy, *not* making an assessment of an objective state of affairs that the analyst can evaluate for truthiness. Further, following the prior discussion, that representation is also potentially implicated in legitimating the response to that world it describes.

This approach implies that *international* status is not a fact "out there" to be discovered, independently recognizable, accessible, and salient to all, and instead treats people's understanding of their state's status as *produced* via practice within localized discourse(s). This move makes it possible for "local" interpretations of international hierarchies to be insulated from foreign representations and, crucially for this book, analyze how these representations of international hierarchies emerge, change, solidify, and perhaps can be contested in the social contexts within which they are articulated and instantiated.[16] Whether the representation matches some objective assessment of the international hierarchy is immaterial unless those alternative assessments feature in the social context within which the actor is operating. What matters for my analysis is whether that representation of international hierarchy was implicated in the legitimation of the policy, and if so, *how*.

Similarly, acts of international (mis)recognition are relevant insofar as they are interpreted and articulated within the policy discourse, but my approach demands that I do not ascribe to them an a priori power to determine the success or failure of a given status theory. Crucially, my discursive approach demands that we leave as an open question how such international acts of (mis)recognition affect theories of status in use within a policy debate. This logically flows from the constructivist ontology by which no act, object, or idea can be assumed to have fixed meaning or consequence across contexts. But it also facilitates empirical analysis: exploring the agency of actors to reinterpret their status in unexpected and imaginative ways when the world resists their preferred status theory. Indeed, chapters 3–5 showcase a range of possibilities here, from discounting international assessments (chapter 4) to uncritically accepting international assessments of status (chapter 5) and several options in between.

A key assumption I make, then, is that for a *social* hierarchy to have political/social effects it must be intersubjectively known and salient to the people involved. However, although the hierarchies must be intersubjectively invoked and produced to have effects, the people involved need not simultaneously understand themselves to be "motivated" by status: they may invoke the grammar of status without consciously reflecting upon it. For instance, when an opposition party seeks to shame the government by making a negative comparison with other states, they may not realize that they are delegitimating the state's behavior by invoking *competitive* status hierarchy.

All this implies quite a substantial ontological shift from most prior status research.[17] It is therefore useful to clarify this difference and its implications by juxtaposition with the paradigmatic definition of international status.

---

[16] To be clear, it is certainly possible for an analyst to construct and position people and states within a hierarchy that they envision to be external to the actors and produce insightful findings. I am merely showing how one can also make hay with a discursive approach to status.

[17] Though not quite *all* extant status research: Pouliot's (2014, 2016) practice-turn approach shares a similar scientific ontology and inductive methodology.

68 THE GRAMMAR OF STATUS COMPETITION

In the seminal edited volume of contemporary research, Paul, Larson, and Wohlforth (2014, p. 7) define "status as collective beliefs about a given state's ranking on valued attributes (wealth, coercive capabilities, culture, demographic position, socio-political organization, and diplomatic clout)." In contrast, I define status as *a position in social hierarchy* and status competition as *a processual-relational, rule-governed competition for relative position*. While they are in the same ballpark, my definition does not require the researcher to access people's beliefs.[18] Instead, my definition of social hierarchy requires only that representations of an international hierarchy be *social*: intersubjectively available (not private or subjective) in a given context.[19] When taken together with the previous chapters' discussion about the difference between individual and group identity and status, this has crucial analytical and methodological implications. Representations of a state's position in an "international" hierarchy still constitute a *social* hierarchy even if the subjects representing the position are all members of the same group.[20] Moreover, following the discussion above regarding legitimation, these context-bound representations—even if they are not shared by members of other groups— can still be meaningful and acted upon by those members of the group. Intersubjectivity need not imply intersubjectivity between *group* "subjects." This move thus negates the difficult methodological task of trying to second-guess the "collective beliefs" different countries' populations or elites hold. Instead, it allows me to zoom in on the discrete discursive contexts whereby representations of international hierarchies are instantiated and contested in the concrete processes of policy (de)legitimation.

Nonetheless, treating status as discursive has been alluded to by leading first-wave status research, even if it has not been fully fleshed out theoretically. Akin to how Stephen Walt (1990) set the stage for securitization theory when he incorporated "threat perception" into his theory of alliance formation, so too does Wohlforth (2009, p. 30) when he theorizes that status competition is likely to occur when "decision makers identify with the states they represent"

---

[18] The other difference is more trivial: I would argue that *any* activity or quality could become constituted as a valued attribute constitutive of a social hierarchy. However, I suspect that Paul, Larson, and Wohlforth (2014) would agree and that their definition did not mean to imply a finite list of status attributes. Certainly, their surrounding theoretical discussion does not suggest as much.

[19] See Jackson (2006) and Buzan et al. (1998) for discussions of the difference between subjectivity and intersubjectivity.

[20] As noted in the introduction, states' status operates differently from individual status in a crucial way. States contain people and groups that can acknowledge and recognize their representations of their group's own status. Unlike the perceptions or beliefs of an individual, representations of a group's status are social: they exist in the intersubjective realm of discourse.

THE GRAMMAR OF STATUS COMPETITION   69

and decide to "*frame* issues as positional disputes over status in a social hierarchy" (my emphasis). Indeed, this formulation strongly alludes to a degree of domestic-interpretative agency to decide what to frame—construct—as a positional competition. However, Wohlforth's theoretical interest—linking polarity to the frequency of status competition—means that he does not flesh out what this framing involves. Nor does he explore the theoretical implications that are implied by framing: that governments (and the opposition too) have agency to "frame" different activities as status competitions. And crucially for this book, nor does Wohlforth consider how domestic actors might frame the same activity in multiple different hierarchical ways: creating and contesting status hierarchies of a group's own making. The next section thus unpacks what is loosely captured by Wohlforth's notion of "framing" to develop a systematic means of recognizing the logic of status competition when it becomes manifested in domestic discourse and implicated in the legitimation of policy.

The Grammatical Units of Status Competition

The previous chapter detailed an idealized logic of status competition: a processual-relational, rule-governed competition for relative position. In the real world, the Olympics and its constituent events embody this logic and constitute a near perfect example of an international status competition. Indeed, individuals competing on behalf of their group (states or city-states) compete in relational contests of strength, agility, speed, and so on. The criteria for victory are agreed upon by all competitors beforehand, and the winning collective reaps both prizes and pride. I argue that the logic embodied in this ideal is manifest, visible, and often consequential in domestic discourse about the international, even if a full-blown status competition is seldom realized. We can recognize the logic by looking out for what I call the "grammar of status competition": a type of discursive representation that embodies, and thus instantiates, the logic of status competition in practice. Following Fierke (2002) and Buzan and colleagues (1998), I use the term "grammar" here to refer to a metalinguistic framework that operates across varying contexts while still retaining a family resemblance:

A grammar is the range of possible expressions belonging to a category of experience. As Wittgenstein said, "A grammar tells us what kind of object

70   THE GRAMMAR OF STATUS COMPETITION

anything is" (Wittgenstein 1958: para. 373). A grammatical investigation is therefore one that looks into the possibilities of phenomena. For instance, we have a grammar of marriage. This would include language games such as saying "I do" in the context of a Christian wedding ceremony or stamping a piece of glass in a Jewish one. This is a speech act in the sense that it is not just saying something; it is acting, with the result of confirming the creation of a marriage. This language game belongs to a larger grammar. (Fierke 2002, p. 344 drawing on Wittgenstein 1958, footnotes removed)

In a similar vein, by developing a grammar of status competition, I am seeking to provide a systematic means of investigating the possible expressions of status competition. It is crucial to note that this grammatical approach to status has a key advantage in that it avoids reifying the criteria for status hierarchies. Instead, like securitization, it is the enactment of the logic embodied in the grammar that determines what constitutes a status hierarchy, not a priori assumptions about what constitutes valued attributes nor the criteria by which they should be counted and compared.[21] Moreover, this approach allows the analyst to ascertain the logic of status competition without the actors themselves using the word "status" or self-consciously understanding themselves to be motivated by status.

I will now elaborate the grammatical units of status competition and illustrate with examples. I argue that the following types of representations invoke and thus constitute competitive status hierarchies: (1) superlatives[22] and competitive comparisons, (2) positional identity constructions, and (3) sports metaphors. I argue that each grammatical unit on its own (no matter how momentary) invokes the logic of status competition and can be used to legitimize and delegitimize particular courses of action. Given iteratively or used with a temporal dimension they can be deployed to produce status narratives, which legitimate action to arrest a decline in status, maintain status, or improve one's position in a status hierarchy. In this sense, like other narratives, representations of status competition imply a course of action and thus tell an actor how to proceed (Ringmar 1996; Subotic 2016; Steele 2008). I will then discuss how the grammar of status serves as a lens to

---

[21] For instance, even though Wohlforth uses the term "framing," he assumes what substantive hierarchies (GDP, military personnel, the navy) matter, and thus how they are measured and the principle of comparison, prior to empirical analysis.

[22] To be clear, I mean "superlative" in the grammatical sense, whereby it demarks the best *or* the worst, most *or* least. Although it overlaps, I should specify that I do not mean the everyday meaning of "superlative," which has an exclusively positive valence.

illuminate my cases in chapters 3–5. The goal of developing this lens is to provide a "systematic production of empirical factual knowledge about political social arrangements" (Jackson 2010, p. 22). The system in question—looking out for how the grammar of status is instantiated and implicated in legitimation processes—serves both to facilitate and order my analysis and also to aid transparency so the reader can assess how I reached my conclusions in the empirical chapters.

Competitive Comparisons

The basic unit of the grammar of status is statements in which a comparison with other, ostensibly similar entities is invoked. As Nicholas Onuf (1989, p. 267) notes, a concern for status *must* always depend upon *global* comparison.[23] By "global" Onuf means comparing how one performs relative to others, rather than "global" in the geographic sense. This "ground of comparison" is necessarily relational to others: one cannot aim to be better or best at something without reference to other participant(s). Thus, global comparisons require the construction of a ranking system: "The set, or whole, then consists of a series of positions occupying a complete and transitive ordering: first place, second place . . . last place. Furthermore, the places in such an ordering come with cardinal values. . . . Only now can she say: I want to be best" (Onuf 1989, p. 266). However, in practice, statements that make competitive comparisons between entities and instantiate a crude competitive hierarchy of status between X and Y whenever they utter a statement akin to X is better than Y at Z. It is crucial to emphasize (again) that to say that something is better than something else requires some principle of comparison by which to evaluate performance. It is thus theoretically impossible to make a competitive comparison without some sort of rule. Thus, even if an explicit ranking of rivals is made, a comparison—*X is better than Y at Z*—also establishes the rules of a hierarchy. Within my framework, these theories of international hierarchies need not be recognized as salient, valued, and credible by international audiences for it to become meaningful, only for audiences whose consent or acquiescence is required for the successful legitimation of an activity.

---

[23] Though Onuf uses the term "standing."

72 THE GRAMMAR OF STATUS COMPETITION

Using the discursive expression of relative comparisons as a basic unit in the grammar of status competition is broadly consistent with all strands of IR status research. Social identity theory is the most explicit; it posits that individuals generate self-esteem from their ability to make positive comparisons with the out-group on salient dimensions (see Tajifel and Turner 1979; Larson and Shevchenko 2003, 2010, 2014). It is via these comparisons that actors assess their relative status and experience shame and pride accordingly. Meanwhile, as noted, large-N status research suggests states (or leaders) compare the relative power of their country to ascertain whether they receive sufficient recognition or deference from their peers (e.g., Renshon 2017; Volgy et al. 2011) While it is not made central to their analysis, it is clear that these causal mechanisms presuppose the ability to make comparisons between states. Finally, Vincent Pouliot's practice-turn approach shares our concern here for how status hierarchies are produced and acted upon in practice. Contra psychologists, who posit an innate urge to make positive comparisons, Pouliot (2014, p. 197) suggests that because people are born into societies in which comparisons with those around them are unavoidable, status hierarchies quickly emerge through practice. Ultimately, making competitive comparisons a basic discursive unit of status hierarchies should be uncontroversial. With the exception of Pouliot (2014), the difference is the ontological status of those comparisons. I suggest they are productive as well as reflective of the social world.

To illustrate how actors may make competitive comparisons in policy debates and how these can exert (de)legitimation effects, let us turn to the United Kingdom's response to the Syrian refugee crisis. As the crisis wore on in 2015, the United Kingdom began to come under pressure to accept more refugees from Syria. The government responded by asserting that it was the second biggest financial contributor to the region in terms of aid. However, the pressure became especially intense when an image of a child (Alan Kurdi), found dead on a beach, captured the world's attention, prompting urgent calls for something to be done (Adler-Nissen, Andersen, and Hansen 2020, p. 76). Critical voices in Parliament and the press drew attention to how the United Kingdom had accepted far fewer refugees than many other countries. For instance, one MP argued in Parliament, "The number of refugees that this Government say they will take . . . is derisory compared with Germany, which in the last few days has taken in 17,000 refugees. . . . We will look back on this Government's mean response to this heart-rending humanitarian crisis and we will be ashamed."[24] Eventually, the U.K. government gave in to pressure and announced it would accept 20,000 refugees over the next five years. A week later France announced it would take 21,000. Little had changed in the meantime to make accepting refugees any more efficient than sending money to the region, yet the government changed policy. It is noteworthy for our purposes here that the government and its critics constituted the United Kingdom as positioned in two *rival* status hierarchies. One theorized status in the moral hierarchy as derived from financial contributions to the region; the other used the number of refugees accepted as the measure for moral status. In short, although an absolute legal standard exists, the specifics of appropriate behavior for the United Kingdom was informed by contestations over which criteria should be used to assess relative moral performance and comparisons with how other countries responded. To be sure, international legal duty, altruistic impulses, and the emotions the image generated provided the pressure to do *something* (Adler-Nissen, Andersen, and Hansen 2020, p. 77). However, the government sought to legitimate the specifics of the policy by reference to a status hierarchy of its own construction, but when challenged, it ceded to a theory based upon the number of refugees admitted into the country. This example illustrates how a government's theory of status can be invoked and contested in practice, and how the grammar of status competition can be involved in the legitimation of the timing and shape of a policy.

Competitive Positional Identities

Closely connected to comparisons of performance are what I call *positional identities*, which also instantiate status hierarchies when uttered. Here I draw upon identity theorists who understand the self and the other as mutually constituted in discourse via boundary-producing performances of difference (Ashley 1989; Campbell 1992; Neumann 1996; Doty 1996; Rumelili 2004; Hansen 2006). In lay terms, the central assumption is that to know what something is, is to know what it is not; to know what we are is to know what we are not. In constructivist terms, the *Self* always necessitates an *Other*. Spelling out the implications of this way of theorizing identity formation, Hansen (2006, p. 2) suggests identity should be understood as

---

[24] Hansard, HC 08 September 2015 Vol 599 cc 267

74 THE GRAMMAR OF STATUS COMPETITION

"discursive, political, relational, and social"; status can be understood in much the same manner. Indeed, like identity, status is relational: to have high status requires another to have low status. Status is discursive: statuses are not given by the entities themselves but are produced through discursive practice. Status is political: people contest and struggle for higher status, and the outcomes of these struggles can have serious consequences. Status is social: a status, by definition, can never be private and can only be constituted intersubjectively. Indeed, following de Carvalho and Neumann (2014), I suggest that status is *a subset of relationally formed identity*,[25] one that constitutes a higher or lower position in a *social* hierarchy. While status is a type of identity, they are not quite synonyms. If identity is who one is, status is also the position *where* one is sat. One can seek higher status, but one cannot seek higher identity. Indeed, one cannot talk about a "high identity," for instance, or "seek identity." Unlike identity, then, the concept of status explicitly contains the *possibility* for competition and improvement: the goal of maintaining or moving up in position in a social hierarchy.[26] Indeed, a status *position* always implies a relationally formed hierarchy, whereas identity implies no necessary structural counterpart (compare Wendt 1992; Katzenstein 1996; Hansen 2006).[27] As chapter 1 noted, however, status clubs and fixed status hierarchies produce different relations between self and other than status competition. Thus, the grammar of status *competition* requires that the positional identity is constituted by relative performance in a changeable quality or attribute.

The archetypal positional identity that invokes status competition is that of the "leader/laggard." From my discursive perspective, when a state

---

[25] I rely here upon the assumption that all identities are socially formed through juxtaposition to some Other (Hansen 2006; Neumann 1997).

[26] One can live up to one's identity, one can seek recognition for an identity, but one cannot improve one's identity. Especially when paired with the logic of appropriateness, this conceptualization struggles to account for change (Towns 2010; Sending 2002) and, I would argue, status competition.

[27] While symbolic interactionists' account of identity struggles to incorporate hierarchy (or arguably structure in general). As Rumelili (2004) notes, symbolic interactionism posits a convergence rather than divergence following interactions. Elsewhere, Towns (2010, 2012) critiques weak constructivists for focusing only on norm diffusion that engenders homogenization and ignoring how the spread of international society also always stratifies, producing hierarchies in the process. Thick constructivist work which posits that meaning construction involves positing a privileged sign contra another necessarily implies a relationally formed identity and broad hierarchy. However, these works have tended to focus on radical difference and Othering rather than status rivalries as they are conceived here. As Hansen (2006) and Rumelili (2004) independently note, this focus on radical othering is an empirical choice, not theoretically necessitated by discursive theories of identity construction. This would open up for frameworks that study systematically nonradical othering such as the rival relations I associate with status competition.

represents itself as the "leader of the free world," it is juxtaposing itself not only to the non-free world but also to other free-worlders and instantiating a competitive hierarchy for leadership position. When protecting that leadership position is invoked to justify a course of action—"We must intervene lest we forsake our leadership of the free world"—then status competition becomes implicated in legitimation processes. To give a concrete example, the British (Labour) government's decision to build a new nuclear weapons system (Trident) was partially legitimated on the (curious) grounds that it was a "leader of nuclear disarmament" (Beaumont 2021). This legitimation was co-constituted with a competitive comparison to other nuclear weapons states. It defined disarmament in terms of (a) the number of nuclear weapons possessed by states and (b) included in the hierarchy only those states defined as "nuclear weapons states" under the Non-Proliferation Treaty (NPT).[28] Only by this very British construction of the disarmament hierarchy could Britain's status as "leader" make sense (Beaumont 2021).

Another, better known, but more ambiguous example of a competitive-positional identity in international relations is that of "great power." It is ambiguous because it is not clear that what constitutes a great power across space and time has always been based upon changeable criteria, nor if all those criteria were relative in nature. For instance, Neumann (2008b) has argued that recognition of greatpowerhood has never been strictly a function of relative power—although this has usually been crucial—but also depended upon a state's system of governance (see also Bull 1977). This latter quality would appear to operate as an absolute standard: in terms of legitimation, it would be quite possible to strive for greatpowerdom by reforming the society in light of an absolute norm that was deemed necessary to entering the club. At other times, a seat at the top table of Europe was also a function of royal blood. As such, although the identity would be positional, it would not invoke a hierarchy that an actor could *compete* within. The upshot of this short discussion is that invoking a positional identity does not in itself invoke the logic of status competition. Instead, the discourse analyst must pay close head to the criteria and mode of comparison that constitute a positional identity, whether it is based upon changeable criteria and relative comparisons.

---

[28] The NPT defines nuclear weapons states as those which tested a nuclear weapon prior to 1967.

76 THE GRAMMAR OF STATUS COMPETITION

Sports Metaphors

Finally, when the metaphor or analogy of sport is used to describe and illuminate a situation it frames the activity as a status competition. As Nietzsche observed, language is inherently and necessarily metaphorical. If sometimes we forget this, it is only because metaphors are so entrenched in our language that we use them habitually without reflection (Lakoff and Johnson [1980] 2003). While they might be unavoidable, the "metaphors we live by" structure our interpretations of reality in important ways that warrant critical reflection. In line with my productive ontology, when a leader invokes a sport metaphor it *does* something: it constitutes the situation as a sport and conjures up the logic of status competition. For instance, Lakoff (1991, p. 29) notes that when war is treated as a "competitive sport like chess, or as a sport, like football or boxing" it provides a

> metaphor in which there is a clear *winner and loser*, and a clear end to the game. The metaphor highlights strategic thinking, team work, preparedness, the spectators in the world arena, *the glory of winning and the shame of defeat*. This metaphor is taken very seriously. There is a long tradition in the west of training military officers in team sports and chess. The military is trained to win. (My emphasis)

In short, likening a social activity to a sport constitutes winning as an end in itself. The metaphor of sport or games does *not* encourage reflection about "payoffs." Quite the opposite: although game *theory* implies rational cost-benefit analysis of outcomes, framing an activity as a game or a sport actually has the effect of reducing the value of activity to winning and losing, success or failure.[29] For instance, it is no good finishing a chess game with higher-value pieces than your opponent if they have checkmated you. Ringmar (1996, p. 3) is especially lucid on this point and is worth quoting at length. Noting that people seldom play games only for the material prizes on offer, Ringmar writes:

> [I]t is worth underlining the obvious, yet easily neglected, fact that we participate in games because we want to *excel over others*. Winning as such is

---

[29] It is somewhat ironic that for all the insights game theory can provide, the logic it embodies is quite unlike almost any competitive game: nobody would bother playing games or sports if they always ended up at Nash equilibria.

what is important, not what-ever additional rewards winning might bring. And why, then, do people want to win? Simply put: because winning is desired by others; we want to win because others want to win. By winning we can manifest our superiority; we become "winners," and everyone else is forced to recognise us as such. (Original emphasis)

For our purposes here, what matters is that when international relations are constructed as a competitive game they constitute the value of an activity in relative terms and constitute states as *rival* players with positional identities: winners and losers, laggards and leaders. As such, the game also theorizes status hierarchy and instantiates the logic of status competition. As the following chapters will illustrate, sporting metaphors that draw upon familiar sports can help render intelligible in terms of international status otherwise complex and distant phenomena. For instance, chapter 4 shows how the Winter Olympics were used to frame Norway's PISA rankings performance as an important status competition. Meanwhile, likening the siege of Mafeking to a game of cricket (chapter 3) helped render the Boer as a rival against whom Brits could express pride at defeating.

Mobilizing the Grammar of Status Competition

Each grammatical unit taken alone invokes a status competition and provides a legitimation to proceed in a particular way. A representation of "laggard" implies striving to regain position; a sports metaphor impels one to compete in the "game." In this way the grammar of status competition enacts a simple plot: we must do X to maintain, improve, or regain our position in Y hierarchy. As such, representations of status competitions enact a narrative that situates the collective in time and space, and legitimates a particular direction of travel (Subotic 2016). In the process, such representations often direct focus away from the rules of the games—which they define in the act of instantiating a hierarchy—and toward strategies to compete. For instance, when the PISA rankings were successfully framed as a crucial status competition in Norwegian politics, it prompted considerable debate among the left and the right about how best to improve performance. The left wanted to spend more on education, and the right wanted to instigate new testing procedures, while traditionalists suggested more discipline was needed. Amid this debate, the veracity and legitimacy of the PISA rankings'

78 THE GRAMMAR OF STATUS COMPETITION

rules were reproduced by both sides as they contested how best to compete. However, although the grammar of status works as a heuristic for identifying representations of status competition and the rules such representations embody, we cannot say a priori whether they will prove successful in legitimating a particular course of action. Instead, this requires close empirical analysis of the social context within which they take place.

When investigating whether and how the grammar of status competition is mobilized to legitimate government activities, it is important to keep in mind alternative logics of legitimation that may have informed an outcome. Beyond the concrete justifications given for particular policies in my cases, it is useful to lay out alternative generic logics of legitimation that might be expected to manifest in my cases and international relations writ large. Surveying IR, and simplifying, there are at least three other generic logics of legitimation that frequently feature in IR scholarship: logic of appropriateness, utility maximization, and securitization. Because each should be immediately familiar to IR scholars (and social scientists), I will emphasize only that the first two are inherently individualistic;[30] meanwhile securitization processes obviously have no necessary relationship to relative position in social hierarchy. Proceeding inductively, the analyst should investigate how the grammar of status—and the logic of status competition it embodies—contests, supplements, or interacts with other modes of legitimation at play in the case in question. Indeed, as Jackson (2010, p. 170) notes, when using an ideal type as a baseline, it is not necessarily the manifestation of the ideal but the divergences from it that generate insight.

Emotional Register

To reduce status competition to its logic alone may lead the analyst to overlook the emotions that animate status competition in practice and risk conjuring away the means through which invoking the grammar generates

---

[30] What is crucial to note is that both are individualist: whether an actor follows the norm or not can be ascertained without reference to whether others do likewise (see Sending [2002] on the individualism of Logic of Appropriateness). To be sure, others may disagree about the interpretation of the norm and whether the action lives up to it, and this will likely affect whether the society within which the actor exists treats the actor as a norm follower or not. However, in the ideal, it is only the relationship between the actor's action and the norm that determines whether it obtains. Meanwhile, regarding utility maximization (absolute gains), the goal is to improve upon their prior situation in some way. Here the actor justifies an action by making an internal comparison to the previous situation or hypothetical alternatives (Onuf 1989, p. 267).

THE GRAMMAR OF STATUS COMPETITION 79

rhetorical power. Fortunately, a burgeoning body of work investigates the role that emotions play in international politics.[31] However, to avoid overstepping my discursive methodology, it is necessary to specify the object of analysis as "emotion discourse" (Koschut 2018a, 2018b). Here, discourse analysis does not involve trying to infer emotions of the author or speaker from texts but recognizes that discourses always embody an "emotional register," which may underpin or undermine a particular discursive performance (see Adler-Nissen, Anderson, and Hansen 2020, pp. 76, 80). While the pathos generated by "name and shame" discourses is straightforward to apprehend, even a dry cost-benefit analysis has an emotional register that helps it function. Indeed, a cost-benefit analysis's credibility and rhetorical power rely upon sanitizing the text of explicit emotional content. Akin to how using "zero-degree writing" to give the illusion of objectivity *is* political (Barthes 1967), minimizing explicit emotional content from a text *is* an emotional register in itself. Remaining sensitive to the emotional register serves two purposes for the study of status competition: methodological and analytical.

Empirically, the logic of status competition is commonly associated with an emotional register of pride, shame, joy, humiliation.[32] Language in this emotional register can serve a basic methodological purpose for flagging the *potential* existence of status being wielded to (de)legitimate a particular course of action. However, unlike the units of the grammar, no single emotional register can be logically tied to status competition.[33] Emotion-laden discourses may prompt urgent "calls for 'something to be done,' but leave the specificity of the 'doing' undecided" (Adler-Nissen, Andersen, and Hansen 2020, p. 77).[34] For instance, the public shame expressed at the death rate in the concentration camps during the Boer War prompted calls to (1) end the war, (2) end use of camps, and (3) measures to improve the conditions in camps. The government undertook only the last and rejected the former two. Indeed, this vagueness of the policy implications of emotion discourse implies that the status analyst must remain sensitive to what the expression

---

[31] See Crawford (2000), Bleiker and Hutchison (2008), Fierke (2013).

[32] This is an observation based upon my research and other status research that tie analysis of status with inner feelings (e.g., humiliation, anxiety, anger, pride).

[33] Although it is worth noting that Koschut's "four ways of communicating emotions in discourse" echo my grammar of status competition: "emotion terms, connotations, metaphors, as well as comparisons and analogies" (Koschut 2018, p. 284).

[34] The authors were referring specifically to the "bundles" of emotions produced by images, but in the context of their discussion, I read it to be a general feature of expressions of emotion in discourse.

80 THE GRAMMAR OF STATUS COMPETITION

of emotions (or lack thereof) *does* in *conjunction* with the grammar of status competition.

Indeed, invoking pride alone need not imply status competition, but invoking this emotional register together with a grammatical unit of status competition may imply that pride and shame were theorized to constitute the stakes that made the game worth playing. For example, expressing anger and umbrage that such a small adversary as the Boer could have the "audacity" to send an ultimatum to Britain, the Marquess of Granby demanded military action against the Boer by arguing that "no Government with one atom of self-respect . . . could by any possibility have accepted [the ultimatum]. . . . There must be no juggling with the fact that there can only be one paramount Power in South Africa, and that that Power must be Great Britain."[35] Indeed, Lord Granby's speech calling for war with the Boer offers an apt example of how emotion discourse—in this case, pride—can co-constitute the value of a status competition and thus help legitimate a particular course of action (and delegitimate inaction). Methodologically, we need not confirm that Lord Granby experienced these emotions personally to study how this type of representation helped constitute the value of the competition (see also Adler-Nissen, Andersen, and Hansen 2020, p. 80). Ultimately, all invocations of the grammar of status will be performed in some kind of emotional register; however, the specifics of *how* the emotion discourse informed legitimation is a matter for empirical analysis.

Conclusion

This chapter has spelled out the assumptions that underpin my approach to investigating how the logic of international status competition informs government policy. I elaborated how status competition can be seen as a mode of *legitimation* (rather than motivation) and how this logic of status competition becomes identifiable and influential in discourse via its grammar. Therefore, rather than treating international status hierarchies as the cumulative beliefs of a multitude of international Others, my approach directs us to investigate the concrete representations—*theories*—of international status hierarchies as they inform political practice in discrete local contexts. While humbling prior status research's grand theoretical pretensions, this switch

---

[35] Hansard HL Deb 17 October 1899, vol. 77, col. 5-7.

allows me to ground the book in empirically observable phenomena (discourse) and avoids the need to make bold assumptions about *international* intersubjectivity or attempt to infer and disentangle motivations. Ultimately, I argue that this ontological shift enables systematic empirical inquiry into how theories of international status are instantiated in domestic politics and to investigate their role in legitimating particular policies.

Moreover, by differentiating between the ideal of status competition and how its logic can become visible in discourse, I have set the stage to investigate how status competition diverges from the ideal when it emerges in practice. Indeed, for reasons that I theorized in the introduction, my central theoretical gambit is that although the *logic* of status competition is at play in international relations, states and their citizens often lack intersubjective agreement about the rules of the game. Thus, although governments may frequently act "as if" the state is involved in a status competition—mobilizing the grammar of status to legitimate their activities—I expect that political parties and citizens would often disagree about the rules of international hierarchies they compete in and thus generate but also attempt to clarify the ambiguity that this contestation generates. Hence this book argues, and the following chapters will illustrate, why it is fruitful to investigate whether and how domestic theories of the rules of international status hierarchies— unlike those in the Olympics—are contested and change during the process of competing and how any such changes and contestation affect the legitimation of policies.

These expectations—that theories of international status hierarchies may be implicated in legitimation of national policies and that the rules of those status hierarchies are unstable—imply two methodological procedures. One resembles the general status MO, reviewing the evidence of the case and determining *whether* the logic of status competition was employed and whether it significantly affected the outcome of the policy (timing, shape, size). However, my theoretical concern with how the rules of the game came to be, or change, also implies close analysis of the *process* of policy legitimation and whether and how the rules of the status hierarchy changed during the process of competition. It is important to note the limited methodological function that the grammar of status competition plays: it allowed me to locate the logic of status competition at play in legitimation, but the substantive content of any concrete theory of status competition and how it changed during a policy process has to be investigated via close inductive analysis.

3

Rational Illusions

Britain and the Boer War

> Even supposing that a war of this kind were in fact a war between two cultures, the value of the victor would still be a very relative one and could certainly not justify choruses of victory or acts of self-glorification. For one would have to know what the defeated culture had been worth: perhaps it was worth very little: in which case the victory of the victorious culture, even if attended by the most magnificent success in arms, would constitute no invitation to ecstatic triumphs.
>
> —Friedrich Nietzsche, *Untimely Meditations* ([1873] 1997)

Introduction

"War, *huh?* What is it good for?" sang Edwin Starr half a century ago. At the same time as signaling his disgust at the horrific loss of life and futility of war, Starr's rhetorical question also expressed the paradigmatic puzzle for scholars studying the political economy of war (e.g., Fearon 1995). Starr's answer, "Absolutely nothing at all," reflects popular wisdom but does not satisfy scholars who deduce that war must be good for something or someone. Yet, so-called rationalist approaches have also foundered upon Starr's question (Fearon 1995; Kirshner 2000); many a war seems to neither secure nor enrich the winner. At first blush, first-wave status research appears well-equipped to address this puzzle. Indeed, for several leading first-wave status scholars, one can deduce status concerns from the very lack of material rationalist explanations.[1] For instance, Deborah Larson and Andrei

---

[1] See Alex Yu-Ting Lin (2023) for a thorough critique of this approach to inferring status motivations.

The Grammar of Status Competition. Paul David Beaumont, Oxford University Press. © Oxford University Press 2024.
DOI: 10.1093/9780197771808.003.0004

Shevchenko (2019, p. 15)—pioneers of status research in IR—suggest that when substantial economic and security costs are incurred pursuing a policy in which prosperity or security could be achieved more effectively another way, it is a tell-tale sign of status driving the policy. In a similar vein, Lilach Gilady (2018) argues that prestige policies by design require conspicuous waste that sacrifices societal welfare. It is easy to see how this logic of explanation—inferring status motivations from the absence of conventional material interests—would offer an enticing explanation for ostensibly irrational conflicts.[2]

There is a hitch, however. As I noted in the introduction, first-wave status research has documented that states often pursue policies—including waging war—that appear to be motivated by status, but has fared less well showing how increased status was forthcoming.[3] As a result, IR scholarship now counts a number of status skeptics among its ranks, who not only question the costs of status-seeking but suggest the "pursuit of status itself may be a chimera" (McDonald and Parent 2021, p. 12; see also Glaser 2018). The most theoretically thoroughgoing example of this skepticism comes from Jonathon Mercer's (2017) well-cited article in *International Security*. Mercer contends that even on its own terms, status-seeking is a futile endeavor because other states face incentives to discount the performance of rivals, and thus preserve their own status. What rewards statesmen think they receive by chasing status, Mercer alleges, are in fact "psychological illusions" based upon "feelings" rather than "analysis" (p. 47). Thus, rather than merely showing that seeking status is wasteful compared to security or wealth maximization, Mercer's claim is bolder: that seeking status is irrational on its own terms because it is pointless to "chase what you cannot catch" (p. 168). Lacking recognition and/or additional deference for one's feats, status-seeking dissolves into "vanity" (p. 168). Mercer illustrates his argument by documenting how the British government portrayed its victory in the Second Boer War (1899–1902) as worthy of acclaim and a boon to its international status, even as international actors—both rivals and allies—remained unimpressed. Mercer describes his findings as "more than a provocation" to status research and contends that skepticism is required of

---

[2] See Lebow (2010a, p. 254) for another influential example of scholarship using this method.

[3] Renshon (2016, 2017) claims international society has systematically rewarded war-wagers across time with greater recognition. However, several have questioned the use of embassies as proxy for status recognition (e.g., Mercer 2017; Wolf 2019; Røren and Beaumont 2019; McDonald and Parent 2021).

84   THE GRAMMAR OF STATUS COMPETITION

any status research that does not "explain or document how actors evaluate" their international status (p. 168).

It is this intra-status debate into which this chapter steps. As I noted in the introduction, these skeptics are quite correct to admonish prior status research for paying insufficient attention to how states assess their international status in practice. Indeed, one of this book's chief goals is to prove a framework for remedying this shortcoming. However, need it follow that if a status-seeking policy elicits little international approval or deference, claims to status dissolve into "little more than vanity"? Showcasing the value of paying attention to the domestic theories of international status, this chapter argues no, and uses Mercer's own case to draw the opposite conclusion: even if the *international* status gains from the war were indeed an illusion, these domestic "illusions" helped to legitimate an otherwise mediocre government and generate expressions of joy and pride among its citizens.

Further, Mercer contends that the belief the war boosted Britain's status stemmed from "feelings" rather than analysis. Against this, using my grammar-of-status framework, I show how in the *process* of re-presenting the war as it unfolded, the government and the press developed a new theory of the war's status value, one that contradicted their own earlier depiction. Indeed, although the war was frequently constructed as a status competition, British mainstream discourse diverged from my ideal type in a crucial way: unlike the Olympics, the *rules* by which comparisons were made and status assigned were contested and revised as the war unfolded. Indeed, I show how the government and press retheorized the status value of war and how this retheorization predated the celebrations at victory. Tracing this process allows me to invert Mercer's claim: rather than pride informing analyses of Britain's status, this new theory of the status competition made expressions of pride possible. These insights illuminate how governments (and domestic actors) possess a hitherto underacknowledged agency to retheorize international status hierarchies for domestic consumption, which I argue can provide a plausible explanation for why and how states compete for "status" even when international rewards appear ephemeral. Rather than a *psychological* "illusion"—as Mercer would have it—that governments will eventually learn to ignore, the illusion of status would be better treated as a sociological construction, one that governments actively seek to protect and maintain.

Finally, utilizing longitudinal research design, the chapter also highlights the agency of critics to contest and disrupt the government's preferred theory of status. Indeed, the latter half of the chapter highlights how opponents of the war developed rival, less flattering theories of how the conflict would impact Britain's status. Drawing on the standards of civilization discourse, they argued—and simultaneously theorized—that Britain's "methods of barbarism" negated any glory from victory. Especially in the latter stages of the war, these critics had considerable success in undermining the popularity and the legitimacy of the government. Hence, the chapter highlights how the pro-war side and the "pro-Boers" developed rival theories of Britain's status that legitimated opposite policy conclusions: prosecute the war; end it early. Ultimately, fully grasping how status affected the government's prosecution of the war and the domestic consequences requires recognizing this diversity of status theories: how rival theories emerged, became salient, and were contested at different times during the war.[4] In doing so, the chapter illustrates that we cannot assume a domestic agreement around the status implications of the war for Britain—the rules of the game—let alone a consensus among international audiences, as first-wave status research is prone to do.

Britain, Great Power Status, and the Boer War

Britain's "New Imperial policy" of the late 19th century and especially the Second Boer War would seem well explained by a standard status model. As J. A. Hobson ([1902] 1965)[5] highlighted at the time and many have argued since, the economic (and demographic) arguments supporting new imperialism were specious. In short, trade did not "follow the flag," but quite the opposite: Britain's trade increased more quickly with foreign countries than with its new colonies, while its colonies tended to increase their trade quicker with foreign countries than with Britain. As Hobson lamented at the time, trade with the new colonies "forms an utterly insignificant part of our national income, while the expenses connected directly and indirectly with the acquisition, administration and defence of these possessions must swallow

---

[4] Hobson ([1902] 1965) famously argued that vested capitalist interests were at the root of Imperialism and used the Boer War as an example. However, he suggests that investor interests were a *secret* motive and that concerns about national prestige and honor were used to pursue these ends. As such, he does not contradict the argument I will make here.

[5] It is important to highlight that Hobson's book contains anti-Semitic passages, where he implies that the financiers, whom he blames for encouraging the war, were Jewish. See Allet (1987) for an extended examination of Hobson's anti-Semitism.

86   THE GRAMMAR OF STATUS COMPETITION

an immeasurably larger sum" (pp. 38–39).[6] In short, scrambling for Africa was a waste of British taxpayers' money.[7]

Few examples illuminate the economic and human folly of British imperialism better than the Boer War. In a war lasting less than three years, Britain and its colonies sent 400,000 men, spent more than £200 million, and suffered at least 22,000 casualties (Pakenham 1979). The costs of the war dwarfed other contemporary imperial wars: The Anglo-Ashanti War of 1873–1874 cost only £900,000, the Zulu War of 1879 £1 million, while a decade of the Maori wars had come to just £3 million (Porter 2000, p. 635). Even the Crimean War with Russia barely exceeded £68 million (p. 635).[8] The long-term accounting looks no better. The victory was short lived: after the Liberal government replaced the Conservative government responsible for the war in 1905, they granted the Afrikaner colonies self-government under the British Crown in 1907 (Ellis 1998, p. 65). Less than a decade after Britain had sent hundreds of thousands of men to fight in a bloody, costly, and brutal war to assert dominance over their South African colonies, on May 31, 1910, the Union of South Africa was born, led by the same Boer leaders Britain had spent so much blood and treasure fighting.

Indeed, the Boer War looks like an open-and-shut case of a status-motivated policy leading a country to adopt economically and strategically irrational policies inimical to the public good. Acquiring an empire was just what "great powers" *did*, and their international status was judged by the size of that empire (Naylor 2018, pp. 99–100; Barnhart 2016). As Barnhart (2016, p. 386) has argued, the "scramble for Africa" among great powers was "an effort to assert their state's great power status . . . in spite of their expectations of high associated costs and heightened strategic vulnerability." Hence, first-wave status research seems to offer a straightforward and compelling explanation: Britain as the leading imperial power annexed the Transvaal at great

---

[6] Hobson's thesis that hidden vested interests—private financiers and gold speculators—were behind the Boer War and Britain's New Imperialism in general has been extensively researched. Yet, despite the Boer War providing the prime example, historians have found scant evidence of gold magnates or financial interests encouraging the war (e.g., Van Helten 1982, p. 411). Insofar as readers may wonder how my explanation relates to this debate, at the level of discourse and public legitimation (rather than motivation) I can state with some certainty that the government *did not* use financial interests to *legitimate* the war; instead, accusations of vested interests were used by its opponents to *delegitimate* the war. For a detailed review of Hobson's many critics, see Stokes (1969).

[7] See, for instance, Davis and Huttenback (1982).

[8] The Boer War also came at enormous human cost to the other side: not only were 25,000 of the Boers killed on the battlefield, most troublingly at least 27,927 Boer civilians and 14,154 native South Africans died in concentration camps set up by Britain during the last 18 months of the war (Roberts 1991, p. 358).

RATIONAL ILLUSIONS   87

cost in order to buttress its great power status. To be sure, some would posit that other motivations played a role; Hobson's ([1902] 1965: ch. 2) thesis resembles what we now call a military-industrial complex that profited from imperial expansion, but even he only claims that financial interests were a *secret* motivation pursued by promoting a "jingoism" in the press that preyed on patriotism, pride, and prestige. If one were content to merely hold together the "two tail ends of the causal chains" (Ringmar 1996, p. 35), we could stop here and point to the Boer War as a particularly egregious example of a great power wasting resources through imperial status competition.

However, the conventional story leaves behind too many puzzles to be satisfactory. As Porter (1990, p. 54) points out with regard to the Boer War, "it is essential to beware reading history backwards . . . from the scale, nature, costs and consequences of the war, to its origins and the intentions of imperial policy-makers." While the ruling Conservative Party and most of the general public supported the empire, leading members of the government doubted whether the public would support annexing the Transvaal.[9] Indeed, the viceroy of South Africa, Alfred Milner, who is widely considered the architect of the war, spent several months preparing the groundwork in public opinion and concocting a crisis that would avoid making Britain look like the aggressor (Pakenham 1979). If imperial expansion was such a popular enterprise that one could spend £200 million and tens of thousands of lives on a war, we would not expect legitimating it to take so much labor. Moreover, although Britain ended up entangled in a long and costly conflict, in the run-up few expected a war, and when it broke out, conventional wisdom was that it would be "over by Christmas."[10] Following Porter, we must avoid reading history backward—assuming the price of the war was the price Britain would pay for prestige—and instead inquire into the crucial processes that made the huge economic and human costs possible.

Second, although at its onset most of the government, press, and public supported the war, few believed it would boost Britain's prestige, but would

[9] See Surridge (1998, pp. 15–57) for an extended discussion of the government debates that took place behind the scenes. It is worth noting that Prime Minister Salisbury was among those skeptical of a military operation against the Boer unless public opinion was sure to favor it (p. 47).

[10] Krebs (2004, p. 32) attributes these words to General Roberts, who led the British army during the first period of the war. However, the expectation of a quick and easy war was widespread (Pakenham 1979). For instance, Arthur Balfour, the leader of the House, closed his speech in a Parliament debate at the onset of hostilities by saying, "[H]aving with us [Britain] the conscience of the Empire and the material resources of Empire, surely we may look forward without undue misgiving to the result of a contest" (HC Deb 17 October 1899). A secret British Military Intelligence report reflected similar confidence: "It appears certain that, after [one] serious defeat, they [the Boer] would be too deficient in discipline and organization to make any further real stand" (quoted in Jones 2009, p. 63).

THE GRAMMAR OF STATUS COMPETITION

only preserve it. Support was present, but it was scarcely enthusiastic and faced a significant minority of critics in Parliament. This presents a puzzle: just nine months later, Brits were dancing in the streets with joy following the relief of Mafeking in May 1900, while the government and press soon began boasting about how the victories in the war could not help but impress the world. Yet, during the latter stages of the war, the public mood shifted, and little enthusiasm or celebration greeted its victorious conclusion. This was the point at which Britain officially won the war and gained a colony, thus we might expect some jubilation at this new addition to the British Empire. But little joy was forthcoming, in fact quite the opposite: the government's popularity sank in the years following victory and they lost in a landslide at the next general election. In short, while status dynamics were imbricated throughout the Boer War, a straightforward status-seeking explanation is inadequate.

Yet, taking a second look through the grammar-of-status lens, focusing on processes of legitimation rather than motivations and outcomes, can shed light on these puzzles and counter Mercer's provocation. To undertake this task, the analysis disaggregates the war into three episodes: 1) the lead-up to the war and its legitimation from 1898 to 1899; 2) the first nine months of fighting in which the Boers inflicted several battlefield defeats before British reinforcements arrived and the tide turned; and 3) the final 18 months of the war, when the Boers fought using guerrilla tactics, and Britain forced thousands of Boer and Black South Africans into concentration camps. Analysing each episode in turn, my grammar-of-status framework illuminates important features of the British discourse that can help explain some of the more puzzling facets of the case and challenge important parts of the theoretical conventional wisdom about how status hierarchies inform foreign policy. Ultimately, the goal is to go beyond showing *that* status mattered and highlight *how* it mattered.

Episode 1: Honor and Hubris

> Lord Roberts and Kitchener,
> General Buller and White
> went out to South Africa
> to teach the Boers how to fight.
> —Popular British schoolyard ditty

RATIONAL ILLUSIONS   89

The run-up to the onset of the war has been researched extensively. Historians have long had privileged access to the official and private correspondence of the viceroy of the Cape, Sir Alfred Milner. There is now little doubt that he intentionally "worked up a crisis" with the Transvaal republic in order to force the British government to intervene on account of the "Uitlanders" (foreign nationals) living under the Boer Rule (Pakenham 1979, p. 26). Indeed, the war is often referred to as "Milner's war because of his outsized role in bringing it about."[11] In short, Milner was pursuing British supremacy in the region—what he saw as befitting a great power and master race[12]—as well as personal status (as the man to do it). However, at stake here is *how* the war was legitimated. Milner believed—and it seems likely he was correct—that neither the British public nor the government would support a war with the Boers for the sake of imperial expansion alone (Surridge 1998, ch.). After all, following defeat at Majuba on the Natal border during the First Boer War (1880–1881) Britain had ceded *internal* independence (suzerain status) to the Boers in the Transvaal instead of sending reinforcements in order to avoid defeat. Thus, it cannot be assumed that Britain—government or public—was willing to pay any price to annex the Transvaal. While Secretary of the Colonies Joseph Chamberlain was supportive of Milner's plans, he considered winning over the public essential and did not consider imperial ambition sufficient or even necessarily useful for this purpose (Pakenham 1979, chs. 2 and 5; also Porter 1996).

Instead, in order to legitimate intervention in the Transvaal, Milner and the government claimed that Britain needed to stand up for the rights of British citizens living under the Boers in the Transvaal. In the year preceding the outbreak of war, Milner circulated stories in the British press about the Boers' mistreatment of "Uitlanders" in order to ferment anti-Boer sentiment in Britain (Pakenham 1979; Surridge 1998). This set in motion a long period of negotiations led by Milner and Paul Kruger (the Boer president) which were (ostensibly) intended to hammer out an agreement about the rights of British citizens in the Transvaal (Pakenham 1979). In particular,

[11] See Marks (1982, p. 105), Packenham (1979)

[12] Milner was a self-described "Imperialist and a British Race Patriot." However, while Milner—and likely other elites—understood the Transvaal as part of a broader competition among the races, Milner clearly did not believe this would convince the British public to support the war, and indeed, as we will see, this argument did not feature in the public *legitimation* for war. To be clear, although it has preoccupied historians, the motivations of Milner or whether he or the Boers were to blame for the war are not of analytical significance for this chapter. Whatever the answers to these questions, they would not change how the war was legitimated in British domestic discourse.

90 THE GRAMMAR OF STATUS COMPETITION

the negotiations centered around the issue of the franchise for Uitlanders living and paying taxes in the Transvaal. The crux of the matter hinged on how many years an Uitlander had to live in the Transvaal before they were granted the electoral franchise. Pakenham (1979) has argued that Milner deliberately drew out negotiations with the intention of "turning the screw" while appearing to act in good faith to Brits at home. The Boers eventually succumbed to Milner's pressure and issued an ultimatum to Britain, which provided the government with a welcome pretext for war. Although the government would express outrage and dismay in Parliament, as a note from Secretary of War Landsdown to Chamberlain shows, the ultimatum was welcomed by influential members of the cabinet: "Accept my felicitations. I don't think Kruger could have played your cards better than he has."[13] The upshot of the ultimatum was that the British government could plausibly present war as defensive and, given the length of the negotiations, that they had tried their best to avoid military intervention and settle matters peacefully.[14] Returning to our theme, then, to what extent and how did theories of Britain's international status become salient within British political discourse during the negotiations and run-up to the war?

The Rules of Britain's Imagined Competition

On the surface, it might appear as though a war with the Boer would serve to buttress Britain's status because it would expand the empire and involve showing off its martial prowess: two activities associated with great power status at the time. However, British discourse at the time does not reflect this view.[15] Instead, the dominant theory of status used by the government explained why Britain could *not* expect the war to bolster its status, but paradoxically why the war could also be presented as necessary.

The government's pro-war discourse invoked complementary theories of its moral and military status in order to legitimate going to war with the Boer.

---

[13] The note came from Lord Landsdown, who was the secretary of state for war (1899). As the note suggests, by this point Chamberlain wanted the war, but had wanted to ensure that he had bipartisan support, something which the ultimatum would all but guarantee (Pakenham 1979, ch. 4).

[14] For instance, Joseph Chamberlain (HC Deb 19 October 1899, vol. 77, col. 266). See also the pro-war speeches (HC Deb 19 October 1899, vol. 77, col. 254-371).

[15] It is also useful to clarify that economic arguments were *not* used to legitimate the war but were used by critics to delegitimate the war. This thesis was to become canonized by Hobson and popularized by Lloyd George during the war (Rintala 1988, pp. 127–129).

RATIONAL ILLUSIONS 91

Even though the Boer were represented as unworthy opponents within such a discourse, their lowly status also implied that Britain could not (be seen to) give in to their demands and *not* intervene. It would have constituted public humiliation for a great power—and its people—and would have undermined Britain's international status. The governments theory of status is well-illustrated by Chamberlain's speech to Parliament following the ultimatum. Legitimating the decision to go to war, he argued that "the man on the street"

> knows perfectly well that we are going to war in defence of principles—the principles upon which this Empire has been founded and upon which alone it can exist. What are those principles? I do not think that anyone—however extreme a view he may take of this particular war, and however much he may condemn and criticise the policy of her Majesty's Government—will dispute what I am going to say. The first principle is this—that *if we are to maintain our position in regard to other nations*, if we are to maintain our existence as a great Power in South Africa, we are bound to show that we are both willing and able to protect British subjects everywhere when they are made to suffer from oppression and injustice.... That is the first principle. It is a principle which prevails always and everywhere, and in every difference which we may have with another country. (My emphasis)[16]

At least two aspects of Chamberlain's speech are worth emphasizing. First, while a great deal of the speech regards the details of the process of negotiation that led to the war, which was the main angle of attack by skeptical members of the Liberal Party opposition, Chamberlain clearly holds that maintaining Britain's status is a goal around which all political parties and citizens can align. Second, for Chamberlain, the moral and material hierarchies were intermingled in legitimation: it was *because* Britain was a great power and had the ability to intervene that it had the moral obligation to do so, lest it forfeit its great power status. Chamberlain's argument encapsulates neatly the dominant line of reasoning by pro-war MPs on the Conservative side.[17]

Indeed, the fact that the Boers were considered so inferior in terms of resources (and, to some, in terms of race and civilization) only multiplied

---

[16] Joseph Chamberlain (HC Deb 19 October 1899, vol. 77, cc 266).

[17] See, for instance, Captain Sir A. Acland-Hood: Hansard (HC Deb 17 October 1899, vol. 77, col. 6).

92   THE GRAMMAR OF STATUS COMPETITION

the necessity of *not* giving in to the Boers' demands. From this perspective, Britain's great power status relied upon its military power, martial prowess, empire, moral and civilizational standing, and, for many, neo-Darwinian notions of being the master race (e.g., Doyle 2008 [1902] *Times*, January 26, 1900; see also Mercer 2017, p. 146). This theory placed Britain atop the international hierarchy, winning a status competition *partly* with rules of its own making.[18] While within British politics at the time, Britain was usually theorized to be at top of the international hierarchy, it was not without rivals: Russia, France, and increasingly Germany were seen as putative rivals to British leading power status.[19] This was patently not how the Boer were represented. Akin to how Liverpool would not expect glory from defeating Doncaster at football, the Boer were considered so far beneath the British in terms of status that there was little glory to be gained from defeating them. As one Irish MP put it in Parliament, "it is a war without one single redeeming feature, a Giant against a Dwarf, a war which, no matter what its ending may be, will bring neither credit nor glory nor prestige to this great British Empire."[20] While the Irish Nationalists could be expected to take an antiwar line, their reading of the status stakes in the war was also reflected among some English MPs. For instance, the MP for Burnley Stanhope reflected a common lack of enthusiasm: "We will succeed, but that will not make the war a justifiable one. We have a feeling—indeed I am not sure that we do not confess—that we do not expect any glory from it. The war must inevitably be an inglorious and an ignoble one."[21]

The way that theories of status informed the legitimation for the war is best highlighted by the umbrage expressed by more avid supporters of the war. These MPs tended to speak in the emotional register of shock and outrage at the lack of deference shown by the Boers.[22] Indeed, it is the sheer *defiance* shown by the ultimatum—and the implied lack of respect for Britain's great

---

[18] To be sure, other international actors may have grudgingly recognized Britain's military power, especially its navy, but it is doubtful—for reasons discussed in the introduction—whether the rest of international society would have recognized Britain's alleged moral or racial leadership.

[19] This is reflected in the primary sources, both *Hansard* and the *Times*, where Germany and France are frequently referred to as rivals. They were also frequently used by opponents of the war to draw unfavorable comparisons to British conduct. Other countries crop up—the views of Russia and the United States appeared in the *Times*—but Germany and France were the main Others in the discourse. This is broadly consistent with the secondary literature, in which France and especially Germany are usually depicted as Britain's main rivals at the time.

[20] Mr. Davitt: HC Deb 17 October 1899, vol. 77, col. 60-160.

[21] HC Deb 18 October 1899, vol. 77, col. 181-228.

[22] This is consistent with Alex Yu-Ting Lin's (2023) argument, which suggests that insubordination from small states is especially concerning for great powers because deference is expected.

power status—that underpinned the need to act.[23] As the prime minister, Lord Salisbury, argued in Parliament, the Boers had "issued a defiance so audacious that I can hardly depict it adequately without using stronger words than are suited to this Assembly"; therefore the need to explain the war had been "wiped away in this one great insult, which leaves to us no other course to pursue."[24] Salisbury was echoed by the Lord Chancellor, who argued that "no Government with one atom of self-respect . . . could by any possibility have accepted [the ultimatum]. It is difficult to say whether the ultimatum is characterized more by audacity or by insanity."[25] Indeed, umbrage that such a *small* adversary could dare send an ultimatum to Britain was pervasive in the Lords debate.[26] For instance, Lord Loch stated that "no one throughout this country" could read "that arrogant message" and for "a moment doubt the absolute necessity and duty of teaching the Boers . . . that we are determined to maintain our rightful position as the dominant power in South Africa."[27] Yet, *why* the ultimatum was so helpful for legitimation is worth spelling out. Although it was taken for granted within British discourse at the time, and by historians later, that Britain could not plausibly give in to the ultimatum, given that Britain had yet to mobilize its massive military advantages, it would have made good "rational" sense to play for time to prepare for war. Yet as the quotes illustrate, it was presented as unthinkable to meet the ultimatum with anything but war. In short, the Boers were of such lowly position—as the prime minister put it, a "wretched little population"[28]—that Britain has no option but to teach them a lesson lest their own status be called into question.

Crucially, reviewing the entirety of the Commons and Lords debates there is not a single member who legitimates the war in terms of a positive quest

---

[23] Interestingly, the Boers also saw fighting the war in terms of status, though in their case as a rite of passage to enter the "state club": "Our volk throughout South Africa must be baptized with the baptism of blood and fire before they can be admitted among the great peoples of the world" (Jan Smuts, future prime minister of South Africa, cited in Judd and Surridge 2013, p. 9). Indeed, the Boers' understanding of the need to fight for recognition resembles Ringmar's (1996) explanation of why Sweden joined the Thirty Years' War. Moreover, it would support Renshon's (2017) argument that "fighting for status" is endogenously encouraged by the hierarchies within international society.

[24] Lord Salisbury, the Prime Minister (HL Deb 17 October 1899, vol. 77, col. 17).

[25] Lord Granby, the Lord Chancellor (HL Deb 17 October 1899, vol. 77, col. 6).

[26] Lord Barnard was one of many who make the size asymmetry explicit: "No nation could receive such an ultimatum as that, even from the most powerful nation in the world, without at once replying to it in a manner which could leave no doubt that it was prepared to defend the territories which were attacked" (HL Deb 17 October 1899, vol. 77, col. 3-39). The emphasis on size was also echoed by the prime minister and others in the Commons and Lords when referring to why Britain could not meet the ultimatum with anything but war.

[27] HL Deb 17 October 1899, vol. 77, col. 3-39.

[28] Quoted in Steele (2000, p. 19).

94   THE GRAMMAR OF STATUS COMPETITION

for status. Instead, most express reluctance to fight in what the leader of the House, James Balfour, referred to in the debate as "this unhappy war." In other words, the Boer ultimatum had forced their hand, and action had to be taken to *preserve* or *maintain* Britain's status.[29] This is why for those who had welcomed war, the ultimatum was a boon to their efforts to legitimate it.[30] Even Liberal MPs who expressed their "protest against what has led up to the war" and who supported an amendment expressing their disapproval[31] admitted that "the ultimatum *undoubtedly* called this country to go to war" (my emphasis).[32]

Yet, seeking to preserve Britain's status by rejecting the ultimatum was theorized as a question not only of national pride but also of prizes, or more precisely, the expectation of punishment should Britain not go to war. This line of argument contended that giving into the Boers' demands would risk other states perceiving Britain as weak (bad in itself) and encourage other colonial uprisings, requiring costly interventions or perhaps even concessions. As such, Minister of the Colonies Chamberlain put it to the cabinet in the run-up to the war that failing to intervene risked "the position of Great Britain in South Africa—and with it the estimate formed of our power and influence in our colonies and throughout the world" (cited in Ovendale 1982, p. 41).[33] The *Times* reflects this concern with preservation of influence, writing, "Had we not acted as we have acted, we should have abdicated our Imperial influence altogether" and insisting that Britain must "see this war through to the end" until "we have *restored* British Prestige fore and aft" (November 6, 1899, my emphasis). This theory was also expressed in the Commons and Lords debates about the decision to go to war (October 17–19). Given the general lack of military force Britain employed to control its colonial possessions,

---

[29] In his speech Balfour used the word "unhappy" three times to describe the war. HC Deb 19 October 1899, vol. 77, col. 254-361.

[30] Prior to the ultimatum, Chamberlain acknowledged to Milner that "the technical casus belli is a very weak one," and this "hindered preparations and resolute action" (cited in Surridge 1998, p. 50). The ultimatum solved this problem.

[31] The amendment read, "But we humbly represent to your Majesty our strong disapproval of the conduct of the negotiations with the Government of the Transvaal which have involved us in hostilities with the two South African Republics." Mr. Stanhope: HC Deb 19 October 1899, vol. 77, col. 254.

[32] Sir Samuel Evans, Hansard, HC Deb 18 October 1899, vol. 77, cc 197-198.
Another self-identifying "radical" Liberal MP, Charles Dilke, put it similarly: "I freely admit that the war in its immediate inception has been forced upon us in circumstances which make it impossible for us not to pick up the gauntlet thrown down." Hansard, HC Deb (17 October 1899, vol. 77, col. 66).

[33] This concern with British influence was also expressed in Chamberlain's address to Parliament. See the quote above and also Hansard, HC Deb 19 October 1899, vol. 77, cc 263-266.

maintaining its position in what realists refer to as the "hierarchy of prestige" (see Gilpin 1983) could be represented as strategically crucial.

Ultimately, in the government and pro-war public discourse the decision to go to war against the Boer was not a question of competing *for* status; it was theorized as necessary to *preserve* its status for reasons of both pride and prizes. The theory that Britain would have forfeited its great power status should it have caved in to the ultimatum was the primary and, I would argue, necessary representation that made the war possible and enabled bipartisan support for the war. Thus, the analysis above highlights an advantage of studying theories of status as a mode of legitimation: that we can study the political effects of theories of status rather than attempting to assess whether they were true or not. Moreover, and crucially, in the government's own words, defeating the Boer should have proven straightforward; a routine exercise in imperial management. Yet, as I will elaborate shortly, Britain struggled to defeat its tiny foe yet would go on to present its eventual victory on the battlefield as glorious, manage to elicit dancing in the streets among its citizens, and contribute to a landslide election in 1900. This establishes the puzzle that the next section answers: How was it possible for the government to present its struggles to defeat the Boer as a boost to its great power status? How and why could these status claims be expected to resonate among the domestic audience?

Episode 2: Emergent Status Competition

> Everyone is splendid: soldiers are staunch, commanders cool, the fighting magnificent. Whatever the fiasco, aplomb is unbroken. Mistakes, failures, stupidities, or other causes of disaster mysteriously vanish. Disasters are recorded with care and pride and become transmuted into things of beauty. Other nations attempt but never quite achieve the same self-esteem.
>
> —Barbara W. Tuchman, *Stilwell and the American Experience in China: 1911–1945* (1970, p. 557)

Within weeks of the onset of war, the government's confidence revealed itself to be hubris. Not only was the war not over by Christmas, but Britain was losing at Christmas. Between December 10 and 17, 1899, the British army suffered humiliating defeats at Stormberg, Magersfontein,

96 THE GRAMMAR OF STATUS COMPETITION

and Colenso. Around 2,776 men were killed. These military defeats became known as "Black Week," which together with the disaster of Spion Kop in January 1900 revealed that the government and the public had severely underestimated the Boers' relative strength, organization, and military prowess. Indeed, in what became known as the first "modern war" and a precursor to the First World War, the Boer victories highlighted the weaknesses of a sclerotic British army, which hitherto had been hidden by fighting opponents lacking modern weaponry.[34] The Boers had not only managed to repel the British threat to their territories (the Orange Free State and the Transvaal); they had seized several towns in Britain's Cape Colony and Natal and laid siege to Britain's strongholds at Ladysmith, Kimberley, and the outpost of Mafeking. These defeats prompted consternation among the public, who directed their ire at the political class they accused of failing to provide the generals with adequate resources. Certainly, it has been widely recognized that the poor planning and personal feuding at the War Office had left a dangerous gap between the onset of the war and the period when sufficient reinforcements would arrive (Surridge 1998). However, the gradual arrival of massive reinforcements eventually saw Britain's asymmetrical resources overwhelm the Boers (at least on the conventional battlefield). Between February and May 1900, they relieved the besieged towns before embarking upon a victorious march on Pretoria in June. The conventional war concluded in September, when General Roberts took Komati Poort, thus effectively cutting the Boers off from the outside world. This would prompt Roberts to declare the war to be "practically over."[35] While thousands of Boers continued to wage a guerrilla campaign, few expected it to last long.

The events in South Africa during this episode interest us here insofar as they were represented within British discourse as evidence of Britain's status in the world and the effects this had upon domestic politics. Given that it was widely expected that Britain would defeat the Boer with ease,[36] the succession of battlefield defeats immediately had ramifications within British discourse. Yet, as Mercer (2017) has highlighted, the British government claimed their eventual triumph in the war as bound to impress international

---

[34] Indeed, one important outcome of the war was to bring about a comprehensive reform of the War Office (Porter 2000, p. 636).

[35] In a speech given to an audience in Durban (quoted in Pakenham 1979, p. 486).

[36] As Jonathon Mercer (2017, p. 152) notes, "the British considered the Boers uncivilized, racially inferior, and amateur soldiers."

audiences, boost Britain's prestige, and thus induce additional deference. At the same time, Mercer shows that international audiences were unmoved and did not show any additional willingness to defer. Yet, what Mercer misses is that the international audience's response is consistent with British discourse in the run-up to the war: even the proponents of the war did not expect a boost in status from beating such lowly opponents; instead, they had legitimated the war on the grounds that only by defeating the Boer could Britain's prestige be preserved. Thus, the puzzle is not only why Britain's theory of status differed from that of the international audience, but how the government could plausibly claim that the war boosted its great power status, given its earlier representation of the Boer as a trifling opponent. Mercer's argument is that Britain based its claims to status upon emotions born from victory. Against this, I show how, through the process of fighting and *re*-presenting the war, an alternative, a more favorable theory of the war's status value was made plausible and salient, one that made the emotional register of pride possible.

War of Words

The Boer War caught the public's imagination as no other had (Donaldson 2018; Morgan 2002). John Gooch (2000, p. xix) probably gets a little too carried away claiming it was the "*first* Media war" (my emphasis), but certainly the level of coverage and breadth of readership was unprecedented. The advent of the popular press, telegraph, and portable camera allowed domestic populations to keep abreast of the latest news from the battlefront with a new immediacy and intimacy (Badsey 2000). Indeed, at least 58 dedicated war reporters were employed in the field on behalf of the British and international press to report the action as it unfolded (Morgan 2002, p. 2). Unsurprisingly, Britain's great power rivals followed the war with interest, especially following Black Week. The press in France, Russia, and Germany had long sided with the Boers even before the conflict, depicting Britain as an interminable bully attempting to coerce the Boers into submission (Lowry 2002, pp. 271–272).[37] Moreover, the *Times* and other newspapers frequently

---

[37] Around 2,500 men volunteered from overseas—including from Russia, Germany, Ireland, the United States, and Holland—to fight on the Boer's side (Lowry 2002, p. 272).

98   THE GRAMMAR OF STATUS COMPETITION

reported international opinion about the war from various European capitals (Krebs 2004, p. 42).

As a result, when Britain suffered a series of unexpected early defeats, "Britain's embarrassment was international" (Williams 2013, p. 493). For instance, Black Week prompted one of the *Daily Mail*'s war reporters to lament, "What shame! What bitter shame for all the camp. All ashamed for England! Not of her—never that!—but for her. Once more she was a source of laughter to her enemies" (G. W. Steevans, cited in Farwell [1976] 2009, p. 83). Another war correspondent, who would write among the first contemporary histories of the war, H. W. Wilson (cited in Porter 2000, p. 638), expressed most clearly why these defeats prompted such outpourings: "The fame of the Army, the prestige of the nation, the very existence of the Empire, were in grievous peril. ... [V]ictory at best could never regain for us what we had forfeited—our reputation before the world." The shame was not merely an elite manifestation but widespread among the working class (Readman 2001). For instance, Frederick Willis, a working-class man, recalled in his memoirs how he felt about the what he saw as a threat to Britain's international status: "[T]o this day I remember the distress [it] gave me. As a citizen of the great British Empire ... I felt I could never face the world's scorn if we ceased to exist as a first-class power" (quoted in Readman 2001, p. 136). In short, shame from suffering defeat at the hands of the Boer was reflected among the elites and ordinary citizenry alike and produced popular demand for the government to salvage Britain's status.[38]

Indeed, the defeats during Black Week prompted a rapid response from the government, which immediately began calling up the rest of the reserves and for volunteers to go to the front. The *Times* rallied, telling its readers that "the urgency of sending further reinforcements with the least possible delay is recognized, we are sure, by the whole of the British people" (December 18, 1899). While the parliamentary debate in January saw widespread recriminations about inadequate preparations for the war,[39] as Blanch (1980, p. 217) put it, even critics now recognized that "even if the war was wrong, it could not be lost."

---

[38] Although some historians have questioned this, most notably Price (1972), who claims that the working class were uninterested in the empire or the exploits of the British army. For a compelling rebuttal of Price, see Mackenzie (1986). Indeed, Price's argument has undergone sustained and compelling critique. (See Beaven 2009, pp. 209–11 for a review.)

[39] See HC Deb 30 January 1900, vol. 78, col. 71-156.

Retheorizing the Status Competition

Beyond the threat of losing territory and men, the early defeats also produced a status predicament. Given how Britain had represented the Boer prior to the war's onset, how could Britain's great power status be reconciled with this wave of military defeats to such a minnow? Even though Britain ultimately defeated the Boers, one might expect that its military defeats on the battlefield would surely have indicated that Britain was not so great after all. Besides sending vast numbers of reinforcements to ensure that at the very least Britain did not lose the war, British discourse underwent considerable adaption that served to mitigate, insulate, and offset the threat defeats posed to Britain's understanding of its status. As we shall see, rather than reevaluating the status position of Britain, the press and government *remade* the rules of the status competition. This section explores how this was achieved in practice.

First of all, the process of fighting and especially suffering defeat at the hands of the Boers led to Britain's reevaluating its enemy on more favorable terms. This became a key line of defense in Parliament, used to exculpate the government from blame for the early losses. Suddenly the government presented its once lowly opponent as having assembled a "vast military machine" armed "with the most perfect weapons ever used in warfare."[40] Meanwhile the secretary of state for war suggested they had underrated the Boers' "value as fighting men," in particular their "tenacity and mobility."[41] While the Boers were still "othered," it became common to emphasize their military pedigree and prowess. In the immediate aftermath of Black Week the *Times* (December 20, 1899) offered a textbook example of how the British press came to retheorize their adversary:

> [B]eing born and bred to the life of the veldt, they possess inherited and acquired instincts which can be imparted to the soldier only after long and careful training in this special kind of country. . . . They are exceedingly stubborn and tenacious in defence, which also might have been anticipated from their national character, since they trace their descent from the stout-hearted seamen who proved our toughest naval antagonists. . . . Highly trained tacticians—and there are many such in the Boer ranks—would, if

[40] HC Deb 30 January 1900, vol. 78, col. 73-75.
[41] HL Deb 30 January 1900, vol. 78, col. 41.

100 THE GRAMMAR OF STATUS COMPETITION

trusted and obeyed, be able to effect much with the excellent material at their disposal.

Beyond a new appreciation of the Boer's fighting prowess, the quote also illustrates several other new criteria through which both the Boer and the war were reevaluated. Indeed, the discourse now reflected a newfound respect for the Boer "race," a new appreciation of the difficult terrain, and a new emphasis on the Boer's "excellent" military capabilities. Indeed, Arthur Conan Doyle ([1902] 2008: location 24 Kindle),[42] who worked as a correspondent and historian of the war, ran with these themes explicitly. Drawing upon the neo-Darwinian discourse of the period, he argued—mobilizing the grammar of status—that the Boer's mix of Dutch and Huguenot heritage and the fact they had spent several generations fighting "savage men" had produced "one of the *most* rugged, virile, unconquerable races ever seen upon earth" and made them the "*most* formidable antagonist who ever crossed the path of Imperial Britain." It is also not coincidental that the Boer War acquired the misleading nickname of the "white man's war" during this period.[43] The cumulative effect of these discursive moves was to grant the Boer a new *status* as worthy enemy, one that Britain could take pride in defeating.

In addition, British discourse during the conflict began to emphasize the logistical difficulty of waging war on a separate continent. Recalling that to make competitive comparisons requires a great deal of discursive labor and abstraction, it is not surprising that the symbolic value of the Boer War in terms of status was ambiguous and contested. Although realist scholars have—post hoc—coalesced around material definitions of who and who was not a great power, more historically oriented scholars highlight that there was considerable ambiguity and disagreement around which countries were great and why (Zala 2017; Naylor 2018; Neumann , 2014). Race, history, proximity to Europe, as well as land and sea power were to varying degrees at play during the 19th century regarding who should count as great among

---

[42] I am citing the 1902 edition; it was first published in 1900, and according to the author, he made minimal alterations to the text with each new update.

[43] It is now widely established that this nickname was a gross misrepresentation; there were thousands of non-Whites involved on both sides of conflict (Roberts 1991; Krebs 2004). It also got the nickname "gentleman's war" (e.g., Fuller 1937), which was both racialized and bitterly ironic given that the British would pioneer concentration camps as a military tactic and undertake widespread farm burning.

the powers.[44] In this context, Britain had some discursive leeway to construct and modify the criteria by which to assess the status value of the war with the Boers, at least to its domestic audience. Indeed, once the war was underway, ever greater numbers of reinforcements were sent to South Africa from Britain as well significant numbers from New Zealand, Australia, and Canada. Rather than a sign of its struggle to defeat its tiny foe, the British government claimed that its ability to call upon its colonies should be seen as symbol of the empire's impressive military capacity.[45] Moreover, the global nature of this operation led the government to emphasize the logistical capacity required to transport hundreds of thousands of men several thousand miles across the oceans. For instance, speaking a month following Black Week, one Conservative MP called upon his colleagues in the House of Commons to

> remember that this war is being carried on at a distance of 6,000 miles from the base, and is in that respect *unprecedented* in the history of the world. It is not an easy matter to send troops to fight 6,000 miles away and to keep up an adequate commissariat supply.[46]

Taken together, this positive reevaluation of their adversary and the logistical difficulty involved in waging the war laid the discursive groundwork for the prime minister to later declare that victory was a "wonderful achievement."[47]

The takeaway point in terms of the theory of status competition that emerged was that while the Boers were by no means a great power in size, the scale of the operation and their newly recognized fighting capacities implied that beating them would display a power projection capacity befitting a great power. To be sure, this drew upon extant discourses about how being a "world power" required global power projection, but at the same time, this theory of why the war should impress de-emphasized the relative *size* of the

---

[44] As Japan would find to its chagrin, the race hierarchy of the time could override the symbolic value of military victories in determining which countries were recognized as great (see Ward 2013; Naylor 2018).

[45] The Duke of Somerset's speech in the House of Lords offers an especially good example of this reevaluation of the war and enemy (HL Deb 30 January 1900, vol. 78, col. 6-8). See also *Times*, February 6, 1900.

[46] HC Deb 30 January 1900, vol. 78, cc 150-151.

[47] Prime Minister Salisbury, speaking to Liberal Unionist Association (quoted in Mercer 2017, p. 153).

102 THE GRAMMAR OF STATUS COMPETITION

enemy, which the government had hitherto used as a reason for why the victory should have been straightforward and thus why status could not be gained but only saved.

"200 Not Out": Narrating the Competition

In addition to reevaluating the enemy and emphasizing the power projection, the style of the press reporting encouraged the country to understand the war as an important round in an international status competition. Accustomed to living vicariously through their country's exploits, the public could follow every blow via the new half-penny press (Morgan 2002). Typically, the asymmetry between the Boers and the British remained in the background, while reports from the front zoomed in on the micro-battlefield dynamics and individual narratives of heroics (Omissi and Thompson 2002). As Jaffe (1995, p. 93) notes, the young "gentlemen" who volunteered to be officers saw the war as a "series of sporting events" whereby the conflict became an extension of the "system of sports, games and physical fitness exercises which characterised British Public schools in the nineteenth century." The press and the war correspondents followed suit.[48] Indeed, as Donaldson 2018, p. 7) notes in reference to the Boer War, "the language exchange between the sporting and military worlds . . . became an increasing feature of popular journalism of the period."[49] What is crucial for our purposes here is to highlight how sporting metaphors provided a discursive mechanism by which the war could became constituted as a status competition against a worthy rival.

Few better illustrations exist of how the conflict was framed as a sporting contest between rival competitors than how the siege of Mafeking was reported in the press. Zooming on the tactical predicament—the Brits were outnumbered—rather than the strategic balance of power, the general charged with the defense of Mafeking, Robert Baden-Powell, could be presented as a plucky hero: fighting against the odds, displaying British virtues of ingenuity, good humor, and bravery in the face of adversity. Indeed, Mafeking became a central narrative in the Boer War, making Baden-Powell famous in the process. For example, in an episode that typifies how the war could be understood as sport, Baden-Powell released a dispatch to the press

---

[48] Indeed, sport had become an "essential frame of reference for society at the turn of the twentieth century" (Donaldson 2018, p. 7).

[49] For a more general discussion of the function of sport metaphors and war, see Lakoff (1991).

relaying his response to the Boer general who had challenged his men to a cricket match:

> Sir, I beg to thank you for your letter of yesterday. . . . I should like nothing better—after the match in which we are at present engaged is over. But just now we are having our innings and have so far scored 200 days, not out, against the bowling of Cronje, Snijman, Botha . . . and we are having a very enjoyable game. I remain, yours truly R. S. S. Baden-Powell. (Cited in Ferguson 2012, p. 277)

The press had a "field day" with the story: "[It] was portrayed back in Britain as the war's most glorious episode. . . . Indeed the press treated the siege as a kind of big imperial game, a seven-month test match between England and the Transvaal" (Ferguson 2012, p. 195). Mafeking was far from the exception: besides cricket, boxing also featured, and even the government joined in (Donaldson 2018, p. 23). The practice of using sports metaphors in reporting was so widespread that it even fomented a backlash. For instance, one letter to the *Manchester Guardian* described as "repellent" depicting "the war in the language of sport when the issue is the making of widows and orphans" (Donaldson 2018, p. 21). And not all those fighting on the front line appreciated the metaphor. For instance, William Elliot Cairns, a captain in the Royal Irish Fusiliers, published a book in 1900 in which he lamented that "active service is regarded rather as a new and most exciting kind of sport, a feeling which has been heightened by our numerous campaigns against savages, than as a deadly serious business where the stakes are the lives of men and the safety of the empire" (cited in Donaldson 2018, p. 17).

While distasteful, the use of sporting metaphors can help explain why Britain would and could end up "behaving as though they had beaten Napoleon" rather than an opponent similar in size to a "second rate English Town."[50] By invoking notions of "fair play," rules, and winners and losers, the widespread use of sports metaphors in the reporting of the war helped constitute it as a salient status competition between *rivals*. Indeed, framing the war using sports metaphors conjured away the power imbalance that had made the Boer a trifling foe, enabling the enemy to be reevaluated as a worthy opponent. The result was that rather than mere relief from humiliation,

---

[50] These are the words of two contemporary critics of the war, John Merriman and Wilfred Blunt, respectively (quoted in Mercer 2017, p. 155).

104 THE GRAMMAR OF STATUS COMPETITION

triumphing in this "contest" could enable a new emotional register—joy and pride—and winning the war could be theorized to bestow glory upon Britain and Brits.

Mediating and Translating International Opinion

We now turn to the final key discursive practice—the British media's translation of international opinion—that helped maintain and insulate Britain's new theory of the Boer War's status implications. While international audiences were paying close attention to the war, the national press mediated international opinion through nationalist lenses. For instance, the *Times* systematically discounted criticism and generally narrated it in a manner that downplayed its significance. The following dispatch from a foreign correspondent a month after Black Week showcases the key techniques of the genre:[51]

> England's privileged situation, her immense, colonial conquests, fertilized by her genius for colonization, the extent of her trade, through vast civilizing influence exercised by her throughout the globe, have aroused the baneful and degrading sentiment of jealousy which rages in the souls of the nations not less than in individual hearts. This, with other motives more degrading still, is the fundamental cause of the treatment of which England is today the object. (*Times*, January 26, 1900)

It goes on to theorize that even if the "regret" is not "publicly displayed"

> [i]t cannot, in fact, be a matter of indifference to a superior mind that the universal patrimony of modern civilization should be despoiled or one of its most considerable factors, and that such a nation as the English should suffer reverses in such surprising conditions as we have seen. This explains why, by an odd contradiction, many people whom I meet, who are not distressed to see England's pride humbled, in reality experience within them sincere regret in beholding England's enemies already hastening to proclaim that her prestige has suffered a death-blow, affirming that her influence, an influence so salutary for the civilization of the world as a whole,

---

[51] Other examples include *Times*, February 7, 1900, and May 24, 1900.

will soon have ceased to be felt. Nothing in the world is more odious for an inhabitant of the Continent than to listen to such utterances on this occasion.

Several aspects are worth emphasizing here: the preamble emphasizing foreign envy of Britain; the assumption that regret must be felt even if it is not expressed; and the irritation with the "odious" assertion that Britain's prestige has suffered a "death blow." Crucially, the dispatch enables the reader to apparently learn about the continental perspective, while at the same time being encouraged to discount it. Making the reasonable assumption that this pattern was widespread in other newspapers reporting international opinion,[52] it would surely offer a significant piece of the puzzle for how the dominant domestic theory of the Boer War's status implications could diverge from international audiences in the manner that Mercer (2017) describes.

Nothing in the preceding sections will strike scholars of the Boer War as controversial. While I have provided only the odd exemplary quote, in each case there were a host to choose from. The marked tendency within British discourse to reevaluate the Boers as worthy enemies and the new emphasis on the logistical demands of the war do not diverge from any ordinary historical account. Nor will it surprise Boer War scholars to learn that the press focused on battles, heroes, and micro-narratives, and that they tended to report international opinion with skepticism. However, taken together and put into the context of status research, these practices can help explain and support a counterintuitive thesis about how states can compete with—and gain domestic political advantages from—status-seeking policies even when international recognition is not forthcoming. In short, the previous section has shown how Britain's government and press constructed a theory of status competition that allowed them and their citizens to express pride at defeating the Boer on the battlefield even when international audiences did not consider the feat worthy of esteem. This, as I will elaborate in the following section, can help solve what I call *Mercer's Puzzle*: why, even if the *international* gains from seeking international status often prove illusionary, "competing" for status may remain rational to states nonetheless.

---

[52] Most of my primary data are based on the *Times*, though it is reasonable to assume the other pro-war press—especially the famously jingoistic *Daily Mail*—would likely have had an even stronger nationalist bias. Indeed, Krebs (1999, p. 53) has argued that the *Times*, while conservative and nationalist, was far more balanced in its reporting of the concentration camps than the *Mail*.

106 THE GRAMMAR OF STATUS COMPETITION

Theories of Status and Domestic Legitimation

As I noted in the introduction, Mercer (2017) highlights how Britain's great power rivals publicly poo-pooed the victory and did not appear to defer any more readily to Britain than before. Yet, at the same time, the government and ordinary Brits—apparently oblivious to international opinion—hailed their victory as symbolic of their greatpowerdom. Ergo, argues Mercer, the Boer War wrought only illusionary benefits, and thus international status is a quixotic pursuit that rational leaders will eventually learn to forgo. Yet, if we treat pleasing the domestic audience as important for legitimating a government, then we can present a compelling and more plausible alternative. Further, drawing on the discussion above, we can show how the government's preferred theory of the status implications of the war emerged through the process of re-presenting the war as it unfolded rather than stemming from feelings of pride at victory. Indeed, I argue it was *analysis* that generated the expressions of pride rather than the other way around, as Mercer claims.

On the first point, Mercer (2017, p. 153) describes in some depth the British public's response to battlefield victory, ostensibly to highlight how it was divorced from international opinion:

> The Oxford English Dictionary added "to Mafik" to capture the euphoric, wild, "Mafeking" crowds. A British war correspondent wrote, "It is good to be an Englishman. These foreigners start too quick and vanish quicker. They are good men but we are better, and have proved so for several hundred years." Each victory led to "Mafeking" crowds, reported the Handsworth Herald: "Staid citizens, whose severe respectability and decorum were usually beyond question or reproach were to be seen parading the streets shouting patriotic songs with the full force of their lungs, dancing, jumping, screaming in a delirium of unrestrained joy." So great was the joy that members of Parliament sang the national anthem to Queen Victoria in the courtyard of Buckingham Palace. (References removed)

Yet, this account surely begs the obvious question: What rational leader would not want to preside over a policy that led to such joy among their subjects that, as Mercer describes, they added a new word for euphoria to their dictionary? One might object that the public celebrations and government

RATIONAL ILLUSIONS   107

support reflected the joy at the increased security or perhaps the economic gains that victory on the battlefield wrought. However, both the secondary literature and my primary sources suggest the positive valence attached to the meaning of the victories was primarily constituted by their implications for Britain's status in the world. For instance, a *Times* article published shortly after Mafeking explained the public mood in the following way:

Week by week the chance grew stronger that, for the first time for a hundred years, a great British army might be forced by famine, by disease, and by the exhaustion of their ammunition to lay down their arms. The military effects of such a calamity would have been serious, but it was not the military effects the nation feared. They feared for the prestige of the flag, and today they are rejoicing with an exuberant gaiety they rarely display, because Sir Redvers Bullen and his gallant troops have removed that fear from their hearts. (March 2, 1900)

Beyond prompting citizens to invent a new word to describe euphoria, the Conservative Party benefited in more tangible ways from theorizing and competing in their own status competition. Indeed, being seen to have successfully restored and even boosted Britain's status as a great power provided immediate gains to the party. The Conservatives actively campaigned for reelection in 1900 on their record in the war: 34 of the 49 campaign pamphlets published during the "Khaki Election" pertained to the war, while only 14 referred to domestic issues (Galbraith 1952). Thus, we can say at a minimum that the government and its supporters actively used its war efforts policy to legitimate its reelection. The crucial function the war played for the government in seeking to get reelected is captured well by the following excerpt from a pro-Conservative election pamphlet:

WORKING MEN! The correspondence of Radical M.P.'s with the enemy, their speeches, actions, and votes show that alas! the party of a small England, of a shrunken England, of a degraded England IS NOT DEAD. But KILL IT NOW by your contempt, your loathing, your manly patriotism, and your votes FOR A UNITED EMPIRE. Electors, be up and doing. Your Children Call Upon You. They will ask you hereafter how you voted in the crisis of the Empire. *Don't let your reply be "For a Small England, a Shrunken England, a Degraded England, a Submissive England."* NO! To the

108 THE GRAMMAR OF STATUS COMPETITION

Poll then, to the Poll to Vote for the Unionist Candidate and for GREATER BRITAIN.[53] (Cited in Galbraith 1952)

This example illustrates how supporting the war was associated with protecting British manhood, strength, and ultimately status among nations. Indeed, it highlights how the Conservatives' campaign explicitly argued that Britain's status in the world depended upon voting Conservative/Unionist. The prime minister's pitch to the country on the eve of the election put the war front and center, arguing first and foremost that "the gravest questions" concerning the "imperial power over the territories of the two South African republics" required reelecting the Conservatives (*Times*, September 24, 1900). Coverage of the election by the Conservative-supporting *Times* also tied together support for the war effort and securing Britain's status in the world with reelecting the Conservative Party.[54] Finally, contemporary accounts—by both Liberals and Conservatives—suggest the war had been at the very least helpful to the Conservatives and a "liability" to the Liberals (Readman 2001, p. 127). As one Conservative MP noted, the 1900 election had given his party "a very much larger majority than we should have secured had there been no war" (cited in Readman 2001, p. 127). Thus, even if the boost to Britain's status was illusionary, it was a useful illusion for the government to produce and maintain.

On Mercer's second point: Did feelings drive the analysis of the war's status implications? Inspecting the evidence that Mercer himself uses reveals how observers did *analyze* but used diverging theories of status. Indeed, lacking an independent adjudicator with the means to define the terms of comparison and circulate an authoritative assessment of Britain's status, the government and the public theorized for themselves the impact of the war on Britain's status. Given the difficulty of this task (see introduction), it is hardly surprising that rival theories existed. Crucially, diverging interpretations need not mean they are derived from emotions; they can instead reflect different assumptions about the nature of international status hierarchy. As Mercer (2017, pp. 153–155) documents, Prime Minister Salisbury assumed that the colonies' support would impress the world; the Liberal critic Hobson assumed that the brutality of the tactics would shame; others such as the influential naval theorist Alfred Mahan assumed beating White people (the

---

[53] Hopefully it goes without saying: emphasis in the original.
[54] For instance, *Times*, September 26, 1900.

Boers) was worthy of esteem. It should go without saying that these are just different approaches to *analysis*. Mercer claims these actors are going on feelings because they do not conduct direct analysis of their audience. Yet, similar to how Mercer argues that states should discount the successes of their rivals in their public pronouncements, as we saw earlier the press systematically discounted the words of international audiences too. Rather than go by what their rivals expressed in public, they preferred to deduce status effects from their assumptions about how international status works. Given that, as Mercer himself argues, foreign governments have instrumental incentives to limit public praise for their rivals, this is not a wholly unreasonable approach. To be sure, the various observers—especially Mahan, the Social Darwinist—might have been working on faulty assumptions, but this is not the same as going on "feelings."

It might be tempting to suggest there is no point adjudicating between feelings and analysis. Yet if we look at the *temporal* development of the British discourse, we can see that these different theories of the status implications were not merely elicited *upon* victory, as Mercer (e.g., 2017, p. 154) claims. Rather, as I documented above, during the process of fighting, the Boers were systematically reevaluated in Britain's discourse as a worthy adversary, setting the stage for conceiving of the war as a competition that Britain could take pride in winning. This process was facilitated by the style of reporting of the battles that focused on micro-dynamics rather than strategic asymmetry, and the tendency for newspapers to insulate the domestic audience from international opinion. Hence, the positive domestic assessments of Britain's status in the aftermath of the first stage of the war relied upon an earlier process of retheorizing the war's meaning. In short, it was this discursive groundwork that enabled Britain's leaders and ordinary Brits to express pride at victory rather than victory itself that prompted pride.

Finally, put into the broader context of status research, this analysis also illustrates how the rewards from framing and treating an activity as an international status competition need not be zero sum in practice. As the Boer War highlights, contradictory theories about status can exist, persist, and have effects simultaneously. This is neatly illuminated by Mercer's account of the allies' apparently contradictory self-understanding of their role in the war. Mercer (2017, pp. 158–160) shows how the British, New Zealanders, and Canadians all *simultaneously* contended that the Boer War demonstrated their *superior* fighting prowess. In other words, akin to the world's many "above average" drivers, multiple countries could simultaneously make

110 THE GRAMMAR OF STATUS COMPETITION

the same claim to superior status—in an imagined international hierarchy of fighting prowess—and "win" according to their own account of the same competition. Meanwhile, the relative insulation from one another's discourses enabled these interpretations to endure and produce effects without their logical contradictions needing to be settled.

Episode 3: "Gentlemen," Guerrillas, and Gender

> When is a war not a war?
> —Henry Campbell-Bannerman,
> leader of the Liberal Party, June 14, 1901

The satisfaction the British government expressed following the battlefield victories of 1900 was relatively short-lived. Thousands of Boers refused to surrender. Initially Britain's leadership expressed confidence that the "Bitterenders" would soon realize their plight was futile and surrender to British rule. This confidence turned out to be misplaced, and Britain became embroiled in an 18-month guerrilla war in which the so-called civilized norms of war were disregarded. In September 1900, Britain began systematically burning the farms of Boer families suspected of aiding the guerrillas. In December that same year it would become official policy to force these now homeless civilians into what the British government would claim were "refugee camps" but would later be known as "concentration camps." Although it was not the ostensible intent of the British authorities, an estimated 27,000 would die in the camps from diseases related to poor sanitation and malnutrition.

When reports of the farm burning and the conditions in the camps eventually reached the British public, they became the new focal point for public debate around war. While the Liberal Party had long been divided over the war, in the early stages the party's official position was to support waging the war but question the government's strategy and the negotiations that led to it.[55] However, as news of the farm burning and the camps emerged, the antiwar faction of the Liberals increased in both number and voice.[56] In December

---

[55] HC Deb 19 October 1899, vol. 77, col. 254-371.
[56] This is reflected by the leader of the Liberal Party's change in position toward the war from begrudging support at its outset—the ultimatum had prompted even radical Liberals to back the war—to outspoken opposition once the high death rate in the camps was publicized (Pakenham 1979, p. 535). For an extended discussion of Liberal divisions, see Jacobson (1973).

1901, the party passed a motion, the General Committee of National Liberal Federation, calling for a negotiated settlement, as well as voicing confidence in their leader Henry Campbell-Bannerman, who by this time had become an outspoken critic of the government's tactics. They also passed a motion condemning the concentration camps.[57]

This tragic episode of the war is relevant to us here because it demonstrates how it was not merely winning the war per se that enabled expressions of pride in the British population and buttressed their faith in their international status. Rather, how Britain fought—playing by the rules of the game—was also crucial. As we saw, the pro-war, government-led discourse retheorized the meaning of the war in a manner that bolstered the status of the Boer, and thus allowed Britain to represent beating them on the battlefield as a major achievement worthy of pride and acclaim. However, while the terms of comparison could to some extent be remade, Britain's tactics in the latter part of the war contradicted long-standing norms about how wars should be fought: victories on the battlefield could elicit pride, but winning by targeting women and children was considered "uncivilized" and thus illegitimate. Indeed, as I will discuss below, critics of these tactics argued the government had breached the "standards of civilization," of which Brits saw themselves as the flagbearers. Indeed, exporting "civilization" to "savage" and "barbarian" cultures was a crucial normative underpinning for Britain's imperial enterprise (see Boisen 2013; Vucetic 2011a, pp. 24–26; Suzuki 2009, pp. 18–20). While the government had leeway to present its actions in South Africa in a positive light—and they certainly attempted to present the concentration camps as a source of pride—when the death tolls from the camps began to emerge in the press and enter public debate in Parliament, it was increasingly difficult for the government to legitimate its tactics and its prosecution of the war in general.

The Concentration Camps: Women, Children, and Civilization

Britain initiated the farm-burning tactic toward the end of the conventional campaign and began using camps in autumn 1900, ostensibly to provide for the families left destitute by these tactics. Especially in the beginning, the camps

---

[57] Reported in the *Times*, December 5, 1901.

112 THE GRAMMAR OF STATUS COMPETITION

suffered from appalling sanitation and "shortages"[58] of food, which led to them becoming rife with illness and a series of lethal epidemics.[59] Given the international and national attention the war had garnered, it is surprising it took so long—several months—before reports surfaced in the press. A letter from Louise Maxwell, wife of Pretoria's military governor, to the *New York Herald* (April 16, 1901, cited in Roberts 1991) first alerted the international and British publics to the conditions in the camps.[60] However, it was Emily Hobhouse's (1901) reports from the camps, published in a penny pamphlet, that sent shock waves through Britain (Roberts 1991). She did not hold back in her condemnation, arguing that even if it was not the intent of the authorities, "[t]o keep these camps going is murder to the children" (Hobhouse 1901, p. 4). Following the public outcry that met Hobhouse's pamphlet, the government was forced to defend the camps in Parliament and promise to address the public's concern. To this end, they sent the Fawcett Commission (comprised of six women) to investigate the conditions in the camps and provide recommendations about how to improve them. Although the commission was expected to whitewash the problems in the camps, they ended up echoing most if not all of Hobhouse's criticisms (Roberts 1991, pp. 265–267; Pakenham 1979, p. 546).

It is in this context that in March 1902 an amendment was tabled by the Liberals "deploring the great mortality in the concentration camps formed in the execution of the policy of clearing the country in South Africa" and demanded the government "state what further measures they intend to take for the preservation of life" inside the camps.[61] The heated parliamentary debate this amendment inspired offers an excellent window into the changing discourse of the third phase of the war. Crucially, powerful criticisms (and critics) came to the fore, which successfully undermined the government's earlier theory that the war constituted a boon for Britain's international status.

Contesting the Government's Theory of the War

The attacks on the government's use of concentration camps rested upon two co-constitutive lines of attack. The first did not require the war to be understood

---

[58] Some of this shortage may have been strategic: critics of the camps claimed that the families of Boer men who were engaged in guerrilla warfare were given even worse rations than those who were not (e.g., MP Owen Humphreys (HC Deb 04 March 1902, vol. 104, col. 406)).

[59] The inmates suffered from measles, bronchitis, pneumonia, dysentery. and typhoid.

[60] Having been publicly rebuked for going public and, even worse, requesting aid from foreign countries, she wrote a letter defending herself in the *Times*, July 31, 1901.

[61] HC Deb 04 March 1902, vol. 104, cc 421-422.

RATIONAL ILLUSIONS 113

in terms of status in order to generate its power: causing the deaths of innocent people was considered morally abhorrent in and of itself. In theory, this argument could have relied only upon the recognition of the norm that killing innocent people is wrong. This was straightforward in 19th-century Britain:[62] women and children were assumed a priori to be innocent, so the deaths in the concentration camps were difficult to present as anything other than the deaths of innocent people (see Krebs 2004, p. 62). As one Irish MP argued:

> Assuming the policy of the war to be perfectly right, assuming it to be a perfectly just and necessary war, surely it does not follow that we ought to pursue a policy of extermination against children in South Africa. The worst of this method of proceeding is that the burden of it is falling not upon the men on the field, but upon the weak and innocent who are outside. Why should the children be punished?[63]

However, in addition to the internal shame of being responsible for the deaths in the camps, this argument was systematically buttressed with theories of how it would affect Britain's international status. In the words of one of the Liberal MPs who tabled the amendment, the tactics employed by Britain would besmirch "the reputation and the honour of the whole nation."[64] Thus, it was "the interests of the Government, and also in those higher interests of humanity, and *for the good name of this Empire*, to let everything be done that is possible to bring about a better condition of things" (my emphasis). Indeed, seldom did those who spoke against of the camps *not* buttress their critique by raising how the camps would reflect upon Britain's status as a civilized nation. For instance, the leader of the Liberal opposition, Campbell-Bannerman,[65] attacked the camps on the same basis: "It is the whole system which they have to carry out that I consider, to use a word which I have already applied to it, barbarous."[66] Indeed, the standards of civilization were invoked by both sides to debate the legitimacy of British's use of concentration camps in the final episode of the war.

---

[62] And today—see Charlie Carpenter (2003) on the gendered discourse of presuming women and children are innocent and how this can imperil innocent men.

[63] HC Deb 17 June 1901, vol. 95, col. 581.

[64] HC Deb 04 March, 1902, vol. 104, col. 413.

[65] He had famously referred to Britain's farm-burning tactics as "methods of barbarism" in a speech he gave at a dinner given by the National Reform Union at the Holborn Restaurant (Kuitenbrouwer 2012, p. 226). He had earlier that day had a meeting with Hobhouse to discuss the situation in South Africa (Roberts 1991, pp. 242–243).

[66] HC Deb 17 June 1901, vol. 95, col. 601-602.

114 THE GRAMMAR OF STATUS COMPETITION

The fact that it was women and children who suffered in the camps prompted particular consternation among the opposition. As Lloyd George emphasized, "We are fighting them, but we are bound to fight them according to the rules of civilized nations, and by every rule of every civilized nation it is recognized that women and children are non-combatants."[67] It was an Irish nationalist MP who expressed the civilizational argument against the camps most sharply, arguing that Britain's "conduct in South Africa in connection with these women and children is conduct which would bring shame to the cheeks of the most savage and most barbarous people in existence."[68] However, several British MPs also explicitly theorized how the treatment of women and children in the camps would affect Britain's status in the world. For instance, one MP belied a patriotic concern for Britain's standing when he argued that the camps were "a disgrace, and if children die and women fall ill it is upon us that the responsibility lies, and upon the fair fame of this country lies the discredit."[69] These MPs were echoing Hobhouse's report—a frequent reference point in the debates in the Commons about the final episode in the war—which had also used the civilizational discourse to attack the use of camps.

Breaching the standards of civilization was seen as particularly damning because Britain was assumed to be not only a civilized nation but the *leading* civilized nation. As illustrated by the *Times* correspondent quoted earlier, British discourse was saturated with glowing representations of its "privileged situation, her immense, colonial conquests, fertilized by her genius for colonization, the extent of her trade, through vast civilizing influence exercised by her throughout the globe."[70] In the House of Commons debates over the legitimacy of the war, countless references were made to Britain's purported civilizing influence (by both pro- and antiwar MPs). Thus, when the camps' critics drew upon the standards of civilization to attack Britain, they aimed at a central basis of Britain's understanding of itself and its position in the world: not merely as *a* civilized country among many but as the *leader* and standard-bearer. Indeed, Byron Farwell (2009 [1976], p. 353) notes, the accusation that Britain had employed "methods of barbarism"

---

[67] HC Deb 17 June 1901, vol. 95, col. 582-583.
[68] HC Deb 17 June 1901, vol. 95, col. 612.
[69] Mr. C. P. Scott (HC Deb 17 June 1901, vol. 95, cc 603-604).
[70] Or as another *Times* correspondent wrote, "The world has to thank England for having led the way in all the great achievements of three centuries in the sphere of politics, economics, and culture" (May 26, 1902).

"horrified" the British public because "for the past two hundred years at least [the British] had regarded themselves as the most civilized people on earth." Thus, the rhetorical question posed by Hobhouse in a public address in Southport—"where is your *boasted* civilization and humanitarianism?" (reported in *Times*, July 4, 1901, p. 10)[71]—could be expected to sting.

Putting women and children in concentration camps also destabilized the meaning of the war as a masculine—read: positive—enterprise.[72] As the election pamphlet quoted in the previous section suggested, Britain's masculinity and virility were represented as being bound up with supporting war and Britain's war performance. Fighting was considered manly and thus positive; opposing the war implied a "shrunken," "degraded," "submissive" England. Yet, as stories of Britain's treatment of women in the camps began to surface[73] it destabilized the pro-war association with masculinity: civilized gentlemen were supposed to protect women, not force them into filthy camps to die (Krebs 2004). As one Irish nationalist asked in Parliament, "What civilized Government ever deported women? Had it come to this, that this Empire was afraid of women?" He went on to pointedly draw an unfavorable comparison with Britain's great power rivals: "The Germans when they conquered France did not deport the women. A pretty pass you have brought the British Empire to."[74] While this counterdiscourse did not bring a halt to the war, it did foment a growing opposition and ambivalence among the British population, and over the long term, according to Porter (2000, p. 647), "spawned disillusionment with Empire."

Forced to defend their use of concentration camps, the government and its supporters used several arguments against their critics. They suggested that the death rates were not necessarily worse than they would have been without the camps, highlighted the improvements that they had instigated since they

---

[71] Although reporting on the meeting, the *Times* featured it under the headline "Pro-Boer Movement." Hobhouse wrote a letter two days later admonishing the *Times* for misquoting her; she asserted she had said "their" rather than "your."

[72] I lack the space to elaborate fully here, but my research suggests there were also racial rules that defined the terms of status competition, which if broken would threaten the positive comparisons and status value of the victory. As I alluded to earlier, neo-Darwinian notions of racial competition were also implicated in the rules of the competition. Britain made great efforts to maintain the image of the war as "White Man's war." For instance, Britain refused offers of support from the Indian viceroy during periods when Britain was otherwise seeking reinforcements, and even denied General Kitchener's requests for Indian troops during the latter stages of the war (Pakenham 1979, pp. 215–216; Omissi 2002). Yet, Britain had used troops from Canada, New Zealand, and Australia.

[73] Crucial here was Hobhouse's firsthand reports from camps that were published in the *Manchester Guardian* between early 1901 and the end of the war. See Krebs (2004).

[74] HC Deb 25 February 1901, vol. 89, cc 1164-1165.

116   THE GRAMMAR OF STATUS COMPETITION

had been alerted to the problems, and suggested the problems were an unpleasant but ultimately unavoidable consequence of war.[75] Some attempted to silence opponents by claiming that criticizing the camps would only help the Boer, undermine the war effort, and thus prolong the suffering.[76] The government was bullish at first. Secretary of State for War Brodrick sought to blame the Boers for "taking advantage" of the British people's "humanity" by pursuing a guerrilla war that used their farms as supply depots, thus turning the concentration camps into a military necessity.[77] Interestingly, the government, and specifically Chamberlain, sought to render the concentration camps as not only legitimate but as a source of pride for Britain. In a radical if doomed attempt to legitimate the camps, Chamberlain theorized the size and scale of the camps as symbolic of Britain's status as a civilized nation.[78] Claiming that the concentration camps were in fact refugee camps, he said:

> Now, let me say that *never in the whole history of the world, so far as we know it, have there been such gigantic efforts* made by any nation to minimize the horrors of war.... [T]aking it as a whole, I repeat what I said at the beginning—no more gigantic task has ever been undertaken by a nation in time of war, no more humane task has ever been so well fulfilled.[79]

However, given that the camps were required as the result of the farmburning strategy, that the government had been forced to admit that inmates of the camps were not free to leave, and that it had become known that the

[75] HC Deb 04 March 1902, vol. 104, e.g. cc 420-433.

[76] HC Deb 04 March 1902, vol. 104, cc 421.

[77] HC Deb 17 June 1901, vol. 95, cc 592-593. These sentiments were also echoed by the *Times*. For instance, one of paper's war correspondents attempted to rebut Hobhouse's claims about the camps (October 19, 1901, p. 11). It also published many letters to the editor questioning Hobhouse's account and accusing her of helping the Boers as well as Britain's enemies on the continent (e.g., *Times*, August 17, 1901, p. 8; March 29, 1902, p. 8). Frequently the criticism of Hobhouse was heavily gendered, suggesting that she was overly emotional and therefore her account could not be trusted. For instance, the *Times* depicts Hobhouse's complaints against its reporting as "an ill-considered ebullition of temper, such as ladies sometimes imprudently indulge in, which we are sure she-ill herself in cooler moments regret" (August 30, 1901). Although hardly balanced, the *Times* did publish (and thus report on) a great number of Hobhouse's letters, her correspondence with government, and some of her fellow critics.

[78] Although not framing it in such bold terms, the *Times* editorial line echoed Chamberlain's attempts to depict the camps as a source of pride: "We do not agree with Hobhouse, and her ilk, but we offer our hearty assent to her view that it is the duty of all right-minded persons to encourage those who are trying to alleviate the miseries of war rather than carp at those good Samaritans. Naturally we differ from her as to who the Samaritans are. She thinks they are the pro-Boer committees. We hold that they are the British Government and their servants in the refugee camps" (August 30, 1901, p. 7).

[79] HC Deb 04 March 1902, vol. 104, col. 446-449.

camps were at least partly a strategy of war,[80] the government's attempts to legitimate and even celebrate the camps rang hollow. Indeed, while the government contested several aspects of its critics' narrative, it could not escape the fact that Britain had been responsible for forcing over 100,000 women and children into camps, where tens of thousands had died. Although the *Times* was on balance sympathetic to the government's line on the camps (and skeptical of their critics, especially Hobhouse), the topic of the concentration camps was a discursive terrain the government's legitimacy suffered from dwelling upon (Morgen 2002, pp. 11–12; Porter 2000, p. 647).

Not Cricket

Notably, the press reported on the guerrilla war considerably less frequently and with less enthusiasm than during the earlier phase (Morgen 2002, p. 9), and the Boers' eventual surrender did not bring about wild celebrations as previous battlefield victories had. Instead, the victory had been tarnished by the means they had used to achieve it. Although the prime minister would attempt to put a positive gloss on the occasion, his speech nonetheless belied a widespread lack of enthusiasm when he opened by saying he "hope[d] that [the surrender] will bring the *lamentable* state of things in South Africa to an end" (my emphasis).[81] The sour taste the war left behind was also apparent in Parliament and is well illustrated by the consternation expressed when MPs were asked to vote on a motion to provide a pecuniary reward for General Kitchener for prevailing in the war.[82] While the government was not wholly unsuccessful in defending its tactics, the attacks on the camps succeeded at the very least in rendering the war's implications for Britain's status ambiguous and contestable in mainstream political discourse.

Indeed, despite the government's rhetorical gymnastics,[83] it proved difficult to square the concentration camp policy with the earlier construction of the war as a sporting contest in which Britain prevailed in a fair competition. Ultimately, once Britain ceased fighting the Boer on the battlefields,

---

[80] HC Deb 17 June 1901, vol. 95, col. 584).
[81] HL Deb 02 June 1902, vol. 108, col. 1086.
[82] HC Deb 05 June 1902, vol. 108, col. 1555-85.
[83] It is also worth noting that many of the officers involved (Surridge 1997, pp. 582–584), as well as Milner and Chamberlain, privately questioned the legitimacy of Britain's counterinsurgency tactics (Pakenham 1979, pp. 541–542).

118 THE GRAMMAR OF STATUS COMPETITION

and because the rules of "the gentleman's war" were clearly being broken, the ideal of the war as a "fair fight" was fatally undermined. Similar to how if your opponent castles with a queen, one cannot be said to be playing chess, so it was that once Britain began to use "methods of barbarism" the war became difficult to present as a rule-governed competition they could take pride in winning. As Williams (2013, p. 494) notes:

> [It] was one thing to celebrate the steadfastness of the defenders of Mafeking, or the battlefield heroism displayed at Paardeberg, but quite another to remain comfortable with the burning of Boer farms and the herding of Boer civilians into squalid and disease-ridden "concentration camps." Public enthusiasm waned, opposition grew more confident, and the newspaper press played its part in articulating a mounting reaction against the war. Few celebrated the actual victory . . . quite the opposite, the guerrilla war was looked upon with growing disquiet and almost outright shame.

Status Competitions of Our Own Making

Using the grammar-of-status framework, this chapter has conducted a close reading of how rival and evolving theories of international status constituted the meaning of the Boer War within mainstream British discourse and how these played into the (de)legitimation of the war. Episode 1 highlighted how bipartisan support for the war relied upon the government's theory that its great power status would be lost if it ceded to the Boer's ultimatum. The Boer's lowly status in this discourse made it essential that Britain put them in their place, but at the same time promised little glory for doing so. This established the puzzle that animated episode 2, how the prime minister managed to hail the long struggle to defeat of the Boer as a "wonderful achievement." Rather than reevaluate Britain's own greatness in light of its struggles, the analysis showed how the government reappraised its adversaries during the course of the war, downplayed their relative size, and emphasized the logistical difficulties involved in fighting the war. Meanwhile, the press's coverage zoomed in on the battlefield heroics of the war, constituting it as a "fair fight," and encouraged its readers to discount any negative foreign views as founded upon jealousy rather than reason. Thus, episode 2 documented how the government could theorize that beating the Boer warranted glory even when international audiences were not impressed. Finally, episode 3 showed the

RATIONAL ILLUSIONS   119

limits of the government's ability to retheorize the status competition in a self-serving manner; Britain's use of concentration camps ran into prevailing gender and civilizational discourses, which critics wielded to delegitimize the war and destabilize the government's claim that the war was a performance befitting a great power.[84]

Taken together, the chapter has sought to demonstrate how my grammar-of-status competition heuristic and processual-relational approach can be used to produce new insights into a well-known case. In so doing, I hope to have illustrated the general utility of (a) conceiving of "international" status as a mode of legitimation rather than motivation and (b) treating status competition as a discursive process, in which the "international" hierarchy may be contested and retheorized within domestic politics. I will now elaborate three theoretical and methodological implications of this chapter for IR status research.

Theorizing Status: Seeming Like a Successful State

Among the most crucial theoretical contributions of this book is to illuminate the interpretative agency located in domestic discourse that enables governments to retheorize the rules of the status competition to their own advantage. Indeed, episode 2 illustrated how domestic theories of international status can develop in relative insulation from the outside world, thus mitigating the zero-sum game for status, at least insofar as a government can legitimate itself to its domestic audience. As the chapter highlighted, a domestically produced and insulated theory enabled Brits to see winning the Boer War as an important round in an international status competition and enabled the emotional register of pride and joy. Hence, my analysis directly challenged the widespread assumption within status research that status claims require international recognition to be worthwhile. Put differently, the case highlights how ambiguity around the international status implications of the war could be exploited by the government to reap domestic advantages from what might otherwise appear to be a disaster for Britian's status.

---

[84] Rather than putting off future governments from using concentration camps, Britain would learn to attempt to keep their brutal tactics hidden. See Elkins (2005), whose research into Britain's use of concentration camps against the Mau-Mau in Kenya led to the British government's admitting the existence of hitherto "lost" archives documenting the use of camps throughout the empire during decolonialization (Anderson 2015).

Indeed, although status scholars have been inclined to focus on the socially creative *policies* that states *do*, the above analysis illuminates another important way that states generate positive status comparisons: via cultivating and insulating a local or "nationalist" theory for interpreting their status in the world, one that accentuates strengths and downplays weaknesses. Like ordinary theories, nationalist theories of status involve slicing up and organizing social life into meaningful categories and relationships that they use for making sense of and acting upon the world. As we saw, Mercer (2017) contends that such self-serving theories are best understood as psychological illusion if they depart from those held by international audiences. However, from the perspective of governments seeking to legitimate themselves, an alternative rationale emerges. Indeed, it is hardly controversial to note that governments have strong incentives to attempt to present themselves as successful and thus legitimate. Moreover, leading an imagined community that is at once aware of "others" in the international landscape but lacking perfect information about their "collective beliefs," governments have both the opportunity and the incentive to develop and insulate theories of international hierarchies favorable to themselves. Given that international comparisons increasingly form the basis for assessing the performance of states and governments, maintaining nationalist theories of status is better seen as a routine and prudent part of statecraft rather than vanity, as Mercer claims.

Not Just the Winning That Counts

Theoretically, the final episode illustrates that when a war is framed as status competition, to elicit expressions of pride from winning may require victory to be achieved according to the domestic understanding of the rules of the game. This insight fleshes out IR's prior understanding of how waging and winning a war can generate the "intrinsic" benefits commonly associated with international status. For instance, Renshon's (2016) influential *International Organisation* paper and his book, *Fighting for Status* (2017), emphasize that it is victory in war that changes the international audience's perceptions and generates pride as a result. However, as the Boer case shows, simply winning a war may not prove sufficient to generate status dividends; it may also require imaginative discursive labor to develop criteria by which winning can appear impressive. Moreover, while episode 2 suggested states may have more leeway to make their own rules than previously envisioned—at least with regard to domestic audiences—this agency is not infinite. Indeed, as the war entered its final stage the tactics that they used to win—putting the enemy's women and children in concentration camps—allowed the war's opponents to draw upon long-standing gendered norms of civilized conduct to delegitimate the war and the government. This chapter thus highlighted how domestic legitimacy and status gains may *depend* upon competing in the right way according to prevailing norms of conduct and/or the ability of the government to theorize the war in a favorable manner. Further research could fruitfully investigate how international recognition is affected by *how* victory in war is achieved—whether breaking the norms of war matter—and the extent to which this is open to retheorization and contestation by states and other onlookers.

Gendered Status

Finally, this chapter highlighted the heavily gendered theories of status, used by both advocates and critics of the war. Although feminists have highlighted how gendered discourses valorize war and military power in domestic and international contexts (Sjoberg 2013; Tickner and Sjoberg 2013), status research has yet to adequately engage with this scholarship (Beaumont and Røren 2018). This is a pity because feminist theories may provide crucial clues to important questions contemporary status research largely leaves answered: Why are military power and war associated with high status, and how is this association reproduced? While Gilady (2018), Renshon (2017), and O'Neil (2006) theorize that it is the intrinsic qualities of status symbol that generate its symbolic utility—variations on conspicuousness, difficulty, and costliness—a gender lens trains our gaze upon the broader discursive practices that may reproduce the status value associated with war in a given context. Indeed, victory in the Boer War was not only theorized as necessary to hold onto great power status but was co-constituted as a test of Britain's masculinity. This is well illustrated by how the tactics employed—specifically the treatment of Boer women—undermined the government's theory that Britain could bask in glory from victory. Ultimately, the Boer case strongly suggests that scholars should put on gendered lenses if they wish to explain how and why certain status value is generated.

4

Organizing and Resisting Status Competition

How PISA Shocked Norway

In 1995, at the first meeting of OECD ministers I attended, every country boasted of its own success and its own brilliant reforms. Now international comparisons make it clear who is failing. There is no place to hide.

—Andreas Schleicher, OECD's head of education research, 2008

Introduction

"Like coming home from the Winter Olympics without any gold medals" was how the education minister described Norway's middling performance in the OECD's inaugural Progamme for International Student Assessment (PISA) ranking. These words would catalyze a decade of education reforms aimed at improving Norway's PISA rank (Sjøberg 2014b). Such international country performance indicators (CPIs) have been termed "governance from a distance" (Rose and Miller 1992), yet every Norwegian student since 2004 cannot help but have been touched by the national testing regime introduced in PISA's wake. Norway's response to PISA was far from unusual: "PISA shocks" rippled throughout the OECD in 2001, as one country after another reckoned with a lower than expected position (Pons 2017). Yet, PISA shocks constitute just one example of a still broader trend in global governance toward using CPIs to prod and pressure governments into changing their domestic policy practices.

Understanding this CPI phenomenon has become an urgent task for IR. Since the 1990s, the number of CPIs has grown almost exponentially, quadrupling in the 1990s and tripling over the next 15 years (Kelley and

The Grammar of Status Competition. Paul David Beaumont, Oxford University Press. © Oxford University Press 2024.
DOI: 10.1093/9780197771808.003.0005

Simmons 2019, p. 493). At the last count, the Global Benchmarking Database (v1.9) estimated that at least 275 country performance indexes exist, most of which emerged in the last decade. These rankings claim to make visible states' relative performance in all manner of social fields, from gender equality to corruption, from ease of doing business to human trafficking (Cooley and Snyder 2015). Until fairly recently, most research tended to focus on CPIs' methodological veracity rather than their influence on the very subjects they rank (Cooley and Snyder 2015). While this has begun to be addressed (Cooley and Snyder 2015; Kelley 2017; Kelley and Simmons 2015, 2019), theorizing about the political, social, and ethical consequences of this new "technology" of governance is far from exhausted (Kelley and Simmons 2019, pp. 504–506). Notably, conventional legal and rationalist approaches offer only limited purchase on why actors would compete for position in a ranking when leading or lagging offers little direct material reward or punishment. Indeed, unlike EU law, which operates through legal-rational authority, or the World Bank, which can offer economic sticks and carrots tied to its structural adjustment packages, many global rankings have no such means to influence policy. This begs the question that animates recent research into CPIs effects: Lacking legal authority and economic incentives, how and why do international rankings influence government policies?

This chapter argues that CPIs can be understood as attempts to organize and inspire status competition and universalize a particular theory of status in a policy field. Where the previous chapter painted a somewhat comfortable picture for states whereby governments can construct their own status hierarchies and insulate their citizens from rival theories of status, this chapter picks up the other end of the theoretical thread. It argues that global governance actors—via CPIs—have developed technologies to overcome this insulation and undermine states' autonomy to construct and maintain national theories of status. Indeed, I contend that CPIs should be understood as a *status Esperanto* in which the numerical nature of a ranking provides a universally legible resource to domestic actors that enable them to wield the CPI's theory of the status competition and overcome the insulation language and geography usually provide. Moreover, the scientific appearance of rankings generates the illusion of objectivity and thus hides the value judgments embodied in rules of the hierarchy that are normally the source of status disagreement across and within states. In making this argument, the chapter theoretically fleshes out recent works suggesting that CPIs can work by wielding social pressure and inducing status concerns (Towns

124 THE GRAMMAR OF STATUS COMPETITION

and Rumelili 2017; Kelley and Simmons 2015, 2019; Rumelili and Towns 2022).[1]

However, whereas prior works studying rankings have tended to stop at showing whether a CPI led to policy change, treating status competition as a discursive process allows for more critical questions pertaining to resistance; for example, once a state has begun competing in a ranking, can it escape that competition? This is important because a wealth of scholarship has documented how many leading CPIs suffer from fatal methodological flaws, present a decontextualized and misleading picture to policymakers, and produce myopic obsession with CPI rank at the expense of other important goals (see Cooley and Snyder 2015; Beaumont and Towns 2021). Critics also contend that CPIs outsource authority to unaccountable technocrats operating beyond national democratic processes (Scott and Light 2004).[2] Yet, for all their work in documenting the pathologies of rankings, CPI scholarship has yet to explore whether, how, and with what success CPIs are resisted over time. Making the most of my longitudinal research design and my assumption that even hegemonic discourses are always in need of reproduction and thus vulnerable to contestation, the chapter thus explores whether and how domestic groups can question the theory of status embodied in a ranking and thereby escape the game.

By way of exploring how CPIs organize status competition and whether and how this process can be contested, this chapter zooms in on Norway's responses to the PISA education ranking. PISA is an excellent case for exploring how and why CPIs can overcome national insulation and encourage status competition: the OECD does not possess any direct material carrots or sticks, which means that looming, more parsimonious explanations of influence under anarchy are easier to rebut.[3] Moreover, PISA

---

[1] *International Organization* recently dedicated a special issue to theorizing and documenting this influence (Kelley and Simmons 2019) Key works in this agenda include Cooley and Snyder (2015); Kelley and Simmons (2015); Davis, Kingsley, and Merry (2012); Kelley (2017); Merry (2016); Broome and Quirk (2015); Broome, Homolar, and Kranke (2018); Freistein (2016); Löwenheim (2008); Anderl (2016); Sharman (2009); Beaumont and Towns (2021).

[2] These decisions once made become very difficult to contest yet are often influential on states' domestic politics (Broome and Quirk 2015).

[3] Perhaps the best-known scholarship seeking to demonstrate how CPIs exert social pressure (Kelley and Simmons 2015; Kelley 2017) analyzes a CPI produced by the United States and consequently leaves doubts about what is doing the work: the ranking or the latent material power of the ranker. Further, although this research mentions status, the Human Trafficking Index, which they study, uses absolute tiers and thus does not produce the same status dynamic as a relative ranking (see chapter 1). Elsewhere, Towns and Rumelili (2017) theorize the social pressure stemming from relative norms but provide only a brief empirical illustration (the Ease of Doing Business Index), which also generates direct external financial incentives (unlike PISA). While my approach departs from both in significant ways, this research has laid considerable groundwork upon which I build here.

is a theoretically and empirically important CPI: it is acknowledged—by both critics and advocates—to have been profoundly influential in shaping education policy over the course of the previous decade (Zhao 2020). By shedding light on how it works and resistance to it, this chapter contributes to both CPI literature and education research which has documented PISA shocks but without adequately theorizing how they work.[4] Finally, Norway's response to international education rankings is a deliberately different case with which to illustrate the utility of my grammar-of-status framework; if it can provide useful insights into such radically different cases as a 19th-century imperial war and the education reforms of a "small state," then it should generate confidence that my framework will have broader "transferability."

CPIs: Universalising Theories of Status Competition

This section ties together my theoretical framework with the growing research into CPIs. To recap, earlier I defined an ideal status competition as one in which competitors share the same understanding of the rules of the game, have near perfect information about one another's relative performance, and share a common understanding of what constitutes winning. This is much more likely to obtain when the organizer of a competition enjoys legitimate authority, the rules are uncontested, and those playing the game join voluntarily. Unsurprisingly, such status competitions are far easier to organize among individuals than among sovereign states. As the introduction argued, the difficulty involved in reaching agreement about both the rules of the game and acquiring credible information about other states' performance undermines the likelihood of agreement over relative position and thus what actions should be undertaken to compete. While these conditions hinder the *ideal* of status competition being reached, I argued that, nonetheless, *the logic* of international status competition may still inform government behavior and (de)legitimate particular policies. This section suggests that CPIs can be understood as an *attempt* to organize and institutionalize a particular theory of status competition among states in particular policy domains. Although such rankings seldom succeed in toto, I argue that CPIs can nonetheless

---

[4] As Pons (2017) notes in his review of PISA literature on PISA shocks, this research has proven successful in documenting its influence but needs to "better conceptualize" how and why the shock works.

126   THE GRAMMAR OF STATUS COMPETITION

enable the grammar of status to be wielded domestically, potentially with significant policy consequences. The section begins by demonstrating how rankings embody the logic of status competition, before drawing on extant research to theorize how and why CPIs can enable the grammar of status to be wielded in domestic politics and potentially overcome the barriers to domestic agreement about the nature of international status hierarchies.[5]

Country Rankings: Embodying the Logic of Status Competition

It is not difficult to conclude that CPIs package information in a manner that embodies the logic of status competition defined in chapter 1. To take the conventional definition of global indicators:

> An indicator is a named collection of *rank-ordered data* that purports to represent the past or projected *performance* of different units. The data are generated through a process that simplifies raw data about a complex social phenomenon. The data, in this simplified and processed form, are capable of being *used to compare* particular units of analysis (such as countries or institutions or corporations), synchronically or over time, and to evaluate their performance by reference to one or more standards. (Davis, Kingsbury, and Merry 2012, p. 5, my emphasis)

I have highlighted the key components of this definition that are theoretically relevant to the logic of status competition. First, a status competition *always* requires a "global comparison" between competitors rather than internal comparison based upon an actor's individual performance (Onuf 1989, p. 267). When indicators are packaged into transitive rankings, they represent an idealized hierarchical context for a status competition. In this way, such rankings provide the structure—or "playing field"—within which status competition between actors can unfold. Second, for status competition to occur, the status attributes must be changeable: if they cannot change (e.g., like a biologically defined racial hierarchy), actors cannot compete, or indeed have a "performance" (chapter 1). Country performance indicators per definition measure social qualities that to varying degrees can change.

---

[5] It is testament to the difficulty of organizing a rule-governed status competition under anarchy that the extant rankings research has dedicated such significant effort to theorizing the conditions under which rankings can influence state behavior (Kelley and Simmons 2015, 2019).

Third, this performance is then problematized via their packaging in relative rankings in which states' comparative performance is illuminated and emphasized. Thus, when circulated to rankees, knowledge of *others'* performance relative to one's own defines good and bad, not the absolute performance itself. It is the emphasis on relative international performance which offers the novelty in this "governance technology."[6] In sum, a relative ranking embodies the logic of international status competition, and when wielded in practice they mobilize the grammar of status.

Indeed, if those ranked by a CPI agreed with the rules and valued the game—like an Olympic competition—then the ideal of a status competition would likely be realized. Yet reality seldom approaches the ideal: it is one thing to place states in an idealized hierarchical context, and it is quite another to get all states to agree to the rules and compete. Indeed, few if any CPIs enjoy such *universal* agreement about the legitimacy and value of the competition they embody and promote.[7] However, we can still ask and theorize: How might rankings foster *more* interstate and intercitizen agreement over the rules and thus sometimes overcome the discursive insulation that states usually enjoy? How might CPIs generate prizes and pride that encourage competition? To answer these questions, we need to take a closer look at the processes through which CPIs are developed, packaged, and circulated and theorize how and why they might be used by domestic actors.

Technocratic Status Competition: How CPIs Theorize Hierarchies

CPIs attempt to establish the rules of the game and assess and allocate states' status within a given field. In this way, CPIs take on the role of a governing body that assesses state performance and allocates status in various fields of policy practice (Kelley and Simmons 2015, 2019; also see Towns and Rumelili 2017). CPIs do this by systematically measuring and quantifying hitherto private and diffuse practices (e.g., gender equality, democracy, corruption) in order to generate equivalence and thus render "performance" in these practices comparable. Thus, when a ranking is created, it *expands*

---

[6] It is worth noting that Miller and Rose (2008) list several "technologies" related to auditing and indicators, but although they leave the door open for rankings, they do not mention them.

[7] Arguably GDP rankings come closest, though several rival measures (e.g., the Human Development Index) contest GDP's near-hegemony as a measure of social welfare and/or economic performance (e.g., Fleurbaey 2009).

128   THE GRAMMAR OF STATUS COMPETITION

the range of activities in which international comparisons can be made and potentially enables intersubjective (interstate and intercitizen) agreement about one another's status performance.

At the same time as expanding the range of policy domains constituted in terms of international status, CPIs also tacitly promote their specific *theory* of international status in the activity in question: the rules of comparison and the empirical basis for assessing performance. As Cooley (2015) points out, *all* rankings tacitly embody theories of what they purport to assess. Regardless of what they wish to measure, CPIs undertake "ontological theorizing" (Guzzini 2013, p. 434) because they must answer questions like "What *is* gender equality" and "What *is* democracy?" before they can even begin to assess performance. This process inevitably involves deciding what to count and what can be left on the cutting-room floor. Even once this is decided, the ranker must still then decide how to weigh the indicator's inputs. Thus, despite their objective-looking end product, CPIs always embody normative and political judgments (Merry and Conley 2011, p. 84; Snyder and Cooley 2015, p. 183), or to paraphrase Cathy (2017, p. 21), CPIs are opinions dressed in math. Thus, the technocratic process of describing, counting (*not* counting), and comparing complex social phenomena establishes the rules of the status competition behind closed doors and beyond domestic politics.

Moreover, in this process of codifying the rules of their ranking and circulating the results, CPIs attempt to *universalize* the criterion by which comparisons are made and status is judged. As I noted in the introduction, without considerable discursive labor it is quite possible for multiple countries to simultaneously believe in their own superiority in any given activity. In the case of public goods provision, the sheer complexity and cost involved in making plausible comparisons insulates states and citizens from unfavorable international comparisons. In such cases, the absence of agreed-upon rules and lack of evidence can prove productive of contradictory theories of international status. For instance, prior to the establishment of the OECD's PISA education rankings, the OECD's head of education research told the *Economist* (2008), "In 1995, at the first meeting of OECD ministers I attended, every country boasted of its own success and its own brilliant reforms. Now international comparisons make it clear who is failing. There is no place to hide." As this quote illustrates, when CPIs are circulated to domestic audiences, they strive to clarify the ambiguity around performance by introducing a new universal theory of international status and thus potentially undermining a state's insulation from unfavorable international comparisons. But why should citizens pay attention to a CPI developed by international technocrats? Indeed, *ceteris paribus*, countries might be expected to be skeptical about the imposition of "foreign" values and reject a ranking for instrumental reasons if it places them lower than they expected (see Towns and Rumelili 2017, p. 11; Mercer 2017).

Status Esperanto: Circulating Science-y Status Stories

CPIs strive to overcome these obstacles in three ways. First, CPIs package and circulate information in rankings in a manner well designed to encourage "reactivity" among states. Since Hawthorne, scientists have known that human subjects react to being observed and evaluated. In mainstream social science this reflexive "reactivity" is often understood as a problem to be minimized, but it is exactly this social effect that organizations seek to harness with rankings (Espeland and Sauder 2016). Indeed, CPIs theorize, assess, and then *circulate* states' status performance to their populations. The plan is clearly to inspire a reaction, one that partly relies upon inspiring status concerns (Towns and Rumelili 2017; Kelley and Simmons 2019; Rumelili and Towns 2022). Yet, for a CPI to become salient in a country's domestic political discourse, it must be publicly known and the ranking must be considered legitimate and credible (Kelley 2017). Regarding legitimacy and credibility, numerical rankings borrow the illusion of objectivity and precision of numbers to generate a science-y appearance. While most leading CPIs are known to suffer from well-known "dodgy data" problems (including PISA), as Broome, Homolar, and Kranke (2018, p. 4) argue, CPIs can nonetheless generate authority from "piggybacking on the status of the organizations that produce them" and the veneer of scientific credibility that their numerical appearance provides.[8]

Moreover, rankings embody what in chapter 2 I called *status narratives*: they construct winners, losers, and, if iterative, simple stories of rising, falling, and stagnation. As with other types of narratives, status narratives construct subject positions and imply and legitimate a course of action (Subotić 2016, p. 312): to compete in the competition and delegitimize alternatives (e.g., letting rivals "win"). Just as with ordinary narratives, CPI's status narratives

---

[8] Indeed, even well-established rankings, such as GDP, suffer from serious validity issues (Jerven 2013).

generate their rhetorical power from their simplicity and their familiarity. However, narratives embodied in rankings travel across borders unusually easily. Crucially, the language of this discourse is a numerical ranking, which has a universal legibility that ordinary languages lack. Thus, we might think of rankings as a status Esperanto. Ultimately, the ability of CPIs to translate status hierarchies across borders stems from combining the credibility associated with science with the legibility of numerical rankings, together with the rhetorical power of narratives.

Counterintuitively, CPIs highlight the importance of agreed-upon rules for status competition precisely because they hide them away. Countries' populations are presented with the outcome of comparisons, whose rules have been decided earlier by technocrats behind closed doors (Broome, Homolar, and Kranke 2018). By hiding the rules—and the value judgments therein—rankings can overcome potential domestic resistance to foreign status hierarchies. Indeed, as we will see, instead of debating value judgments embodied in the hierarchy, a successful CPI may inspire debate about how best to triumph in the hierarchy. This process of contestation over *how* to compete rather than *whether* to compete serves to reinforce and reproduce the legitimacy of the rules of the competition. However, this is not a one-off event; it necessitates persistent discursive labor to maintain the salience or dominance of any one theory of status. As such, the hidden value judgments embodied in a CPI are always potentially contestable and vulnerable to challenges. Moreover, as I argued earlier, at least some domestic actors will face incentives to contest a theory of status in which their state ranks poorly.

Generating Pride and Prizes

So far I have elaborated how international rankings embody the grammar of status, while simultaneously universalizing and hiding value judgments that generate the rules of the competition. Further, I argued that the packaging of information in the form of rankings enables easy narratives of winning and losing to cross national borders and can generate legitimacy from their scientific appearance (scientism). However, that alone would likely not prove enough; as chapter 1 suggested, a status competition requires some prizes or pride to be at stake to encourage players to compete. These are similar to those that I outlined in chapter 2 and therefore I will provide only a brief sketch.

First, a CPI can offer external incentives to compete: prizes. By compiling valuable information about states' qualities that would be costly and difficult for interested parties to obtain individually, CPIs can establish and operate as a focal point around which international actors organize and distribute rewards (Cooley and Snyder 2015, p. 24).[9] Second, CPIs are well-designed to manufacture the symbolic utility associated with status: pride and self-esteem. As Lilach Gilady (2018) notes, for something to become an international status symbol it must be conspicuous, difficult, costly, and exclusive (see also O'Neill 2006). Until international rankings burgeoned in the 1990s, performance in public policy areas like education, healthcare, and gender equality (etc.) could not meet this demand for conspicuousness and thus made poor status symbols (see Gilady 2018; O'Neill 2006). Yet, by packaging performance in a relative transitive ranking, CPIs can both make performance conspicuous and accentuate the scarcity and difficulty of achieving a good performance. Relatedly, rankings enable easy relative comparisons in performance among the global population that is ranked by the CPI. Thus, on top of the symbolic value for finishing on top, CPIs enable and encourage competition for position between rivals and peers lower down the rankings. Third, competing in a CPI may be required to please the group: the citizens, if CPIs become accepted as a measure of a state or government's performance. In such cases, the CPI supplants domestic standards and will provide incentives for the government to compete in the CPI-defined hierarchy.

Three points are necessary to emphasize. The final two mechanisms indicate that CPIs can generate rewards and punishments quite apart from any international material carrots or sticks. While prior social psychology–inspired work has typically focused on interstate practices of recognition, as the second point suggests, CPIs can be treated as an actor bestowing status recognition upon a target. Thus, it is consistent with prior status work to suggest that CPIs can inspire status competition by generating "intrinsic" rewards for high position and punishments for low position (pride and shame, respectively). Additionally, the final mechanism—replacing internal standards for assessing government performance with international status comparisons—is largely overlooked by extant status work, which has

---

[9] For instance, firms use the Ease of Doing Business Index to inform their investment decisions and thus reward countries that compete according to their definition of easy business (Schueth 2015). Conversely Transparency International's corruption index informs several important actors' development aid decisions. States may also receive international praise and back-patting for good performance on a CPI.

132 THE GRAMMAR OF STATUS COMPETITION

overwhelmingly treated status-seeking as a matter of motivation rather than domestic legitimacy. Finally, prior work has generally taken for granted the intersubjective agreement over the rules of any given status competition and eschewed investigating the introduction of new rules of international status competition. Yet, because CPIs are ontologically meaningful to statesmen and their populations, and not just (potentially) epistemologically useful to researchers, we can empirically study the emergence of a CPI's theory of status, whether and how it travels, and the extent to which it is used and contested. This is quite different from the approach taken by large-N status research (e.g., Renshon 2017; Volgy et al. 2011), where they may refer to "subjective" status hierarchies, but these are invariably constructed by the analyst (e.g., rankings of diplomatic recognition) rather than being intersubjectively present in the "real world."

International Rankings and Domestic Politics

Even if a CPI is visible and credible and offers incentives to participating states, whether a ranking informs policy will necessarily depend upon domestic political processes. Rather than deducing whether the ranking motivated an outcome, my approach demands I investigate whether and how its theory of international status was mobilized and invoked by domestic actors as grounds for undertaking a policy. Following the lead of other CPI research, rather than directly causing an effect, rankings—and the theories of status they embody—can be understood as providing *discursive resources*: potentially salient information that may be mobilized in the domestic sphere to legitimate policy change or attack political opponents. In this way, and when amplified by the press, it may provide the "catalytic" that may be used by domestic actors to successfully demand reforms (Kelley 2017, p. 13; Kelley and Simmons 2019, pp. 499–501).

Kelley and Simmons (2019, pp. 499–500) provide a useful starting point here for understanding how rankings get used in domestic politics. They suggest that domestic groups may use the comparisons provided by the rankings to demand reforms aimed at improving the ranking: via the ballot box, critiques in the media, as well as through lobbying and traditional forms of protest. However, they go on to suggest that "in responsive regimes" such demands "might elicit policy change" or at least provide incentives for the "government to claim they are addressing the issue" (p. 500). The authors go

ORGANIZING AND RESISTING STATUS COMPETITION   133

on to claim that "where institutions repress public input and suppress political demands, governments may respond not with reform, but by denigrating the GPI or its creator" (p. 500). Thus, "denigrating" the ranking becomes a response associated with repressive regimes, while responding to rankings implies a "responsive regime." Yet, it is quite possible for domestic actors to use a dubious CPI to call for change that a responsive regime may quite reasonably reject (by denigrating the ranking). Meanwhile, a repressive regime may itself wield a ranking to legitimate reforms its citizens may otherwise object to. Finally, a responsive regime may include various political parties and supporters that disagree about the legitimacy of a particular CPI, and thus some may prefer to use it to legitimate reforms while the other may not. In fact, as I will show, being responsive may involve denigrating a ranking.

When should we expect a CPI to become saliant to domestic audiences? Typically, international status concerns are said to develop when states snub another state that believed it warranted deference or social recognition (e.g., Wohlforth 2014), Taking a similar tack, I suggest that rankings can be used to produce a "status shock" when a collective receives new and compelling evidence that their status is lower than they had theorized it to be. Thus, there needs to be credible *new* information regarding the status of a state in a given hierarchy, and this new information needs to diverge to some significant degree from what the previous status was or was assumed to be. Crucially, it is thus not finishing *low* itself that would cause a status shock, but finishing lower than expected or lower than rivals.[10] New rankings are well suited to induce this type of status shock because they often measure and render equivalent previously opaque social qualities that would not otherwise be readily comparable. Administering a status shock can enable a domestic actor to enact a plot that "something must be done" to remedy the lowly position in the ranking. Akin to how securitization theorizes how the grammar of security enables the breaking of normal rules of politics, so does such a status shock enable action to remedy a status shortcoming.

However, we cannot assume status shocks automatically induce policy change. Rather I suggest there is a degree of contingency: while states may seek to make policies to redress their low-status position in the rankings, the collective may also realign their expectations to mediocrity, or they may

---

[10] Conversely, lots of countries finish low in lots of indicators, and it may not induce status concerns, let alone a shock. For example, Saudi Arabia's ranking low on gender equality is unlikely to cause a status concern because they would expect and even want to place low.

134   THE GRAMMAR OF STATUS COMPETITION

reject the rankings methodology and/or legitimacy altogether (Kelley 2017; Towns and Rumelili 2017). However, when a state *does* choose the first, the rankee may find themselves routinely theorized as a player in an ongoing status competition.

If players do get "taken by the game"(Pouliot 2014, p. 198), this implies that rankings will provide a constant supply of discursive resources to legitimate the never-ending logic of status competition in the policy domain. Competing in the rankings may even become institutionalized. For instance, Espeland and Sauder (2016) document how concern for *U.S. News and World Report* law school ranking has become embedded in the day-to-day organization practices in which the effect on performance is routinely taken into account in decision-making. Although it has hitherto not been investigated or theorized, it is also possible that players may give up on the game, even once they have begun playing. Indeed, this book treats intersubjective agreement around a theory of international status as the triumph of ongoing discursive labor. This approach thus implies there is value in exploring whether and how a CPI's theory of international status competition remains in use, how rival theories are marginalized and paying attention to emergent contestation of the ranking. Indeed, as the empirical analysis will demonstrate, the process of competition may prompt critical reflexivity among players about the value of the game itself.

PISA Rankings and Education Status Competition

The previous section established how international rankings can *potentially* introduce a new theory of international status in a policy domain, one that can be used to administer status shocks and instigate the logic of status competition. This section explores this possibility by investigating how Norway responded to the OECD's PISA education rankings. PISA seeks to measure the educational performance of students (age 15) across the OECD and other participating countries. Since 2000, PISA has assessed science, reading, and math levels of participating countries' students on a triannual basis (OECD n.d.). PISA rankings do not directly compare the actual education practices. In order to simplify these complex phenomena and render equivalence, PISA tests "the skills and knowledge" of 500,000 students from the participating countries and uses the numerical scores it generates as a proxy for the quality of their "education systems" (OECD n.d.). While PISA has many critics within academia,[11] because states *pay* for the privilege of taking part in PISA, they tacitly grant it legitimate authority in education. Indeed, PISA itself is widely circulated and recognized as a credible indicator of education (Carvalho 2012). Critically for our purposes here, PISA packages its studies in relational transitive ranking.

A great deal of research has been dedicated to outlining methodological and normative issues associated with PISA (e.g., Pons 2011; Singe and Braun 2018); however, to understand how PISA attempts to organize status competition, we need foreground only three characteristics of its rankings process. First, PISA defines what constitutes literacy, math, and science skills and thus sets the rules for its international comparisons. Second, and more controversially, PISA frequently presents these scores as a measure of the quality of countries' "national education system" and uses its indicators as a means to highlight and promote (allegedly) best practices. Hence, PISA's official policy papers "are packed with policy recommendations regarding schools and educational governance" (Sjøberg 2019, p. 658). Thus, not only does PISA propose a theory of what constitutes good literacy, math, and science, but it tacitly proposes a grand theory of the quality of education. Third, while PISA makes the absolute performance and individual case studies available, PISA itself promotes the league tables and thus encourages the press to focus on the relative performance in the rankings (Sjøberg 2019, pp. 681–682). It is thus not a coincidence that national media tend to present the results in a manner akin to the Olympics (e.g., Figure 4.1). In short, PISA is well designed to overcome national insulation in the manner described above and encourage states to participate in its status competition.

The next section investigates whether PISA worked in the manner theorized here, or was merely a spurious accompaniment to reforms that would have occurred regardless. Thus, I answer the following questions: *How did PISA enable policy reform? Was the grammar of status competition key for legitimating the timing and substance of Norway's education reforms?* Here, I pay attention to whether and how grammar of status in the PISA rankings was mobilized in order to legitimate action or delegitimate inaction. Part of this interpretative process involves assessing whether the policies changed in accordance with the values embedded within the rankings methodology: the extent to which policy reforms were aimed at improving the

---

[11] In 2014 dozens of leading education academics wrote an open letter to the head of PISA calling for a moratorium on PISA testing on the grounds that it was "damaging education worldwide" (*Guardian* 2014).

Which countries are best at reading?	Which countries are best at maths?
📰 Top 12	🏅 Top 12
01 Singapore ★	01 Singapore ★
02 China: Hong Kong ★	02 China: Hong Kong ★
03 Canada ★	03 China: Macao ★
04 Finland	04 Taiwan
05 Ireland	05 Japan
06 Estonia	06 China: Beijing, Shanghai, Jiangsu and Guangdong
07 South Korea	
08 Japan	07 South Korea
09 Norway	08 Switzerland
10 New Zealand	09 Estonia
11 Germany	10 Canada
12 China: Macao	11 Netherlands
	12 Denmark

Figure 4.1 League Tables Used by the BBC to Report the PISA Results in 2015. Source: BBC (2016).

PISA position. I will also pay heed to other looming alternative logics of legitimation associated with the policy field in question, striving to meet an absolute standard of education quality or addressing absolute problems identified by PISA. Second, I will address the critical question that a longitudinal discourse analysis makes possible: To what extent did PISA's theory of international education status meet resistance, and when, why, and how did rival theories emerge and with what consequence? Finally, although not a rival explanation, it is of theoretical interest to explore empirically whether and what sort of prizes, pride, and group-pleasing domestic actors theorized to be at stake in PISA's education status competition.

Pre-PISA Reforms: Norwegian Education Was Not Always an International Competition

In order to generate analytical traction on Norway's PISA period (2000–present) it is necessary to sketch the policy landscape before PISA. Norway's education system has undergone several major reforms—often expansions of provision—over the course of the past century.[12] We need not dwell on the history of reform nor the makeup of the Norwegian system, but three characteristics of Norway before PISA require highlighting. First, both PISA advocates and critics agree that prior to PISA there was a lack of evidence with which to assess Norwegian schools, which fostered considerable disagreement about how to assess the quality of Norway's education. For instance, the state secretary for education during Norway's PISA shock, the social scientist Helge Ole Bergeson (2006, p. 42), claimed that before PISA Norwegians' beliefs about the quality of the school system were ideologically driven rather than data driven. If Bergeson might be expected to present PISA as a new dawn, Norway's most prominent PISA critic agrees with him:

> Norwegian schools lived for a long time in an innocent state. The community trusted that the schools were good and that the teachers did their job. We did not participate in international tests, we did not have national tests, we did not have national inspectors who came to school to collect data or give advice. Some felt that we had the best schools in the world, while others claimed they were at the bottom. The two extremes had one thing in common, namely that they had no data to substantiate the claims. The quality of the school was a matter of faith—and the school was then also under the Ministry of Church and Education. Now it's called the Ministry of Education. (Sjøberg 2014b, p. 30)[13]

Thus, although international comparisons could be made, they lacked an empirical basis. Nonetheless, this would not stop Norwegian politicians from frequently proclaiming the Norwegian education system to be the best in the world (Bergeson 2006, p. 39). Hence, although the school system had its critics, especially among the right, they had little evidence to challenge claims Norway's schools were the envy of the world (Bergeson 2006, p. 39). Amid this ambiguity, Norway's nationalist theory of its international status in education could flourish.

Second and relatedly, at an academic and policy level Norway had fostered an "exceptionalist frame of mind" regarding the quality of its education (Isaksen 2015, p. 59). This point of view emphasized how the education

---

[12] See Telhaug and Aasen (1999) for a historical overview. See Bergesen (2006, ch. 1) for a critical review from the liberal perspective that would inform the government's post-PISA reforms.
[13] Sometimes with the help of a dictionary and occasionally my partner, I translated all the Norwegian quotes from primary and secondary sources.

138 THE GRAMMAR OF STATUS COMPETITION

system in Norway—and in other Scandinavian countries—offered a more far-ranging education on citizen responsibility. Rather than assessing outcomes, the Norwegian tradition since the Second World War had regarded quality as a function of the structure of the system and the broad values promoted in the curriculum (Isaksen 2015, p. 60). This is reflected in the substance of the last major education reform prior to the PISA era, Reform 97, which provided an expanded and, some argue, an excessively comprehensive taxonomy of educational aims (Bergeson 2006, p. 35). Noticeably, the reform offered no institutionalized means of assessing these aims' realization. While not universally endorsed (e.g., Bergeson 2006), this framework for understanding quality in terms of inputs and structural quality had been historically dominant at the government policy level and among Norwegian academics prior to PISA (Isaksen 2015, pp. 60–65).

Third, Norway's preference for assessing education by the quality inputs made it resistant to the sort of national testing regime that OECD had long recommended and that PISA is used to promote. Indeed, in 1987 the OECD had explicitly recommended that Norway implement national testing in the late 1980s (Isaksen 2015, p. 52). However, having taken it into consideration, the government-sponsored research into the question ended up rejecting all forms of national evaluation. While the question of introducing some kind of education output evaluation would be debated throughout the 1990s, it got bogged down over what to measure and how to define it (Isaksen 2015, pp. 75–77) Indeed, just a couple of years prior to the first PISA results, a report to Parliament, *Aiming for Higher Goals*, concluded that Norway did not need a national assessment system (Isaksen 2015, pp. 76–77). Although the idea was in circulation then, prior to PISA there was little public pressure to introduce national evaluation. Moreover, it would need to overcome historical opposition to national testing from the teacher's union (Isaksen 2015, p. 67; Bergeson 2006).[14]

These three conditions in Norway's education politics prior to PISA provide crucial context to the analysis that follows: (1) the lack of evidence with which to compare Norwegian schools' education output performance internationally, (2) a policy-level preference for evaluating quality via inputs and the values Norwegian education provide, and (3) ambivalence toward national testing (despite OECD recommendations). If Norway was generally

---

[14] Historically, Norway had even taken pride in their rejection of national testing. According to an OECD report in 1987, Norwegian educators regarded the abolishment of national testing as one of the major achievements of Norwegian policy" (OECD 1987, p. 86, cited in Isaksen 2015, p. 60).

ORGANIZING AND RESISTING STATUS COMPETITION 139

eager to follow OECD education advice prior to PISA, then it might suggest that legitimation via PISA performance was merely window-dressing to reforms that would have happened anyway. However, this is patently not the case, and thus we can ask: How did PISA change the education policy discourse such that it became possible to enact a raft of new reforms, including some that had been explicitly rejected just a couple of years earlier?

What Was the Shock in Norway's "PISA Shock"?

It is well established that Norway suffered what has become known as a "PISA shock" (Breakspear 2012; Østerud 2016; Sjøberg 2014a). In short, a PISA shock refers to the public outcry that results from a country being disappointed with its PISA rank, prompting widespread calls for "something to be done." Germany, Switzerland, and Norway are usually cited as examples (Breakspear 2012) of countries that have experienced PISA shock. But what exactly constitutes the shock in the PISA shock remains unclear (Pons 2017). This chapter contends that the PISA shock is partly constituted by a *status shock*: the discovery that a valued attribute or quality that a social collective considered important for their collective self-esteem, the state's legitimacy, and/or a symbol of superiority over outgroups, gets undermined or challenged. The effects of a status shock include expressions of public opprobrium at the lower-than-expected position in an international hierarchy and urgent calls to remedy the low status. As we shall see, Norway's response to PISA displays these characteristics. Again, to emphasize, for it to qualify as a status shock the *problem* must be primarily articulated in reference to being worse than or falling behind other peers, *not* concern for the absolute performance in or quality of the activity itself.

Both the press reports and the politicians' response to PISA indicate that what most shocked Norway was their lower-than-expected *position* in the rankings. The first ever PISA results were published in December 2001, and Norway ranked around the OECD average in math, science, and literacy. *Dagbladet* led the story with the headline "Norway Is a School Loser" (Ramnefjell 2001). The article goes on to complain, "Norwegian 15-year-old students are just average compared with their peers in the other 31 OECD countries." Nowhere in the article does *Dagbladet* refer to the absolute performance in terms of the standards that Norwegian students reached. These examples were reflective of broader public response; for instance, Per Østerud

140   THE GRAMMAR OF STATUS COMPETITION

(2016, p. 15) reflects, "The shock that Norwegian schools were not among the best in the world created a situation of fear and perplexity and it was expected that someone [would] intervene quickly and put things right." What might appear strange, though, is that Norway did not perform badly: its scores were average among the OECD and, in absolute terms, not so far away from the leader, Finland. Indeed, as Sjøberg (2014b, p. 33) notes, the debate the PISA rankings inspired in Norway focused on relative position and overlooked how the absolute differences separating country performances were often so small they scarcely warranted political or educational alarm.

Administering a Status Shock: Problematizing PISA Position and Framing a Status Competition

It would be misleading to treat Norway's "PISA shock" as the direct result of PISA. Although PISA's packaging in ranking and dissemination practices facilitates the enactment of status narratives, in Norway PISA could also rely upon a new government willing to actively render PISA as a crucial status competition, amplify domestic status concerns, and thus administer a status shock. Indeed, the results were jumped on by the recently elected Conservative government, which had long wanted to reform Norway's school system but knew that they would likely face stiff resistance from teachers, unions, and opposition parties (Bergeson 2006). At the press conference where Minister of Education Kristin Clemet (2001–2005) announced the results, she provides a near ideal example of how an international ranking can be transformed into a powerful status narrative. Framing the results to the press, Clemet likened Norway's performance to the archetypal status competition (chapter 1): "This is disappointing. It is like coming home from the Winter Olympics without a gold medal. And this time we can't blame the Finns for doping" (quoted in Ramnefjell 2001).[15] It is not a coincidence

---

[15] This comment on doping was misleading. Indeed, several countries "game" the rankings, whether intentionally or unintentionally; for instance, Finland has very low levels of migration, while South Korea spends the equivalent of 2.5% of GDP on private tutoring (Singer and Braun 2018; Simola 2005). Both factors influence PISA scores, yet the rankings promoted by PISA and the press overlook this. The irony would become explicit a decade later, when, reporting accusations of cheating in PISA, *Aftenposten* did not forget to recount Clemet's words from 2001 (Svarstad, 2013). For its part, Norway itself has increasingly excluded weaker students from the tests. The exclusion rate rose 250% between 2000 and 2015 (the sharpest rise among OECD countries in the period), and by 2015 Norway had the fourth highest exclusion rates among participating countries (Aursand 2018, pp. 20–22). Whether this is intentional "doping" or not, as Sjøberg (2019, p. 660) has pointed

ORGANIZING AND RESISTING STATUS COMPETITION   141

that she used for her analogy the *Winter* Olympics, a status competition that Norway excels and expects to excel in. It is also not surprising given her framing that *Dagbladet* (2001) chose to lead with "Norway is a school loser," while *VG* suggested Norwegian students were "this week's losers."[16] Notably, the Norwegian researchers involved in PISA were surprised that finishing around the OECD average generated so much attention, though they also note that Clemet "underlined" the fact on several occasions (Kjaernsli et al. 2004, p. 1; e.g., Clemet 2002; UFD 2004). Indeed, Clemet, aided by her ministry and the press, can be understood as a key domestic actor who mobilized the discursive resources provided by PISA's rankings to administer a status shock in Norwegian discourse.

Clemet and the government were certainly successful—arguably too successful for their own good—in framing PISA as crucial status competition. As *Aftenposten* (2014) noted a decade later, it would set in motion a decade of PISA "hysteria." The following rounds of PISA in 2002, 2005, and 2008, would bring no solace to Norway, despite the introduction of reforms directly targeted at improving Norway's PISA performance (see below). Instead, each round wrought a new wave of consternation and calls for something to be done: better teacher training, more classroom discipline, more resources, and/or learning from Finland (e.g., Width 2002; Solveig 2008; Ramnefjell 2002).[17] Particularly following the 2006 scores, when Norway's results fell below the PISA average in all three categories, the results prompted an intense political debate about how to improve the Norwegian school system.[18] As an *Aftenposten* (2008) leader put it, "There is broad political consensus that the performance of Norwegian school pupils is too poor compared to the results of pupils in other countries." However, there was little agreement about how to rectify it nor who was to blame.

Crucially, while the left-side and the right-side parties disagreed about how best to improve Norway's PISA rank, they did not contest the premise of

---

out, Norway's improvements in the 2015 PISA tests dissolve once the higher exclusion rate is taken into account.

[16] Cited in Kjaernsli and colleagues (2004, p. 16).

[17] Leading Norwegian politicians and educators quite literally went to Finland to reform their school system (reported in Ramnefjell 2002; Ertesvåg and Lynau (2002). Thanks to PISA, Finland had overnight gained the status of leader in education. Indeed, before PISA, few paid attention to Finland's education system, and the Finns themselves were as surprised as anyone that they topped the first PISA rankings (Simola 2005).

[18] The number of articles in the three newspapers covered peaked in 2007 and 2008 in the months following the publication of the 2006 scores. See appendix.

using PISA position as both a measure of performance and a goal. Instead, by using PISA uncritically as a reason to act, these debates reproduced the rules of the competition and contributed to legitimizing PISA's theory of international status hierarchy in education. The use of PISA in this way had become so predictable that by 2007, education experts attempted to preempt the outcry by warning in the week leading up to PISA's publication, that Norway must avoid "staring blindly at the results of the OECD-implemented PISA" (*Dagbladet* 2007).

The policy documents that supported the government's plans to reform go into more depth about the problems identified by PISA, but they routinely used PISA's relative country comparisons to illuminate and emphasize the problems they aimed to address. As we saw, Clemet was keen to emphasize that Norway should aim for higher than the OECD average—itself a relative comparison that instantiates an international status hierarchy—but the policy documents also mobilize relative comparisons of the disaggregated results. For instance, the government policy document that contributed to the intellectual basis for the reforms, *Culture for Learning* (UFD 2004, p. 12), stated that PISA shows Norway is "one of the OECD countries with the *biggest* problems with unmotivated students and low working hours." A page later it notes, "Although a large group of students achieve good academic results in school—and 55 percent of Norwegian students who participated in PISA outperform the international OECD average—Norway is among the five countries with the *largest spread* in reading skills" (p. 13). Surveying the press coverage and use of PISA by the government, it is clear that PISA served as a means of highlighting a problem in Norway's education system defined in terms of relative comparison to peers—that is, not being best, or being merely average. While critical voices existed in public discourse (see below), especially in the first decade of PISA tests, the dominant use of PISA among the press and the government was to identify relative international position as a problem and thus legitimate something to be done.

Legitimating Competing for Position

While Renshon (2017) suggests status dissatisfaction may trigger war as a means to rectify a country's low position, this would have been unlikely to remedy Norway's PISA score. However, the PISA results did enable and facilitate educational reform. There is little doubt that PISA has contributed to

ORGANIZING AND RESISTING STATUS COMPETITION 143

both the timing and the substance of educational reforms in Norway between 2001 and 2009. The OECD's Norwegian representative estimated PISA was "highly influential" on education in Norway (Breakspear 2012). Meanwhile, the government-sponsored research group charged with analyzing PISA and guiding policy, PISA+,[19] stated in 2004:

> The PISA results from 2000 revealed some alarming weaknesses at the Norwegian school, and both school officials and politicians agreed that many of them were both necessary and possible to do something about. In all likelihood, *PISA* has played a significant role in both academic and educational policy in our country. (Kjaernsli et al. 2004, pp. 18–20)

As the education secretary at the time recounted, the results of the PISA test "offered us [a] flying start" and gave the government a "mandate" to push through education reforms (Bergesen 2006, p. 42). The substance of the reforms was also clearly shaped by PISA. For the New National Quality Assessment System in 2004 reflects closely PISA's "best practice" recommendations: introducing more country-wide standardized testing, which Norway had hitherto proven reluctant to implement.[20] Similarly, in 2006 the substance of the "Knowledge Elevation" reforms indicated a clear goal to improve PISA performance (Elstad and Sivesind 2010; Kjaernsli et al. 2004; Sjøberg 2014b).[21] Moreover, Elstad and Sivesind (2010, p. 14) note how PISA influenced not only Norway's education politics but also its education evaluation practices.[22] As Svein Sjøberg (2014b, pp. 34–37), a Norwegian education professor, summarizes, the government "were liberating[ly] honest to emphasize" how they "let Pisa be the basis for almost every measure in their school policy," and given the "countless" references to PISA tests in parliamentary reports and school documents, it "does not require profound analysis to suggest they have had an enormous influence on policy making."

Notably, when the new Red-Green government took over in 2005, they followed through with the "Knowledge Elevation" reforms that had been mooted under the previous government and continued to make PISA central

---

[19] The PISA+ project was implemented on behalf of the Directorate of Education.

[20] Indeed, the creators of the new curriculum were explicitly given a "mandate" by Clemet to ensure the tests were informed by PISA (NOU 2002, para. 1.9).

[21] The original Norwegian is "Kunnskapsløftet," which has a double meaning: knowledge promise and knowledge elevation.

[22] Questions from the PISA tests were used in Norway's own national tests.

144 THE GRAMMAR OF STATUS COMPETITION

to Norway's education policy (Elstad and Sivesind 2010, p. 23). Indeed, the new prime minister, Jens Stoltenberg, made PISA central to his New Year's speech in 2008, telling voters that he had "got the message" that Norway's PISA scores must improve (quoted in Skjeggestad 2016). Not to be outdone, and indicating the cross-party consensus about the significance of PISA, the leader of the opposition (and future prime minister) Erna Solberg in 2009 offered a "guarantee" that if elected her party would improve Norway's PISA performance (Skjeggestad 2016). As Sjøberg has noted, this constituted a shift from policymaking based upon the standards Norway set itself, to those set by international organizations:

> [I]f we look at parliamentary reports and other school documents in the early 2000s, including with the red-green government [the new government that took over in 2005], there are not many references to the purpose paragraph [general principles supposed to guide the education policy]. Nor are there many references to the general part of the curriculum. . . . Nor does the word formation or general education appear in recent parliamentary reports or government assessments regarding Norwegian schools. On the other hand, there are countless references to PISA, TIMSS[23] and "OECD experts." (Sjøberg 2014b, p. 199)

In sum, during this first decade of PISA testing, there emerged a cross-party concern—some would say obsession—with PISA performance. This manifested in a series of reforms legitimated by reference to Norway's relative PISA position. In other words, a cross-party consensus emerged that the PISA education ranking's rules should also become Norway's: the OECD's theory of education status competition had succeeded in overcoming national insulation and inducing Norway to play their education game.[24]

The Stakes of the Competition: Prizes, Pride, or Something Else?

Reviewing how PISA enabled the grammar of status competition to inform Norwegian policy also provides insight into what value was theorized to

---

[23] TIMSS is another international education assessment: Trends in international Mathematics and Science.

[24] According to Bergesen (2006, p. 43), the perception that PISA offered a "scientific" basis for policy was crucial for overcoming objections.

ORGANIZING AND RESISTING STATUS COMPETITION   145

be at stake in Norway's education status competition. Though PISA is not connected to any direct carrots or sticks, one might suspect that it was fears about future economic competitiveness that drove the PISA shock. Yet, reviewing the public outcry across the period, little mention is made of the economic implications of scoring average among OECD countries on PISA. In fact, quite the opposite, the main group that mentions this in the press are those who criticize PISA: they use the OECD's focus on economically useful skills as a reason why Norway *should not* pay so much attention (e.g., Johnson and Østerud 2002a). To be sure, economic motivations provide a general overall motivation of Norway's education policy reforms during this period (UFD 2003, 2004, 2005), but economic anxiety was clearly not the reason for the *public* outcry about PISA that constructed the demand and thus the pressure for reforms. An article in *VG* written by the education minister following the first round of PISA illustrates this nicely. She does not mention economic concerns when she explains her mooted education reforms, but instead focuses on how Norway should expect to be best and thus strive to be best: "I am convinced that we are already the best in the world in many areas. . . . The question is how we can pull more students 'upwards' so that even more can enjoy the very best" (Clemet 2002).

Indeed, what enabled the government to administer the shock and create the need for urgent action was that many in Norway *expected* to finish on top. Before the first PISA in 2001, many Norwegians tended to believe their education system was the best in the world (Baird et al. 2011; Østerud 2016). This fits with prior research into PISA shocks more broadly. Reviewing the distribution of PISA shocks as a whole, Martens and Niemann (2013) find no correlation between a country's rank in the PISA test and its level of reaction, noting that low position in itself is not sufficient to trigger a national education debate and reforms. Instead, they suggest that countries who held their education system in high esteem found even average results "shocking," while states with widely acknowledged problems in education did not suffer from a PISA shock (e.g., the United States). Martens and Niemann do not make the link to status: failing to meet expectations can be based upon a failure to meet an internally generated standard rather than a score relative to that of peers. However, my status framework foregrounds the *relational* component of the PISA shock and allows us to explore the stakes that were theorized to be on the line in the competition.

Indeed, the education discourse in both the press and policy documents indicates that unfavorable comparisons with Norway's Scandinavian peer

146 THE GRAMMAR OF STATUS COMPETITION

group helped the PISA shock reverberate. This tallies with recent work in IR, which has drawn upon Frank (1985) to emphasize how "status concerns" are especially likely to emerge out of negative comparisons with "significant others" (Renshon 2017; Røren 2019). In the context of Norway, this implies that the friendly "neighborhood rivalry" with fellow Nordic countries would be the most salient (Røren 2019): The PISA debate reflects this too. What stung was not only that Norway was merely average, but that it was ranked lower than its peers. For instance, Finland was frequently used in the school debate throughout the first decade of PISA as a model to be envied and indeed mimicked (e.g., Width 2002; Solveig 2008). However, these significant others were not used only because they are Norway's long-standing "sibling" rivals. The Norwegian government reports systematically use Nordic countries as a benchmark for comparison for scientific-rational reasons. In the policy documents Norway frequently refers to its Nordic neighbors as "natural" countries to which to compare themselves. Besides sibling rivalry, the justification for comparison rested upon the comparative logic that because the Nordic countries share a similar culture, a similar "Nordic economic model" and are relatively wealthy, Norway should expect to perform at least as well as they do.

My analysis cannot confirm what the motivation was for the outcry, but the emotional register of much of the discourse was consistent with SIT: that Norwegian's self-esteem was on the line. For instance, Bergeson (2006, p. 41) claimed the results were a "national humiliation." However, the government's dominant line of reasoning when legitimating their policy reforms was neither economic concerns nor any "intrinsic" concerns for Norway's status. Instead, the expectation that Norway should perform better on PISA was based upon a comparison of relative spending on education. Hence, at the first press conference, Clemet argued:

> We are at the top of the OECD when it comes to the use of resources at school, our education level is high and we are a rich country. Therefore, we should have higher ambitions than average. We owe that to our children. (Quoted in Ramnefjell 2001)

The policy documents that underpinned the calls for reform reproduce Clemet's logic. For instance, the *Culture for Learning* paper, which discusses the PISA results and what to do about them, explained that reform was necessary because PISA showed that Norway was not getting "value for money"

ORGANIZING AND RESISTING STATUS COMPETITION   147

(UFD 2004; see also Bergeson 2006, pp. 40–46). Meanwhile, the PISA+ team, which led government-sponsored research about how to respond to PISA, also reproduced the value-for-money discourse:

> The problematic findings that gained focus through the PISA results are assessed from an international perspective and on the basis of national priorities, attention and resource allocation. They can be summarized as follows: 1. Around or below average performance in all areas (math, science and reading) relative to the OECD, and a decline from 2000 to 2003. Based on strong focus and high resource use in schools, politicians and the general population consider this unsatisfactory. (Klette et al. 2008, pp. 2–3)

Embedded within this "value for money" discourse is the assumption that PISA provides an objective and commonsensical means of assessing value: relative position in the PISA rankings is compared with relative spending on education.[25] The value judgments that inform PISA's rules thus become reified as an objective means of assessing the "value" provided by the school system.[26] In other words, the combination of new information based upon a new mode of comparison—ranking in PISA's math, literacy, and science tests—made possible a new measure of education performance, one that seemed to suggest Norway did not excel. Given that Norway generally holds the quality of its public good provision in high regard, the representation of being not only "mediocre" but inefficient generated additional salience within the PISA-Clemet-inspired education debate. What this value-for-money argument occluded, of course, was that there were many alternative means of assessing the value of education. Indeed, whether it was economic value of education or more broadly defined goals, PISA was far from the only option, nor, as many pointed out, an unproblematic one (see below; also Singer and Braun 2018).

---

[25] This value-for-money discourse was combined with the argument that because PISA results were not closely correlated with spending, improvements could be made without spending more money. (See Bergeson 2006 for an extended discussion of this debate.) Although it is not central to this chapter, it is worth noting that there are serious problems with this line of argument. For instance, South Korea was held up as an example of a country that gets value for money, yet its citizens spend the equivalent of 2.5% of GDP on private tutoring on top of the 3.6% spent by the government (Singer and Braun 2018, p. 39).

[26] This discourse is also reflected in recent qualitative research into how school leaders perceive PISA (Aursand 2018, p. 66).

148   THE GRAMMAR OF STATUS COMPETITION

The value-for-money discourse around PISA thus illustrates a *via media* explanation for why a state may compete in an international status competition. PISA's relative ranking became the primary barometer through which citizens judged the state's public good provision in education, and thus the legitimacy of the government. Therefore, besides external pride or privileges, the case illustrates how performance in international status hierarchies can affect a government's and state's legitimacy (see also Ward 2017a).

Instrumentalizing Status for Other Ends: Government and Press

Before moving on to the critical discourse, this analysis begs the question: Why was the government so willing to defer authority for the evaluation of Norwegian education to the OECD, given it meant amplifying negative status comparisons? The advantage of disaggregating the state in analysis is that it highlights how different domestic groups may not have equal incentives to maintain positive international status comparisons. Indeed, the Conservative Party (Høyre) that entered into office in 2001 was not responsible for the previous education reforms and thus had little legitimacy resting upon schools' international performance. In fact, PISA was a boon to the government as they could use it as a stick to beat their major rival (Arbeiderpartiet).[27] Moreover, Høyre had long wanted to introduce more accountability into the system; PISA provided them with that opportunity as well. This would explain why the government not only did not attempt to insulate the country from PISA's unflattering theory of Norway's education system's status, but they actively sought to amplify it. However, as we saw, once the government had framed PISA and legitimated its use, the press accepted the rankings and began reproducing the rules of the competition independent of the government's actions. Thus, in the first decade of the 21st century, both sides of the political spectrum faced domestic incentives to compete for position in the PISA rankings.

At least in the first decade, then, the PISA rankings enabled the logic of status competition to manifest within Norwegian education policymaking and saw Norway embroiled in a "race to the top" (Bieber and Martens 2011, p. 103) whereby consecutive governments undertook policies specifically

---

[27] A center-left or social democratic party, which historically has been the biggest party in Norwegian politics.

ORGANIZING AND RESISTING STATUS COMPETITION 149

designed to compete in the OECD-defined education game. Indeed, the way PISA rankings engender a status concerns could be understood to constitute a peculiar type of "external shock" which opens a "window" for government actors to undertake large-scale reform (Kingdon 1995). The interesting thing about PISA, and other CPIs, is that the window they open may stay open by virtue of the way they *package* knowledge in an iterative ranking. As noted, this logic of status competition implies that one can improve one's performance in absolute terms and still move down a ranking if the other competitors improve by more. Notwithstanding an unprecedented improvement, it might have appeared as though the PISA rankings could have been used to legitimize education reforms for as long as Norway did not reach the summit.

Rebellion, Reflexivity, and Escaping Status Competition

So far we have concentrated upon one type of reactivity the PISA rankings formented: a status shock and subsequent competitive measures whereby Norway responded to the rankings by striving to improve its performance. Norway's initial response to PISA may seem like an open-and-shut case of rankings overcoming national insulation, successfully imposing a new theory by which to make international comparisons, and thus inspiring status competition in the policy field (education). However, a second, more reflexive and critical response to the rankings emerged and became more pronounced throughout the period (2001–2019). Zooming in on the domestic response to PISA *across time*, we can also see how several groups in Norway sought, eventually with some success, to undermine the theory of the international education hierarchy found in PISA and thus mitigate and escape the status competition that it had enabled and encouraged.

Taking a longer lens and looking more closely at the response shows how nationalist theories of status can emerge anew within domestic societies. As noted, governments and citizens face incentives to avoid negative comparisons with out-groups. In Norway this is illustrated by how the education sector became demoralized by the PISA shock (Johnson and Østerud 2002b). Indeed, one of the protagonists in the government who led the call for reform in PISA's wake admitted that by the second round of results that they deliberately softened the comparisons they used to refer to Norway's scores (Bergesen 2006, p. 47): instead of using "mediocre" to describe Norway's

150   THE GRAMMAR OF STATUS COMPETITION

performance, they began to use "middling good."[28] Moreover, although they were a minority voice in the early years of PISA, education academics fought back in several op-eds in national newspapers (e.g., Johnson and Østerud 2002; Sjøberg 2007; Fretland 2007), while resistance to PISA's influence in Norway emerged in Norwegian academic fora. For instance, in a well-cited article titled "PISA Syndrome," Sjøberg (2014b, p. 36) took aim at the very premise of making interstate comparisons using relative rankings, arguing that statistically insignificant changes in position had taken on political potency in Norwegian politics they scarcely warranted. Meanwhile, an edited volume titled *PISA: The Truth about School?* was published in 2010, in which leading Norwegian education experts directly questioned PISA's outsized influence on Norwegian education policy. As one chapter put it, "[V]ery many [Norwegian researchers] seem to have accepted PISA's quality judgment without discussing the durability of the conclusions. The fact that there is now a Norwegian book that does not take all Pisa's conclusions for granted is thus an important event" (Langfeldt and Birkeland 2010, p. 96).

The substance of many of these critiques constituted a rejection of PISA's theory of the international education status hierarchy. First of all, several academics questioned the validity of the tests. For instance, a group of natural scientists who were asked by NRK[29] to assess the PISA tests were scathing. Professor Sissel Rogne argued that it "must be exceptionally difficult to test a student's knowledge based on such a test." Another reported that they found the tests "messy, inconsistent and confusing" and worried that PISA scores were "given so much weight in Norway" (cited in Fretland 2007). Writing the following week, Sjøberg (2007) argued that Norwegian (and Swedish and Danish) students would be especially unlikely to be "patient enough to do their best and fight through these long, strange and linguistically awkward tests" that offered no clear value to their studies. This sort of argument served to delegitimize PISA's international hierarchy and insulate Norway from negative international comparisons.

However, rather than merely reject PISA's tests, several critics explicitly posited an alternative theory of educational performance, one more favorable to Norway. For instance, Jan Johnson and Per Østerud (2002) reflected a common argument found among educators: that the Norwegian education

---

[28] This sounds strange in English but makes more sense in Norwegian. I am translating here "Middelmådige" and "middels god."

[29] NRK stands for Norsk rikskringkasting (Norwegina Broadcasting Corporation). Basically, it is Norway's version of the BBC.

ORGANIZING AND RESISTING STATUS COMPETITION   151

system prioritizes other qualities that are "hardly measured" in PISA, such as encouraging students to "develop tolerance for other ethnic groups" and "create an understanding of democracy and individual rights." Thus, they suggested Norwegian schools likely performed better in a "number of places that are not reflected in the PISA survey's ranking list."[30] Along similar lines, some critics emphasized that PISA's priorities reflected the narrow priorities of the OECD rather than the broader principles Norwegians might want their education to be based upon (e.g., Sjøberg 2007; Clausen 2010). However, rather than an entirely *new* theory of Norway's education status, this argument is better seen as a reiteration of the Scandinavian exceptionalism discourse predating PISA.

This skepticism toward PISA eventually spread to the press and political parties. Indeed, the "PISA shock" itself has reflexively become reconstituted in the past decade as a lesson from history about the folly of paying too much heed to the PISA results. While this critical discourse did not become entirely dominant among the national daily newspapers, it was increasingly found in the mainstream commentary (beyond op-eds written by academics). For instance, reflecting on Norway's best results since PISA began,[31] regular *Aftenposten* columnist Helene Skjeggestad was less than euphoric. In an article titled "15 Years with the Test That Shows What You Want It to Show," Skjeggestad (2016) looked back on Norway's "PISA shock" and how PISA had primarily been used to score cheap political points and as a blunt rhetorical instrument for legitimating reforms.[32] Reflecting upon the 2015 PISA scores, *Aftenposten* (2016) is less critical but notably prefaces its positive response by saying that Norwegians are "allowed to enjoy [the results], even if neither PISA or the TIMSS survey, which were presented last week, tells the whole truth about Norwegian schools."

Notably, when in 2019 the Conservative Party—which had instigated the PISA shock in 2001—initiated the most significant education reform since "Knowledge Elevation," the substance and rationale of the reforms

---

[30] Qualitative research based upon school leaders' understanding of PISA, undertaken in 2015, suggests these views are also found at the school level. As Leah Aursand (2018, p. 66) reports, "Several interviewees mentioned feeling that PISA's results do not accurately reflect the values behind a country's education system." The example the researcher quotes reflects Johnson and Østerud's (2002a) argument: "Maybe we can tolerate that we don't come out on top in these tests because we have made other choices about what we think is important to spend time on in school—raising students socially, building democratic skills, and becoming a critically thinking person."

[31] Norway came above the OECD average in maths, literacy, and science in the same year for the first time.

[32] See also Skjeggestad (2016).

152 THE GRAMMAR OF STATUS COMPETITION

explicitly reflected the criticisms of competing in PISA. Even though Norway remained in the same position that had first prompted the PISA shock, PISA was scarcely mentioned in the government's legitimation of the "Professional Renewal" reforms in the policy documents (Kunnskapsdepartementet, 2016) or its public launch (*Aftenposten* 2019;). Instead, following a large-scale consultation with teachers, unions, schools, and other education interest groups, "Professional Renewal" was presented as a "values lift" which aimed to embed democracy, citizenship, and sustainable development across the curriculum. The reforms also simplified the curriculum and reduced the amount of testing with the aim of encouraging "deep learning." In an assessment of the intention and content of reforms, an Oslo University report noted that rather than simply a *renewal*, the reform also constituted a *corrective* to the path Norway had followed over recent decades, and specifically the "narrow view of knowledge" promoted by PISA and the national testing regime (Karseth 2020, p. 28). Notably, the government's primary strategy document, laying out the rationale for the reform, mentioned relative position in PISA just once and was careful to emphasize that Norwegian understanding of democracy is overlooked by PISA and that its results "do not cover all subjects in the school or the full breadth of the subjects" (Kunnskapsdepartementet 2016, p. 13). Hence, the consensus on, if not quite hegemony of, PISA's theory of education status within Norwegian politics had become significantly undermined.

This critical reflexivity about the value of competing in PISA is well illustrated by how Clemet's Olympics metaphor has become emblematic for PISA's opponents. Indeed, the Olympics analogy she used in 2001 has now been reconstituted as a means of questioning the use and abuse of PISA rankings. More than a dozen articles since 2013 quote Clemet's Olympic analogy, mostly sardonically. For instance, a professor of education and long-term PISA critic Sjøberg has published several critical op-eds quoting Clemet's Olympics analogy to highlight the pathological influence of PISA on Norway's schools and to question the sense of competing (e.g., Sjøberg 2014, 2014a). The reconstitution of Clemet's metaphor as an attack on competing in PISA has also been mobilized by left-leaning political parties. For instance, the shadow education minister of the largest opposition party wielded Clemet's words in an op-ed in *Dagbladet*, criticizing the use of PISA in Norwegian education policy. In "Testing Is the Wrong Medicine," Torstein Tvedt Solberg (2020) sarcastically suggests that the education minister might like to say the results of the 2018 PISA tests were

ORGANIZING AND RESISTING STATUS COMPETITION   153

disappointing—like coming home from the Winter Olympics without a single medal—but he couldn't, because it is the Right who is responsible for these numbers. For too long, the right has been defined too much by school policy in Norway, and they have used the PISA figures to whip up a turmoil for their own political gain.

Solberg goes onto to declare that "PISA has never told the whole truth about Norwegian schools." It is important to note that Solberg belongs to the same political party—Arbeiderpartiet—whose previous leader declared back in 2008 that the PISA results were unacceptable and publicly prioritized improving Norway's position.

Crucially, opposition to even participating in PISA is now a policy position of several major parties. In 2016 two parties of the left that had hitherto been in the government that had made rising in PISA a priority made it their official policy to support opting out of PISA altogether. Citing the support of the teachers union, the Socialist Left Party (SV)—which held the education ministerial post in government between 2005 and 2013—began to argue that PISA's focus does not offer a comprehensive picture of the quality of schools, and as such, competing on PISA's terms had "harmed" Norwegian education (quoted in *ABC Nyheter* 2016; see also Kruger 2019). While in 2013, SV's education spokesmen still proclaimed that "PISA results are important" (quoted in Brønmo 2013), their party's working program in 2020 promised to "get PISA out of schools" (Socialist Left Party n.d.). Reasserting Norway's earlier national theory of status, the education spokesperson for the Centre Party has argued that "Norway must have the balls to rely on ourselves and the school we have developed over many years. Norwegian students are good in other areas, such as understanding democracy" (quoted in Kruger 2019; see also Sandvik, Grønli, and Myklebust 2016). Their 2017 election manifesto promises to "terminate Norway's participation in PISA" (Centre Party 2017, p. 66).

The 2021 election saw the Centre Party enter into a coalition government with Arbeiderpartiet, which, as we saw, has become increasingly ambivalent toward PISA (e.g., Solberg 2020). Given the coalition also depends upon the Socialist Left Party's support, the possibility that Norway may leave PISA has become a real possibility. Regardless of whether this occurs, the possibility that PISA could be used to instigate another status shock has become significantly less likely.

The eventual spread of dissent to the political class indicates that competing in PISA is not an all-or-nothing decision: the process of competing ran parallel to critical reflexivity about the value of the competition itself. This critical discourse began in academia and among teachers but over the past decade has become a major force in mainstream politics. Moreover, the substance of this discourse reflects the *reassertion* of a nationalist theory of status hitherto privileged in the pre-PISA era: an alternative value system upon which to make international comparisons. This is consistent with the argument that citizens face incentives to maintain a theory of international status that is favorable to themselves. To be sure, prior research has suggested that states may reject—in a discrete one-off act—rankings that they score poorly in (Towns and Rumelili 2017). However, my approach highlights the dynamic aspect: how contestation of an international hierarchy may emerge and strengthen over time and undermine the competition that a state had hitherto accepted. Relatedly, tracing the emergence of this anti-PISA discourse shows that this cannot be said to be a strategic state-led enterprise, but one driven by civil society (in this case by academics and teachers). This would suggest that status scholars should avoid treating domestic actors as a homogeneous a group that strives to maximize positive status comparisons; some groups—including governments under some circumstances—can and often do have interests that override the incentives to maintain positive international status comparisons.

A Healthy Competition?

Without belaboring the obvious, how to govern sovereign states in "anarchy" is a central problematic in international relations and in IR. Maybe the promise of institutions is false, but whatever way one cuts it, international organizations, and the global governance initiatives they manifest, usually feature in the problem, the answer, and/or the solution. Stimulating status competition via rankings offers one novel solution to overcoming the challenge of governance under anarchy. At a high level of abstraction, this chapter can be seen as an additional case of how and why a country responds to a CPI: because their government and citizens decide to pursue status in the field defined by the ranking. Thus, it adds empirical ballast to Towns and Rumelili's (2017) theorization of how relative international hierarchies exert social pressure, as well as Kelley and Simmons's (2015, 2019) growing body of work on how rankings influence their targets.

However, juxtaposing the findings with prior research reveals that the chapter makes least three further contributions to the IR status agenda. First, the chapter showcases the value of treating status as legitimation rather than motivation; it highlights how the grammar of status can be mobilized to achieve outcomes that are conventionally rational: Norway introducing national testing. This runs against conventional (rationalist) wisdom whereby seeking status is associated with inefficiency and sometimes recklessness (e.g., Gilady 2018). This analytical move thus significantly expands the range of activities that a status lens can help account for beyond the materially "irrational." Second, my theorization of international status hierarchies as an ongoing discursive achievement enabled me to illustrate not only how status competition can be encouraged by CPIs but also how these competitive processes can be successfully contested and undermined at the domestic level. I would suggest that this is one avenue IR's status research agenda would do well to pursue, and my TIS framework can offer a useful heuristic for rendering these processes tractable: tracing how and why a specific theory of status rises to prominence and dominance *and* how and why it becomes contested and its influence withers. Indeed, while prior status research has focused on how international measures of "accommodation" can mitigate status competition (e.g., Larson and Shevchenko 2010), this chapter's argument suggests it is also worth exploring how domestic resistance can undermine the domestic consent for competing in an international hierarchy. Finally, the chapter illuminated a "third way" of how status can inform policy that does not rely on either external incentives or the assumption of intrinsic psychological rewards: by redefining *legitimate* public policy performance in terms of a relative international hierarchy.

Normative Implications

One reading of this theorization and analysis would be that—contra the conventional wisdom in IR—the logic of status competition might sometimes be healthy. Historically, status-seeking is normally associated with waste and even war; for instance, the "Veblen effect" describes how a concern for symbolic (status) utility rather than primary utility directs resources toward conspicuous consumption. This leads to overconsumption of battleships and underconsumption of less conspicuous but otherwise more efficient policies like submarines or health insurance (Gilady 2018). If one accepts that rankings can organize status competition and make the hitherto private social qualities public and comparable, then this may offer a corrective to the distortion created by Veblen effects.

Yet, from a democratic perspective, allowing international organizations to set the rules of the game and thus the value judgments underpinning public spending is also highly problematic. As the critical CPI literature has illuminated, rankings embody value judgments that become hidden and thus insulated from democratic politics (Broome and Quirk 2015). Yet, as the analysis showed, this depoliticization is not final: the subjects of the rankings may learn to question the values of the theory embodied in the methodology. Indeed, reactivity to rankings can operate in divergent directions. The iterative feedback loop theorized as status competition can simultaneously engender a critical reflexivity among players that leads them to question the legitimacy of the ranking and thus undermine the pressure to compete. This *tentative* finding suggests international rankings may *not* offer a never-ending discursive resource for legitimating policy reform, but can lose salience as the domestic audience reflects upon its meaning and implications (e.g., for democracy). This is important because critical rankings research has hitherto provided a comprehensive taxonomy of pathologies associated with CPIs (see Beaumont and Towns 2021 for a summary), without theorizing or investigating instances of resistance. This chapter provides both an analytical framework for highlighting such resistance as well as an empirical illustration of how it can occur in practice.

5

Symmetry over Strategy

How Status Suckered the Superpowers at SALT

The real issue is the impact what we agree on will have on the decision-makers in Washington and the decision-makers in Moscow. Our view of our advantages or disadvantages will determine whether we can pursue an aggressive or timid foreign policy. The same will be true for the Soviets. If we all recognize we are not at a substantial disadvantage as [to] the Soviets, we have great potential and power.

—President Nixon, National Security Council
meeting, March 8, 1973

Introduction

It was not only peaceniks who argued that the Cold War nuclear arms race was mad. A litany of realist luminaries and cold warriors argued that the "nuclear revolution" should have removed the need to compete for relative gains (Jervis 1989). The argument runs that once both sides acquired a second-strike capability by the early 1970s, striving for nuclear superiority became futile. The theory of the nuclear revolution resonated with academics and policymakers alike. For instance, during his time as secretary of state, Henry Kissinger stated that "when each side has thousands of launchers and many more warheads, a decisive or politically significant margin of superiority is out of reach" (quoted in Reston 1976). Acquiring further weapons, beyond this capacity would be redundant, as Winston Churchill is reported to have remarked, "Why make the rubble bounce?"[1] The late Kenneth Waltz put it

---

[1] Churchill first used this line in reference to the Allied bombing during the Second World War; however James Reston (1969) credited Churchill with using it to refer to the folly of nuclear arms racing. For the first reporting of this expression being related to nuclear arms racing, see Reston (1969).

The Grammar of Status Competition. Paul David Beaumont, Oxford University Press. © Oxford University Press 2024.
DOI: 10.1093/9780197771808.003.0006

more bluntly: "[T]he logic of deterrence eliminates incentives for strategic arms racing." While Waltz glossed over the puzzling disjuncture between his theory and superpower practice,[2] Charles Glaser (1994, p. 87) was more explicit: "[T]he nuclear arms race should have ground to a halt and the full spectrum of the most threatening nuclear forces should have been limited either by arms control agreements or unilaterally"; therefore its continuation "must be explained by other theories." Indeed, the final 20 years of the Cold War confound conventional realist wisdom and beget a puzzle: If the nuclear revolution should have negated the nuclear arms race, why did the Soviet Union and the United States race to around 40,000 warheads apiece by the end of the 1980s? While various domestic, psychological, and strategic explanations have been proffered for this "suboptimal" outcome, the nuclear arms race remains the longest-standing, and most significant, puzzle of conventional security studies (Kroenig 2018: Green 2020).

Moreover, the long-term deterioration of Russian-American relations, the invasion of Ukraine in 2022, and the subsequent nuclear threats issued by Putin have made the Cold War nuclear arms race alarmingly salient again.[3] The prospect of a new Cold War and nuclear arms race has been refracted within security studies, where a new wave of nuclear scholarship has emerged around contemporary strategic challenges and generated renewed interest in the late Cold War nuclear puzzle. Indeed, a recent wave of revisionist (and hawkish) scholarship has sought to solve the puzzle by contesting both the empirical and the theoretical basis of the nuclear revolution and its pacifying policy implications.[4] For instance, Keir Lieber and Daryl Press (2020) argue that nuclear stalemate is far harder to obtain and maintain than conventional wisdom appreciates. In order to deter conventional threats, they contend, it is quite rational to develop large, flexible arsenals like those of the United States during the Cold War. Similarly, Brendan Green (2020, p. 7) provides a historically rich account of how, contra the nuclear revolution, consecutive U.S. administrations considered the nuclear balance to be "delicate" and that advantages could thus be gained from nuclear competition. The upshot of this revisionism has been to rationalize the madness of arms-racing during the Cold War and fundamentally question the revolutionary character of the nuclear era in general. Needless to say, this scholarship has profound, and

---

[2] Waltz (1981, pp. 25–26) merely noted in passing, "This should be easier for lesser nuclear states to understand than it has been for the US and the USSR."

[3] Not to mention the buildup in Chinese nuclear capabilities (Broad and Sanger 2021).

[4] Green (2020); Kroenig (2018); Lieber and Press (2017, 2020); Snyder et al. (2018).

arguably bleak implications for the prospects of avoiding new nuclear arms races in the 21st century.

This chapter follows in the footsteps of the revisionist scholarship to the extent that it uses recently declassified archives to address the puzzle of the nuclear revolution that wasn't. By highlighting the key role that *theories of status* played in stopping the nuclear revolution in its tracks, I offer an alternative explanation this scholarship has hitherto overlooked.[5] Indeed, this chapter tackles the Cold War nuclear puzzle by investigating how status concerns affected the SALT negotiations between the Soviet Union and the United States that took place between 1969 and 1980. My central methodological gambit is that the negotiations offer an excellent window into the status value of nuclear arms during the Cold War period of (allegedly) mutually assured destruction (MAD), and as such can offer insight into whether and how status concerns affected the arms control process and the nuclear arms race in general.

The SALT processes also constitute an empirical puzzle in their own right. SALT was premised on the idea the superpowers shared an interest in reducing the risk of nuclear war by implementing more stable force structures and reducing the costs of strategic arms-racing that would leave neither side safer, only poorer. As such, SALT was premised on arms *control* rather than disarmament. Rather than strive to remove nuclear weapons from the world, arms controllers strove to manage the risk of the nuclear era.[6] The SALT processes spanned a decade and three presidencies (Richard Nixon, Gerald Ford, and Jimmy Carter)[7] and initially seemed successful. SALT I led to the signing and ratification in 1972 of the ABM treaty, which limited each side to two antiballistic missile (ABM) sites apiece,[8] and the "Interim Agreement," which froze for five years the level of submarine-launched ballistic missiles

---

[5] By advancing a status explanation for the post-MAD puzzle, I also address a crucial case for the new status research agenda in IR. While some status scholars have argued that military policy is a hard case for status theory (Pu and Schweller 2014), I do not aver. After all, nuclear weapons have long been considered a major, and arguably *the* major, status symbol in international society (O'Neill 2006). Further, if one extends the logic of deterrence, states armed with survivable nuclear weapons—the so-called ultimate deterrent—should have plenty of leeway to pursue other priorities with their arms acquisitions without fear of being "selected out" of the system. Given these grounds, it is not only curious that status research has hitherto had little to say about the Cold War nuclear arms race, but crucial that it shows it can.

[6] There has long been frequent conflation between the two in practice, which is one reason why antinuclear activists have historically been disappointed with the fruits of arms control.

[7] Arguably one could include Lyndon Johnson in this list. His administration tried to initiate arms control with a letter in 1967, but he was rebuffed by the Soviets (Brands 2006).

[8] The full title is Treaty between the United States of America and the Union of the Soviet Socialist Republics on the Limitation of Anti-Ballistic Missile Systems (ABM Treaty).

160 THE GRAMMAR OF STATUS COMPETITION

(SLBMs) and land-based intercontinental ballistic missiles (ICBMs) at 1972 levels.[9] The SALT II process would eventually lead to the SALT Treaty,[10] which limited both sides to 2,250 strategic nuclear missiles and 1,320 missiles equipped with multiple reentry vehicles (MIRVs).[11] However, the SALT II treaty took over six years and three U.S. presidents to negotiate, and while it was eventually signed 1979, it would never reach the Senate for ratification.[12] The difficulty of SALT II is thus as a subpuzzle of the post-MAD nuclear era. Spanning the decade in which destruction had become mutually assured, the SALT talks should have proven quite straightforward, according to the logic of Glaser, Jervis, and Waltz. After all, why would it be difficult to limit redundant weapons? Instead, the talks were laborious, filled with contention about relative gains, and (especially SALT II) scarcely successful in limiting strategic arms.

To answer this question and shed light on the broader puzzle of the post-MAD nuclear arms race, I focus on the process through which the U.S. SALT strategy was legitimated. While a significant body of research has already convincingly suggested that status concerns played a significant role in driving Russian/Soviet nuclear policies (Ringmar 2002; Neumann 2008b; Götz 2018; Larson and Shevchenko 2003; Clunan 2014), the United States has been largely neglected by IR status scholarship.[13] To be sure, prima facie, status seems likely to be implicated in SALT: nuclear weapons are arguably international society's most potent status symbols (O'Neill 2006), while status *competitions* imply intense concern for relative gains (see chapter 3; Wohlforth 2009). Yet, deducing status motivations from outcomes depends upon a universalist conception of rationality, which is especially problematic in this case because different modes of rationality point to the same outcome. Indeed, among the "rational world of defence intellectuals" (Cohn 1987) many called for nuclear policies that cut against the rationality of Waltz, Glaser, and Jervis and promoted policies striving for superiority in number of nuclear weapons, even after MAD had been established (e.g., Gray 1979). Therefore, to ascertain whether and how status (or other goals) shaped the

[9] The full name of the treaty is Interim Agreement between the United States of America and the Union of Soviet Socialist Republics on Certain Measures with Respect to the Limitation of Strategic Offensive Arms.
[10] Full name is Treaty between the United States of America and the Union of Soviet Socialist Republics on the Limitation of Strategic Offensive Arms (SALT II).
[11] MIRVs enabled multiple warheads to be launched from the same missile and hit independent targets.
[12] The administration canceled the vote following the Soviet invasion of Afghanistan.
[13] With some notable exceptions: Wohlforth (2009), Lake (2013), Glaser (2018).

SYMMETRY OVER STRATEGY   161

U.S. SALT strategy, I conduct a longitudinal analysis of the archived SALT I and II top-level security meetings.[14] Using the grammar of status competition as a lens, the goal is to ascertain whether and how theories of international status were used to (de)legitimate SALT negotiating positions. Rather than a priori assuming one approach to nuclear policy is rational, this involves asking how one mode of rationality overcame the others. How did the government and members of the bureaucracies involved represent their SALT policy as legitimate and desirable? How was the social value and costs associated with nuclear weapons theorized in these legitimation processes? Here I will pay special attention to the process of how the "rules of the game"—the specific criteria used to understand who was winning the arms race—were represented, contested, and wielded to legitimate specific policies and delegitimize others.

The central argument of this chapter is that the U.S. SALT strategy was substantially hindered by consecutive administrations' expectations about how the agreements would affect domestic and international audiences' perceptions of U.S. status in the nuclear competition. Reviewing U.S. top-level SALT negotiations and preparations reveals how concerns about how domestic and international audiences would respond to numerical inequality were used as *the* primary means of legitimating prioritization of relative position. Moreover, tracing the front-stage (public) and back-stage (private) discourse reveals how the process of arms control itself saw the emergence, contestation, and solidification of the theory of international status (TIS) at play in SALT. Indeed, I show how the process of debating SALT I domestically produced and reified a particular mode of evaluating the nuclear arms race—in terms of total number of nuclear launchers—that structured SALT II negotiations despite the key bureaucracies explicitly doubting its strategic sense. Specifically, I show how equality in *aggregate launchers* took on growing symbolic value that, at different times during SALT, was prioritized over both hawkish and dovish strategic objectives. Finally, I argue that the process of conducting highly public bilateral arms control negotiations, by facilitating intersubjective agreement about the

---

[14] This chapter draws on recently declassified archives providing minutes and summaries of top-level security meetings (e.g., NSC, Verification Panel), memoranda, and policy papers pertaining to SALT I and SALT II. These are available online in *Foreign Relations of the United States* (*FRUS*) at U.S. Department of State, Office of the Historian. They include more than 1,000 documents totaling more than 3,000 pages. Beyond this, I have also conducted an analysis of the public discourse via the archives of the *New York Times* and *Foreign Affairs*, as well as selected other contemporary sources from secondary reading.

162 THE GRAMMAR OF STATUS COMPETITION

criteria through which nuclear forces should be judged and publicizing the agreement, intensified the status stakes involved in arms control and helped constitute SALT as a focal point for the broader superpower status competition.

To be clear, this argument does not refute the revisionists in toto; it is clear from the historical record that the United States did indeed strive for unilateral advantages throughout SALT in a manner consistent with the revisionists' assertions that the nuclear balance was far more delicate than previously acknowledged. However, as I show, from SALT II (1972) onward, these objectives were subordinated to ensuring the United States avoided *looking* like the sucker at SALT, which was not the same thing as what U.S. strategists considered *being* the sucker. This left the U.S. negotiators prioritizing an exact equality in launchers that neither hawks nor doves could justify strategically, except in reference to what they explicitly considered to be onlookers' misguided preferences. Unilateral strategic advantages were indeed pursued, but only *within* this symbolic hierarchy, whose rules were set by international and especially domestic audiences.

This chapter makes this argument in three moves. I first elaborate the theoretical puzzle of the Cold War arms race and in the process sketch the context to the SALT negotiations. Drawing on "soft" game theory, I take Charles Glaser's (1994) argument to its logical conclusion: not only should the prisoner's dilemma of the nuclear arms race dissipate following the establishment of MAD, but it should have been inverted. Rather than a prisoner's dilemma, I argue, it resembled what I call a *Wild West duel*, whereby each additional weapon offers not extra advantage but additional burden. Thus, the superpowers should have had an interest in the other side's wasting money on guns rather than investing in butter. This crystallizes the puzzle that my TIS approach is well placed to solve. By training our analytical gaze beyond considerations of nuclear deterrence, my framework can illuminate whether and how other social prizes and punishments— theorized to be at stake in the negotiations—informed U.S. negotiation positions during SALT I and II. Given the nuclear arms race is such a well-known and significant puzzle, I also elaborate in more depth than the other chapters how my status approach relates to alternative explanations for the arms race. The final section puts the framework to work and traces how the U.S. positions on SALT were contested and formed and how this affected the SALT negotiations.

The Nuclear Era: Security, Status, and the Prisoner's Dilemma

To understand why the post-1970s arms race is normally considered a puzzle it is necessary to sketch the standard Herzian formulation of the security dilemma: why it implies prioritizing relative power, and why nuclear deterrence is expected to negate this pressure (see Herz 1950). In short, IR realists argue that to guarantee security under anarchy, states must rely on themselves (Mearsheimer 2001; Glaser 1994; Waltz 1979; Jervis 2001). Uncertainty about the other's intentions requires states to acquire the means of defending themselves. However, defensive capabilities are difficult to distinguish from offensive capabilities. As such, states that arm themselves merely to defend themselves may inadvertently threaten those around them, triggering others to arm themselves in response, which may in turn appear threatening, prompting, a counterresponse. The tragedy is that this arms race "spiral" can occur even when the states involved have only benign intentions. This so-called tragedy is compounded by uncertainty about how much force a state requires to defend itself. As George Simmel noted, "the most effective presupposition for preventing struggle" would be "the exact knowledge of the comparative strength of the two parties" (cited in Waltz 1981, p. 7). Yet, prior to the nuclear era, the proxies for assessing an adversary's relative power left much to the imagination. As such, miscalculation and overconfidence abound in the historical record of interstate war.

Nuclear weapons by themselves are not expected to mitigate this predicament. A nuclear deterrent requires "possession of sufficient nuclear capabilities to assure one's relevant adversaries of their destruction in the event of war" (De Mesquita and Riker 1982, p. 289) and thus deter the adversary from aggressive actions they might otherwise undertake. Nuclear weapons make near-ideal deterrents, according to Waltz (1981, p. 4), because "they make the cost of war seem frighteningly high and thus discourage states from starting any wars that might lead to the use of such weapons." Yet, just possessing nuclear weapons does not automatically alleviate the pressure to compete for relative firepower. Before a second-strike capability is assured, in the world of hyperrational defense intellectuals, a merciless foe may be tempted to undertake a preventative "bolt from the blue" to destroy the other's forces, lest the adversary get there first (Wohlstetter 1959, pp. 153–154). Although both sides would prefer not to build new weapons in order to save money, a rational risk-averse state should match or exceed their

164 THE GRAMMAR OF STATUS COMPETITION

opponent in numbers or risk falling prey to a first-strike attack and annihilation. In a pre-MIRV world, whereby one missile equals one warhead, it is theoretically logical to try to match and exceed one's opponent in aggregate number of missiles. Therefore, judging one's force size by reference to one's enemy's makes sense, even if it may lead to an arms spiral (see also Glaser 2000). Thus, the 1950s and 1960s arms race between the superpowers is well-explained by the security dilemma.

Indeed, the "missile gap" furor during the 1950s provides a good example of how vulnerability, uncertainty, and poor information can inflame an arms race. Here, poor quality intelligence, combined with taking Soviet boasts at face value, led the United States to overestimate the rate of missile production in the Soviet Union. The United States subsequently began crash-building ICBMs in the late 1950s in order to stop a "missile gap" from emerging in the 1960s that some in the military claimed would threaten deterrence (Linklider 1970, p. 614). But the impending missile gap was "illusory" (Treverton 1989, p. 115): American intelligence estimates had dramatically exaggerated the Soviet buildup, leaving the United States with a large missile gap in their favor (Treverton 1989, p. 115; see also Norris and Cochran 1997). In response, the Soviets launched their own crash program. This period of the Soviet-U.S. competition corresponds to the classic action-reaction cycle theory of arms races in general and, because of the centrality of poor intelligence, Glaser's defensive realist theory of arms races in particular. Indeed, because neither side had an *assured* second-strike capability, the (theoretical) potential for their nuclear weapons to mitigate the pressure to arms-race—the nuclear revolution—could not yet be realized.

Post-MAD World

Yet, by the 1970s, following several technological advances, defensive realists argue that the uncertainty around relative power should have become moot and thus the pressure to compete for position in number of nuclear weapons curtailed (Waltz 1981; Jervis 1978; Glaser 1994). Before a stable deterrent can be assured, nuclear-armed states need to ensure a sufficient number of weapons can survive first-strike attack, ready to respond with a suitably devastating blow on the enemy: "a second-strike capability" (Wohlstetter 1958). Although hardened missile silos and long-range

SYMMETRY OVER STRATEGY 165

bombers offered a reasonable—if temporary—second-strike capability in the 1960s,[15] the gold standard became and remains SLBMs. Both the United States and the USSR had developed SLBMs at the end of the 1950s, and by the turn of the 1970s, although the United States was ahead in terms of range and accuracy, both sides possessed a secure second-strike SLBM capability. Further, the late 1960s saw advances in satellite surveillance that allowed each side to accurately monitor the testing of new weapons systems and their deployment (Burr and Rosenberg 2010, p. 102). Thus, both sides had little doubt about the other side's capacity to inflict devastation on them. In short, the era of MAD had begun, as well as the era of mutual awareness of MAD.

The upshot of MAD should have been that the pressure to match the number and quality of weapons of one's adversary subsided. As Bernard Brodie (1973, p. 321) noted, "weapons that do not have to fight their like do not become useless because of the advent of newer and superior types." Instead, the weapons need only survive, which in the era of SLBMs was a considerably easier problem to solve than matching an opponent's technology. A second-strike capability should also remove the need to match an adversary's power or number of weapons. A country need not concern itself with the relative power; it need only ensure it can inflict the requisite absolute level of devastation upon an adversary deemed necessary to deter. Beyond a certain point, extra weapons equate to paying to make the rubble bounce. Thus, as Kenneth Waltz (1981, pp. 5–6) argued, "variations of number mean little within wide ranges. . . . Nuclear weapons make military miscalculations difficult and politically pertinent prediction easy." In sum, by the 1970s this technical innovation in delivery vehicles had seemingly realized nuclear weapons potential for escaping the security dilemma and removing the imperative to prioritize relative nuclear firepower. Indeed, in Glaser's (1994, p. 87) view, the superpowers' accurate surveillance combined with their massive second-strike capability should have led to the nuclear arms race petering out in the 1970s.

Several prominent academics argued both before and after that concern for nuclear relative gains should have been blunted by MAD. However, if this view was limited to the ivory tower, it might be unrealistic to expect it to

---

[15] Hardening the silos of U.S. Minutemen was a stop-gap solution. Once the Soviets began MIRVing missiles, improving accuracy, and increasing the size, even hard silos could not survive attack. Indeed, worrying about the survivability of U.S. ICBMs became a long-term obsession for military and defense analysts throughout the Cold War (e.g., Nitze 1976, p. 229).

166 THE GRAMMAR OF STATUS COMPETITION

overcome the historic modus operandi of great powers. However, the logic of nuclear revolution was not only found in mainstream U.S. nuclear discourse, but it fundamentally informed the *official* U.S. nuclear doctrine during the 1960s. Indeed, between 1961 and 1967 the United States maintained a nuclear doctrine quite consistent with unilateral arms-control measures and the ability to accept relative numerical asymmetries. Secretary of State Robert McNamara (1960–1967) had attempted to put into practice the theory with what he called the "assured destruction" doctrine—soon after nicknamed MAD—which rejected the relevance of nuclear superiority or even equality to U.S. security. In a famous address in San Francisco, McNamara (1967) explained the logic that underpinned the Nixon administration's nuclear philosophy: that counting launchers or gross megatonnage was an "inadequate indicator" of assured destruction capability because even with "*any* numerical superiority realistically attainable, the blunt inescapable fact remains that the Soviet Union could still with its present forces, effectively destroy the United States."[16] Rather than *relative* power, what mattered was "an ability to inflict at all times and under all foreseeable conditions an unacceptable degree of damage upon any single aggressor, or combination of aggressors—even after absorbing a surprise attack" (McNamara 1968, p. 47.). This was estimated to require the ability of the second strike to destroy 20% to 33% of the Soviet population and 50% to 66% of its industrial capacity (Freedman 1989, p. 246).[17]

While morbid, this doctrine embodied the logic that Glaser, Waltz, Jervis, and Co. have long articulated: the United States could largely ignore relative numerical differences. Indeed, the country's own calculations showed how diminishing returns on force quickly set in: even using the most conservative estimates, their own war-gaming predicted that doubling the number of warheads from 400 to 800 would destroy only 1% more population and 9% more of the Soviet Union's industrial capacity (Freedman 1989). Hence, the "nuclear revolution" idea was not merely an ivory tower theory of little salience; it was both politically salient and available within the prevailing U.S. elite and official discourse.[18] This only adds another reason to consider

---

[16] The speech was given to United Press International editors and publishers (quoted in the *Bulletin of the Atomic Scientists* (McNamara 1967).

[17] This logic was also embodied in British nuclear doctrine during the Cold War, which defined its force levels according to the "Moscow Criterion": the absolute level of destruction that the government estimated was required to deter the Soviets.

[18] As McNamara's quote above illustrates.

the post-1970s nuclear arms race among the superpowers *the* major puzzle of nuclear scholarship.

Summing up, the nuclear revolutionists' expectation of nuclear cooperation under MAD can be formulated as a collective action *non*dilemma. If the marginal military utility of building extra nuclear weapons falls to zero and we assume nuclear weapons are costly, then not only does the prisoner's dilemma change,[19] but it ceases to be a dilemma at all. Assuming that once a sufficient second-strike capability is achieved and all spending on additional weapons becomes waste, then the payoff matrix is inverted. In such circumstances, the optimum outcome for a state faced with a nuclear adversary would be to invest in butter and hope that the adversary invests in additional guns. The situation thus resembles a Wild West duel whereby each additional gun offers diminishing returns, before inverting as the cowboy collapses under the weight of his arsenal. In short, power is still relational, but it is poorly evaluated by either the relative number or the aggregate firepower. Indeed, this nondilemma would appear to illuminate China's attitude to nuclear weapons during and after the Cold War: it required little cooperation or negotiation for China to eschew nuclear arms racing, despite its rivalry with both Russia and the United States.[20] Indeed according to defensive realists, this should be the norm: once a sufficient second-strike capability is assured, it should not require active cooperation or negotiation for a nuclear arms race to dwindle. Although Glaser (1994, 2000) does not put it in terms of an inverted prisoner's dilemma, this is implied by his expectation that after MAD, states could stop nuclear arms races "unilaterally."

This is a hyperstylized account but helps us clarify the puzzle: If secure second-strike nuclear weapons remove both the ambiguity in the cost-benefit analysis of conflict and dramatically reduce the marginal utility of additional aggregate power (beyond a certain threshold), why did the superpower arms race persist and even accelerate in the latter half of the Cold War? What were the incentives for racing well past MAD? What was the value to the U.S. of matching the Soviet Union's nuclear buildup?

---

[19] The prisoner's dilemma "game" was used to describe and explain suboptimal collective action outcomes, the security dilemma, and arms racing: it ostensibly explains why "rational" actors would choose to engage in costly arms racing when all sides would seemingly benefit from arms control. See O'Neill (1994), Schelling and Halperin (1961), Axelrod and Keohane (1985).

[20] Despite joining the nuclear club in 1962, China had until very recently pursued a minimalist nuclear doctrine that explicitly eschewed the arms race of the superpowers (Yunzhu 2008).

168 THE GRAMMAR OF STATUS COMPETITION

Filling in the Blanks: The Social Prizes of SALT

The Cold War is often used as the paradigmatic example of a security competition, yet it was also a competition for international status (Glaser 2018; Wohlforth 2009). The stakes in the competition were not only physical survival but the perceived superiority of their respective social-economic systems and ideologies. As such, several public metrics emerged that served as proxies for status comparisons: from space exploration to Olympic Games performance. As Nicholas Onuf (1989, p. 283) noted, Cold War superpower competition produced a "climate of contest and spectacle—an unending tournament, rounds of play in many arenas, all of us a captive audience." However, given military capabilities have long been the most important status markers defining great powers (Neumann 2008; Gilady 2018), we would expect their relative military power to become especially salient for their international status. In particular, nuclear weapons came to symbolize technological mastery and modernity, qualities both superpowers were keen to display (O'Neill 2006, p. 10). Hence, although the nuclear arms race during the 1950s—which rapidly put considerable quantitative and qualitative distance between the superpowers and the rest of the world—may well have been driven by the security dilemma, it also necessarily affected the participants' international status. Analogous to how status of the "leader" and the "challenger" emerges during the process of an Olympic sailing race, so the growing gap between the United States and the Soviet Union and the rest saw the emergence of a new status category: *the superpower*. While willingness to pursue global ends and fight proxy wars also constituted the status of superpower (Buzan 2011), as Ringmar (2002, p. 128) notes, "nuclear armaments were what defined a superpower as such." Yet, given the United Kingdom, China, and France joined the nuclear club, but not the superpower club, it is more accurate to say it was the ability and willingness to *compete* in the nuclear arms race that became the crucial status marker for superpowerdom.

Moreover, we have grounds to expect that SALT processes themselves would enable and intensify concerns for status at SALT. Although largely bracketed by extant status research, status competition requires some agreement over the rules of the game in order for status competitions to unfold. In this regard, SALT facilitated intersubjective agreement over both what was valuable and how to measure it. While additional information about the other's forces is expected by Glaser (1994, 2000) to help mitigate arms races and improve arms control, my theories of status approach suggests

SYMMETRY OVER STRATEGY 169

that conspicuous relative comparisons would facilitate the construction of SALT as a status competition and thus hinder trade-offs. Indeed, the negotiations took the form of a public spectacle and thus encouraged highly public comparisons of force levels (not unlike the CPIs discussed in the previous chapter). Although the previous administration had questioned the relevance of relative comparisons of force levels post-MAD, the relational structure of SALT negotiations insisted upon them. Moreover, the U.S. government knew that such comparisons, publicized in the treaty, would be widely circulated, publicized, and pored over by international and domestic audiences. This "information," once circulated about the relative capabilities, could be imbued with a social value beyond its military purpose. Indeed, as the analyses will show, the U.S. government keenly analyzed how their possible SALT negotiating positions could be interpreted by their alliance partners, nonaligned countries, and domestic audiences. Ultimately, SALT seemed well designed to become a focal point for assessing the superpowers status. While the superpowers may have enjoyed the attention,[21] how those interested parties interpret the meaning of SALT—the rules of this public game—were beyond the superpowers' control.

All these are preliminary reasons to suggest that more was at stake in the nuclear arms race and SALT than deterring the enemy. Prima facie it offers a plausible explanation for why the prisoner's dilemma quality of the nuclear competition did not disappear with the onset of MAD and, specifically for our purposes here, why arms control would prove so difficult and ultimately founder. However, at this point it is only conjecture; to evaluate whether and how status mattered to SALT we must dig into the archives.

The grammar-of-status heuristic can help illuminate and evaluate the significance of the social prizes at stake at SALT. Recall that in status competitions, audiences bestow prizes on the winner and punishments on the loser and that these prizes are independent from whether the protagonists consider the rules of game are just or fair. Ostensibly, the main social prize on offer was the successful deterrence of the enemy.[22] However, the nuclear competition did not take place in a vacuum: international audiences were

---

[21] The archives reveal how keen President Nixon was on summitry, even if he attempted to play it cool with the Soviets. Meanwhile, as several authors have noted, the Soviets placed a high value on SALT because arms control was the one arena where the United States treated them as an equal before the world (Anderson and Farrel 1996, pp. 70–77; see also Ringmar 2002).

[22] No matter how powerful a state's nuclear weapons, they cannot deter if they are kept a secret. As *Dr. Strangelove* illustrates, even a Doomsday Device cannot work if the enemy is oblivious.

170 THE GRAMMAR OF STATUS COMPETITION

expected to reward good performance with practices of deference and loyalty. Meanwhile, from the U.S. administration's perspective, the domestic audiences could also bestow electoral prizes and punishments. Indeed, the grammar-of-status framework operates here as a lens that can help clarify and illuminate the social prizes theorized to be in play when the administration weighed up potential SALT negotiation positions, beyond deterrence or other narrow military objectives.

This method will allow me to adjudicate between potential reasons for the U.S. negotiating positions at SALT. This is important because at the time of SALT, there were members of the strategic community who advocated for equality or superiority in nuclear force levels on military grounds that had little to do with international or domestic audiences' assessments. For instance, to deter the Soviets, some influential members of the strategic community argued it was important to match or exceed the Soviets' force level such that the United States could guarantee "escalation dominance" and/or undertake limited nuclear wars (e.g., Kahn 1965). Paul Nitze (1976) argued that failing to at least match the Soviet levels risked granting the Soviets leverage in crisis situations. Some even argued that it was possible for the United States to achieve nuclear superiority such that they could "win" a nuclear war (e.g., Gray 1979; Gray and Payne 1980). Indeed, these arguments would lead to a similar *outcome*: arms control would be severely hindered by concerns for relative gains in the treaty negotiations. However, while the outcome would be similar, the mechanism would differ. To ascertain which was in operation we need to go back over the U.S. preparations for SALT and ask: How was the U.S. SALT strategy legitimated backstage? Was it primarily legitimated in reference to deterrence or other rationale related to influencing Soviet behavior? Or did a theory of status with other social prizes and punishments dominate, such as how international and domestic audiences would respond, take precedence? We will also be in a good position to assess whether the "nuclear revolution" discourse featured and how it was marginalized backstage.

Beyond investigating how the SALT strategy was legitimated, my status grammar heuristic can also enable me to trace whether and how the rules of the nuclear status hierarchy were shaped by the SALT process itself and the public discourse around it. As chapter 2 argued, state status competitions seldom approach the ideal of an Olympic competition: a state's activities may be constituted with the grammar of status competition, but participants may lack intersubjective agreement over the rules of the game. Instead, the criteria upon which states, and their publics, assess international status may be heavily contested and/or diverge (also see Pouliot 2014). Therefore, the framework opens up another vector of analysis: paying attention to the *process* of how the rules of the game emerged and were contested and how a particular theory for evaluating the competition marginalized alternatives.

A few clarifications are in order regarding rationality and motivations. First, I am investigating competing rationali*ties*, rather than "rational deterrence" versus "irrational status" concerns. As Jonathon Renshon (2017, p. 45) has pointed out, so long as the means are suitable to pursue the ends, social goals like status can be just as rational as "strategic" goals like security. Second, I make no claims to be able to access the protagonist's motivations; I am interested only in how the policy was legitimated (see Krebs 2015), what was the argument that was used to successfully justify the position the United States took, and how this affected the negotiation processes of SALT I and II. As some suspected at the time, the military and members of the bureaucracy may not have been arguing in good faith and may have been driven by alternative motivations than those that they expressed in meetings and memoranda.[23] Meanwhile, it is perfectly possible to legitimate a SALT policy on the grounds of international status and be motivated by security or fear. Both these possibilities and other discrepancies between public legitimation and private motivation could well be the case, but it makes no difference to my argument one way or the other.

Alternative and Complementary Explanations

In one sense, I am following the lead of scholars who have sought to explain "suboptimal" foreign policy outcomes by exploring how domestic politics affects foreign policy.[24] I agree with their overall assessment: structural pressures are indeterminate, and governments, especially superpowers, have considerable leeway to pursue questionable policies without getting

---

[23] For instance, General Scowcroft wrote to Kissinger that he suspected "that the JCS don't want an agreement and will pursue any convenient argument to prevent it." Message from the President's Assistant for National Security Affairs (Scowcroft) to Secretary of State Kissinger, Washington, January 22, 1976, 0501Z, *FRUS 1969–1976*, vol. 33, p. 572.

[24] Perhaps by far the most influential strand of this type of theorizing is neoclassical realism that posits domestic factors as intervening variables that explain how states respond to the structural pressures of anarchy. For influential reviews of neoclassical realism research, see Rathbun (2008) and Rose (1998).

172 THE GRAMMAR OF STATUS COMPETITION

punished by the system. Regarding defense policy, this strand of research has focused on how bureaucratic politics (Tal 2017; Allison and Halperin 1972), variation in government structures (Risse-Kappen 1991), and perception bias (Jervis 2017; Wohlforth 1993) have led to diversions from structural realism's expectations. My argument does not directly contradict these explanations. In fact, some can be read as facilitating conditions to my status argument.

For instance, my status approach complements rather than contradicts the argument that bureaucratic politics—variations on the military-industrial complex—fueled the arms race.[25] These explanations disaggregate the state into a series of actors, which are said to have vested interests encouraging the nuclear arms race (Sagan 1997). The state becomes a series of competing bureaucracies seeking to protect and expand their budget. To achieve this, the military are said to use their authority and expertise to exaggerate threats, thereby helping to legitimate new weapons systems and increase their relative power among other bureaucracies. It becomes a military-industrial *complex* once the arms industries and the democratic representatives are involved in the same process. The thin version of this argument would suggest this is a subconscious effect of the strategic culture of preparing for the worst-case scenario. A thick version of this argument verges on a conspiracy: the military and its dependents knowingly inflate threats to buttress their budget or please their financiers (Rosen 1973). To be sure, the archives reviewed here provide plenty of support for the "thin" thesis: the Joint Chiefs of Staff (JCS) and various military men provide consistently pessimistic interpretations of the arms race and frequently used this to hinder arms control (also see Tal 2017). However, if bureaucratic politics posits an explanation for why certain groups had vested interests in pushing for more weapons, my argument explains *how* this was done in practice. The military had to be able to provide a legitimate rationale for their demands, which could not simply be "to expand our budget and bureaucratic power." Indeed, as we will see, the U.S. military bureaucracy frequently relied quite explicitly on status arguments to legitimate their insistence upon equal aggregates and thus prioritize relative gains in the SALT negotiations.

---

[25] The concept was coined in a speech by Eisenhower in 1961 and quickly caught the public and academia's imagination. Eisenhower, D. (1961), Public papers of the presidents of the United States, Dwight D. Eisenhower, vol. 8 (Washington, DC: US GPO)

The Role of Congress in U.S. Treaty Ratification

The U.S. treaty ratification process provides a crucial condition and mechanism for how the domestic politics (bureaucratic, party-political, and domestic status concerns) could influence the arms control process. Because international treaties require approval by a two-thirds majority in the Senate, leading senators could wield outsized influence and hold the executive hostage (Trimble and Weiss 1991, p. 646) Consequently, the executive has excellent reason to take into account domestic politics, and as my analysis will show, during the preparations and negotiations of SALT they frequently did. The U.S. ratification process is thus a facilitating condition for my argument. It can also help explain why, according to Henry Kissinger, there was a "near majority" of senators who believed in minimum deterrence and the nuclear revolution, yet the United States could not pursue arms control in a manner that reflected these ideas.[26] While the "doves" were sometimes taken into account, the minutes of the security meetings reveal that the chief audience Presidents Nixon, Ford and later Carter were most anxious to appease was the right.[27] Although the left was underwhelmed by SALT I and II and frustrated by the modesty of its proposals, they could be relied upon to prefer limited arms control to no arms control.[28] The same could not be said for the right.[29] In terms of the arms control debate, the right, comprised of "cold warriors"—from both parties—were skeptical of the very idea of arms control on the basis that they doubted a mutually beneficial deal was possible, and even if such a deal were possible, whether the Soviets could be trusted to keep it.[30] However,. the degree of skepticism among these critics of arms control varied from outright opposition to mere suspicion that could be assuaged with a combination of consultation, reason, and horse-trading

---

[26] Memorandum from the President's Assistant for National Security Affairs (Kissinger) to President Ford, Washington, October 18, 1974, *FRUS 1969–1976*, vol. 33. P.344

[27] Though Nixon had some advantages here: he could lean on his cold warrior credentials from his earlier career (Platt 1991, p. 270).

[28] Though disillusionment with arms control was widespread on both sides by the 1970s: it failed to live up to expectations of antinuclearists, while cold warriors claimed it had resulted in U.S. nuclear inferiority. See Kruzel (1981).

[29] For an extended discussion of the criticism from the right during SALT I and II, see Tal (2017, pp. 113–117, 266–269), Caldwell (1991), and for an example, see Nitze (1976).

[30] Although Republicans comprised the majority of critics of SALT, it would be a mistake to suggest it was divided neatly along party lines. For instance, in 1976 an influential a bipartisan group of Jackson Democrats and Conservative Republicans established the Committee of Present Danger, which campaigned against arms control and any arms control deal with the Soviets (Bohlen 2003, p. 14).

174 THE GRAMMAR OF STATUS COMPETITION

(Platt 1991, pp. 251–260). These conservative groups were a crucial audience for SALT negotiations whose understanding of the rules of nuclear competition were frequently taken into account by all the administrations—Nixon's, Ford's, and Carter's—that took part in the SALT negotiations.

The next section explores whether and how various theories of international status informed U.S. negotiating positions and ultimately the outcomes of SALT I and II. What follows is not an argument for why specific arms programs were legitimated, but how status concerns hindered the ability of the United States to pursue its preferred strategic objectives, and how and why SALT II proved far more difficult than leading realists expect. Beyond this headline argument, the analysis advances three interconnected theses. First, the United States prioritized equality *in launchers* during SALT II because of its importance in the eyes of domestic and international audiences for assessing status, rather than strategic reasoning related to deterrence or nuclear war-winning.[31] Not only were alternative theories of equality available, but these were recognized by those involved as making more strategic sense than the theory of equality in launchers that was eventually settled upon. Second, the particular theory of nuclear status that made negotiating SALT II arduous emerged out of SALT I and became dominant only through the process of negotiating SALT II. In short, the domestic public's backlash to SALT I was successfully mobilized by hawks to specify the rules of the game and insist upon equality in launchers. Third, prioritizing status led the United States to forgo other important strategic objectives of *both* hawks and doves, slowed down the process, and ultimately contributed to the failure to ratify SALT II. Thus, I argue that status concerns suckered SALT II and were to a large extent of the United States' own making. To support these claims, the following sections trace and analyze the U.S. arms control policymaking process from SALT I to SALT II.

SALT I: Strategy over Symmetry

The Johnson administration first approached the Soviet Union about the possibility of arms control in 1967. Initially the Soviets refused to countenance

---

[31] The meaning of the term "strategic" is not my invention but how the protagonists in the negotiations understood their goals, in which "strategic" referred to any military goal that had direct implications for deterring the Soviets, the stability of deterrence, and/or the ability for one side to conduct a first or second strike.

SYMMETRY OVER STRATEGY   175

the idea of limiting arms while they lagged behind the United States (Burr and Rosenberg 2010). However, by 1969 the Soviets fast approached numerical parity, and most observers agreed the superpowers were militarily stalemated (Burr and Rosenberg 2010). Moreover, after initial befuddlement, arms control theories[32] had begun to catch on among Soviet Union strategists and diffuse into elite circles (Adler 1992, pp. 134–137). Thus, when the United States announced plans to develop the Sentinel ABM system in the late 1960s, the Soviets were primed to reconsider their attitude to nuclear arms control. For their part, Nixon and Kissinger[33] were keen on SALT I as a means to pursue containment through détente. Indeed, recent revisionist scholarship has highlighted how the United States aimed to use SALT to structure the nuclear arms race so that it played to American strengths (Maurer 2022). Nixon also saw SALT as an opportunity to play "peacemaker" and thus offset his troubles in Vietnam (Burr and Rosenberg 2010, p. 107).[34] Although the Soviet Union's invasion of Czechoslovakia delayed the onset of SALT, negotiations formally began in November 1969.

To understand how theories of international status structured the SALT II negotiations, we must begin with SALT I. The first SALT agreement limited ABM sites to two apiece, while the Interim Agreement on offensive nuclear weapons "froze" the number of SLBMs and ICBMs for a duration of five years (1972–1977). Looked at in isolation, the ABM agreement was the most important result of SALT I and was rightly hailed as a major arms control achievement. In short, it cut off at source what many predicted would have been a rapid arms spiral, whereby each side would build the missiles necessary to overwhelm the opposing side's ABM defenses. However, as I will show, the missile freeze would lead to significant downstream effects upon SALT II, and therefore it is this part I will focus on here. Although the exact numbers were omitted from the treaty text, in practice the freeze meant that the United States was permitted 1,054 ICBMs and 656 SLBMs, while the Soviets were allowed 1,618 ICBMs and 950 SLBMs. While these

---

[32] For instance, that missile defense systems would cost a fortune and ultimately hinder rather than help security (Brennan 1961).

[33] Henry Kissinger, who was chief security advisor to the president in SALT I and secretary of state during SALT II was a crucial figure in both Nixon's and Ford's SALT policy. However, as the Watergate scandal hit and Ford took over (1973–1976), his political capital fell as SALT II negotiations got underway (Tal 2017).

[34] One reason why the SALT I agreement was reached so rapidly was President Nixon's keenness for the Moscow summit to take place prior to the 1972 election. Indeed, his eagerness to organize the summit quickly is palpable throughout the minutes recorded in the archives.

176 THE GRAMMAR OF STATUS COMPETITION

numerical differences were offset by U.S. qualitative superiority in other areas, one might have expected that agreeing to unequal numerical limits would have proved a tough sell to Congress. Yet, following considerable lobbying and no little horse-trading, the House and the Senate approved both agreements with comprehensive majorities.[35] Although the treaties eventually passed with relative ease, the shape the interim agreement eventually took could have been quite different. In fact, it may not have been concluded at all had dissenting voices within the military been heeded by the administration.

SALT I: Accepting "Inequality"

The military had pushed for the United States to insist upon a treaty with equal aggregate launchers throughout SALT I negotiations.[36] While this might not be surprising in itself, the rationale the military used to push for equality rested less on strategic concerns than on managing public perceptions of status. For instance, in a paper prepared for the U.S. National Security Council (NSC), which discussed the significance of the Soviets being permitted more submarines than the United States under the interim agreement, the authors conceded that "the strategic advantages to the Soviets of continuing to build Y class subs are not great." However, they insisted that "the political, diplomatic, and psychological advantages could be significant."[37] Even in the months running up to the final Moscow Summit, the military—via the JCS—was still pushing for numerical equality. Again, their reasoning speaks to perceptions and psychology as much as strategy:

> There are those who argue that, at the high levels of strategic weapons possessed by the United States and the USSR, simple numerical advantages are not significant. The Joint Chiefs of Staff do not accept that view. *Superiority, equality, and inferiority* have not only a military but also a political and *psychological impact* on US security interests. The United States should never sign an agreement which places it in a position that other nations, including

[35] The Senate passed both the ABM Treaty and the Interim Agreement with majorities of 88–2.
[36] See Memorandum from the Acting Chairman of the Joint Chiefs of Staff (Zumwalt) to Secretary of Defense Laird, Washington, July 31, 1971, *FRUS 1969–1976*, vol. 32, pp. 578–582.
[37] Issues paper prepared by the National Security Council Staff, Washington, n.d., NSC MEETING ON SALT, March 17, 1972, *FRUS 1969–1976*, vol. 32, p. 706.

SYMMETRY OVER STRATEGY   177

the other party to the agreement, could *perceive* as a position of US strategic inferiority.[38]

However, the military's theory of status did not resonate at SALT I, and their opposition to accepting numerical inequality was eventually overruled. Kissinger, the national security advisor to the president during SALT I, strongly opposed the military's demand for an agreement with equal numerical aggregates.[39] He argued that the various U.S. capabilities that fell outside the agreement (MIRVs, forward-based systems, bombers) offset any numerical disparity, and that given the United States lacked any plans or programs to build either new SLBMs or ICBMs, any freeze on the Soviet side would be to the advantage of the United States.[40] Thus, it was better to limit the Soviets than not at all; the United States would make relative gains regardless of the perception of inequality. Ultimately, the military did not get their way: the interim agreement that emerged out of SALT I froze the SLBMs and ICBMs at levels whereby the United States were permitted fewer submarine- and land-based launches. Kissinger would see this result as a remarkable negotiating feat. As he put it, the United States had not been "stopped" from doing anything they had planned, while the Soviet build-up had been halted. In fact, Kissinger considered it "miraculous" that the United States had managed to limit submarines and ICBMs "when we had next to no chips."[41] Here we can clearly see how Kissinger's concern for relative gains, which paid little heed to the status implications, did not necessarily mean being allowed more launchers than the Soviets under the treaty, but relative to what would have transpired without a treaty.

In retrospect, it seems reasonable that rather than a "miracle," the Soviets were taking more social prizes into account than Kissinger was. As

---

[38] Memorandum from the Chairman of the Joint Chiefs of Staff (Moorer) to Secretary of Defense Laird, JCSM-99-72, Washington, March 6, 1972, *FRUS 1969–1976*, vol. 32, p. 692, my emphasis.

[39] Nixon invested considerable authority in Kissinger in the SALT negotiations, which, at least prior to Watergate, lent his views on SALT positions special authority. For a more detailed discussion of the interpersonal politics of SALT, see Tal (2017).

[40] Kissinger would end up defending SALT I along these lines throughout the SALT II negotiations. See Minutes of a Meeting of the National Security Council Washington, June 20, 1974, 3:10–5:10 p.m.; Minutes of a Meeting of the National Security Council Washington, September 14, 1974, 10:08 a.m.–noon; Minutes of a Meeting of the National Security Council Washington, January 19, 1976, 9:57–11:40 a.m., all in *FRUS 1969–1976*, vol. 33.

[41] Conversation among President Nixon, Senator John Stennis, the President's Assistant for National Security Affairs (Kissinger), the Assistant to the President (Haldeman), and the President's Deputy Assistant for Legislative Affairs (Korologos), Washington, June 13, 1972, *FRUS 1969–1976*, vol. 32, p. 957.

178 THE GRAMMAR OF STATUS COMPETITION

the United States' own intelligence indicated, the Soviets were said to be "obsessed" with numbers. As such, it seems likely that institutionalizing *publicly* unequal aggregates in the interim agreement provided them with a valuable social prize in itself. Indeed, the fallout from SALT I would suggest that more had been at stake in the negotiations than Kissinger appreciated.[42] To be sure, the strategic community was generally positive to SALT I. A symposium published in *Survival* reflecting on SALT I and the interim agreement considered the agreement to be just and the numerical disparities to be "of no security significance" (Scoville et al. 1972, p. 210). Meanwhile, the initial reaction upon signing the treaty saw President Nixon bask in the unlikely acclaim of the *New York Times* (1972b), which reported that the agreements were "probably the most important accords of the postwar period." Nonetheless, SALT I did suffer public criticism. For instance, John Ashbrook (Republican from Ohio), who was standing for the Republican presidential nomination, claimed on the House floor that the SALT agreements would "lock the Soviet Union into unchallengeable superiority" and "plunge the United States and its allies into a decade of danger" (quoted in Platt 1991, p. 241). Moreover, following the acclaim that met its signing and ratification, conservatives turned against SALT I and arms control through the course of the 1970s.[43] While the SALT I agreements were widely hailed at the time as a harbinger of what détente could achieve, as the 1970s wore on and tensions and political crises between the Soviets and the United States persisted, SALT I became a symbol of the folly of détente for a growing number of the right. Especially following Jimmy Carter's election, the right rallied around opposition to SALT II.[44]

---

[42] The backlash against SALT I often featured in the top-tier discussions, infuriating Kissinger, who frequently lamented that the SALT I agreements were misunderstood and that the military had failed to defend them against claims that SALT had institutionalized inferiority. For instance, in a Verification Panel meeting in 1974, he lamented, "These constant attacks on SALT I as a sell-out must stop. We had no missile program. Not one US program was stopped by SALT I. It may be that some Soviet programs were stopped. Indeed, several US programs were accelerated. . . . These attacks are untrue and they're phony and they have to stop." Minutes of a Meeting of the Verification Panel, Washington, April 23, 1974, 10:19–11:45 a.m., *FRUS 1969–1976*, vol. 33, p. 244.

[43] Kissinger complained in 1974, "[W]e [Americans] have talked ourselves into a national psychosis on how far behind we are." Minutes of a Meeting of the Verification Panel, Washington, April 23, 1974, 10:19–11:45 a.m., *FRUS 1969–1976*, vol. 33, p. 251.

[44] Among many anti-SALT groups, the Committee on the Present Danger was "the single most effective organization within the Washington beltway opposing the treaty" (Caldwell 1991, pp. 326–327). Formed just three days after Carter's election, it counted a formidable list of former generals and high-ranking government officials, including Paul Nitze, who had been a member of the previous administration's SALT delegation.

One senator's amendment during the ratification process and the administration's response to it would take on particular significance in the next round of SALT. A crucial thorn in the side of the government throughout SALT I (and later SALT II) was Senator "Scoop" Jackson.[45] A leading Democratic hawk with presidential ambitions, nicknamed "the Senator from Boeing" because of his ties to the defense giant (Bloodworth 2006, p. 71), Jackson was a persistent critic of the SALT negotiations and the eventual agreement. His stature as an expert on defense matters, a leading member of Senate's Armed Services Committee, and the chairman of the subcommittee on Salt made him a senator consecutive administrations sought to woo into supporting SALT I and II (Platt 1991; Tal 2017; Caldwell 1991). True to form, Jackson had publicly spoken out against the SALT I Interim Agreement's provisions, arguing that the freeze froze the United States into a position of "sub-parity" and would put the United States at a disadvantage.[46] Jackson thus sought to attach a congressional understanding to the interim agreement. The Jackson Amendment, as it became known, demanded that any future SALT agreement must have "equal numbers of intercontinental strategic launchers taking account of throw weight"[47] and initially demanded that the U.S. government reserve the right to abrogate the treaty should the USSR undertake any missile modernization during the interim period that threatened U.S. Minutemen missiles.[48] As the *New York Times* (1972a) noted at the time, Jackson's nuclear counting was misleading:

> There is no doubt that, to the layman, the numerical edge in the interim offensive pact appears to give the Soviet Union an advantage, although the Pentagon and its supporters know that this is not so. President Nixon showed political courage in agreeing to the Moscow terms. To undermine this achievement and further arms control prospects by concessions to Mr. Jackson and the military-industrial complex would be the height of folly.

---

[45] Jackson features prominently in the NSC and Verification Panel meetings of the Nixon, Ford, and Carter administrations; even the Soviets mentioned his name during the negotiations.

[46] Reported in *New York Times* (1972a).

[47] Throw-weight usually refers to the total weight of a nuclear missile's warheads, reentry vehicles, penetration aids, and missile guidance systems: generally everything besides the launch rocket booster and launch fuel.

[48] Senate Joint Resolution 241 on the Interim Strategic Offensive Arms Agreement, August 7, 1972. The amendment mandated equality in U.S. and Soviet strategic arms.

180   THE GRAMMAR OF STATUS COMPETITION

Yet, the way the administration defended SALT I emphasized that the asymmetry on launchers was equalized by the asymmetry on warheads. The upshot of this position was that while it helped get SALT I ratified, it also tacitly legitimated the theory that relative numbers were a reasonable way of evaluating both the SALT agreements and the status of the competitors in the nuclear arms race in general. Moreover, the Nixon administration, eager to win the support of Jackson and his followers, endorsed Jackson's demand for future offensive weapons agreements to be based upon the "principle of equality" in aggregate numbers of launchers. The government's rationale for supporting Jackson's amendment was as short term as it was pragmatic: it would allow the administration to ratify SALT. Some have suggested that the Nixon administration was playing an intricate two-level game here: endorsing an amendment that restricted the U.S. negotiation position in order to strengthen U.S. hands in future negotiations (Platt 1991, p. 252). However, this reading seems unlikely given that Kissinger, who was the dominant voice during SALT, frequently argued against insisting on equal aggregates in both the SALT I and the SALT II negotiations. Moreover, prioritizing equal numbers would mean forgoing other strategic priorities. Instead, it seems far more likely that they endorsed the "Jackson Resolution" primarily to smooth ratification prior to the upcoming 1972 election.

The reasonable-sounding principle of "equal aggregates" would have significant downstream effects in the later SALT II negotiations. First, demanding "equality" embodied a demand for (joint) top position and constituted the nuclear arms race as a zero-sum status game. The representations of inferiority and inequality, when based on aggregate number of launchers, produced a clear competitive status hierarchy and simultaneously legitimated demanding equality in the future and delegitimating "inequality." While the demand for equality in itself was not controversial, Senator Jackson also *specified* a particular means of assessing the nuclear hierarchy and SALT: aggregate numbers of launchers.[49] This was not an inevitable mode of comparison: the back-stage and front-stage debates around SALT I indicated several other plausible ways to evaluate the U.S. nuclear position, of which counting launchers was only one strategically questionable, albeit straightforward,

---

[49] As Patrick Thaddeus Jackson (2006, p. 44) explains, "specification" is a rhetorical move employed by political actors to corner opponents by taking a widely accepted value and defining it precisely in a particular context to support one's agenda (and delegitimize the agenda of one's opponents). Here "equality" is a taken-for-granted moral value; equality with the Soviet Union was difficult to argue against, but far more controversial is the claim that equality in nuclear weapons is best measured by number of launchers.

measure. However, by endorsing Jackson's amendment, even though it was only advisory, the government legitimated using the number of nuclear launchers as the principle means of evaluating the relative power of the United States and the USSR. As we will see, the demand for equality in aggregates of launchers would eventually solidify into cross-party conventional wisdom of what was an appropriate goal for SALT II.

SALT II: Specifying Equality

> We noted the Soviet position of 27, U.S. of 28. Gromyko said this difference was so slight that the public would be amused if it were published.
> —Telegram from Secretary of State Vance to the
> White House, Brussels, December 24, 1978,
> 0038Z, *FRUS 1969–1976*, vol. 33, p. 924

If in SALT I the social value of equality in launchers had not been clarified, or not yet produced, as negotiations for SALT II got underway it would eventually become taken for granted and prioritized above all else. Across the first two administrations that took part in SALT II negotiations—Nixon's and Ford's—equal aggregates were debated and eventually settled upon as the primary negotiating priority. Perhaps surprisingly, while President Carter strove for greater reductions in the total level of the aggregates, his administration's position never wavered from the demand for equal aggregates. The priority given to equal aggregate of launchers was reflected in the minutes of security meetings, as well as all the official documents spelling out the formal negotiating position of each administration from Nixon's to Carter's.[50]

This is puzzling for several reasons. First of all, there were several alternatives under consideration that suggest measuring equality by aggregate launchers was far from an inevitable outcome.[51] Indeed, as Kissinger

---

[50] For instance, Memorandum from the President's Assistant for National Security Affairs (Kissinger) to President Nixon, Washington, November 8, 1972; Memorandum from Helmut Sonnenfeldt of the National Security Council Staff to the President's Assistant for National Security Affairs (Kissinger), Washington, December 1, 1972; Minutes of a Meeting of the Verification Panel, Washington, January 8, 1974, 10:12–11:32 a.m.; Presidential Directive/NSC–71 Washington, March 23, 1977, all in *FRUS 1969–1976*, vol. 33.

[51] This is not even to mention (a) that the mode of counting "equality" ignored U.S.-sponsored "tactical" nuclear weapons in Europe, which were capable of hitting the Soviet Union, and (b) that U.S. NATO allies, who possessed strategic nuclear weapons, explicitly targeted the Soviet Union (the United Kingdom's strategic doctrine was based upon the "Moscow Criterion").

182 THE GRAMMAR OF STATUS COMPETITION

pointed out early in the process of SALT II, equality could means several different things:

> Everyone agrees that one of our most fundamental objectives in SALT Two is equality. The real question is, how do we define equality. Do we mean (1) equality in first-strike capability, (2) equality in second strike capability, (3) equality in numbers of launchers and re-entry vehicles, or (4) equality in assured destruction capability.[52]

Second, the fiercest proponents of equality in launchers in the backstage negotiations readily admitted that launcher equality was a poor way of evaluating the nuclear balance. Third, the United States did not end up matching the Soviets' aggregate force level, and it was doubtful that the military even planned to. Finally, although the Jackson Amendment demanded equality in launchers, it was not legally binding, and both Nixon and Ford considered alternatives. Given all this, why did equality become settled as a priority in SALT II, and why was aggregate equality defined in the way it was? Moreover, what were the opportunity costs of insisting upon equality of launchers?

First of all, the archives show how the domestic audience and Congress structured the administration's SALT negotiation strategy from the outset. President Nixon was keen to be presented with options for SALT negotiating positions and for their relative merits to be debated and defended before any decision was made. Throughout the preparations for SALT I and SALT II, whether an option could be "sold" to Congress was frequently asked and treated as a deal-breaker. It was not only concern for hawks that structured the SALT discussion; doves, and sometimes even Nimbys,[53] were taken into account too. Put simply, the Nixon administration sought to avoid looking like they were fueling the arms race but also not losing it either. This balancing act is nicely illustrated by Kissinger's dismissal of a potential negotiating position:

> I believe we are unanimous in saying that the Soviets probably will not accept it and that it is not salable in this country. . . . You would be vulnerable to the right because it has no constraints on Backfire [a type of Soviet strategic bomber]; and vulnerable to the left because there are no constraints

[52] Minutes of a Meeting of the National Security Council, Washington, March 8, 1973, 10:10–11:30 a.m., *FRUS 1969–1976*, vol. 33, p. 50.
[53] Minutes of a Meeting of the National Security Council, Washington, September 17, 1975, *FRUS 1969–1976*, vol. 33, p. 471.

on cruise missiles. People will say this is a phony agreement and that it jeopardizes our national interest.[54]

Indeed, throughout the SALT I and SALT II negotiations, U.S. decision-makers theorized how the domestic audience would respond and discount various options as "[un]sellable."[55] In this way, the administration's theorizations of the expected domestic response to specific arms control proposals structured the negotiations. The archives show quite clearly that the administration acted upon what they believed the domestic preferences were, even if they went against what the administration considered reasonable or plausible. This is a useful starting point—showing that domestic politics influenced the ostensibly high-politics of arms control—but it will not surprise many American political scientists. Indeed, given that ratifying an international treaty requires a two-thirds majority in the Senate, it would be remarkable if the administrations did not take Congress into account.

Theorizing the Domestic and International Rules of the Game

More theoretically interesting is how *through* the backstage SALT process, saleability would eventually become defined primarily in terms of "equality" in aggregate number of launchers. As we will see, this position had to be justified vis-à-vis alternative measures of equality (e.g., throw weight), against proposals to offset disparity in launchers with MIRVs, as well as during discussions regarding how to count the aggregate. Thus, the archives provide a clear window into *what* value equality in launchers was represented to provide for the United States, and *where* that value was said to be derived from.

First of all, the archives make clear how the process of ratifying SALT I played a crucial role in specifying "equality" and defining the domestic prizes and punishments associated with alternative SALT negotiating positions. Even though it was only advisory, and even though it lacked a "strategic" rationale, the Jackson Amendment came to symbolize the domestic pressure to insist upon equality in aggregates. For instance, during the preparations for SALT II, a memorandum from Helmut Sonnenfeldt of the

---

[54] Minutes of a Meeting of the National Security Council, Washington, January 8, 1976, *FRUS 1969–1976*, vol. 33, p. 518.

[55] This metaphor was frequently used across all the administrations to theorize which SALT position would or would not make it past Congress.

184 THE GRAMMAR OF STATUS COMPETITION

NSC illustrates how Jackson came to embody rhetorical shorthand for the political and domestic pressure for "equality":

> For political-diplomatic reasons, the perpetuation of unequal numbers is regarded by a certain body of opinion, reflected by Senator Jackson, as an unacceptable long term arrangement, and acceptable in the short-term only because we still have technological advantages and strategic systems not covered by the agreement, and because theoretically at least, we can break out after 5 years. . . . The forward base issue is probably perceived by the Soviets in much the same way as we perceive at least a part of the problem posed for us by the numerical disparities contained in the Interim Agreement. That is, they find these bases obnoxious mostly for diplomatic/ political/psychological reasons rather than because they pose serious military threats, much as we find the 62:41 submarine ratio *politically* unacceptable as a long-term arrangement.[56]

In other words, inequality in numbers was seen as "obnoxious" quite independently from its strategic importance. It's clear that these "political" and "psychological" reasons must have been important if they could trump strategic reasoning.[57] It was Secretary of Defense James Schlesinger who emphasized Jackson and the *domestic* concern for equality most vociferously in the SALT II top-level meetings. For instance, in an NSC meeting when the administration was considering again whether to resist the Soviet request for unequal aggregates to offset the U.S. forward-base systems (FBS),[58] Schlesinger does not make the strategic case but leans instead upon the presumed opposition of Jackson and his ilk:

---

[56] Memorandum from Helmut Sonnenfeldt of the National Security Council Staff to the President's Assistant for National Security (Kissinger), Washington, November 3, 1972, *FRUS 1969–1976*, vol. 33, p. 18.

[57] Although Sonnenfeldt mentions in the same memo that unequal aggregates also posed a problem for the vulnerability of U.S. land-based missiles, as the next two years of U.S. deliberations made clear, this problem *could not* be solved by insisting on equal numbers of launchers, only with limitations on throw weight and/or limits on the number of MIRVed heavy missiles. See, for instance, Memorandum from the President's Assistant for National Security Affairs (Kissinger) to President Nixon, Washington, November 8, 1972, *FRUS 1969–1976*, vol. 33, p. 24; Memorandum from the President's Assistant for National Security Affairs (Kissinger) to President Ford, Washington, October 18, 1974, *FRUS 1969–1976*, vol. 33, p. 345. Sonnenfeldt himself admits this when reflecting on the advantage of equality in launchers without a significant sublimit on MIRVs or throw weight; he concedes that it offers "[n]othing in terms of survivability of the ICBM force." Minutes of a Meeting of the Verification Panel, Washington, April 23, 1974, 10:19–11:45 a.m., *FRUS 1969–1976*, vol. 33, p. 252.

[58] The nuclear weapons in Europe that were capable of hitting the Soviet Union.

SYMMETRY OVER STRATEGY   185

Inherently, this kind of decision is simple to make. The question is whether militarily, diplomatically, and politically, you want to move rapidly toward the Soviet proposal of giving the U.S. inferiority in numbers. This would be very difficult to justify. Unequal numbers would not have much Congressional support, and would violate the *Jackson Amendment* which requires equal numbers. It would be difficult to persuade the American public that any position other than equal aggregates, especially as our going-in position, is the correct one.[59]

Later Schlesinger expressed the priority for the diplomatic and political advantages even more bluntly, rounding off his contribution to an NSC meeting on SALT by saying, "On the question of equal aggregates, it is politically and diplomatically crucial. Perhaps, *it is the most critical feature.* We can live with an increase in instability, but it would be difficult not to come up to their level."[60]

However, the appearance of equality of aggregates was not only important for domestic consumption, but was theorized to matter for international audiences too. Here, the international response to the SALT I treaty provided a discursive resource for legitimating the priority of equal aggregates in SALT II. For instance, Secretary Schlesinger recounted a conversation he had with the Japanese minister of defense about SALT I as evidence for theorizing why equal aggregates were crucial: "He asked me why we accepted an unequal agreement in 1972. I answered him that we had a technological advantage. But this is to point out that the perception is there in third parties."[61] But, Schlesinger went on, it was not only the Japanese: "there is a problem of *appearance* in Europe. The agreement is perceived as unequal."[62] Backing up Schlesinger, the JCS frequently emphasized perceptions of equality rather than the importance of equality per se:

> The point is that it is much more important to achieve agreement on equal aggregates of central systems, even at the 2500 level, than it is to accept an

---

[59] Minutes of a Meeting of the National Security Council, Washington, October 7, 1974, 2:55–4:35 p.m., *FRUS 1969–1976*, vol. 33, p. 364.

[60] Minutes of a Meeting of the National Security Council, Washington, October 18, 1974, 3:40–5:45 p.m., *FRUS 1969–1976*, vol. 33, p. 367, my emphasis.

[61] Minutes of a Meeting of the National Security Council, Washington, October 18, 1974, 3:40–5:45 p.m., *FRUS 1969–1976*, vol. 33, p. 364.

[62] Minutes of a Meeting of the National Security Council, Washington, October 18, 1974, 3:40–5:45 p.m., *FRUS 1969–1976*, vol. 33, p. 374.

186   THE GRAMMAR OF STATUS COMPETITION

agreement which is asymmetrically in favor of the Soviets in numbers of launchers. . . . I believe that the approach outlined above is the maximum initiative that can be taken without undue risk. Further, it: a. Reflects the firm US resolve with regard to non-central systems; b. *Incorporates equal aggregates and will, therefore, protect our standing with third countries, our allies and our adversaries. Provides for essential equivalence from a military as well as political image point of view.*[63]

Finally, both Ford and Nixon also raised concerns about how various audiences would interpret any deal that did not appear equal. At an NSC meeting in 1973, President Nixon asserted that the United States must take into account how SALT *"appear[s]* to other countries, since this is what affects our foreign policy."[64] All this brings to mind Robert Gilpin's famous claim, that prestige rather than power is the "everyday currency" of international politics. These quotes also clearly embody the grammar of status competition. The rules of the competition are simple: inferior and superior statuses in the international hierarchy of power are represented to derive from the relative number of nuclear weapons each superpower is allowed under the treaty. Failure to get equality in number, they *theorize*, will jeopardize U.S. influence with other countries, even if by their own "strategic" calculations such numerical differences would not matter. In short, interest in influence collapsed into interest in international status.

Thus, the seemingly reasonable demand for "equality" produced a fear of being seen as inferior that structured the SALT II process. Although in SALT I other metrics had been taken into account, the total number of launchers became *the* primary—and increasingly conventionalized—*proxy* for making this calculation during the SALT II backstage negotiations. Crucially, none of those involved in formulating the U.S. SALT II position earnestly argued that aggregate launchers *were* the best way of either measuring equality or assessing deterrence. Rather than relying on their own assessments of what was required for deterrence, even those passionately in favor of numerical equality argued that it was needed because this was how various audiences would evaluate the U.S. position: domestic

---

[63] Memorandum from the Chairman of the Joint Chiefs of Staff (Moorer) to the President's Assistant for National Security Affairs (Kissinger), Washington, May 2, 1973, *FRUS 1969–1976*, vol. 33, p. 77.

[64] Minutes of a Meeting of the National Security Council, Washington, March 8, 1973, 10:10–11:30 a.m., *FRUS 1969–1976*, vol. 33, p. 50.

critics in Congress, the general public, as well as allies and third-party countries.[65] From my grammar-of-status perspective, it does not matter whether their analysis was correct; it matters only that this theory of international and domestic audiences' criteria for assessing U.S./Soviet status is what legitimated the U.S. government's insistence upon total equal aggregates.

Opportunities Lost

The salient question, then, is how this concern for status affected arms control. The conservative answer is that at a minimum it made arms control considerably more difficult—and the process longer—than if the administration had gone only by their own "strategic" calculations. Again and again during the first two years of the SALT II negotiations, the U.S. position hit up against the Russians' refusal to accept the equal aggregate principle. It is not an exaggeration to say that this was *the* sticking point that held up negotiations. However, as a result of the Soviet position, the U.S. demand for equal aggregates had to be defended and legitimated at NSC and Verification Panel meetings as the United States sought to find compromise. These discussions give a direct window into both what constituted the value of equal numbers and why it had to be prioritized.

At the outset of SALT II negotiations in 1972, Kissinger established why launcher equality mattered: "Our SALT Two agreement can't result in serious inequalities in numbers of delivery vehicles, if *for no other reason* than those other countries *will look at these differences* and assume we are inferior. Therefore, it will affect our foreign policy."[66] Thus, from the very beginning status concerns limited the negotiating options available. However, as Kissinger's use of the word "serious" implied, he believed that there was wiggle room at the margins to offset slight differences in launchers with inequalities in other areas. While Kissinger was skeptical about prioritizing equality in aggregates above all else, he nonetheless accepted the necessity to *appear* to offset inequality in aggregates with inequality in MIRVed missiles,

---

[65] International audiences are referred to rather vaguely in the SALT archives, but it is reasonable to infer that these were primarily NATO allies in Europe, which the so-called U.S. nuclear umbrella was supposed to protect.

[66] Minutes of a Meeting of the National Security Council, Washington, March 8, 1973, 10:10–11:30 a.m., *FRUS 1969–1976*, vol. 33, p. 50.

188 THE GRAMMAR OF STATUS COMPETITION

even if it were "superficial."[67] Thus, with Nixon's and then Ford's blessing, Kissinger would float several such deals to the Soviets.[68] However, through the course of 1973 and the first half of 1974 it became apparent that the Soviets were not willing to offset inequality in launchers with inequality in MIRVs to the extent that the U.S. side wanted.[69] Instead, by 1974 the Soviets were proposing what the U.S. side agreed to be a strategically unimportant inequality in launchers together with equal limits on MIRVs.[70] At this point it is worth asking why the U.S. side considered it worthwhile to insist upon offsetting or removing a strategically trivial difference at all.

To be sure, Kissinger himself was open to allowing the Soviets slightly more launchers but with an equal MIRV limit, but pressure from the military saw that this was ruled out. By mid-1974 there was what amounted to a united front among the military bureaucracies against accepting even trivial differences in aggregate numbers. Kissinger considered their arguments "shoddy" and wrote in memorandum to President Ford that despite Defense Secretary Schlesinger's, the JCS's, and Senator Jackson's demand for "absolute equality in the number of central system launchers," he did "not believe the Congress, the American people, or our Allies have such a simplistic view of the strategic balance that they ignore all considerations other than the number of missiles and bombers."[71] Yet, a fortnight later, with public criticism of SALT mounting domestically and because of the latent threat by the military to publicly oppose any deal with unequal aggregates,[72] Kissinger

[67] Memorandum from the President's Assistant for National Security Affairs (Kissinger) to President Ford, Washington, n.d., *FRUS 1969–1976*, vol. 33, pp. 375.

[68] For instance, Note from the United States to the Soviet Union, Washington, n.d. [circa March 1974], *FRUS 1969–1976*, vol. 33, pp. 211–212. During these early days, the military and its bureaucracies were also open to the idea of slight inequality in aggregates but provided the Soviets accepted equality in throw weight at a level equivalent to the United States. This was an extremely one-sided offer that would have required the Soviets to completely restructure their nuclear forces and stop several programs, while the United States would need to change little of their existing program. It was thus not surprising that the Soviets rejected this idea out of hand.

[69] Memorandum of Conversation Oreanda, June 30, 1974, 3:15–5:45 p.m., *FRUS 1969–1976*, vol. 33, p. 278–289. The argument here is not that the Soviets would pay *any* price for unequal aggregates in launchers; the negotiations strongly suggest that they considered equality in MIRVs to be important too. Yet as the Schlesinger quote above indicates, at the higher levels being discussed equality in MIRVs was also partly a symbolic concern.

[70] Memorandum from the President's Assistant for National Security Affairs (Kissinger) to President Ford, Washington, n.d. [circa October 1974], *FRUS 1969–1976*, vol. 33, p. 375.

[71] Memorandum from the President's Assistant for National Security Affairs (Kissinger) to President Ford, Washington, October 18, 1974, *FRUS 1969–1976*, vol. 33, p. 345.

[72] As Kissinger explained forlornly to Ford, "[T]he arguments [for equal aggregates] were shoddy, but they have put you in a box. You will be accused of moving under pressure at my advice, misusing the NSC system, and that you could have had a better deal by waiting six months." Memorandum of Conversation, Washington, October 8, 1974, 9 a.m., *FRUS 1969–1976*, vol. 33, p. 338.

SYMMETRY OVER STRATEGY 189

and Ford succumbed to the military's theory of status. It is in this context that Kissinger sent a memorandum to Ford during the preparations for the Vladivostok Agreement that stated explicitly the perceived payoff of insisting upon equal aggregates:

> [The] aggregates in Brezhnev's proposal essentially comes down to 2400 launchers for the Soviets versus 2200 for the U.S. In strategic or programmatic terms, such an arrangement would present few difficulties; the problem with it is *political* in that it might not provide the "perception of equality."[73]

Beyond the fact that, by his own account, the difference was of negligible strategic value, it is crucial to note how by this point equality could not be rough, but had to be *exact* to the final detail. The appearance of equality in aggregates had become all or nothing. As a result, the equality in aggregates took on a value quite independent from and disproportionate to what were considered to be its military implications. This seemingly curious obsession with equal numbers—down to the final launcher—makes sense from a status perspective, as Wohlforth (2009, p. 33) notes: "Once linked to status, easily divisible issues that theoretically provide opportunities for linkages and side payments of various sorts may themselves be seen as indivisible and thus unavailable as avenues for possible intermediate bargains." Rather than being able to bargain away a trivial difference in number, the United States was stuck insisting upon it. As I will elaborate further, U.S. insistence on equal aggregate launchers would hold up the negotiation process and deprive the United States of a bargaining chip that could have been used to attain other goals.[74]

To make the claim that the high social value—international and domestic audience perception of equality depended upon the nuclear aggregate—emerged out of SALT I and was *the* salient reason for insisting upon numerical equality, we must address a looming counterargument. One could try to argue that the external strategic situation had caused this change: because the Soviets had not yet developed MIRVs and because bombers were excluded

---

[73] Memorandum from the President's Assistant for National Security Affairs (Kissinger) to President Ford, Washington, n.d. [circa October 27, 1974], *FRUS 1969–1976*, vol. 33, p. 374.

[74] Although the Soviets were clearly not willing to accept unequal MIRVs in return for unequal launchers, there were other goals that the United States could have pursued, such as limits on heavy MIRVed missiles (see below).

190 THE GRAMMAR OF STATUS COMPETITION

from the aggregate, the United States could more readily accept inequality at SALT I.[75] However, this argument cannot explain why the United States did not just insist upon equal aggregates in *MIRVed* missiles rather than equal ·aggregates in all missiles. Indeed, this option was feasible in terms of verification and openly considered.[76] As Kissinger explained to Ford, "On the Soviet side, the extra 200 launchers they would be permitted would consist entirely of unMIRVed missiles, since neither side could have more than 1320 MIRVed missiles."[77] He added, "Given the tremendous difference in military capability between MIRVed missiles and single warhead missiles, these 200 launchers would be worth very little in strategic terms."[78] At this point, one might expect that the United States could try to leverage the fact that the Soviets were pushing for a strategically trivial advantage in aggregate numbers. Instead, Kissinger advised the opposite: "Nevertheless, given the adverse political reaction you might suffer if you accepted this disparity in launchers, I believe we must press Brezhnev to accept numerical equality."[79]

The discussions in the NSC during the run-up to Vladivostok provide even more specifics on what was theorized to be the value of equal aggregates in launchers vis-à-vis MIRVs. Interestingly, ensuring relative equality in MIRVed missiles was *not* considered by the military to be a priority. At an NSC meeting prior to Vladivostok Defense Secretary Schlesinger, a longtime advocate of equal launcher aggregates, specified what constituted the relative value of equality in launchers versus equality in MIRVed missiles. Echoing the nuclear sufficiency discourse of McNamara, he argued, "Once you are

[75] It is worth noting that while the Soviets were catching up with MIRVs, the United States had developed a new qualitative advantage in cruise missiles that allowed their long-range bombers to penetrate the Soviet air defenses in a manner they had not been able to do previously.

[76] One might be tempted to suggest that given the problems with verifying MIRVs counting the balance via launchers was a practical solution to the counting problem. However, the national means of verification by satellite had reached the point where the United States could distinguish between missile types and which ones had been tested with MIRVs. The final agreement was thus able to keep a MIRV sublimit within the launcher limits by assuming that whatever missiles had been tested with MIRV and deployed were counted as MIRVed.

[77] Meanwhile, even to reach 2,200, according to Kissinger, the United States would "have to retain some combination of 224 obsolete Polaris missiles and B-52 bombers. To go above 2200, we would have to retain even more obsolete systems (at high operating costs), or build additional Tridents and B-1s (at very high procurement costs)." Memorandum from the President's Assistant for National Security Affairs (Kissinger) to President Ford, Washington, n.d. [circa October 27 1974], *FRUS 1969–1976*, vol. 33, p. 375.

[78] Memorandum from the President's Assistant for National Security Affairs (Kissinger) to President Ford, Washington, n.d. [circa October 27, 1974], *FRUS 1969–1976*, vol. 33, p. 375.

[79] As the next section will suggest, among the casualties of prioritizing equal aggregates was the administration's prior strategic goal to seek equal throw weight and to stop the Soviets from developing heavy missiles that could threaten U.S. ICBMs.

over about 600 to 700 MIRVed missiles, the additional 300 have considerably less value. I would be less inclined to trade off the visually very important equality in aggregates to get 300 less MIRVed missiles. . . . If the U.S. is perceived as being unequal in numbers, it would be very harmful. But the political perceptions are not so strong on numbers of MIRV missiles."[80] In other words, Schlesinger argued that the extra MIRVs would only make the rubble bounce. Therefore, although MIRVed missiles were several times more powerful and generally had more strategic utility than unMIRVed missiles,[81] beyond the 700-missile threshold diminishing returns rapidly set in. Therefore, because superiority in launchers aggregate was more symbolically valuable domestically and internationally, it would be worthwhile to accept relative inferiority in MIRVed missiles for relative numerical superiority in total aggregates.

Ultimately, maintaining equality in launchers had taken on a higher social value between SALT I and SALT II. However, this higher estimation was not constituted by new military utility but by new appreciation—consensus around a theory—of how domestic and international audiences would perceive any agreement with unequal aggregates. The fallout from SALT I, both domestically and internationally, had established the salience of "equality" and the audience's preferred means of measuring it: launchers. In this way, domestic and international audiences set the rules of the superpowers' nuclear status competition.

Symmetry over Strategy: Reaching an Agreement at Vladivostok

President Ford did not take any chances with international or domestic perceptions and insisted on both equal aggregates of MIRVed and unMIRVed missiles going into Vladivostok. The agreement established that the United States and the Soviet Union would be permitted a total of 2,400 launchers, with no more than 1,320 MIRVed missiles. Estimating the opportunity costs of prioritizing symbolic equality by pursuing equality of launchers requires

---

[80] Minutes of a Meeting of the National Security Council, Washington, October 7, 1974, 2:55–4:35 p.m., *FRUS 1969–1976*, vol. 33, p. 332. Schlesinger himself considered equality in throw weight (together with a limit on aggregates) to be the optimum measure, but by this point in the negotiations this would be ruled out as unrealistic.

[81] Because of their capacity to overcome ABMs and the fact that one missile could take out several missiles, they were far more suitable for a counterforce strike.

192   THE GRAMMAR OF STATUS COMPETITION

counterfactual analysis. Reviewing the process of the negotiations, I argue that U.S. insistence upon equal aggregates (a) delayed the negotiations and ultimately the signing and (b) sacrificed other strategic goals in order to insist upon strict numerical equality. However, for this counterfactual to be plausible, it is necessary to demonstrate that the U.S. negotiators were aware that the Soviets prized the symbolic value of numerical advantages.

First of all, it is clear that the U.S. administration believed the Soviets placed a high value on aggregate launchers because it was believed to be crucial to maintain the *perception* of strength. The following snippet of conversation between the chief U.S. SALT negotiator, Secretary of State Kissinger, and Defense Secretary Schlesinger at a national security meeting in the months leading up to the Vladivostok summit illustrates how this idea was accepted across key actors on the U.S. side of the SALT negotiations:

AMBASSADOR JOHNSON: They [Soviets] will always choose the higher aggregates.[82] They want a perception of a higher aggregate—
SECRETARY SCHLESINGER: Exactly the reason why we want equal aggregates.
SECRETARY KISSINGER: I think they want the perception of the higher aggregates more for their own internal bureaucracy rather than for third countries.[83]

Among the president and his leading staff, the Soviet concern for the appearance of strength was taken as commonsensical. In the background papers and in Verification Panel and NSC meetings, when the Soviet position and objectives were discussed, their concern for "appearing ahead"[84] and for "visible military power,"[85] and their "obsession"[86] with equality were frequent refrains. Moreover, the NSC discussed positions prior to Vladivostok that recognized that some negotiation advantages could be gained from allowing the Soviets to have a trivial lead in aggregate launchers. After floating two

[82] In this context, it is clear they are referring to aggregate launchers, not MIRVs.
[83] Minutes of a Meeting of the National Security Council, Washington, October 18, 1974, 3:40–5:45 p.m., *FRUS 1969–1976*, vol. 33, p. 364.
[84] Minutes of a Meeting of the National Security Council, Washington, March 8, 1973, 10:10–11:30 a.m., *FRUS 1969–1976*, vol. 33, p. 50.
[85] Memorandum Prepared in the Central Intelligence Agency, Washington, May 3, 1977, *FRUS 1969–1976*, vol. 33, p. 711.
[86] For instance, one national intelligence memorandum argued about the Soviets, "In their view, the SALT process is one of the means for: —registering and reinforcing the *co-equal superpower status* of the USSR; —keeping the Soviet Union in the forefront of US foreign policy and security concerns." National Intelligence Memorandum 1 NIM 77-025, Washington, September 19, 1977, *FRUS 1969–1976*, vol. 33, p. 760, my emphasis.

SYMMETRY OVER STRATEGY   193

negotiating position options with "offsetting asymmetries"—allowing the Soviets a lead in total aggregates in return for a lower limit on MIRVs— the first advantage Kissinger outlined was "that it may be more negotiable than equal aggregates."[87] The major downside was that "unequal aggregates might mean that some would perceive a U.S. inferiority."[88] In short, Kissinger considered it easier to negotiate because he believed the Soviets valued the perception of superiority. Ultimately, President Ford chose to insist upon equal aggregates of launchers *and* equality in MIRVs, thus forgoing the gains that might have been available by leveraging Soviet preferences for a symbolic lead in launchers not offset by a symbolic inequality in MIRVs.

Beyond merely slowing down the negotiations, other strategic goals were sacrificed in order to prioritize strict numerical aggregates. From the outset of SALT II, the U.S. Verification Panel and NSC meetings had frequently expressed the goal of stopping or at least limiting the deployment and/or MIRVing of the Soviet SS-18 heavy ICBMs.[89] The heavy ICBM was considered strategically important because it could potentially deliver high-yield warheads that the U.S. military believed would be capable of breaching the hardened silos of U.S. ICBMs. Indeed, the vulnerability of U.S. ICBMs was a long-term matter of strategic concern and fueled public anxiety about a threat of a first strike (e.g., Nitze 1976, pp. 220–222). Given that prior to Vladivostok, both back stage and front stage, the administration had set a goal to ban or at least limit these weapons, it is all the more remarkable— and indicative of the high symbolic value they attached to exact equality in numbers—that when the issue arose at Vladivostok the United States chose not to press home the issue even when it appeared the Soviets were divided.[90] Instead they preferred to prioritize equal aggregates on total launchers with an equal limit on MIRVs.[91] Nonetheless, the administration was delighted by the outcome. In the NSC meeting a fortnight following Vladivostok the consensus among participants—somewhat unusually—was that the outcome was a triumph. As Ford put it, "The main accomplishment [of Vladivostok] was that we went from nonequivalence to equivalence. We agreed on a limit

---

[87] Minutes of a Meeting of the National Security Council, Washington, October 18, 1974, 3:40–5:45 p.m., *FRUS 1969–1976*, vol. 33, p. 360.
[88] Minutes of a Meeting of the National Security Council, Washington, October 18, 1974, 3:40–5:45 p.m., *FRUS 1969–1976*, vol. 33, p. 360.
[89] It had also been a matter of public concern for conservatives (Caldwell 1991, p. 285).
[90] Memorandum of Conversation, Vladivostok, November 24, 1974, 10:10 a.m., *FRUS 1969–1976*, vol. 33, p. 383.
[91] Memorandum of Conversation, Vladivostok, November 24, 1974, 10:10 a.m., *FRUS 1969–1976*, vol. 33, p. 384.

194 THE GRAMMAR OF STATUS COMPETITION

of 2400 on the aggregates and 1320 on the number of MIRV missiles."[92] In short, the long-term strategic goal of limiting the MIRVing of large ICBMs had been sacrificed to pursue the symbolically important equality in launchers. There is a certain irony that the U.S. administration considered the Soviets to have an "obsession with equality" yet were blind to the social value they placed on the same thing.[93] As we saw, the United States could have pursued strategic goals more effectively or tied up an agreement sooner had they not prioritized the symbolic value of relative numerical equality.

Downstream Costs of Equality

The cost of insisting upon exact equality in aggregates did not end at Vladivostok. It would take another four years for the SALT II treaty to be finalized and signed. Partly this was because nailing down the technical questions of verification, definitions, and when and how to count the aggregate were extremely complex. However, the obsession with the perception of equality in launchers would make negotiations on what to count in the aggregate far harder than they needed to be. Most notably, the JCS and Defense Secretary Schlesinger threw a major wrench into the works by insisting upon counting the Soviet Backfire bomber in the aggregate despite intelligence showing it would have only a "peripheral, non-strategic role."[94] Echoing the debate around the value of 200-unMIRVed missiles in the run-up to Vladivostok, the argument for counting the Backfire in the aggregate turned around how it would be perceived rather than fears about its implications for the military balance.[95] As Kissinger put it, "[I]n

[92] Minutes of a Meeting of the National Security Council, Washington, December 2, 1974, 10:40–11:35 a.m., *FRUS 1969–1976*, vol. 33, p. 393.

[93] Memorandum from William Hyland of the National Security Council Staff to Helmut Sonnenfeldt of the National Security Council Staff, *FRUS 1969–1976*, vol. 33, p.112.

[94] Memorandum from Jan Lodal of the National Security Council Staff to Secretary of State Kissinger, Washington, November 30, 1974, *FRUS 1969–1976*, vol. 33, p. 390. The Backfire was a new Soviet bomber which U.S. intelligence estimated could reach the United States on a one-way mission. While the Soviets disputed U.S. estimates of its range, even if it could reach the United States, its strategic value was extremely limited. Memorandum from the President's Assistant for National Security Affairs (Brzezinski) to President Carter, Washington, March 18, 1977, *FRUS 1969–1976*, vol. 33, p. 669.

[95] Kissinger would later put it bluntly: "The dilemma is that if we don't count the Backfire, we have a political problem within the US. If we do count it we have a negotiating problem with the Soviets." Minutes of a Meeting of the National Security Council, Washington, September 17, 1975, *FRUS 1969–1976*, vol. 33, p. 465. As the minutes show, the United States would end up making it a negotiating problem for four years before giving in and accepting they would have to tackle the political problem of not including it in aggregates.

theory we can make an overwhelming case that these 100 are not strategic bombers." Yet the case for counting Backfire did not rest upon strategy, as Schlesinger made clear: "On Backfire, equal aggregates were obtained at Vladivostok and everyone recognized that. We must be careful to *not appear* that they can now escape from that. If it becomes open-ended, we will lose the advantage of equal aggregates."[96] Much to Kissinger's chagrin, domestic perceptions of equality were being used to drive and thereby limit the U.S. SALT strategy again.[97] As Kissinger wrote in a memo to Ford in 1975, "Disturbingly, the Backfire has become something of a public issue, and the longer the issue drags on the more people will dig in their heels and claim it is a heavy bomber."[98] Kissinger's prediction would prove prescient: whether to count Backfire would become a major point of contention in both the Ford and Carter administrations.[99] Though the United States never did get close to persuading the Soviets to count it in the aggregate,[100] their persistent attempts to do so would succeed in enraging the Soviets and wasting considerable negotiating time and energy.

Curtailing the Dove's Flight

With the election of Jimmy Carter in 1976, *ceteris paribus* one might have expected that a president who explicitly supported disarmament and opposed nuclear weapons would make arms control negotiations easier. Instead, President Carter set back the process months, if not years. To a large extent the archive material supports the conventional narrative for how Carter's

---

[96] Minutes of a Meeting of the National Security Council, Washington, July 25, 1975, 4:15–5:37 p.m., *FRUS 1969–1976*, vol. 33, p. 349, my emphasis.

[97] Although this chapter is concerned only with legitimation, it is worth noting that some explicitly doubted the military motivations in insisting on counting Backfire. Message from the President's Assistant for National Security Affairs (Scowcroft) to Secretary of State Kissinger, Washington, January 22, 1976, *FRUS 1969–1976*, vol. 33, p. 572.

[98] Memorandum from the President's Assistant for National Security Affairs (Kissinger) to President Ford, Washington, n.d. [circa July 1975], *FRUS 1969–1976*, vol. 33, p. 434.

[99] Like the previous administration, Carter also considered Backfire's importance to be of crucial symbolic importance for the public: "The Backfire is politically almost as important as all the rest of the issues put together. Nothing equals it for Congress and the public. Other issues are more important militarily and strategically. But the whole tone of how we enter SALT III and the progress we make will be shaped by Backfire." Memorandum of Conversation, Washington, September 2, 1978, 9–10 a.m., *FRUS 1969–1976*, vol. 33, p. 872.

[100] They would settle instead for a unilateral declaration containing assurances that Backfire was a medium-range bomber, that the Soviets would not extend the capacity of the Backfire such that it could conduct intercontinental missions, and that they would not increase its production rate. *FRUS 1969–1976*, vol. 33, pp. 943–945.

196 THE GRAMMAR OF STATUS COMPETITION

administration inadvertently hindered SALT II and why it was ultimately never put before the Senate for ratification (Caldwell 1991). For instance, the archives indicate that the transition brought about a loss of expertise and institutional memory that disrupted the negotiation process. In particular, the transition made possible Carter's opening faux pas, which called for far deeper cuts to the overall aggregates than had hitherto been agreed at Vladivostok.[101] It is easy to see in retrospect how he stumbled into this and why the Soviets took umbrage. The Carter team then wasted considerable time and effort arguing with the Soviets over whether to count cruise missiles launched from bombers as MIRVed missiles, unaware and unable to believe that they were reneging on what had been suggested by the previous administration.[102] The conventional story has it that all this dawdling led to external events catching up with the administration (the Soviet invasion of Afghanistan). Had the administration moved faster, they would likely have been able to get SALT II through Congress (Caldwell 1991).

I do not disagree but would add that the whole process was also hindered by President Carter's insistence on equal aggregates. Indeed, early in the process the president established a priority of equal aggregates using the language of "balance." Again, this was explicitly domestically driven; for instance, he said in 1977, "[W]e must maintain an overall balance in order for the American people and Congress to accept it. It has to be balanced."[103] This was also explicitly the rationale the Carter administration used when trying to legitimate the treaty to the public following the signing. If anything, Carter questioned the requirement for equal aggregates less than his predecessors did. Unlike the previous administrations, which had frequently brought the matter up for discussion, the archives show no evidence that anything other than equal aggregates was ever considered by the Carter administration. Indeed, it appears that by 1976 equality had been specified and reified as the standard by which the treaty would be judged. Thus, although President

---

[101] Memorandum from President Carter to Secretary of State Vance and the Director of the Arms Control and Disarmament Agency (Warnke), circa September 9, 1977, *FRUS 1969–1976*, vol. 33, pp. 758–759.

[102] See President Carter discussing how he saw no record of the idea of counting ALCM-equipped bombers as MIRVs: Memorandum of Conversation, Washington, September 23, 1977, 10:30 a.m.–1:30 p.m., *FRUS 1969–1976*, vol. 33, p. 767. Yet, the NSC meeting of 1976, for example, reports an offer to "count heavy bombers with 600–2500 kilometer ALCMs in the 1320 MIRV ceiling." Minutes of a Meeting of the National Security Council, Washington, July 30, 1976, 9:30–11 a.m., *FRUS 1969–1976*, vol. 33, p. 623.

[103] Memorandum of a Meeting of the National Security Council, Washington, March 22, 1977, 4–5:25 p.m., *FRUS 1969–1976*, vol. 33, p. 674.

SYMMETRY OVER STRATEGY   197

Carter certainly strove for the goal of fewer nuclear weapons, he had a priori ruled out the only negotiating chip he could have used for achieving it.

To be sure, the U.S. demand for equality did not directly jeopardize its security,[104] but it added a major additional hindrance to arms control. As Nitze stated in the preliminary SALT II meetings, the United States was attempting to achieve "equality in reality *and* in appearance."[105] Clearly, they were not the same thing. Moreover, negotiating a deal that *appeared* equal was an additional complicating factor that became a constant sticking point with the Soviets. Thus, although there remained considerable technical and political labor to come on how to define "equal" and what should be included in the aggregate, the status value attached to relative equality in launchers prestructured this wrangling and thus dramatically slowed negotiations.

Relative Gains and "Winning" the Negotiations

Another crucial mechanism by which status concerns hindered and held up negotiations was that the negotiations themselves became constituted as a sporting contest. Not unlike how Onuf (1989, p. 283) suggests the Cold War became treated as a "contest and spectacle—an *unending* tournament" with several rounds of play, so too did SALT become treated as a sport or a game[106] in which there had to be winners and losers who would enjoy public acclaim or suffer public shaming accordingly. This is certainly how President Nixon believed that international and especially domestic publics understood SALT:

> Needless to say, as you recall, after our China trip, they took a communiqué, which had very little to do with substance, but the whole—but many said, "Who won? Who lost?" Well, in a way because that was a good deal for both

---

[104] Though assessing matters in retrospect and more broadly, the failure of SALT II probably contributed to the decline of detente, the rise of Reagan, and the onset of the "second Cold War."

[105] Minutes of a Meeting of the Verification Panel, Washington, August 15, 1973, 3:04–4:31 p.m., *FRUS 1969–1976*, vol. 33, p. 105.

[106] It should be noted that various administrations also constituted the negotiations through sporting metaphors: poker, baseball, football, and even tic-tac-toe. However, the tic-tac-toe reference, unlike the others, was used to stress the potential pointlessness of the arms race. Smith uses it to warn of danger if they fail to get an ABM agreement: Conversation among President Nixon, the Chief of the Delegation to the Strategic Arms Limitation Talks (Smith), and the President's Deputy Assistant for National Security Affairs (Haig), Washington, March 21, 1972, *FRUS 1969–1976*, vol. 32, p. 732.

198 THE GRAMMAR OF STATUS COMPETITION

sides. But, in this instance, this is a highly substantive matter, as you know. And everybody is going to be watching the darn thing. *Who won? Who lost?* Is the United States in an inferior position to the Soviet Union? Did we get, you know, suckered here by these people and the rest?[107]

As President Nixon complained to his Deputy Assistant for National Security during SALT I negotiations, not only did the United States have to worry about getting a deal "that is sound" but "that about half of this battle— maybe a little more than half—it's got to appear that way. It's got to appear that way."[108]

A similar symbolic cost emerged around making concessions. Not only did the U.S. negotiating team need to consider whether a concession would be worthwhile, but they needed to consider how making concessions from earlier positions would look to the public. Rather than setting out a bold negotiating position that the administration could fall back from, Kissinger was explicitly concerned with avoiding providing "a check list for opponents if there is any deviation" as it "would just give them examples of how we had caved."[109] Rather than assessing the final deal on its merits, the prior history in the negotiation would be used to make a scorecard to assess who "won." President Carter would discover this to his cost, after he had initially proposed new reductions to the Soviets that went far beyond the limits agreed at Vladivostok. As his security advisor explained in a private memorandum in 1977:

> First, the most dangerous dimension of the current campaign of criticism—
> and, in fact, the engine which powers so much of the anxiety and attacks—
> is the argument that we were forced to make concession after concession
> and gave up far more than we got. The Moscow proposal is generally held
> up as the measure of how far we have collapsed. For much of the public
> and many on the Hill, this is the level at which they evaluate what has been
> done—not the specifics of the agreement.[110]

---

[107] Conversation among President Nixon, the Chief of the Delegation to the Strategic Arms Limitation Talks (Smith), and the President's Deputy Assistant for National Security Affairs (Haig), Washington, March 21, 1972, *FRUS 1969–1976*, vol. 32, p. 721, my emphasis.

[108] Conversation among President Nixon, the Chief of the Delegation to the Strategic Arms Limitation Talks (Smith), and the President's Deputy Assistant for National Security Affairs (Haig), Washington, March 21, 1972, *FRUS 1969–1976*, vol. 32, p. 723.

[109] Minutes of a Verification Panel Meeting, Washington, November 23, 1973, *FRUS 1969–1976*, vol. 33, p. 135.

[110] Memorandum from the President's Assistant for National Security Affairs (Brzezinski) to President Carter, Washington, November 4, 1977, *FRUS 1969–1976*, vol. 33, p. 793.

SYMMETRY OVER STRATEGY   199

Compounding and constituting the cost of concessions was a masculinized discourse of needing to "display toughness" and avoid looking weak.[111] The upshot of this was an outsized and even perverse obsession with details. Concerned with limiting relative losses on the record, the negotiators often spent time haggling over what both sides recognized as trivialities. For instance, Kissinger freely admitted to the Soviets that their nearly obsolete diesel-powered submarines were of trivial strategic significance, but he explained that the United States could not let it go because of how it would look to their domestic critics.[112] Later, when the Carter administration was trying to finalize SALT II, a sticking point became whether the United States would be allowed to have 27 or 28 cruise missiles on a bomber. In a moment of gallows humor, Andrei Gromkyo made fun of the trivial nature of the Soviet and American disagreement, saying the "difference was so slight that the public would be amused if it were published."[113] The irony here is that a significant part of why the United States was such a stickler for details stemmed from trying to ensure that the record would show how strongly they had held to their positions and how they fought to avoid concessions, no matter how trivial.

In the latter stages of SALT I President Nixon explained why the details mattered. He stressed that his administration needed to be prepared for domestic opponents to undertake "a great exercise in nit-picking—who won, who got suckered, etc."[114] As his use of game theory language neatly illustrates, the major risk of relative losses was social as well as strategic: not only did U.S. administrations need to avoid *being* the sucker, but they needed to avoid *looking like* the sucker too. It is extremely difficult to evaluate exactly the relative effect of the social pressure to avoid the status of the sucker post-SALT. A conservative conclusion would be that at the very least it slowed down negotiations. Given that the conventional wisdom for why SALT II failed is timing, this is not an insignificant finding.

---

[111] Memorandum from the President's Assistant for National Security Affairs (Brzezinski) to President Carter, Washington, November 16, 1977, *FRUS 1969–1976*, vol. 33, p. 795.

[112] Whether and how to count the diesel submarines with short-range missiles was debated at some length, with the Soviets and backstage U.S. meetings. See Minutes of a Verification Panel Meeting, Washington, June 7, 1972, 3:04–4:15 p.m.; Conversation among President Nixon, the President's Assistant for National Security Affairs (Kissinger), and Assistant to the President (Haldeman); Memorandum of Conversation, Moscow, May 25, 1972, 5:20–6:35 p.m. and 11:30 p.m.–12:32 a.m., all in *FRUS 1969–1976*, vol. 33.

[113] Telegram from Secretary of State Vance to the White House, Brussels, December 24, 1978, 0038Z, *FRUS 1969–1976*, vol. 33, p. 924.

[114] Memorandum for the Record, Washington, SUBJECT Meeting of the President with the General Advisory Committee on Arms Control and Disarmament, March 21, 1972, 3:00 p.m. in the Cabinet Room, *FRUS 1969–1976*, vol. 32, p. 719.

200 THE GRAMMAR OF STATUS COMPETITION

Summary

Consecutive U.S. administrations theorized several significant social prizes to be at stake at SALT beyond deterrence of the Soviet Union. Reviewing the backstage discussions showed how domestic and international audiences' perceptions of "equality" were crucial for legitimating prioritizing relative aggregate number of missiles in the SALT II negotiations. Yet the rules of this game were not fixed like the Olympics. The notion that the country which had the most launchers was superior or "winning" the nuclear arms race was only one of several alternative ways of evaluating the race. However, the debate that followed the SALT I agreement had the downstream effect of specifying aggregate launchers as the rule by which the SALT II agreement would be publicly evaluated. Moreover, even though the various administrations explicitly doubted the relevance of this measure for strategic calculations, by 1974 the theory became sufficiently salient to legitimate equal aggregates becoming *the* primary objective of SALT II. Thus, out of the public process and backlash against SALT I emerged the theory of status for evaluating SALT II. The goal of "equality" and the zero-sum game it produced were explicitly not legitimated on the grounds of strategic necessity but to ensure international and domestic audiences would not *see* the United States as the sucker of SALT. This then structured the way the consecutive administrations theorized the social prizes at stake in SALT. Ultimately, the emergence of this "equality" rule would lead the United States to take negotiating positions that significantly slowed down SALT II and thus contributed to its ultimate failure.

The chapter provides evidence that can help contest the common notion that the Cold War arms race was primarily a tragedy born of the security dilemma. Instead, I argue that a full account of the post-MAD arms race must include international and domestic status concerns, which produced *additional* social and political costs upon being seen to fall behind in the arms race, quite besides worries about a "bolt from the blue" attack. While the U.S. negotiators were indeed obsessed with relative gains, it was the result of a specific theory of status that had emerged out of the SALT process, the rules of which were to a significant degree of the United States' own making.

To be clear, I am not suggesting that status was prioritized *instead* of deterrence. Rather, I argue that status was prioritized *on top* of deterrence, adding a powerful incentive to prioritize *one particular*—and strategically questionable—means of assessing relative gains, which in turn significantly hindered and slowed the SALT II negotiations. Moreover, the nuclear revolution discourse did not lose all salience. The various administrations frequently expressed confidence that the risk of a Soviet attack was minimal and expressed little outward concern that deterrence would fail if they did not match the Soviets' numbers. Hence, the advocates of numerical equality frequently talked about *perceptions* of strength, *perceptions* of balance, *perceptions* of inferiority. This spoke to a tacit assumption that the United States already had sufficient nuclear capability; it was just that the rest of world and domestic society could not be trusted to understand it. Thus, this chapter contests the way we think of status and security as an "either/or" motivation. Instead, maintaining status *is* what constitutes security when it comes to maximizing influence among allies and keeping the domestic audience happy.

This chapter also allows us to mount a defense of the dogmatic army general of popular imagination. Generals are always preparing to fight the last war, the old aphorism runs. As conservative as they are dogmatic, they prepare to attack on horses when they should practice sitting in trenches. This tendency is usually deemed at best inefficient and at worst tragic. Yet, the preceding analysis can shine a more sympathetic light upon our imaginary generals. Deterring enemies requires they appreciate the implications of waging war. Maintaining allies requires they appreciate the *potential* of one's military power. Indeed, deterrence and deference do not depend upon what would *really* happen in war. Instead, it is social: it depends upon what others theorize would occur, and this may not be the same thing. If your enemies and allies are preparing for the last war, then deterrence of the enemy and ally loyalty will require the prudent general to do so too. Although the U.S. military and secretary of defense accepted that the relative aggregate number of launchers had been rendered moot strategically, because this was the salient criterion by which international and domestic audiences evaluated military position, they could not afford to ignore it. In short, U.S. generals had to prepare for the last war *and* the next war at the same time.

Finally, the chapter highlights the utility of the grammar of status as a framework for analysis. Leaving concern for motivations behind allowed the chapter to zoom in on how the rules and the prizes of the nuclear status competition emerged, were contested, and eventually solidified in U.S. top-level discourse. Of particular theoretical interest here is the term "equality." It highlights how the logic of status competition can come cloaked in seemingly unobjectionable moral language. It scarcely needs mentioning that "equality" as an ideal enjoyed commonsense appeal beyond nuclear affairs.

202 THE GRAMMAR OF STATUS COMPETITION

As Krause and Latham (1998, p. 30) note, U.S. arms control policy discourse embodied a "cultural predisposition to see 'balance' as being inherently good." Yet, Senator Jackson's demand for "equality" in the context of SALT produced a competitive status hierarchy: it constituted the United States as "inferior" while simultaneously legitimating measures to remedy that inequality. Moreover, baked into Jackson's demand was a rule for measuring equality, one that was not only eminently contestable but lacked a strategic rationale. However, rather than attempting to contest the dubious definition of equality and the rules of the game it produced, consecutive administrations preferred to follow and reinforce it instead. Therefore, this chapter showcases how the grammar of status can illuminate the "code words" by which the logic of status competition is invoked, and rules specified, but without the word "status" needing to be uttered as a rationale.

Conclusion

Domesticating "International" Status

This book has tackled the central paradox facing status researchers: status-seeking abounds in world politics, yet the status hierarchies within which status is sought are notoriously difficult to empirically ascertain. Indeed, in laying out the challenge for would-be status researchers, Wohlforth (2009, p. 38) explained why status hierarchies elude the analyst: "Status is a social, psychological, and cultural phenomenon. Its expression appears endlessly varied; it is thus little wonder that the few international relations scholars who have focused on it are more struck by its variability and diversity than by its susceptibility to generalization." This remains the methodological puzzle facing status researchers today: How can we systematically identify international status hierarchies and their effects when we see them?[1] Robert Gilpin (1983, p. 33) indicated the size of the challenge when he argued that the difficulty involved in assessing international status makes it, "ultimately, an imponderable." This book does not aver. Instead, it has sought to make a strength out of this ambiguity: because states, statesmen, and citizens care about and pursue status *despite* its difficulty to assess, I argued we can study international status hierarchies via actors' ponderings of the imponderable. Indeed, states and citizens must grapple with the same status ambiguity with which status scholars struggle. Thus, this book's crucial methodological and theoretical move was to redirect investigations from unobservable international status hierarchies and onto the *theories* of international status (TIS) that states, governments, civil society, and citizens use to make sense of those alleged hierarchies.

I contended that not only is it likely that different states disagree about the nature of international hierarchies and produce rival TIS, but that domestic actors can and do produce divergent theories of their own state's international status. In other words, the ambiguity around international status is productive of rival theories of international status that may be made and

---

[1] And in my case, without reifying the rules of the hierarchy prior to analysis.

The Grammar of Status Competition. Paul David Beaumont, Oxford University Press. © Oxford University Press 2024.
DOI: 10.1093/9780197771808.003.0007

204 THE GRAMMAR OF STATUS COMPETITION

remade and perhaps dwindle in salience within domestic politics. Moreover, and contra the existing literature, I argued that these domestically produced TIS do not require international acceptance to become salient and influential. Instead, they need only be credible to the target audience to help or hinder the legitimation of particular policies.

These theoretical expectations provided the premise and the promise of studying the TIS that domestic actors use and act upon. However, were any one of these TIS internationally hegemonic, my approach would provide only a secondhand means of apprehending status. It would be the equivalent of investigating the outcome of the Olympics by listening to the commentary; it would work, but it would be better to just watch the action live. Therefore, to demonstrate the usefulness of my theoretical assumptions and the value of the approach they inspired, I needed to (1) develop a new framework for identifying actor-defined theories of status and how they change and become contested and (2) illustrate how this approach can provide novel insights into how international status hierarchies affect government policy.

This framework constitutes the primary theoretical contribution of the book. Indeed, the gestalt switch needed to go from studying international status to investigating the *theories* of international status required considerable conceptual labor: changing the locus of action from motivation to legitimation and reconceptualizing international hierarchies as discourse rather than collective beliefs (chapters 1–2). While these moves went a long way to solving the conventional methodological puzzle facing status scholars, they beget a new one: How can such actor-defined theories of status be analyzed systematically if one begins from the premise that status is inherently contestable and open to different interpretations? To meet this challenge, I first narrowed my theoretical concern to one particular type of status dynamic: status competition. I then posited a new framework for identifying its logic as it manifests in discourse: what I called the *grammar of status competition*. To do this, I used the Olympics—the archetypal international status competition—to model the essential features of a status competition and to extract its distinct processual-relational logic. The logic of status competition, I argued, is substantially different from the logics underpinning different types of status-seeking—striving to enter a club and resisting domination.[2] I then theorized three "grammatical units" which, upon utterance,

---

[2] I also distinguished the logic of status competition from other logics of legitimation: abstract-rule following, individual utility maximization, and securitization.

CONCLUSION 205

always instantiate the logic of status competition: relative comparisons, positional identities, and sports metaphors.

This grammar of status provided a heuristic device for identifying concrete theories of international status competition within discourse. It thus enables the systematic empirical study of whether and how such renderings are used to (de)legitimate particular policies within domestic politics. Further, because the grammar of status is contingent upon the relations formed through its grammar rather than the substance of the hierarchy, it opened up the possibility of analyzing change in the rules of the hierarchy. To generate analytical purchase and explore the plausibility of whether and how particular theories of international status changed and/or were contested across time, it was therefore essential that I treated theorizing status competition as a discursive *process*. Thus, the book's empirical chapters investigated the iterative process by which domestic groups theorized the status hierarchy (1) prior to a policy, (2) while it was being undertaken, and (3) how they evaluated it afterward. In particular, I was skeptical about the "rules of the game" remaining constant (as they are in the Olympics).[3] Here the grammar-of-status framework was used to identify how rules of particular hierarchies changed, were contested, or remained stable, and above all, the consequences of these TIS. I used this procedure on three purposefully different cases— Norwegian education policy reforms, Britain's legitimation of the Boer War, and the U.S. negotiating positions during SALT I and II—in order to showcase the transferability of my framework and provide insights into how status hierarchies informed the respective outcomes in each case.

Drawing upon my cases, the next section answers the questions: How does the grammar-of-status framework contribute to the study of status in world politics? What sort of research agenda does a TIS framework enable that was hitherto foreclosed? If one accepts that my grammar-of-status framework did provide useful insights into the cases, I contend that this would have major implications for status research in IR.

Domesticating "International" Status: A Research Agenda

While a TIS approach departs quite radically from the pioneering first wave of status research within IR, it is useful to clarify how it diverges from its

---

[3] Here, the rules remain the same and only position changes as the competition unfolds.

206　THE GRAMMAR OF STATUS COMPETITION

nearest and dearest theoretical antecedents within the second wave and in adjacent research agendas. Although several works theorize the domestic, and sometimes discourse, they still analytically privilege "international" actions in their models. For instance, Steven Ward (2013, 2017a) has done most to lay the groundwork for theorizing and investigating the domestic audiences and discourses. However, Ward's approach is a "second image reversed" theory whereby acts of international denial trigger status concerns in citizens that domestic actors exploit in domestic politics. Further, Ward's approach remains grounded in social identity theory and thus requires inferring motivations.[4] Conversely, my approach has much in common with "international" sociological theories, which are also ambivalent about motivations. Here, international/systemic factors—for example, norms (Towns 2010; Towns and Rumelili 2017) or the rules governing the entrance to international status clubs (Naylor 2018, 2022) or relations of amity/enmity among neighboring countries (Røren 2019)—explain particular status-seeking behaviors. Not unlike Ward's oeuvre is Ann Towns's pathbreaking work on the social pressures exerted by international hierarchies, partly inspired my TIS approach. Towns (2010, 2012) theorizes that international norms produce hierarchies that exert social pressure upon those placed low, thereby explaining how normative change often occurs "from below." My TIS approach shares Towns's foregrounding of rules; however, her theory illuminates general patterns of state behavior and normative change, whereas my TIS approach analytically prioritizes domestic interpretative agency rather than international social pressure. This allowed my framework to illuminate how ambiguity around international hierarchies produces leeway for domestic actors to produce hierarchies of their own making and highlight the diversity of theories of status contesting one another within domestic politics.

Indeed, this book treated international status as a sociological phenomenon (remaining ambivalent about motivations), while at the same time granting causal priority to domestic factors (the discursive reproduction of

---

[4] This also puts blue water between my work and domestic-psychological theories, which explain international status-seeking by reference to domestic factors and psychological needs, for instance, Ann Clunan's theorization of how Russia's status-seeking strategy needed to "fit" with elites' historical conception of Russia's historical role (Clunan, 2008). Clunan relies upon SIT here, and thus the drive to pursue status in the first place is provided by an innate motivation for status. Likewise, Freedman (2015) builds upon social psychology to argue that China has a distinct, domestically produced ontology for comprehending its status in the world and that this explains its status dissatisfaction. Again, the theory explains behavior by reference to internal drives.

CONCLUSION 207

theories about international status) rather than *international* social pressures, acts of recognition, or incentives. While international goings-on are not ignored in my approach, they have no privileged status as a factor informing which particular TIS become influential in domestic politics. Although taking this approach may appear like a lonely enterprise within "status" research,[5] considering thick constructivist frameworks in IR more broadly, I stand in good company. For instance, Lene Hansen's (2006) foreign policy-identity framework bears a close family resemblance;[6] so too does Rebecca Adler-Nissen's (2017) stigma-inspired hierarchy framework. The common analytical move that makes these approaches possible is treating language as productive rather than reflective; this implies that the referent by which actors justify their actions is internal—intertextual—to other discourses rather than necessarily "out there" in international relations. One reasonable objection, then, could be that TIS should not be a priori limited to the domestic: they extend as far as they are found in discourse, and discourses cannot (and should not) be fixed into one level of analysis (Hansen 2006). Of course, discourses can and do cross borders. However, as I argued in the introduction, discourses about national status—like those about national identity—often do not travel well. Thus, pragmatically speaking, a TIS approach is *likely* but not inevitably a primarily domestic framework.[7]

This begs the question: Why and when should status researchers take up a TIS approach? The value of a TIS approach hinges upon the degree of agreement about the nature of international status hierarchies at the domestic level. Where domestic groups have interpretative agency to exploit ambiguities about international status hierarchies, I would expect them to be able to contest and/or remake the rules with consequential effects upon legitimation. Chapters 3–5 demonstrated how we can systematically study this interpretive agency: via longitudinal analysis of domestic discourse. However, my approach will offer less insight when and where the rules of an international status competition are well-defined and accepted, as in the Olympics.

---

[5] Though increasingly less so (e.g., Lin and Katada 2022).

[6] As chapter 2's references should make clear.

[7] My grammar-of-status framework could theoretically be used to analyze any group which exists among more than one other group and undertakes some kind of collective action that requires legitimation. I would argue that international society has some specific features that make it particularly suitable for TIS analysis: the fact that all group members are generally aware of the existence of other groups, consider those groups consequential, yet except for a few select representatives (political class) seldom interact in settings where their respective state's status among other states would be easy to ascertain. Though Svendsen (2022) makes a compelling case for how social media is changing this state of affairs.

208 THE GRAMMAR OF STATUS COMPETITION

In the introduction, I provided a theoretical argument for why agreement about the nature of international hierarchies is likely to be quite rare. While my empirical cases cannot be *generalized*, they do confirm that it is *possible* for rival theories of international status to change, become contested, and influence outcomes in the manner I theorized. As such, these cases would be better understood as "plausibility probes" into whether such an approach is worth pursuing in other cases. In my view, the probe came out positive, and it points toward the fruitfulness of developing a research agenda exploring the emergence, spread, and contestation of rival theories of international status.

The Promise of a TIS Research Agenda

A TIS agenda would both broaden and parochialize the horizons of status research. On the one hand, a TIS approach is humbler about the ontological status of international hierarchies: theories of international hierarchies extend their influence only as far as the discourse within which they are manifested. In this sense, my TIS approach parochializes status research, but also puts it on firmer empirical footing—analyzing discourses rather than beliefs, legitimation rather than motivation. On the other hand, and crucially, investigating TIS expands the range of activities that a status framework can help account for. I will now elaborate why and how this opens up productive avenues for further research. To be clear, my overarching analytical move to investigating TIS can be unmoored from the specific analytical toolkit I developed; it is quite possible to study effects of TIS without using my grammar-of-status framework.

First, a TIS approach can generate analytical traction upon policies that are ostensibly aimed at improving international status yet seem poorly designed to succeed. Trump's "Make America great again" discourse is the paradigmatic example here. Indeed, Trump's theorizing of international hierarchies bears little resemblance to those found in the IR status literature. For instance, the longest-standing status research agenda that investigates how "status deficits" or "discrepancies" prompt feelings of dissatisfaction (Renshon 2016) or frustration (Volgy et al. 2011) would struggle to understand why Americans might find Trump's narrative compelling, given that by their measures the United States receives more than adequate recognition. Moreover, as Trump illustrates, such TIS can be mobilized to legitimate policies that are ill-suited to increase what status scholars consider to

CONCLUSION 209

be international status. A TIS approach overcomes this problem because it allows the empirical study of such status theories and their effects, without requiring international hierarchies to provide the determining referent. In the process, a TIS approach offers the advantage of addressing the riddle of chapter 3: why states seek status even when the international gains are often ephemeral and possibly illusionary. To be sure, higher international recognition is welcome if it comes, but as Trump shows, domestic audiences can take pride and the government can generate legitimacy among its supporters even if international recognition is not forthcoming. In this sense, just like the Brits during the first part of the Boer War (chapter 4), many states may well theorize, compete, and win in status hierarchies partly of their own making. A TIS approach renders such status "illusions" rational, tractable, and amenable to analysis.

Second, a TIS framework provides insight into activities where the policy outcome appears rational by conventional theories yet requires legitimation in reference to status hierarchies. As I have already noted, a great deal of prior status research uses conventional rationalist theories as a baseline and uses status to explain the excess. This produces what I call a *rationalist baseline bias*: it a priori grants conventional rationalist theories privileged status that (especially mainstream security theories) do not warrant.[8] As I showed, by doing a longitudinal analysis and using a status competition ideal-type baseline, the grammar-of-status framework provided useful insights into how theories of status informed outcomes, without relying on a material-rationalist baseline. This procedure allowed me to highlight how references to the PISA hierarchy were necessary to the legitimation of a raft of ostensibly "rational" reforms, as well as how the rules of the superpower nuclear hierarchy became solidified backstage only through the process of negotiating SALT. In short, this TIS approach helps explain the size and shape of policies that one could claim post hoc were conventionally rational, and thus would remain overlooked by first-wave status research that explains only the residue conventional rational theories leave behind. Therefore, "the gap" that TIS can investigate here is as large as the influence that TIS have had upon outwardly rational policies. This will have to await further empirical study, but my hunch is this is a rather large lacuna.

---

[8] My point is not that realism is always wrong; rather the family of realism(s) that constitutes this research agenda does not have a sufficiently strong empirical record of explaining or predicting international relations such that it warrants use as a conventionalized baseline for analysis (see also Lin 2023). See Guzzini (1998), Gusterson (1999), Kratochwil (1993).

210 THE GRAMMAR OF STATUS COMPETITION

Third, a TIS approach dramatically extends the range of domains that a status lens can plausibly be used to account for because it does not require *international* intersubjective agreement to have effects. A TIS approach requires only that the target audience finds the theory of status credible and adequate to (de)legitimate a given activity. This means that we can go beyond broad-brush analysis about the effects of well-established international rankings and investigate how status theories inform action in less well-known policy domains where interstate agreement seems (even) less likely. Further, and counterintuitively, parochializing status research in this manner (limiting it to its discursive manifestations) enables investigating the spread of specific status theories among groups within states, across borders, and potentially to regions. Thus, we can map and attempt to account for the travel of TIS and their effects.

Conversely, a TIS approach also enables the systemic study of the reproduction and contestation of TIS from below. Indeed, if scholars can spot that competing for status is wasteful or undesirable, it is reasonable to assume the domestic groups can too. As my PISA and Boer War cases illustrate, a TIS approach opens up for studying how domestic groups can undermine a state-endorsed status competition, even while other states and domestic groups continue to consider the competition valuable. Thus, by parochializing status research, a TIS approach enables two sorts of questions, illustrated by my PISA case in chapter 4: How do TIS manage to cross borders? How can and how do domestic groups resist TIS? This latter question unlocks the critical potential of status research, hitherto foreclosed in theories that treat the state as unitary or as a human. Indeed, studying how groups within civil society can contest a dominant TIS offers one promising means by which states might escape unhealthy status competitions without requiring international cooperation or accommodation (e.g., Larson and Shevchenko 2010).

Fourth, the empirical chapters provide strong hints that the wielders of various theories of status were using them for other purposes than those written on the tin. Although I foregrounded legitimation rather than motivation in my analysis, there is evidence in each case that those wielding TIS had other motivations beyond striving for status and may not have fully believed in their own theory. For instance, despite claiming in Parliament that Britain's concentration camps were a symbol of its civilizational superiority, the preeminent historian of the war writes that Chamberlain "no doubt" also thought they were "barbarous" (Pakenham 1979, p. 542). Meanwhile, Bergeson's (2006) memoirs on Norway's PISA shock give the impression that

CONCLUSION 211

the first PISA rankings were amplified instrumentally to engineer a shock. Finally, Kissinger and his allies suggested in private that the U.S. military bureaucracy did not believe in the import of equal aggregates but used this theory of status as a "convenient" means to hinder arms control (). In other words, each case alludes to the value of flipping of the normal way IR thinks of status as a hidden motivation; instead, status becomes the publicly legitimate means to achieve other, more subterranean ends. Thus, utilizing a different methodology than I have done here, future research could explore the divergence between TIS wielded in public and the broader, perhaps unstated objectives of the protagonists.

Fifth, a TIS approach broadens the scope of actors that are implicated in international status-seeking. For instance, chapter 4 illuminated how academics played a significant role in legitimating and delegitimating PISA's theory of international status within Norwegian politics. Meanwhile, Emily Hobhouse's critique of the Boer War shows how civil society groups can contest governments' status theory. Indeed, a TIS approach can illuminate civil society and academia's influence upon status dynamics and make it analytically tractable. Ultimately, although it need be central to the analysis, a TIS approach implies scholars pay attention to the role academia and civil society play in reproducing or contesting the theories of status wielded by the government.

Sixth, future research could further develop the grammar-of-status framework I used to identify and analyze domestic policy processes. My grammatical units may not exhaust the means through which activities are framed as a status competition, and the grammar presented here could no doubt be refined. Moreover, future research could also develop a "grammar" of other types of status hierarchy: status clubs and hierarchies of domination. This book focused on identifying how different theories of status *competition* were made and remade over time, and how these theories informed policy legitimation. Leveraging the possibility of disagreement over the nature of the international hierarchy further than I have done here, a TIS approach could analyze how contestation cuts across types of hierarchy. For instance, Brexiteers often present the EU as a prison (Daddow 2019)—a metaphor of domination—while Europhiles tend to theorize the EU as a desirable status club. My suspicion is that TIS pertaining to other types of hierarchies will be less contested at the domestic level because the process of ascertaining whether one is in a club or not is less complex than theorizing where one stands in relative ranking among states. Yet how much value there would be in using a TIS approach to investigate other types of hierarchy is a matter for further research.

Further development of the grammar might prove fruitful because it could address a tacit Eurocentrism in status scholarship. One specific advantage of my framework is that it can identify and "decode" the logic of status competition even when the words "status" and "prestige" are not used. This is useful because of the prevalence of the norm against explicitly using status to legitimate policy (Sagan 1997; Gilady 2018, p. 24). Because this norm is especially prevalent in "Western" countries, it seems to have deflected the gaze of status scholars onto countries where stating explicit status goals is considered acceptable (BRICS).[9] Aiming to remedy this tendency, my framework allows the analyst to identify the logic of status competition as it manifests in discourse even when it is superficially hidden from view: when "status" is not uttered explicitly. For instance, chapter 5's inquiry into the SALT case highlighted how the concept of "equality" enabled various domestic actors to mobilize the grammar of status to legitimate their position and delegitimate alternatives. Similarly, at times Norway's pro-PISA discourse hid the logic of status competition beneath bureaucratic discourse of "value for money."

A Reply to Skeptics

There are a number of critiques that could be raised to this book's core argument and the research agenda that it seeks to inspire. The first is conceptual and almost semantic: *Is it really status that TIS refer to?* I would respond that while TIS do not have any *necessary* relationship to international collective beliefs about rank, neither does the rest of status research. For instance, the status discrepancy research agenda uses the rather convoluted method of ranking countries according to how many embassies they host to generate a proxy for status. While this approach can be justified theoretically, as Macdonald and Parent (2021, p. 367) warn, it is "less plausible" that policymakers use this "baroque" technique themselves for assessing international status. Meanwhile, embassies can be stationed in countries for reasons that have little to do with status (Røren and Beaumont 2019; Mercer 2017). Thus, whatever correlations status discrepancy researchers

---

[9] Although Western countries are not entirely missing from status scholarship, status has proven especially popular for understanding rising powers. This becomes borderline Eurocentric when status concerns in these countries are treated as irrational, thereby reproducing orientalist tropes.

CONCLUSION 213

uncover, it is questionable whether it is really status that is doing the work. Similarly, scholarship that reduces status to club membership suffer from a related problem: "States join clubs for a variety of reasons, too, only some of which may be tied to status aspirations" (McDonald and Parent 2021, p. 8). Thus, even conventional approaches to status struggle to operationalize status by their own definition. While my TIS approach does not solve once and for all these problems, it does provide advantages over conventional approaches. First, it restricts inquiries *only* to international hierarchies that are represented and used by concrete actors in international politics, thus overcoming the proxy problem. Second, and crucially, by insisting on calling them *theories*, TIS build in a helpful scientific humility (see Beaumont and de Coning 2022) about these representations' relationship to real status, which, I agree with Gilpin (1981, p. 33), will always remain to a significant extent imponderable.

If this is the robust defense, there is also a more conciliatory and constructive means of reconciling TIS with prior status work, especially first-wave research. My TIS approach and first-wave status research can be understood as analyzing different aspects of the same phenomenon: (1) the study of the effects of social facts and (2) the study of the construction and contestation of social facts. The first approach is analogous to what IR scholars after Wendt (1999, p. 2), call "thin constructivism"; taking their cue from Durkheim, they recognize that the state, international law, and status are social constructions but suggest that their meaning is sufficiently reified that they can be treated as if they are "things" that have independent effects (Neumann 2004). This concern with the effects of social facts animates most status scholarship, for instance, when they recognize that a military weapon's status value is a social construction but hold that this symbolic value is *sufficiently* stable and shared that it can produce systematic effects: a similar kind of status-seeking among states (e.g., Gilady 2018). Indeed, one could tell a "big picture" status story in each of my cases about how *relatively* stable symbolic hierarchies associated with empires, nuclear weapons, and education led to status-seeking behavior. These would not necessarily be wrong, but as my chapters indicate, they would overlook crucial parts of the story of how status dynamics affected the policy outcomes. My approach follows in the path trodden by thicker constructivist scholarship, which points out that these social facts' stability is an illusion brought about through continuous discursive labor (see Hansen 2006; Campbell 1992; Neumann, 1999; Leira, 2019). Look closely and the facticity of social facts tends to become unstuck, or at least becomes more ambiguous than hitherto assumed. Hence, my chapters zoomed in and showed how status hierarchies that look like "social facts" from a distance and in retrospect were more contested and malleable in practice. Only by paying attention to these processes of contestation and reinterpretation could we get a fuller picture of how status concerns inform domestic policy processes and address major puzzles existing status theories leave unsolved. Finally, my approach opens the door to studying the genesis, reproduction, and change of status hierarchies, which remains a significant gap in existing scholarship (Zarakol 2017; Macdonald and Parent 2021).

Ultimately, I would contend that my TIS approach and conventional status frameworks stand in a productive tension with one another that can help further the IR status research agenda. Indeed, a TIS approach offers a useful empirical check upon the universal theoretical ambitions of first-wave status research. Where this research tends to jump quickly to assuming that status hierarchies are widely shared among states, a TIS approach enables the empirical analysis of where, to what extent, and among whom these status hierarchies are actually shared. In short, a TIS approach's focus on discursive manifestations of status can help *bound* conventional analysis in time and space. While this will certainly humble the more grandiose claims of status scholars, it will also strengthen their empirical basis.

Additionally, critics might also buy the argument that domestic actors in Britain, the United States, and Norway had "interpretative agency" to develop hierarchies of their own making but question whether this is a privilege that poorer or weaker states enjoy. This argument would highlight that while my cases are "deliberately different" in some regards, they are all relatively wealthy Western states that can make plausible claims to ranking high, even if the world does not exactly share their view. Do governments or domestic actors in Somalia share this same privilege? What discursive resources are available to citizens from poorer states to develop TIS that place them above Western states? I would counter that humans have a demonstratable capacity to invent and sustain criteria that enable positive comparisons that run counter to dominant understandings of rank. For instance, if you speak to football fans of less successful teams, they may well acknowledge that other teams have better players and win more—how could they deny this? However, they will also often disparage the fans of successful teams as mere "glory hunters" and express pride in their loyalty to their losers. Meanwhile, many football teams' fans simultaneously claim they have the best "atmosphere," without ever needin it to be settled. Similarly, while poorer states may

CONCLUSION   215

not be able to credibly claim they are superior to Western states based on socioeconomic criteria, they may develop alternative means to stigmatize Western states and valorize the in-group. For instance, religious discourses and relative comparisons of piety may serve this purpose. However, ultimately, I would acknowledge that this book's claims should not be too hastily generalized; instead, the extent to which weaker states can and do develop their own favorable theories of international status should be an empirical and theoretical question for future research.

Finally, some may object to my use of the domestic as an analytical category and accuse me of reifying and reproducing the domestic/international boundary. I would respond that the international/domestic binary is not *a priori* problematic, but only when it is used unreflexively as a convention.[10] That is not what I am doing here; as my introduction argues, there are good reasons to expect that domestic discourse will differ systematically from discourse found in other countries. Put bluntly, different states' domestic discourses are substantially different from one another for the simple reason that most citizens do not care much about international relations in general but have good reasons to care about and pay attention to their own state's relations. Thus, they end up, at a minimum, generally better informed about their own state's policies and history. Further, it is not controversial to assume that in the main governments and opposition tend to seek the approval or at least acquiescence of their citizens first and foremost. Thus, most governments spend most of their time addressing their domestic citizens, even when they are theorizing their state's status in the wider world. Again this provides plenty of leeway for systematic divergences between states ostensibly discussing the same international hierarchy. However, the empirical work in this book can only support the contention that domestic audiences *can* and sometimes do produce rival TIS and that important policies *can* be affected by the results of the contestation over TIS. Whether domestic discourse is the optimal scale to study contests over TIS is an open question; some TIS may be better studied at a regional or even global level. Indeed, with the advent of the internet and global interconnectivity among interest

---

[10] Instead, I am opposed to anarchic/state-centric conceptions of the international becoming *the standard* to which all scholarship must adhere. I think this is what the poststructuralists of the 1980s were taking issue with. I would agree that insofar as realism becomes common sense it risks producing the problems it names (and excluding lots of other problems and questions). However, I do not think realism (or any one state-centric perspective) is dominant or even privileged any more in the discipline. Thus, whether to use the international/domestic distinction can be justified on analytical grounds.

216 THE GRAMMAR OF STATUS COMPETITION

groups, one rival hypothesis to my claim that domestic politics insulates TIS is that political cleavages around TIS may cut across countries. However, this would require further research to substantiate.

The Social Function of Ambiguity

> Ambiguity and heterogeneity, not planning and self-interest, are the raw materials of which powerful states and persons are constructed. (Padgett and Ansell 1993, p. 1259)

To conclude, I will draw out a major counterintuitive policy implication of my research: status ambiguity among states and publics is a social good to be cherished. Indeed, the cases provide preliminary evidence that suggests intersubjective agreement about the international hierarchy is an important condition that facilitates a state's willingness and ability to compete for international status and/or affect the rewards from competing. Put differently: ambiguity around the hierarchy in a given domain hinders states' ability to compete in zero-sum games for status. Status thus becomes a theoretical reason why ambiguity among policymakers has often been considered "constructive." To be clear, I do not claim to be the first to note that status hierarchies are ambiguous, nor that status-seeking is often about pleasing the domestic audience. However, none to my knowledge has identified how these features of international status dynamics in *combination* can provide systematic opportunities for individual states to use in order to please their domestic audience, nor theorized how this may help reduce the prevalence and mitigate the intensity of status competition globally.[11]

The Benefits of Ambiguity and the Costs of Clarity

Across the cases, domestic agreement over TIS fostered status competition. In the run-up to SALT I the lack of agreement about the nature of the status hierarchy and the prizes on offer for "equality" of launchers enabled Kissinger to negotiate a treaty in which the United States accepted possessing fewer

---

[11] A related though somewhat different argument is put forward by Rumelili and Towns (2022), who suggest that the systemic effect of multiple country performance indicators is to generate status ambiguity. This ambiguity undermines the ability for such rankings to foment progressive change.

CONCLUSION 217

launchers than the USSR. However, over the course of SALT II the rules became clarified domestically such that equality was considered essential, and this left the United States obsessed with ensuring equality in number down to the last obsolete submarine. Meanwhile, in Norway lack of agreement over the nature of the international education hierarchy enabled some to claim Norway was best, while others claimed the opposite. As a result, attempts to reform based upon international advice were stymied. Following the PISA status shock, agreement over the "rules of the game" emerged across parties that saw Norway exerting considerable effort to compete in the PISA rankings. However, in the past decade PISA's theory of international education status has become heavily contested, undermining the ability of parties to legitimate competing in PISA. Finally, during the Boer War agreement at the domestic level about the impossibility of letting such a small adversary get away with an ultimatum enabled Britain to compete—via war—to maintain its position. The rules of the game were remade domestically, if not internationally, such that celebration was in order upon victory in the conventional war. However, during the final phase of the war, a rival theory emerged to contest the status value of the war, one that undermined the government's legitimacy and the status value of winning.

Along with domestic ambiguity around "international" status hierarchies, status ambiguity among states was also latent even if it was not foregrounded in the analysis. While mainstream discourse in Britain saw conventional victory as impressive, Mercer and the foreign correspondents reporting in the British press suggest this was far from universal. However, this did not stop Brits inventing a new word for euphoria upon victory. Meanwhile, it seems highly unlikely that anyone other than Norwegians considered their education system the best in the world prior to PISA. Yet the lack of agreement about the hierarchy at an interstate level enabled this idea to persist and remain influential until PISA shocked Norway during the 2000s. And the lack of agreement between the United States and Russia about the nature of the nuclear status competition seems to have allowed both sides to—temporarily—believe they had "won" the SALT I negotiations and reach an agreement sooner than if they had agreed upon the rules of the status game.

Thus, we have theoretical reasons and some provisional evidence to support the claim that the ability of states to legitimate competing in an international hierarchy is undermined by disagreement—ambiguity—about the rules of the game and the nature of the international hierarchy. Conversely, domestic agreement—clarity—about the nature of the international

218 THE GRAMMAR OF STATUS COMPETITION

hierarchy facilitates status competition. I argue that this provides preliminary grounds to make the opposite claim to Wohlforth (2009): ambiguity mitigates and undermines the pressure to compete and potentially allows one to generate internal rewards (pride and legitimacy) without succumbing to the sort of zero-sum competition commonly considered a pathology of status. If this is correct, what are the normative or policy implications?

In Defense of Ambiguity

Ambiguity bedevils IR scholars. Indeed, striving to clarify the ambiguous is a major part of our field's modus operandi. Does nuclear deterrence work (Mueller 1988)? What is the European Union: suprastate, neomedieval empire, normative power, or something else entirely (Diez1999)? What is "the state" anyway: a collection of bureaucracies, an organism or a bundle of sensory impressions (Ringmar 1996)? How can one recognize *recognition* itself (Gustafsson 2016)? To be sure, these are all legitimate puzzles, ones IR has yet to solve. On the other hand, normatively, IR scholars also see ambiguity in social life as a problem. Indeed, when not envying physics, mainstream IR yearns to become more like economics (Hoffman 2009, p. 434). From Waltz's market metaphor to the rational actor assumption embedded within all manner of IR "games," mainstream IR has imported economic theory en masse. Economics doxa has to a large extent become IR (mainstream) doxa. It is perhaps unsurprising, then, that many IR scholars also share economics' tacit normative assumption that perfect information is a dream worth striving for. Economists assume that more information is always better than less; for perfect markets to function they require perfect information so people can efficiently select the product that will maximize their utility. Deviance from this impossible dream provides one common explanation for why markets seldom function like economists' models. Similarly, within mainstream IR, theories abound that blame misinformation, rhetoric, propaganda, misperception for world politics' many ills. The tacit assumption becomes that more and better information among actors and subjects would help international society avoid tension and war and ultimately function smoother. Conversely, in the exception that proves the rule, realists' pessimism about the possibility of acquiring perfect information (at least about the future) underpins what they (self-consciously) recognize as a *pessimistic* outlook on the prospects for peace in world politics. Again, lack

CONCLUSION 219

of information and ambiguity is a curse. Thus, IR scholars typically see ambiguity as an epistemological challenge set by our objects of analysis, or an ontological pathology that causes problems for states.

Yet, security and economics are not the only interests in town. Social hierarchies also produce social pressures and social pleasures that do not operate according to the same logic. Accordingly, ambiguity in the social realm serves a different, oftentimes positive function. This book suggests ambiguity may not be so bad after all. For social groups, and in particular the state, ambiguity about international hierarchies may enable states to keep their populations satisfied and reach international agreements and may even help legitimate their existence. Further, ambiguity about international status at the domestic level will make legitimating competing for it difficult. Indeed, my book suggests that ambiguity about where peoples and their states stand in relation to one another often functions as a social blessing for states rather than a curse. Put theoretically, ambiguity around status helps international society avoid frequent, costly, and inefficient zero-sum status competitions, where to move up, another must move down. In short, ambiguity helps international *society* hang together with less friction and helps states *keep on keeping on* without their people discovering that they are not special.

Ultimately, knowing where one stands may not be all it is cracked up to be. In fact, it might drive people to despair; individuals who are capable of accurately assessing their own abilities are prone to depression.[12] States, at least in this instance, are like people; we should be glad if they do not always agree on the terms by which they should be compared. Indeed, contra the axiom that perfect information and rule agreement are ideals to strive for, socially this may prove a dystopia rather than a utopia.[13]

[12] This is called "depressive realism" in psychology (Moore and Fresco 2012).
[13] While Foucault's concern with the panopticon shares this unease with perfect information, his worry is with *control* and freedom; my argument concerns esteem and social well-being.

APPENDIX

Studying Status via Discourse

Text Selection and Interpretative Procedures

While it is common for academic books to eschew a full discussion of methods for readability, I consider this to be an unhelpful convention that runs counter to science, and specifically the aspiration to make one's research practices as transparent and as trustworthy as possible. This is particularly important for this book, as interpretivist work like this is often critiqued for being unsystematic. Hence, this appendix explains, critiques, and defends my method: what I did, why I did it, and how these choices affect the epistemological basis of my conclusions.[1]

While I am not going to launch a full-blown defense of interpretivism here,[2] a few notes justifying my overall approach are necessary. Following Jackson (2010, p. 22), I share a pluralist definition of scientific research: "systematic production of empirical factual knowledge about political social arrangements." Different *systems* of knowledge production imply that different principles and practices animate "good research." Crucially, interpretative scholarship like mine does *not* share the same tests of validity as neopositivist methods (Yanow and Schwartz-Shea 2015). For instance, interpretivists do not "test" a formal hypothesis against "reality."[3] My approach fits best what Jackson calls "analyticism" in which an ideal type (in this case, my rule-governed status competition) provides the framework for producing explicitly case-specific explanations (Jackson 2010, p. 152). It is not just allowed but desired that through the process of investigation, the research departs from expectations and new concepts and factors necessarily are needed to make sense of the case (Yanow and Schwartz-Shea 2015).[4] Instead of seeking generalizable or falsifiable hypotheses, the claims made should be judged by its "pragmatic consequences for ordering the facts of the world": whether they reveal useful insights into the puzzle under

---

[1] I have chosen to eschew the passive voice because I do not want to feign detachment from the social world I study and create a false illusion of a "view from nowhere."

[2] For those interested, I have made the case at length elsewhere (Beaumont and De Coning 2022) for why maintaining epistemological pluralism (one includes interpretivist methodologies) is necessary to giving scholars the best chance of understanding complex phenomena (such as, but not limited to, world politics).

[3] Not least because the notion of testing a hypothesis presupposes a mind-independent world, which interpretivists reject. For analysts using ideal types the idea of "testing" a deliberately and *ideal* type against the world is especially nonsensical: per definition the ideal would not prove to be an accurate representation of reality. See Jackson (2010, chs. 1, 2, and 5) for an extended explanation. Also see Yanow and Schwartz-Shea (2015).

[4] Instead of formal hypotheses, interpretivists take a more flexible approach: they "begin their work with what might be called informed 'hunches' or puzzles or a sense of tension between expectations and prior observations, grounded in the research literature and, not atypically, in some prior knowledge of the study setting" (Yanow and Schwartz-Shea 2014, p. xvi).

222   APPENDIX

investigation (p. 115). Usefulness, however, depends on having applied the framework proficiently and convincing the reader. As Dunn (2008, p. 92) suggests, for discourse analysis the "goal as a researcher[is] to provide an argument about why my interpretation is valid, so that I can convince others that mine is one of the best interpretations out there." Although interpretivist scholarship does not share the *same* procedure of knowledge production as positivists, it does demand systematic application of "logic and argumentation" (Yanov and Schwarz-Shea 2015a, p. xvi) and that the research process is transparent such that the reader has faith in its "trustworthiness" (Schwartz-Shea 2015, p. 31).[5]

To be clear, then, not everything goes. The standards of interpretivist scholarship demand that a reader be convinced of (a) the internal logic and coherence of my arguments on the page, (b) the *usefulness* and insight they offer, and (c) the proficiency and trustworthiness of the research process. I aimed to account for (a) and (b) via the rest of the book. However, to facilitate (c) (a prerequisite to (a) and (b)), the following sections discuss my research process in the most transparent terms permitted by space constraints. Trustworthiness in this context refers to

> the many steps that researchers take throughout the research process to ensure that their efforts are self-consciously deliberate, transparent, and ethical— that the researchers are, so to speak, enacting a classically "scientific attitude" of systematicity while simultaneously, in the spirit of doubt . . . allowing the potential revisability of their research results. (Schwartz-Shea 2015b, p. 131)

Thus, having already justified my case selection in the introduction, this appendix explains and reflects upon my procedure for gathering, mapping, and analyzing the texts. The following section discusses epistemic limitations of my approach, while also anticipating, countering, but also creating a space for potential criticism. I will also provide a list of my primary sources and how they can be accessed. I conclude by reflecting upon how my position vis-à-vis my subject matter will likely have informed both my work and interpretations of the evidence. By laying my biases on the table like this, I hope to give the reader the best opportunity possible to adjudicate how they have prejudiced my analyses.

Episode Construction and Text Selection

While the grammar-of-status framework helps identify the logic of status competition in discourse, as chapters 1 and 2 explained, I do not expect the ideal of status competition to be reached. Instead, I use the ideal type as a conceptual baseline to model "some of the relevant features of the object or process under investigation" and thus provide "a conceptual baseline in terms of which actual outcomes can be comprehended" (Jackson 2010, pp. 146–147). In particular, I expected that the rules governing the status competitions instantiated in discourse would prove far less fixed than in the ideal "rule-governed" competition for position described in chapter 2. Thus, besides identifying whether the logic of status was at play, the grammar of status operates as a heuristic to *map and trace*

[5] Throughout this appendix I will use interpretivist methodological terminology (e.g., transferability, "trustworthiness," "transparency") in order to avoid the epistemological baggage—built-in presuppositions—of neopositivist methodological criteria (see Schwartz-Shea 2015).

the representations of the rules of status competitions as they *potentially* change across time and/or diverge from the ideal in other ways. In this regard, my grammar of status shares more than a familial resemblance with the work of discourse analysts who use the self/other theory of identity formation to map how identity constructions have changed across time and how they make possible particular practices while precluding others (e.g., Hansen 2006; Neumann , 1999). Part of this reading strategy involved paying heed to alternative explanations, specifically, mapping other patterns of representation related to and justifications for the policy. Crucially, this allowed me to remain open and flexible to assess what other logics of legitimacy were at play, as well as any "incidental factors" that may have affected the outcome (Jackson 2010, p. 170).

While each case is deliberately different in terms of substance, each analysis employed a similar methodology: studying the public legitimation of policies in a particular discursive context. Ascertaining what mattered for legitimation at various points in these processes and sifting through the noise required mining the archives of newspapers, policy documents, parliamentary records, and government speeches (see Table A.1). Moreover, my theoretical expectation was that not only would international hierarchies be implicated in the legitimation process, but that the "rules" of the international hierarchy would emerge, change, become contested, and perhaps solidify rather than remain relatively stable. Therefore, it required that I analyze not only a snapshot act of legitimation of a particular policy but a longer *process* of legitimation.[6] The following documents the reasoning behind the steps I took in each case to delimit the cases, select texts, and construct the analytical narrative.

Chapter 3: Rational Illusions

The first empirical chapter investigates how various theories of international hierarchy and competition were mobilized to (de)legitimate the Boer War (1899–1902) and the U.K. government's undertaking of it. The process that led to my selecting this case was formative to my whole approach. My interest in the Boer stemmed directly from Jonathon Mercer's (2017) well-received article in *International Security*, where he argued that status-seeking is prone to prove futile because rivals have strong incentives to discount each other's achievements. He used the Boer War to illustrate his argument. The article was formative for my work because it illustrated several common shortcomings with contemporary status research. To understand my methodology in this book is to understand what I hold is wrong with Mercer's approach.

Three main[7] theoretical and theoretical-methodological moves by Mercer inspired this book. First, Mercer ignores the value for a government of pleasing their citizens, which underpins his claim that gains from status are a psychological illusion. Second,

---

[6] To reiterate, I would expect—or at least not be surprised by—movement *within* the hierarchy to which my objects of analysis refer. Like a cyclist overtaking her competitor, this is absolutely normal. Instead, I was interested in how the rules of the game, what counts as valuable—so determining winners, losers, and rising and falling—changed in ways consequential to the outcome.

[7] Other problems that are less salient to my book's argument but nonetheless important include Mercer's (1) drawing an unduly sharp distinction between prestige and security that is not supported by the realist thinkers he draws upon and (2) naïve reading of the historical sources whereby he does not consider that political leaders have instrumental reasons to present an optimistic picture of the state's status.

224 APPENDIX

Table A.1 Sources Used for the Case Studies

Document Type	Date	Search Criteria	Via
Chapter 3			
Parliamentary records, Hansard	Key Debates 1899–1902[8]	Searching "Boer" and "South Africa"	Available here: https://hansard.parliament.uk
Times archives	Selected Periods 1899–1902	Searching "Boer" "South Africa"	Available here: www.thetimes.co.uk/archive/
Contemporary literature, e.g., histories, reports, pamphlets, academic writings	1899–1902	Via references in secondary literature and primary sources	Mostly online, but sometimes the physical books.
Chapter 4			
Government education policy documents	2000–2019	Browsing government education archive	Online government archive of government policy documents and reports: Regjeringen.no
Academic articles and books related to PISA	No specific dates	Various search terms using PISA+ plus (education words, Norge/Norway)	Google Scholar and Google
Newspaper articles pertaining to PISA	2000–2019 2004–2006	Articles in VG, Dagbladet, Aftenposten referring to "PISA" "Kunnskapsløftet"	ATEKST – (Online archive of Norwegian Newspapers from 1945-present) Via: www.nmbu.no/om/biblioteket/
Official PISA reports and data, 2001–2019	Browsing of the PISA data and reports	Norwegian results in comparison with the OECD average and other countries	Available here: http://www.oecd.org/pisa/

[8] In particular, the Hansard debates of October 17–20, 1899; January 30–February 7; June 17, 1901; March 14, 1902; June 2–5, 1902.

APPENDIX 225

Table A.1 Continued

Document Type	Date	Search Criteria	Via
Chapter 5			
Official archives pertaining to SALT I and Salt II	1970–1980	SALT I and II minutes of meetings and memoranda deemed significant by Office of the Historian	Available here: https://history.state.gov/
Archives pertaining to general foreign policy of the United States and relations with the Soviet Union	1970–1979		Available here: https://history.state.gov/
New York Times articles pertaining to SALT I and II	Selected periods	Search "strategic arms limitation"	Available here: www.thetimes.co.uk/archive/
Foreign Affairs articles pertaining to SALT I and II	1970–1981	All articles coded "Arms Control"	Available here: www.foreignaffairs.com/issues/archive

he claims divergence between domestic actors' understanding of status can be accounted for by "feelings" rather than analysis. He thereby ignores the political incentives that the politicians faced to put either a positive or a negative spin on the war and instead attempts to infer feelings of pride or shame from words (Mercer 2017, pp. 154–156). He does not consider that alternative discourses may allow for alternative interpretations. (Reasonable people can disagree on many things, especially status.) Third, Mercer treats a three-year war as a single event rather than a process: he tests hypotheses on primary data with little regard to when during the war the person in question was speaking (pp. 154–155).[9] In contrast, my approach uses the grammar-of-status framework to investigate how the status value of the war was retheorized and contested during the war and how understanding these processes can provide an alternative explanation for those "illusions" Mercer deemed irrational.

To analyze how theories of international status affected the legitimation of the war and study the meaning of the war as a process unfolding within domestic discourse, I divided the war into episodes.[10] Here, I mirrored the conventional approach of historians

---

[9] For instance, he compares a speech in November 1900 by the prime minister expressing pride at victory in the conventional war (which ended in September 1899) with quotes from opponents expressing shame at the counterinsurgency tactics of the latter 18 months of the war. As chapter 3 illustrated, treating the whole war as one single event gives a misleading impression of how representations of status legitimated both the war and the government.

[10] I use "episode" here deliberately to indicate analytically separable but interlinked periods that can facilitate intracase comparison.

226 APPENDIX

studying the Boer War by dividing the war into three: (1) the run-up to the war's onset and its legitimation; (2) the legitimation of conventional war from September 1899 to September 1900, when the government had to legitimate sending reinforcements; and (3) the insurgency-guerrilla war that lasted for the next 18 months, until May 1902, when the government had to defend its use of concentration camps. Although it is conventional, my empirical inquiries also indicated that analytically distinct practices of legitimation were at play in these episodes. Therefore, I reasoned that dividing the war in this way would offer a useful analytical device for illuminating how the rules of the status competition changed during the process of war.

Following Hansen's (2006, pp. 53–55) model of foreign policy discourse analysis, I focused on the government and opposition discourses. This involved analyzing speeches, government debates, and newspaper articles: texts where the war was legitimated and/or delegitimated by those close to the levers of power. For practical reasons I had to limit the primary material to what I inductively determined were key periods of legitimation. I did this by triangulating secondary reading with the online Hansard (parliamentary records) tool that allowed me to check for the frequency of debates about the war in Parliament (using the search terms "Boer" and "South Africa"). I then read the debate in Hansard together with the reporting of it in the *Times* newspaper. I reasoned that this would offer a good window into the mainstream establishment discourse. (See Table A.1 for the list of primary sources.) I also cross-referenced my interpretation with secondary readings, which also provided me with further primary sources. This approach is not perfect (more texts would always be better), but it worked to the extent that the politics of the war became comprehensible in terms of the patterns of representation and legitimation. To be clear on the limitations of this approach: it can provide a window into whether and how theories of international status were employed in *British* political discourse and contributed (de) legitimation of the war and government; it cannot provide any insight into the "real" status implications of the war internationally: whether or not international collective beliefs changed as a result. Moreover, my approach can shed light only on what was used to legitimate the war to the public. I do not doubt that some involved were motivated by investment interests or that broader geopolitical motivations were important for others; however, these would become salient to my analysis only insofar as they were used to justify the war to the public. Finally, conducting an analysis of elite discourse has the consequence of reproducing the elite's marginalization of subaltern voices (see Bertrand 2018; Hansen 2000). In particular, by focusing on the mainstream British discourse around the Boer War, my analysis occludes from view the role and suffering of Black South Africans during the war. To attempt to mitigate this silencing effect but without undermining my research design, I raise Black South Africans' hidden role in war in the context section and footnotes and provide references to research that foregrounds it.[11]

Chapter 4: Organizing and Resisting Status Competition

This chapter analyzes how the OECD's PISA education rankings have influenced Norwegian education policy from 2001 to 2019. This involved tracing the way that PISA has been used and contested within Norwegian politics across two decades and whether and how PISA had enabled the education policy to become framed in terms of

---

[11] In this way I am hoping to encourage this research.

international status.[12] Norway's response to PISA came to my attention in 2016, when the country was ruminating on its most recent round of results. Although I was later to change my mind, my initial theoretical purpose was to investigate whether international organisations could manipulate status concerns for the public good (contra conventional wisdom that understands status competition as a pathology).

I thus investigated a relatively long period when different parties were in office. Indeed, looking beyond the initial "PISA shock" allowed me to ascertain whether PISA's account of the international education hierarchy was used by only one party, or whether its theory of international education status crossed the political divide. Tracing how it was used by both the Conservative governments (2001–2005, 2013–2020) and the left-coalition government (2005–2013) allowed me to investigate this possibility. Studying this long period enabled me to status in a processual, open-ended fashion: investigating what insight can be gained by critically examining several rounds of "status competition" and whether PISA retained its ability to legitimate policy change. As it transpired, this would enable me to discover and posit that the wider status literature should pay greater heed to reflexive processes and the longue durée of status competition: how interpretations of earlier rounds of competition feed back into the discourse and can potentially undermine the game. To gain further analytical traction on the question of whether PISA was crucial to legitimating the reforms in question, I also compared the PISA period with the pre-PISA period. In particular, I needed to investigate and show that the reforms undertaken in the name of PISA—using the grammar of status competition—would have been difficult to legitimate otherwise. This comparison would also help me probe the plausibility (Eckstein 2000) of my broader theoretical point: that new international rankings in general enable, organize, and thus facilitate status competition in a wider range of activities than would be possible otherwise.

The main texts I used to analyze the processes of legitimation included government policy documents and newspaper articles covering the education reforms, as well as secondary sources that discussed the "PISA shock" in Norway and elsewhere. Again, I wanted to focus on government legitimation to the public. Therefore, I analyzed the government documents pertaining to the reforms and the mainstream press reports of the reforms and the PISA education debate. To do this I searched the government database and an online Norwegian archive for sources (Atekst) with the word "PISA" as well as "Kunnskapsløftet," the name given to the raft of education reforms undertaken in PISA's wake (see Table A.1).[13] The newspapers I selected were the three most read newspapers in Norway (*VG*, *Dagbladet*, and *Aftenposten*). The first two are tabloids, while the last is a more serious centrist newspaper that covers opinions from the mainstream left and right. These sources provided me with what I consider an ample window into the debate that ensued following each round of the PISA results: the discursive context that the government policy reforms both inspired and responded to. Moreover, the texts made tractable the emerging opposition—among some of the smaller parties—to using PISA as a basis for education policymaking. As well as functioning as primary sources, the newspaper articles served as a pointer toward how nongovernment parties' policy toward PISA shifted. (This was not available by searching the government database.) The secondary sources I used to triangulate my analysis become primary sources through the process of

---

[12] It is useful to clarify that the contestation involved rejecting the legitimacy of PISA for use in domestic education policy decisions. It did not (yet) involve questioning the rules of PISA internationally in the manner that SIT theorists might characterize as "social creativity."

[13] This has a double meaning: "knowledge promise" and "knowledge elevation."

228 APPENDIX

conducting research. As I would learn, academia and academics played an important role in both legitimating PISA and contesting its value.

Chapter 5: Symmetry over Strategy

This chapter investigates how various theories of international status informed the U.S. position during the negotiation of the SALT treaties. The process of legitimation of these positions involved studying a different level of analysis (legitimation within the government bureaucracy) and thus involved a different procedure than the other cases. I will thus elaborate in a little more depth the method and justification. While chapters 3 and 4 traced how the respective governments (de)legitimated particular policies to the domestic public, chapter 5 traces how SALT positions were (de)legitimated at the top level of bureaucracy. (Legitimation to the domestic audience provides the omnipresent but delayed backing track.) One objection could be that the top-level bureaucracy was not "public," and therefore paying heed to patterns of legitimation does not work in the same manner. But this takes the term "public" too literally and narrowly. Methodologically, the size of the audience and the number of people party to the discursive context need not matter. The process of legitimation operates when a person needs to justify their action to one or more others lest those others inhibit the action or punish it. As noted, these reasons are social in that they must refer to some logic or rule that exists quite apart—intersubjectively—from the individual person providing the reason.[14] The top-level discussions around SALT embody this requirement; although few in number, all civilian and military participants were expected to proffer their preferred position and legitimate to it to the group by way of logic and evidence. Moreover, the outcome of these discussions directly led to the policy position that the United States took with the Soviets. While the U.S. president had the final say, in the context of SALT the president's hands were tied to the extent that bureaucratic support (especially from the military) would prove crucial for persuading Congress to ratify the treaty. Thus, although SALT meetings were kept "secret" from the general public (until they were declassified a decade or so ago), these top-level meetings do contain public legitimation of policy positions to a small but important audience of top-level civilian and military staff.

As the analysis shows, the requirement for congressional and public approval was seldom far from discussion at these meetings. Although SALT ostensibly involved the *highest* politics, the U.S. SALT negotiation position evolved quite explicitly through reference to what would "sell" to the domestic audience and to a lesser extent the international audience. It is useful to highlight the methodological advantage focusing on legitimation offers, contra trying to grasp "real" motivations or by referring to some kind of "objective" international hierarchy. Imagine that with a new and wondrous methodological invention, we could go back in time and find out how the domestic audience, U.S. allies, and members of the nonaligned movement would have reacted had the United States agreed to a SALT treaty allowing it to have 900 ICBMs and the Soviet Union 1,000. Then imagine we discover with 100% certainly that these foreign and domestic audiences would have only shrugged their shoulders. Would this be valuable to explaining why the SALT II negotiations were so difficult? At best, it would provide grounds to blame the

---

[14] Thus, legitimation, even in contexts with a small audience, is never subjective. See Jackson (2006) for an extended discussion of the intersubjective nature of legitimation.

APPENDIX 229

protagonists, but offer little to explain their actions. Similarly, if we discovered that a secretary of state had been bribed by the defense industry to hinder SALT II, would that make it any less important *how* he managed to insist upon hawkish positions? Rather like my interest in becoming a professional football player, it does not matter how strongly an actor might wish to do something; if the discursive resources are not available, that motivation is moot.

My choice of texts in the SALT chapter was a function of my analytical requirements and pragmatic limitations.[15] Analytically, I needed texts which embodied the legitimation of the various U.S. negotiation positions. Here I relied upon the judgment of the editors of the U.S. State Department's Office of the Historian. Their method for deciding what texts to include in their *Foreign Relations of the United States* (*FRUS*) explains their mandate to ensure that "the published record should omit no facts that were of major importance in reaching a decision; and nothing should be omitted for the purposes of concealing a defect in policy" (U.S. State Department, Office of the Historian 2013, p. III). In an ideal world it would have been more trustworthy to ascertain for myself what was significant for explaining SALT, especially given that my theoretical concern with status and legitimation might not be "seen" with a historian's scientific ontology. However, several reasons provide confidence that the texts analyzed were sufficient and that the texts omitted would not significantly undermine the thesis.

Most important, the nature of the SALT decision-making processes combined with the substance of the *FRUS* texts give me confidence that nothing crucial was omitted. Both SALT I and SALT II involved an iterative series of meetings prior to the United States formalizing its negotiation position (of which there were several in each round). This means that it is possible to see how the meetings' discussions were manifested in the policy positions eventually taken. If the discussions related poorly to the position taken, this would indicate that either (a) the meetings had little bearing on the negotiation position, or (b) the *FRUS* editor had excluded crucial evidence. However, across both SALT I and II all the negotiations contained within the archives correspond to the policy positions taken. Second, this problem is more severe for the analyst seeking to access motivations rather than legitimation. This approach needs to go beyond legitimation in context and look for potentially external or even hidden factors—whether personal, economic, or bureaucratic—that operated outside the reasons given. In contrast, my approach requires analysis of what was adequate in the discrete discursive context to legitimate particular positions, with special attention to how representations of international status were implicated (or not).

In order to triangulate, I also read and analyzed the broader discursive context—both bureaucratic and the national discourse. The former was in order to get an idea of how SALT was situated and discussed as part of the broader U.S. foreign policy. Here, I again relied upon the documents selected by the Office of the Historian. While little of this background features in my analysis, understanding how SALT related to the policy context provided a potential check on my analysis and helped generate a meta-understanding

---

[15] I will not dwell on the practical limitations because they are intuitive and largely generic: time and money are scarce, and reading everything is impossible. Thus, I did not go to the archives physically but relied upon the Office of the Historian of the U.S. State Department. However, as I argue below, I strongly suspect that for my purposes going to the archive myself would not have altered my analysis in a substantive way. I would also add, following Ward (2019a), that academia is supposed to be collegial; unless we have good reason to doubt the historians' selection of the texts (given one's purpose), it is not clear why duplicating their work would be valuable.

230 APPENDIX

of SALT's place in each administration's broader foreign policy agenda. To open a window into the broader discursive context at a national level I selectively drew upon contemporary academic security sources and the *New York Times* at key points during the negotiations (e.g., signings, ratification, and summits). I also relied upon secondary literature and historical accounts of the national politics around arms control. To be sure, it would have been preferable to go deeper and broader into the national discourse. However, the chapter investigates top-level discursive *legitimation* within bureaucratic contexts; therefore, strictly speaking, the domestic audience's real response to SALT mattered only insofar as how it was represented within these bureaucratic meetings and whether those representations informed the legitimation of a given negotiating position. As such, there is little reason to believe that a deeper analysis of the national discourse around SALT would substantially alter my analysis or conclusions.

Reading Strategies and Limitations

Moving from tracing patterns of continuity and change in the textual material to constructing an "analytical narrative" is a big step, one too often hidden. It is necessary to flag some potential weaknesses in these procedures—missing texts and misreading—and how I addressed them. Trustworthiness and faith in the process are tricky to establish, but being transparent about one's procedure helps. First, it is worth clarifying a common misconception regarding discourses: they are not intended "to capture the whole of actuality, but instead to help us bring some analytical order to our experiences" and illuminate relations of the social world that would otherwise remain obscured by pure description (Jackson 2010, p. 154). In the same way that neopositivists "fillet a meat mountain" of data, so must the discourse analyst not only (a) interpret what is often an overwhelming mass of "data" but (b) decide what evidence is significant and sufficient to account for the outcome and (c) decide what is the best way to present that evidence. In practice, steps (b) and (c) cannot involve detailing every nuance of a discourse, and therefore necessarily involve (perhaps sinisterly or cynically) *silencing* what is deemed incidental to answering the research questions. Similar to how we must trust the neopositivist has not "p-hacked" their way to a significant correlation, omitted crucial variables, or all manner of other ways one can manipulate statistics backstage, so discourse analysis depends to a considerable degree upon trust in the researcher. Concerns about malpractice can never be entirely assuaged, but they can be mitigated by openness about one's procedures that can build trust but also facilitate critique.

First of all, the main criteria for deciding what was significant for understanding an outcome involved asking the counterfactual questions: Was a pattern of representations significant for the legitimation of the policy taking place? Could one imagine it taking place in the way it did without this representational practice? What other logics were in play that could have been important? To answer these questions required careful analysis of meanings as they were used in practice; I could not, for instance, count words and infer their significance to the outcome. Indeed, interpreting discourse should not be confused with content analysis; brute frequency is not necessarily a sign of significance. Indeed, all the cases involved debates around the topic in question that occurred with great frequency and heat in the textual material but were ultimately only incidental to the legitimation of the policy. For instance, in the case of how PISA shaped Norwegian school policy, it prompted a great deal of debate about the cause of Norway's poor performance in PISA. While the left and the right proffered different solutions to the problem of Norway's lowly

APPENDIX 231

position in the ranking, at least in the first decade both sides accepted it as a reason to reform. Similarly, during the Boer War there was a great deal of public rumination about
the British struggles in the early stages of the war and who was to blame—government
strategy, equipment, manpower? However, these debates concerned practical discussions
that did not question whether Britain should persist, but rather how to ensure Britain
triumphed. The legitimacy of continuing to fight was taken for granted in this debate.
Analogously, the U.S. SALT negotiation team undertook lengthy technical discussions
about how to ensure there were no loopholes in any agreement and that definitions did
not allow one side an unfair advantage. This slowed down the negotiations; however, the
difficulty involved in the technical discussions was produced by the prior framing of the
negotiations as a status competition. This is certainly not an exhaustive list of what I left
out, but hopefully it provides a useful window into my exclusionary practices that might
preemptively tackle criticism, but also open the door for constructive criticism.

I should also justify the validity of my exemplars in the construction of my analytical
narrative. Crucially, I did not select these representations because they were very different
from other representations; quite the opposite: they were selected precisely because they
were good examples of *regularities* in the discourse. In all cases in which I use a quote to
illustrate a representation, several others reflecting similar sentiments/logic could have
been used; the criteria of selection here become aesthetic and rhetorical: how to illuminate the point best using the fewest words. This should be contrasted with how an analyst
might strive to get at the real motivations of a policymaker. Here, the task might involve
downplaying the public pronouncements as mere deceptions that played to the crowds,
and (quite rightly given their goal) privileging diary entry or a private letter (Ringmar
1996, pp. 41–42). In contrast, by my methodology, what works to please "the crowds" and
was adequate to legitimate is privileged over the secret motivation. The advantage here is
that few of the quotes I use will come as a particular surprise to anyone familiar with the
cases; the novelty and insight stems (hopefully) from my theoretical lens—the grammar
of status—that helps us see it in a new light, ideally in the manner of a gestalt switch.

However, as Neumann (2008a) suggests, pulling off a good discourse analysis relies
heavily on the researcher. Therefore, what is probably a much bigger problem than the
chances of missing texts is the possibility that I have misread the texts, missed important
representations and patterns, and generally conducted a less than convincing discourse
analysis. While some of these potential problems will become apparent in the analysis if
they are present, I can help the reader apprehend dubious interpretations by being open
about how my social identities and relationship to my research subjects may have affected
my analysis. Indeed, as Doty (2004 contends, scholars should "undertake a continual in-
terrogation of [their] own identities," and "any body of thought, perspective, approach, or
critical attitude that uses the rhetoric of social construction and takes this notion seriously
must include oneself in the equation or admit to a deceit." Of particular salience here are
my political orientations and specific normative stance toward some of the issues I am
studying.[16] First, I became opposed to PISA during the research process and engaged in
the public debate (Beaumont 2019b). As a check upon whether my reading of the discourse was "fair," I ran the chapter past a friend who is on the other side of the political
spectrum and was an active member of the party that administrated the PISA shock at the

---

[16] To be clear, this is not an exhaustive discussion of either my identities or my attempts to reflect
upon and mitigate bias. Instead, it is those I consider the most salient to include given my space
limitations.

232   APPENDIX

time.[17] While he had some quibbles,[18] overall he agreed with my interpretation.[19] Second, I have conducted research and training on behalf of organizations campaigning for the abolishment of nuclear weapons.[20] At a minimum, this informed my case selection; I had considerable prior knowledge of the Cold War arms race and nuclear scholarship in general. However, recognizing the danger of "antinuclearist" bias, I took special care to ensure I presented a fair reading of pro-nuclear scholars (e.g., Waltz, Jervis, Glaser), and I specifically reached out to Charles Glaser to check my rendering of his argument.[21] Ultimately, despite my best efforts, it is unlikely that I can fully apprehend how my prior socialization may have affected my research (see Alejandro 2018, pp. 203–204). Therefore, beyond aiding transparency and trustworthiness, these reflections also aim to provide the reader with the best possible chance to join the dots where my attempts at reflexivity may have failed.

Final Thoughts

According to Dvaro Yanow (2015, p. 5), self-conscious reflexivity is the "hallmark" of good interpretivist science. This necessitates the constant questioning of one's methodological choices, presuppositions, and interpretations throughout the research process. This appendix has attempted to open a window into that reflexive process with the goal of ensuring trustworthiness but also to facilitate critique. My discussion of cases, texts, and my identities aimed to serve these purposes. Yet as Yanow (2009) argues, the interpretivist scholar should proceed with "passionate humility," ready to recognize that their analysis might be wrong. Indeed, I hope the rest of the book will demonstrate that I have managed to generate compelling findings despite my various biases, but it would be hubristic and self-defeating—given my ontology and analytical approach—to claim that my book's arguments are definitive (Dunne 2008, p. 92).

---

[17] I also ran the text past several other politically engaged Norwegians, though they were all from the left, and thus likely to suffer bias to similar my own on this issue.

[18] He thought I could have emphasized that the reforms undertaken in the name of PISA were good policies on their own terms. I did not incorporate this advice into my chapter because this sort of normative evaluation of the policies is beyond the scope of my analysis (and expertise).

[19] Running my analysis past someone who was involved at the time, and also on the opposing political side, serves a similar methodological purpose to doing "informant feedback" (see Shwartz-Shea 2015, p. 135).

[20] I wrote several policy papers for the International Law and Policy Institute on their [Anti] Nuclear Weapons Project (2013–2014) and I trained "young leaders" for the International Campaign for the Abolishment of Nuclear Weapons.

[21] To his credit, Charles Glaser—whom I have no professional or personal relationship with— got back to me within 48 hours to say that at first blush he did not have a problem with the paragraphs and or the 2-by-2 matrix in question.

References

ABC Nyheter. (2016). "Pisa-tester splitter de rødgrønne." October 20. https://www.abcnyheter.no/nyheter/politikk/2016/10/20/195250418/pisa-tester-splitter-de-rodgronne.

Abizadeh, A. (2005). "Does Collective Identity Presuppose an Other? On the Alleged Incoherence of Global Solidarity." *American Political Science Review* 99(1): 45–60.

Adler, E. (1992). "The Emergence of Cooperation: National Epistemic Communities and the International Evolution of the Idea of Nuclear Arms Control." *International Organization* 46(1): 101–145.

Adler-Nissen, R. (2017). "Are We 'Nazi Germans' or 'Lazy Greeks'? Negotiating International Hierarchies in the Euro Crisis." In A. Zarakol (Ed.), *Hierarchies in World Politics* (pp. 198–218). London: Cambridge University Press.

Adler-Nissen, R. and Tsinovoi, A. (2019). "International Misrecognition: The Politics of Humour and National Identity in Israel's Public Diplomacy." *European Journal of International Relations* 25(1): 3–29.

Adler-Nissen, R., Andersen, K. E., and Hansen, L. (2020). "Images, Emotions, and International Politics: The Death of Alan Kurdi." *Review of International Studies* 46(1): 75–95.

Adler-Nissen, R. and Gammeltoft-Hansen, T. (Eds.) (2008). *Sovereignty Games: Instrumentalizing State Sovereignty in Europe and Beyond.* New York: Palgrave Macmillan.

Aftenposten. (2008). "Skolepolitikkens kannestøpere." February 5. https://www.aftenposten.no/meninger/leder/i/GQ2zx/skolepolitikkens-kannestoepere?

Aftenposten. (2014). "Advarer mot PISA-hysteri." March 6. https://www.aftenposten.no/unknown/i/bK0MB/advarer-mot-pisa-hysteri?

Aftenposten. (2016). "Norske 15-åringer Klatrer på PISA-listene." *Aftenposten,* December 17.

Aftenposten (2019). "Nye læreplaner i skolen: Mer praktisk skoledag for de yngste." *Aftenposten,* December 18. https://www.aftenposten.no/norge/i/9vePGE/nye-laereplaner-i-skolen-mer-praktisk-skoledag-for-de-yngste.

Alejandro, A. (2018). *Western Dominance in International Relations? The Internationalisation of IR in Brazil and India.* London: Routledge.

Allett, J. (1987). "New Liberalism, Old Prejudices: J. A. Hobson and the 'Jewish Question.' " *Jewish Social Studies* 49(2): 99–114.

Allison, G. T. and Halperin, M. H. (1972). "Bureaucratic Politics: A Paradigm and Some Policy Implications." *World Politics* 24: 40–79.

Anderl, F. (2016). "The Myth of the Local." *Review of International Organizations* 11(2): 197–218.

Anderson, B. (1991). *Imagined Communities: Reflections on the Origin and Spread of Nationalism.* New York: Verso Books.

234 REFERENCES

Anderson, D. M. (2015). "Guilty Secrets: Deceit, Denial, and the Discovery of Kenya's 'Migrated Archive.'" *History Workshop Journal* 80(1): 142–160.

Anderson, M. and Farrel, T. (2016). "Superpower Summitry." In D. H. Dunn (Ed.), (*Diplomacy at the Highest Level: The Evolution of International Summitry* (pp. 67–88). London: Springer.

Ashley, R. K. (1989). "Living on Border Lines: Man, Poststructuralism, and War." In M. J. Shapiro and J. Der Derian (Eds.), *International/Intertextual Relations: Postmodern Readings of World Politics* (pp. 259–321). Lanham, MD: Lexington Books.

Aursand, L. R. (2018). "What [Some] Students Know and Can Do: A Case Study of Norway, PISA, and Exclusion." Master's thesis, University of Oslo. https://www.duo.uio.no/handle/10852/64242.

Axelrod, R. and Keohane, R. O. (1985). "Achieving Cooperation under Anarchy: Strategies and Institutions." *World Politics: A Quarterly Journal of International Relations* 38(1): 226–254.

Badsey, S. (2013). "War Correspondents in the Boer War." In D. Gooch (Ed.), *The Boer War* (pp. 187–202). Routledge.

Baird, J., Isaacs, T., Johnson, S., Stobart, G., Yu, G., Sprague, T., and Daugherty, R. (2011). "Policy Effects of PISA." Pearson UK. https://ora.ox.ac.uk/objects/uuid:26c9fccd-ae47-424e-ba40-0c84ebedfc3e/download_file?file_format=pdf&safe_filename=Policy%252Beffects%252Bof%252BPISA.pdf&type_of_work=Report.

Balzacq, T. (2015). "The 'Essence'of Securitization: Theory, Ideal Type, and a Sociological Science of Security." *International Relations* 29(1): 103–113.

Barnhart, J. (2016). "Status Competition and Territorial Aggression: Evidence from the Scramble for Africa." *Security Studies* 25(3): 385–419.

Barnhart, J. (2020). *The Consequences of Humiliation: Anger and Status in World Politics.* Ithaca, NY: Cornell University Press.

Barthes, R. (1967). *Writing Degree Zero.* London: Macmillan.

BBC. (2016). "Pisa Tests: Singapore Top in Global Education Rankings." 6 Dec. https://www.bbc.com/news/education-38212070.

Beaumont, P. (2017a). "Brexit, Retrotopia and the Perils of Post-colonial Delusions." *Global Affairs* 3(4–5): 379–390.

Beaumont, P. (2017b). "Socializing Status in International Politics: Have You Read Onuf." Paper presented at 58th Annual Convention of the International Studies Association, Baltimore.

Beaumont, P. (2019a). "Brexit and EU Legitimation: Unwitting Martyr for the Cause?" *New Perspectives* 27(3): 15–36.

Beaumont, P. (2019b). "Ut Av Pisa." *Klassekampen*, 17 Dec. https://klassekampen.no/utgave/2019-12-17/ut-av-pisa.

Beaumont, P. (2021). *Performing Nuclear Weapons: How Britain Made Trident Make Sense.* Cham, Switzerland: Palgrave Macmillan.

Beaumont, P. and Coning, C. D. (2022). "Coping with Complexity: Toward Epistemological Pluralism in Climate-Conflict Scholarship." *International Studies Review* 24(4): viac055.

Beaumont, P. and Glaab, K. (2023). "Everyday Migration Hierarchies: Negotiating the EU's Visa Regime." *International Relations.* Online first: DOI:10.1177/00471178231205408.

Beaumont, P. and Røren, P. (2018). "End of Theory Doctoring: Diagnosing the Shallow Pluralism of Status Research." Paper presented at 11th Pan-European Conference on International Relations, Barcelona.

REFERENCES 235

Beaumont, P. and Røren, Pål. (2019). "The Unrepresented Peoples and Nations Organisation, Ontological Security and the Struggle for Status." Paper presented at ISA Annual Convention, Toronto.

Beaumont, P. and Røren, P. (2020). "Brazil's Status Struggles: Why Nice Guys Finish Last." In P. Esteves, M. Gabrielsen, and B. de Carvalhode (Eds.), *Status and the Rise of Brazil: Global Ambitions, Humanitarian Engagement and International Challenges* (pp. 31–48). London: Palgrave Macmillan.

Beaumont, P. and Towns, A. E. (2021). "The Rankings Game: A Relational Approach to Country Performance Indicators." *International Studies Review* 23(4): 1467–1494.

Beaumont, P. and Wilson Rowe, E. (2023). "Space, Nature and Hierarchy: The Ecosystemic Politics of the Caspian Sea." *European Journal of International Relations* 29(2): 449–475.

Beaven, B. (2009). "The Provincial Press, Civic Ceremony and the Citizen-Soldier during the Boer War, 1899–1902: A Study of Local Patriotism." *Journal of Imperial and Commonwealth History* 37(2), 207–228.

Bergesen, H. O. (2006). *Kampen om Kunnskapsskolen.* Universitetsforlaget.

Bertrand, S. (2018). "Can the Subaltern Securitize? Postcolonial Perspectives on Securitization Theory and Its Critics." *European Journal of International Security* 3(3): 281–299.

Bettiza, G. (2014). "Civilizational Analysis in International Relations: Mapping the Field and Advancing a 'Civilizational Politics' Line of Research." *International Studies Review* 16: 1–28.

Bieber, T. and Martens, K. (2011). "The OECD PISA Study as a Soft Power in Education? Lessons from Switzerland and the US." *European Journal of Education* 46: 101–116.

Blanch, M. D. (1980). "British Society and the War." In P. Warwick (Ed.), *The South African War: The Anglo-Boer War, 1899–1902* (pp. 210–238). Harlow: Longman.

Bleiker, R. and Hutchison, E. (2008). "Fear No More: Emotions and World Politics." *Review of International Studies* 34(S1): 115–135.

Bloodworth, J. (2006). "Senator Henry Jackson, the Solzhenitsyn Affair, and American Liberalism." *Pacific Northwest Quarterly* 97(2): 69–77.

Bohlen, A. (2003). "The Rise and Fall of Arms Control." *Survival* 45(3): 7–34.

Boisen, C. (2013). "The Changing Moral Justification of Empire: From the Right to Colonise to the Obligation to Civilise." *History of European Ideas* 39(3): 335–353.

Brands, H. (2006). "Progress Unseen: US Arms Control Policy and the Origins of Détente, 1963–1968." *Diplomatic History* 30(2): 253–285.

Breakspear, S. (2012). "The Policy Impact of PISA: An Exploration of the Normative Effects of International Benchmarking in School System Performance." OECD Education Working Papers 0_1.

Brennan, D. G. (Ed.) (1961). *Arms Control, Disarmament, and National Security.* New York: G. Braziller.

Broad, William, J. and Sanger, David E. 2021. "A 2nd New Nuclear Missile Base for China, and Many Questions about Strategy." *New York Times*, July 26. https://www.nytimes.com/2021/07/26/us/politics/china-nuclear-weapons.html.

Brodie, B. (1973). *War and Politics.* New York: Macmillan.

Broome, A., Homolar, A., and Kranke, M. (2018). "Bad Science: International Organizations and the Indirect Power of Global Benchmarking." *European Journal of International Relations* 24(3): 514–539.

Broome, A. and Quirk, J. (2015). "Governing the World at a Distance: The Practice of Global Benchmarking." *Review of International Studies* 41(5): 819–841.

236 REFERENCES

Brønmo, H. (2013). "Kristin Halvorsen: Ingen grunn til å svartmale situasjonen." *Aftenposten*, December 4. https://www.aftenposten.no/norge/i/Eo73l/kristin-halvor sen-ingen-grunn-til-aa-svartmale-situasjonen?

Browning, C. S. and Joenniemi, P. (2017). "Ontological Security, Self-Articulation and the Securitization of Identity." *Cooperation and Conflict* 52(1): 31–47.

Browning, C. S., Joenniemi, P., and Steele, B. J. (2021). *Vicarious Identity in International Relations: Self, Security, and Status on the Global Stage*. Oxford: Oxford University Press.

Bruner, C. M. and Abdelal, R. (2005). "To Judge Leviathan: Sovereign Credit Ratings, National Law, and the World Economy." *Journal of Public Policy* 25(2): 191–217.

Buarque, D. (2019). "Brazil Is Not (Perceived as) a Serious Country: Exposing Gaps between the External Images and the International Ambitions of the Nation." *Brasiliana: Journal for Brazilian Studies* 8(1–2): 285–314.

Buarque, D. (2022). "Upside-Down Diplomacy: Foreign Perceptions about Bolsonaro's Intentions and Initial Transformations of Brazil's Foreign Policy and Status." *Third World Quarterly* 43(10): 2450–2466.

Bull, H. (1977). *The Anarchical Society: A Study of Order in World Politics*. London: Palgrave Macmillan.

Burr, W. and Rosenberg, D. (2010). "Nuclear Competition in an Era of Stalemate, 1963–1975." In M. P. Leffler and O. A. Westad (Eds.), *The Cambridge History of the Cold War* (pp. 88–111). Cambridge: Cambridge University Press.

Buzan, B. (2011). "The Inaugural Kenneth N. Waltz Annual Lecture: A World Order Without Superpowers: Decentred Globalism." *International Relations* 25(1): 3–25.

Buzan, B., Waever, O., and De Wilde, J. (1998). *Security: A New Framework for Analysis*. London: Lynne Rienner.

Caldwell, D. (1991). "The SALT II Treaty." In M. Krepon and D. Caldwell (Eds.), *The Politics of Arms Control Treaty Ratification* (pp. 279–353). New York: Palgrave Macmillan.

Campbell, D. (1992). *Writing Security: United States Foreign Policy and the Politics of Identity*. Minneapolis: University of Minnesota Press.

Carpenter, R. C. (2003). "'Women and Children First': Gender, Norms, and Humanitarian Evacuation in the Balkans 1991–95." *International Organization* 57(4): 661–694.

Carvalho, L. M. (2012). "The Fabrications and Travels of a Knowledge-Policy Instrument." *European Educational Research Journal* 11(2): 172–188.

Centre Party. (2017). "Prinsipp- og handlingsprogram 2017–2021: Vi tar hele Norge i bruk." Party Program.

Clarke, M. (2012). "The (Absent) Politics of Neo-liberal Education Policy." *Critical Studies in Education* 53(3): 297–310.

Clausen, H. K. (2010). "TIåret da Skolen gikk til Pisa." *Aftenposten*, January 2.

Clemet, K. (2002). "Kvalitet i Skolen." *VG*, April 17.

Clunan, A. L. (2009). *The Social Construction of Russia's Resurgence: Aspirations, Identity, and Security Interests*. Baltimore: JHU Press.

Clunan, A. L. (2014). "Historical Aspirations and the Domestic Politics of Russia's Pursuit of International Status." *Communist and Post-Communist Studies* 47: 281–290.

Clunan, A. L. (2019). "Contribution to 'ISSF Roundtable 10-27 on Steven Ward: Status and the Challenge of Rising Powers.'" *H-Diplo*. 10(27). https://networks.h-net.org/node/28443/discussions/4099020/h-diploissf-roundtable-10-27-steven-ward%C2%A0-sta tus-and-challenge.

Cohn, C. (1987). "Sex and Death in the Rational World of Defense Intellectuals." *Signs: Journal of Women in Culture and Society* 12(4): 687–718.

REFERENCES   237

Cooley, A. (2015). "The Emerging Politics of International Rankings and Ratings: A framework for analysis." In A. Cooley and J. Snyder (Eds.), *Ranking the World: Grading States as a Tool of Global Governance* (pp. 1–39). Cambridge: Cambridge University Press.

Cooley, A. and Snyder, J. (2015). *Ranking the World: Grading States as a Tool of Global Governance*. Cambridge: Cambridge University Press.

Crawford, N. C. (2000). "The Passion of World Politics: Propositions on Emotion and Emotional Relationships." *International Security* 24(4): 116–156.

Crawford, N. C. (2002). *Argument and Change in World Politics: Ethics, Decolonization, and Humanitarian Intervention*. Cambridge: Cambridge University Press.

Daddow, O. (2019). "GlobalBritain™: The Discursive Construction of Britain's Post-Brexit World Role." *Global Affairs* 5(1): 5–22.

Dafoe, A. and Caughey, D. (2016). "Honor and War: Southern US Presidents and the Effects of Concern for Reputation." *World Politics* 68(2): 341–381.

Dafoe, A., Renshon, J., and Huth, P. (2014). "Reputation and Status as Motives for War." *Annual Review of Political Science* 17: 371–393.

Dagbladet. (2007). "Frykt for PISA." November 26. https://www.dagbladet.no/nyheter/frykt-for-pisa/66409429.

Dagbladet. (2001). "Norge er skoletaper." December 5. https://www.dagbladet.no/nyheter/norge-er-skoletaper/65772609.

Davis, K. E., Kingsbury, B., and Merry, S. E. (2012). "Indicators as a Technology of Global Governance." *Law & Society Review* 46(1): 71–104.

Davis, L. E. and Huttenback, R. A. (1982). "The Political Economy of British Imperialism: Measures of Benefits and Support." *Journal of Economic History* 42(1): 119–130.

De Carvalho, B. and Neumann, I. B. (2015a). "Introduction: Small States and Status." In B. De Carvalho and I. B. Neumann (Eds.), *Small States and Status Seeking: Norway's Quest for International Standing* (pp. 1–21). Oxford: Routledge.

De Carvalho, B. and Neumann, I. B. (Eds.) (2015b). *Small State Status Seeking: Norway's Quest for International Standing*. Oxford: Routledge.

De Maria, W. (2008). "Measurements and Markets: Deconstructing the Corruption Perception Index." *International Journal of Public Sector Management* 21(7): 777–797. https://doi.org/10.1108/09513550810904569.

De Mesquita, B. B. and Riker, W. H. (1982). "An Assessment of the Merits of Selective Nuclear Proliferation." *Journal of Conflict Resolution* 26(2): 283–306.

Deng, Y. (2008). *China's Struggle for Status: The Realignment of International Relations*. Cambridge: Cambridge University Press.

Diez, T. (1999). "Speaking 'Europe': The Politics of Integration Discourse." *Journal of European Public Policy* 6(4): 598–613.

Diez, T. (2004). "Europe's Others and the Return of Geopolitics." *Cambridge Review of International Affairs* 17(2): 319–335.

Donaldson, P. (2018). "'We Are Having a Very Enjoyable Game': Britain, Sport and the South African War, 1899–1902." *War in History* 25(1): 4–25.

Doty, R. L. (1996). *Imperial Encounters: The Politics of Representation in North-South Relations*. Vol. 5. Minneapolis: University of Minnesota Press.

Doty, R. L. (2004). "Maladies of Our Souls: Identity and Voice in the Writing of Academic International Relations." *Cambridge Review of International Affairs* 17(2): 377–392.

Doyle, A. C. ([1902] 2008). *The Great Boer War*. New Delhi: Prahbat Books. [Kindle edition]

238 REFERENCES

Dunn, K. C. (2008). "Historical Representations." In A. Klotz and D. Prakash (Eds.), *Qualitative Methods in International Relations: A Pluralist Guide* (pp. 78–92). Basingstoke: Palgrave Macmillan.

Duque, M. G. (2018). "Recognizing International Status: A Relational Approach." *International Studies Quarterly* 62(3): 577–592.

Economist. (2008). "Top of the Class." June 26. https://www.economist.com/internatio nal/2008/06/26/top-of-the-class.

Eisenhower, D. (1961). *Public Papers of the Presidents of the United States, Dwight D. Eisenhower*, vol. 8. Washington, DC: US GPO.

Elkins, C. (2005). *Imperial Reckoning: The Untold Story of Britain's Gulag in Kenya*. London: Macmillan.

Ellis, J. S. (1998). " 'The Methods of Barbarism' and the 'Rights of Small Nations': War Propaganda and British Pluralism." *Albion* 30(1): 49–75.

Elstad, E. and Sivesind, K. (Eds.) (2010). *PISA: Sannheten om skolen?* Oslo: Universitetsforl.

Epstein, C. (2013). "Constructivism or the Eternal Return of Universals in International Relations: Why Returning to Language Is Vital to Prolonging the Owl's Flight." *European Journal of International Relations* 19(3): 499–519.

Epstein, C. (2015). "Minding the Brain: IR as a Science?" *Millennium* 43(2): 743–748.

Ertesvåg, F. and Lynau, J. P. (2002). "Vil Utdanne Superlaerere." *VG*, June 18.

Espeland, W. N. and Sauder, M. (2016). *Engines of Anxiety: Academic Rankings, Reputation, and Accountability*, New York: Russell Sage Foundation.

Farwell, B. ([1976] 2009). *The Great Boer War*. Barnsley: Pen and Swords.

Faulkner, N. (2012). *A Visitor's Guide to the Ancient Olympics*. New Haven, CT: Yale University Press.

Fearon, J. D. (1995). "Rationalist Explanations for War." *International Organization* 49(3): 379–414.

Ferguson, N. (2012). *Empire: How Britain Made the Modern World*. London: Penguin.

Fierke, K. M. (2002). "Links across the Abyss: Language and Logic in International Relations." *International Studies Quarterly* 46(3): 331–354.

Fierke, K. M. (2013). *Political Self Sacrifice: Agency, Body and Emotion in International Relations*. Cambridge: Cambridge University Press.

Finnemore, M. and Sikkink, K. (1998). "International Norm Dynamics and Political Change." *International Organization* 52(4): 887–917.

Fleurbaey, M. (2009). "Beyond GDP: The Quest for a Measure of Social Welfare." *Journal of Economic Literature* 47(4): 1029–1075.

Foucault, M. (1980). *Power/Knowledge Selected Interviews and Other Writings 1972–1977*. Ed. C. Gordon. Trans. C. Gordon, L. Marshall, J. Mepham, and K. Soper. Harlow: Prentice Hall.

Frank, R. H. (1985). *Choosing the Right Pond: Human Behavior and the Quest for Status*. New York: Oxford University Press.

Freedman, J. (2016). "Status Insecurity and Temporality in World Politics." *European Journal of International Relations* 22(4): 797–822.

Freedman, J. (2020). "Back of the Queue: Brexit, Status Loss, and the Politics of Backlash." *British Journal of Politics and International Relations* 22(4): 631–643.

Freedman, L. (1989). *The Evolution of Nuclear Strategy*. London: Palgrave Macmillan.

Freistein, K. (2016). "Effects of Indicator Use: A Comparison of Poverty Measuring Instruments at the World Bank." *Journal of Comparative Policy Analysis: Research and Practice* 18(4): 366–381.

REFERENCES 239

Fretland, R. (2007). "Slakter PISA-prøven." *Dagbladet*, December 7.

Foucault , M. (1972). *The Archaeology of Knowledge*. Trans. A. M. Sheridan Smith. New York: Pantheon Books.

Fuller, J. F. C. (1937). *The Last of the Gentleman's Wars: A Subaltern's Journal of the War in South Africa 1899–1902*. London: Faber and Faber.

Galbraith, J. S. (1952). "The Pamphlet Campaign on the Boer War." *Journal of Modern History* 24(2): 111–126.

Galtung, J. (1964). "A Structural Theory of Aggression." *Journal of Peace Research* 1: 95–119.

Gilady, L. (2017). "Triangle or 'Trilemma': Rousseau and the 'Kantian Peace.'" *Journal of International Relations and Development* 20: 135–161.

Gilady, L. (2018). *The Price of Prestige: Conspicuous Consumption in International Relations*. Chicago: University of Chicago Press.

Gilpin, R. (1983). *War and Change in World Politics*. Cambridge: Cambridge University Press.

Glaser, C. L. (1994). "Realists as Optimists: Cooperation as Self-Help." *International Security* 19(3): 50–90.

Glaser, C. L. (2000). "The Causes and Consequences of Arms Races." *Annual Review of Political Science* 3(1): 251–276.

Glaser, J. (2018). "Status, Prestige, Activism and the Illusion of American Decline." *Washington Quarterly* 41(1): 173–197.

Global Benchmarking Database, v1.9, Centre for the Study of Globalisation and Regionalisation, University of Warwick. Available at: www.warwick.ac.uk/globalbench marking/database.

Gooch, J. (2000). *The Boer War: Direction, Experience and Image*. Routledge.

Götz, E. (2018). "Strategic Imperatives, Status Aspirations, or Domestic Interests? Explaining Russia's Nuclear Weapons Policy." *International Politics* 56(6): 1–18.

Gray, C. S. (1979). "Nuclear Strategy: The Case for a Theory of Victory." *International Security* 4(1): 54–87.

Green, B. R. (2020). *The Revolution That Failed: Nuclear Competition, Arms Control, and the Cold War*. Cambridge: Cambridge University Press.

Guardian [open letter]. (2014). "This Article Is More Than 9 Years Old OECD and Pisa Tests Are Damaging Education Worldwide—Academics." *Guardian*. Available here: https://www.theguardian.com/education/2014/may/06/oecd-pisa-tests-damag ing-education-academics.

Gustafsson, K. (2016). "Recognising Recognition through Thick and Thin: Insights from Sino-Japanese Relations." *Cooperation and Conflict* 51: 255–271.

Gusterson, H. (1999). "Missing the End of the Cold War in International Security." In J. Weldes (Ed.), *Cultures of Insecurity: States, Communities, and the Production of Danger* (pp. 319–345). Minneapolis: University of Minnesota Press.

Guzzini, S. (1998). *Realism in International Relations and International Political Economy: The Continuing Story of a Death Foretold*. London: Routledge.

Guzzini, S. (2013). "The Ends of International Relations Theory: Stages of Reflexivity and Modes of Theorizing." *European Journal of International Relations* 19(3): 521–541.

Hansen, L. (2000). "The Little Mermaid's Silent Security Dilemma and the Absence of Gender in the Copenhagen School." *Millennium* 29(2): 285–306.

Hansen, L. (2006). *Security as Practice: Discourse Analysis and the Bosnian War*. London: Routledge.

240 REFERENCES

Haugevik, K. and Svendsen, Ø. (2023). "On Safer Ground? The Emergence and Evolution of 'Global Britain.'" *International Affairs* 99(6): 2387–2404.

HC Deb (17 October 1899). vol. 77, col. 60-160. Available here: https://api.parliament.uk/historic-hansard/commons/1899/oct/17/first-days-debate.

HC Deb (18 October 1899). vol. 77, col. 181-228. Available here: https://hansard.parliament.uk/Commons/1899-10-18/debates/524ff236-2eff-4f3c-9093-116737445b4d/CommonsChamber.

HC Deb (19 October 1899). vol. 77, col. 254-371. Available here: https://api.parliament.uk/historic-hansard/commons/1899/oct/19/third-days-debate

HC Deb (30 January 1900). vol. 78, col. 71-156. Available here: https://api.parliament.uk/historic-hansard/commons/1900/jan/30/first-days-debate

HC Deb (25 February 1901). vol. 89, col. 1069-105. Available here: https://api.parliament.uk/historic-hansard/commons/1901/feb/25/south-africa-surrenders-of-troops

HC Deb (17 June 1901). vol. 95, col. 573-629. Available here: https://api.parliament.uk/historic-hansard/commons/1901/jun/17/south-african-war-mortality-in-camps-of

HC Deb (4 March 1902). vol. 104, col. 402-67. Available here: https://api.parliament.uk/historic-hansard/commons/1902/mar/04/south-african-war-concentration-camps

HL Deb (30 January 1900). vol. 78, col. 5-44. Available here: https://api.parliament.uk/historic-hansard/lords/1900/jan/30/address-in-answer-to-her-majestys-most%205-44 ·

HL Deb (17 October 1899). vol. 77, col. 3-39. Available here: https://api.parliament.uk/historic-hansard/lords/1899/oct/17/address-in-answer-to-her-majestys-most

HL Deb (2 June 1902). vol. 108, col. 11086-9. Available here: https://api.parliament.uk/historic-hansard/lords/1902/jun/02/south-african-war-terms-of-peace

Herz, J. H. (1950). "Idealist Internationalism and the Security Dilemma." *World Politics* 2(2): 157–180.

Hobhouse, E. (1901). *Report of a Visit to the Camps of Women and Children in the Cape and Orange River Colonies*. London: Friars.

Hobson, J. A. ([1902] 1965). *Imperialism: A Study*. Ann Arbor: University of Michigan Press.

Hobson, J. M. (2012). *The Eurocentric Conception of World Politics: Western International Theory, 1760–2010*. Cambridge: Cambridge University Press.

Hoffmann, S. (2009). "International Relations Theory and Its Problems." *French Politics* 7(3–4): 432–436.

Hughes, D. (2015). "Unmaking an Exception: A Critical Genealogy of US Exceptionalism." *Review of International Studies* 41(3), 527–551.

Huysmans, J. (2000). "The European Union and the Securitization of Migration." *JCMS: Journal of Common Market Studies* 38(5): 751–777.

Isaksen, L. S. (2015). *The Norwegian Accountability Reform 2001–2009—Education Policy as Imitation*. PhD Dissertation. University of Vienna.

Jackson, P. T. (2006). *Civilizing the Enemy: German Reconstruction and the Invention of the West*. Ann Arbor: University of Michigan Press.

Jackson, P. T. (2010). *The Conduct of Inquiry in International Relations: Philosophy of Science and Its Implications for the Study of World Politics*. London: Routledge.

Jackson, P. T. and Nexon, D. H. (1999). "Relations before States: Substance, Process and the Study of World Politics." *European Journal of International Relations* 5(3): 291–332.

Jacobson, P. D. (1973). "Rosebery and Liberal Imperialism, 1899–1903." *Journal of British Studies* 13(1): 83–107.

REFERENCES 241

Jaffe, J. (1995). "The Gentleman's War: The Ideology of Imperialism in Arthur Conan Doyle's *The Great Boer War*." *Alternation* 2(2): 90–105.

Jerven, M. (2013). *Poor Numbers: How We Are Misled by African Development Statistics and What to Do about It*. Ithaca, NY: Cornell University Press.

Jervis, R. (1978). "Cooperation under the Security Dilemma." *World Politics* 30(2): 167–214.

Jervis, R. (1979). "Why Nuclear Superiority Doesn't Matter." *Political Science Quarterly* 94(4): 617–633.

Jervis, R. (2001). "Was the Cold War a Security Dilemma?" *Journal of Cold War Studies* 3(1): 36–60.

Jervis, R. (2017). *Perception and Misperception in International Politics*. New edition. Princeton, NJ: Princeton University Press.

Johnson, J. and Østerud, P. (2002a). "Medienes fordreide skolebilde." *Aftenposten*, April 3.

Johnsen, J. and Østerud, P. (2002b). "Høgskolen Mediene svartmaler skolen." *Aftenposten*. April 29, p. 14.

Johnston, A. I. (2001). "Treating International Institutions as Social Environments." *International Studies Quarterly* 45(4): 487–515.

Jones, S. (2009). "The Influence of the Boer War (1899–1902) on the Tactical Development of the Regular British Army 1902–1914." PhD dissertation, University of Wolverhampton.

Judd, D. and Surridge, K. (2013). *The Boer War: A History*. New York: Palgrave Macmillan.

Kahn, H. (1965). *On Escalation: Metaphors and Scenarios*. Westport, CT: Praeger.

Karseth, B., Kvamme, O. A., and Ottesen, E. Fagfornyelsens læreplanverk: Politiske intensjoner, arbeidsprosesser og innhold. Report no 1. *Universitetet i Oslo. Det Utdanningsvitenskapelige fakultet*.

Katzenstein, M. F. (1996). *The Culture of National Security: Norms and Identity in World Politics*. New York: Columbia University Press.

Kelley, J. G. (2017). *Scorecard Diplomacy: Grading States to Influence Their Reputation and Behavior*. Cambridge: Cambridge University Press.

Kelley, J. G. and Simmons, B. A. (2015). "Politics by Number: Indicators as Social Pressure in International Relations." *American Journal of Political Science* 59(1): 55–70.

Kelley, J. G. and Simmons, B. A. (2019). "Introduction: The Power of Global Performance Indicators." *International Organization* 73(3): 491–510.

Khong, Y. F. (2019). "Power as Prestige in World Politics." *International Affairs* 95(1): 119–142.

Kingdon, J. W. (1995). *Agendas, Alternatives, and Public Policies*. Boston: Little, Brown.

Kirshner, J. (2000). "Rationalist Explanations for War?" *Security Studies* 10(1): 143–150.

Kirshner, J. (2015). "The Economic Sins of Modern IR Theory and the Classical Realist Alternative." *World Politics* 67(1): 155–183.

Kjaernsli, M., Lie, S., Olsen, R. V., and Turmo, A. (2004). *Rett spor eller ville veier? Norske elevers prestasjoner i matematikk, naturfag og lesing i PISA 2003*. Oslo: Universitetsforlaget.

Klette, K., Lie, S., Ødegaard, M., Anmarkrud, Ø., Arnesen, N., Bergem, O. K., and Roe, A. (2008). *Rapport om forskningsprosjektet PISA+*. Oslo: Norges forskningsråd.

Koschut, S. (2018a). "The Power of (Emotion) Words: On the Importance of Emotions for Social Constructivist Discourse Analysis in IR." *Journal of International Relations and Development* 21(3): 495–522.

Koschut, S. (2018b). "Speaking from the Heart: Emotion Discourse Analysis in International Relations." In M. Sanger and E. Clement (Eds.), *Researching Emotions in International* Relations (pp. 277–301). London: Palgrave Macmillan.

242 REFERENCES

Kratochwil, F. (1993). "The Embarrassment of Changes: Neo-realism as the Science of Realpolitik without Politics." *Review of International Studies* 19(1): 63–80.

Krause, K. and Latham, A. (1998). "Constructing Nonproliferation and Arms Control: The Norms of Western Practice." *Contemporary Security Policy* 19(1): 23–54.

Krebs, P. M. (2004). *Gender, Race, and the Writing of Empire: Public Discourse and the Boer War*. Vol. 23. Cambridge: Cambridge University Press.

Krebs, R. R. (2015). *Narrative and the Making of US National Security*. Cambridge: Cambridge University Press.

Krebs, R. R. and Jackson, P. T. (2007). "Twisting Tongues and Twisting Arms: The Power of Political Rhetoric." *European Journal of International Relations* 13(1): 35–66.

Krickovic, A. and Chang, Z. (2020). "Fears of Falling Short versus Anxieties of Decline: Explaining Russia and China's Approach to Status-Seeking." *Chinese Journal of International Politics* 13(2): 219–251.

Kroenig, M. (2018). *The Logic of American Nuclear Strategy: Why Strategic Superiority Matters*. Oxford: Oxford University Press.

Kruger, L. (2019). "Senterpartiet vil avvikle PISA-undersøkelsen." *NRK*, December 3. https://www.nrk.no/norge/senterpartiet-vil-avvikle-pisa-undersokelsen-1.14806458.

Kruzel, J. J. (1981). "Arms Control and American Defense Policy: New Alternatives and Old Realities." *Daedalus* 110(10): 137–157.

Kuitenbrouwer, V. (2012). *War of Words: Dutch Pro-Boer Propaganda and the South African War (1899–1902)*. Amsterdam: Amsterdam University Press.

Kustermans, J., de Carvalho, B., and Beaumont, P. (2023). "Whose Revisionism, Which International Order? Social Structure and Its Discontents." *Global Studies Quarterly* 3(1): ksad009.

Kunnskapsdepartementet. (2016). "Melding til Stortinget Fag—Fordypning—Forståelse En fornyelse av Kunnskapsløftet." *Meld. St.* 28.

Laffey, M. and Weldes, J. (1997). "Beyond Belief: Ideas and Symbolic Technologies in the Study of International Relations." *European Journal of International Relations* 3(2): 193–237.

Lake, D. A. (2013). "Authority, Status, and the End of the American Century." In T. V. Paul, D. W. Larson, and W. C. Wohlforth (Eds.), *Status in World Politics* (pp. 246–272). Cambridge: Cambridge University Press.

Lakoff, G. (1991). "Metaphor and War: The Metaphor System Used to Justify War in the Gulf." *Peace Research* 23(2–3): 25–32.

Lakoff, G. and Johnson, M. ([1980] 2003). *Metaphors We Live By*. Chicago: University of Chicago Press.

Langfeldt, G., and Birkeland, N. (2010). "PISA i lys av styringsteori." In Elstad, E. and Sivesind, K. (Eds.), *PISA: sannheten om skolen?* Oslo: Universitetsforlaget (pp. 83–97).

Larson, D. W., Paul, T. V., and Wohlforth, W. C. (2014). "Status and World Order." In T. V. Paul, D. W. Larson, and W. C. Wohlforth (Eds.), *Status in World Politics* (pp. 3–32). New York: Cambridge University Press.

Larson, D. W. and Shevchenko, A. (2003). "Shortcut to Greatness: The New Thinking and the Revolution in Soviet Foreign Policy. *International Organization* 57(1): 77–109.

Larson, D. W. and Shevchenko, A. (2010). "Status Seekers: Chinese and Russian Responses to US Primacy." *International Security* 34(4): 63–95.

Larson, D. W. and Shevchenko, A. (2014). "Managing Rising Powers: The Role of Status Concerns." In T. V. Paul, D. W. Larson, and W. C. Wohlforth (Eds.), *Status in World Politics* (pp. 33–57). Cambridge: Cambridge University Press.

REFERENCES   243

Larson, D. W. and Shevchenko, A. (2019). *Quest for Status: Chinese and Russian Foreign Policy*. New Haven, CT: Yale University Press.

Leira, H. (2019). "The Emergence of Foreign Policy." *International Studies Quarterly* 63(1): 187–198.

Licklider, R. E. (1970). "The Missile Gap Controversy." *Political Science Quarterly* 85(4): 600–615.

Lebow, R. N. (2010a). "The Past and Future of War." *International Relations* 24(3): 243–270.

Lebow, R. N. (2010b). *Why Nations Fight: Past and Future Motives for War*. Cambridge: Cambridge University Press.

Lieber, K. A. and Press, D. G. (2017). "The New Era of Counterforce: Technological Change and the Future of Nuclear Deterrence." *International Security* 41(4): 9–49.

Lieber, K. A. and Press, D. G. (2020). *The Myth of the Nuclear Revolution: Power Politics in the Atomic Age*. Cornell University Press.

Lerner, A. B. (2022). *From the Ashes of History: Collective Trauma and the Making of International Politics*. Oxford: Oxford University Press.

Lincoln, Y. S. and Guba, E. G. (1985). "Establishing Trustworthiness." *Naturalistic Inquiry* 289(331): 289–327.

Lin, A. Y. T. and Katada, S. N. (2022). "Striving for Greatness: Status Aspirations, Rhetorical Entrapment, and Domestic Reforms." *Review of International Political Economy* 29(1): 175–201.

Lin, A.Y.T (2023). "Looking for Status: Beyond Material Suboptimality." Unpublished manuscript.

Lin, A. Y. T. (2024). "Contestation from Below: Status and Revisionism in Hierarchy." *International Studies Quarterly*. Available at SSRN: https://ssrn.com/abstract=4592 955 or http://dx.doi.org/10.2139/ssrn.4592955.

Linton, R. (1936). *The Study of Man: An Introduction*. Oxford: Appleton Century.

Löwenheim, O. (2008). "Examining the State: A Foucauldian Perspective on International 'Governance Indicators.'" *Third World Quarterly* 29(2): 255–274.

Lowry, D. (2002). "'The World's No Bigger Than a Kraal': The South African War and International Opinion in the First Age of 'Globalization.'" In D. E. Omissi and A. S. Thompson (Eds.), *The Impact of the South African War* (pp. 268–288). London: Palgrave Macmillan.

MacDonald, P. K. and Parent, J. M. (2021). "The Status of Status in World Politics." *World Politics* 73(2): 358–391.

Mackenzie, J. M. (1986). *Propaganda and Empire: The Manipulation of British Public Opinion 1880–1960*. Manchester: Manchester University Press.

Mälksoo, M. (2021). "Militant Memocracy in International Relations: Mnemonical Status Anxiety and Memory Laws in Eastern Europe." *Review of International Studies* 47(4): 489–507.

Marks, S. (1982). "Scrambling for South Africa." *Journal of African History* 23(1): 97–113.

Martens, K. and Niemann, D. (2013). "When Do Numbers Count? The Differential Impact of the PISA Rating and Ranking on Education Policy in Germany and the US." *German Politics* 22(3): 314–332.

Mattern, J. B. and Zarakol, A. (2016). "Hierarchies in World Politics." *International Organization* 70: 623–654.

Maurer, J. D. (2022). *Competitive Arms Control: Nixon, Kissinger, and SALT, 1969–1972*. New Haven, CT: Yale University Press.

244 REFERENCES

Mcconaughey, M., Musgrave. P., and Nexon, D. H. (2018). "Beyond Anarchy: Logics of Political Organization, Hierarchy, and International Structure." *International Theory* 10(2): 181–218.

McCourt, D. M. (2014). *Britain and World Power since 1945: Constructing a Nation's Role in International Politics*. Ann Arbor: University of Michigan Press.

McNamara, R. S. (1967). "Remarks by Secretary of Defense Robert S. McNamara." *Bulletin of the Atomic Scientists* 23(10): 27–31.

Mearsheimer, J. J. (2001). *The Tragedy of Great Power Politics*. New York: W. W. Norton.

Mercer, J. (2017). "The Illusion of International Prestige." *International Security* 41(4): 133–168.

Merry, S. E. (2016). *The Seductions of Quantification: Measuring Human Rights, Gender Violence, and Sex Trafficking*. Chicago: University of Chicago Press.

Merry, S. E. and Conley, J. M. (2011). "Measuring the World: Indicators, Human Rights, and Global Governance." *Current Anthropology* 52(S3): 83–95.

Miller, P. and Rose, N. (2008). *Governing the Present: Administering Economic, Social and Personal Life*. London: Polity.

Milliken, J. (1999). "The Study of Discourse in International Relations: A Critique of Research and Methods." *European Journal of International Relations* 5(2): 225–254.

Mitzen, J. (2006). "Ontological Security in World Politics: State Identity and the Security Dilemma." *European Journal of International Relations* 12(3): 341–370.

Moore, M. T. and Fresco, D. M. (2012). "Depressive Realism: A Meta-analytic Review." *Clinical Psychology Review* 32(6): 496–509.

Morgan, K. O. (2002). "The Boer War and the Media (1899–1902)." *Twentieth Century British History* 13(1): 1–16.

Mueller, J. (1988). "The Essential Irrelevance of Nuclear Weapons: Stability in the Postwar World." *International Security* 13(2): 55–79.

Murray, M. (2010). "Identity, Insecurity, and Great Power Politics: The Tragedy of German Naval Ambition before the First World War." *Security Studies* 19(4): 656–688.

Murray, M. (2018). *The Struggle for Recognition in International Relations: Status, Revisionism, and Rising Powers*. Oxford: Oxford University Press.

Naylor, T. (2018). *Social Closure and International Society: Status Groups from the Family of Civilised Nations to the G20*. London: Routledge.

Naylor, T. (2022). "Social Closure and the Reproduction of Stratified International Order." *International Relations* 36(1): 23–39.

Neumann, I. B. (1996). *Russia and the Idea of Europe: A Study in Identity and International Relations*. London: Routledge.

Neumann, I. B. (1999). *Uses of the Other: "The East" in European Identity Formation*. Minneapolis: University of Minnesota Press.

Neumann, I. B. (2003). "Encompassing Russia: North of East of Central?" In B. Petersson and E. Clark (Eds.), *Identity Dynamics and the Construction of Boundaries* (pp. 21–42). Lund: Nordic Academic Press.

Neumann, I. B. (2004). "Beware of Organicism: The Narrative Self of the State." *Review of International Studies* 30(2): 259–267.

Neumann, I. B. (2008a). "Discourse Analysis." In A. Klotz and D. Prakash (Eds.), *Qualitative Methods in International Relations: A Pluralist Guide* (pp. 93–113). Basingstoke: Palgrave Macmillan.

Neumann, I. B. (2008b). "Russia as a Great Power, 1815–2007." *Journal of International Relations and Development* 11(2): 128–151.

REFERENCES 245

Neumann, I. B. (2014). "Status Is Cultural: Durkheimian Poles and Weberian Russians Seek Great-Power Status." In T. V. Paul, D. W. Larson, and B. Wohlforth (Eds.), *Status in World Politics* (pp. 85–114). Cambridge: Cambridge University Press.

New York Times. (1972a). "President Backs Compromise Move on Arms Control Accord." August 8.

New York Times. (1972b). "The World: Light through 'the Cloud of Doom." May 28.

Nietzsche, F. ([1873] 1997). *Untimely Meditations.* Cambridge: Cambridge University Press.

Nitze, P. H. (1976). "Assuring Strategic Stability in an Era of Détente." *Foreign Affairs* 54(2): 207–232.

Norris, R. S. and Cochran, T. B. (1997). "Nulcear Weapons Databok: US-USSR/ Russian Strategic Offensive Nuclear Forces 1945–1996." Natural Resources Defense Council.

NOU. (2002). "Førsteklasses fra første klasse: Forslag til rammeverk for et nasjonalt kvalitetsvurderingssystem av norsk grunnopplaering."

OECD. (1987). "Reviews of National Policies for Education: Norway."

OECD. (n.d.) "PISA Database." Accessed January 14, 2024. http://www.oecd.org/pisa/data/.

Omissi, D. E. (2002). "India: Some Perceptions of Race and Empire." In *The Impact of the South African War* (pp. 215–232). London: Palgrave Macmillan.

Omissi, D. E. and Thompson, A. S. (Eds.) (2002). *The Impact of the South African War.* Basingstoke: Palgrave.

Onea, T. A. (2014). "Between Dominance and Decline: Status Anxiety and Great Power Rivalry." *Review of International Studies* 40(1): 125–152.

O'Neill, B. (1994). "Game Theory Models of Peace and War." *Handbook of Game Theory with Economic Applications* 2: 995–1053.

O'Neill, B. (2006). "Nuclear Weapons and National Prestige." Discussion Paper No. 1560. Cowles Foundation.

O'neil, C. (2017). *Weapons of Math Destruction: How Big Data Increases Inequality and Threatens Democracy.* Crown.

Onuf, N. G. (1989). *World of Our Making: Rules and Rule in Social Theory and International Relations.* Colombia: University of South Carolina Press.

Oren, I. (1995). The Subjectivity of the "Democratic" Peace: Changing US Perceptions of Imperial Germany. *International Security*, 20(2):147-184.

Ovendale, R. (1982). The South African Policy of the British Labour Government, 1947-51. *International Affairs (Royal Institute of International Affairs 1944-)*, 59(1),:41-58.

Østerud, S. (2016). "Hva kan norsk skole laere av PISA-vinneren Finland?" *Nordisk tidsskrift for pedagogikk og kritikk* 2(2): 14–35.

Padgett, J. F. and Ansell, C. K. (1993). "Robust Action and the Rise of the Medici, 1400–1434." *American Journal of Sociology* 98(6): 1259–1319.

Paikowsky, D. (2017). *The Power of the Space Club.* Cambridge: Cambridge University Press.

Pakenham, T. (1979). *The Boer War.* New York: Random House.

Paul, T. V., Larson, D. W., and Wohlforth, W. C. (Eds.) (2014). *Status in World Politics.* Cambridge: Cambridge University Press.

Platt, A. (1991). "The Anti-Ballistic Missile Treaty." In M. Krepon and D. Caldwell (Eds.), *The Politics of Arms Control Treaty Ratification* (pp. 229–277). New York: Palgrave Macmillan.

246 REFERENCES

Pons, X. (2011). "What Do We Really Learn from PISA? The Sociology of Its Reception in Three European Countries (2001–2008)." *European Journal of Education* 46(4): 540–548.

Pons, X. (2017). "Fifteen Years of Research on PISA Effects on Education Governance: A Critical Review." *European Journal of Education* 52(2): 131–144.

Porter, A. (1990). "The South African War (1899–1902): Context and Motive Reconsidered." *Journal of African History* 31(1): 43–57.

Porter, A. (1996). "The Origins of the South African War." *South African Historical Journal* 35(1): 155–161.

Porter, A. (2000). "The South African War and the Historians." *African Affairs* 99(397): 633–648.

Pouliot, V. (2014). "Setting Status in Stone: The Negotiation of International Institutional Privileges." In T. V. Paul, D. W. Larson, and W. C. Wohlforth (Eds.), *Status in World Politics* (pp. 192–215). Cambridge: Cambridge University Press.

Pouliot, V. (2016). *International Pecking Orders: The Politics and Practice of Multilateral Diplomacy.* Cambridge: Cambridge University Press.

Price, R. (1972). *An Imperial War and the British Working Class: Working-Class Attitudes and Reactions to the Boer War, 1899–1902.* London: Routledge.

Pu, X. (2019). *Rebranding China: Contested Status Signaling in the Changing Global Order.* Stanford: Stanford University Press.

Pu, X. and Schweller, R. L. (2014). "Status Signaling, Multiple Audiences, and China's Blue-Water Naval Ambition." In T. V. Paul, D. W. Larson, and W. C. Wohlforth (Eds.), *Status in World Politics* (pp. 141–162). New York: Cambridge University Press.

Ramnefjell, E. (2001). "Norge er skoletaper: Hermed er det solid dokumentert: Det er typisk norsk å vaere middels!" *Dagbladet*, December 5.

Ramnefjell, E. (2002). "Kvalitet for penga." *Dagbladet*, February 14.

Rathbun, B. (2008). "A Rose by Any Other Name: Neoclassical Realism as the Logical and Necessary Extension of Structural Realism." *Security Studies* 17(2): 294–321.

Readman, P. (2001). "The Conservative Party, Patriotism, and British Politics: The Case of the General Election of 1900." *Journal of British Studies* 40(1): 107–145.

Renshon, J. (2016). "Status Deficits and War." *International Organization* 70(3): 513–550.

Renshon, J. (2017). *Fighting for Status: Hierarchy and Conflict in World Politics.* Princeton, NJ: Princeton University Press.

Restad, H. E. (2014). *American Exceptionalism: An Idea That Made a Nation and Remade the World.* New York: Routledge.

Reston, J. (1969). "Laird Used Word for Hawks as Well as Doves." *New York Times*, January 31.

Reston, J. (1976). "Why Make the Rubble Bounce?" *New York Times*, March 31.

Rhamey, J. P., Jr. and Early, B. R. (2013). "Going for the Gold: Status-Seeking Behavior and Olympic Performance." *International Area Studies Review* 16(3): 244–261.

Ringmar, E. (1996). *Identity, Interest and Action: A Cultural Explanation of Sweden's Intervention in the Thirty Years War.* New York: Cambridge University Press.

Ringmar, E. (2002). "The Recognition Game: Soviet Russia against the West." *Cooperation and Conflict* 37(2): 115–136.

Ringmar, E. (2012). "Performing International Systems: Two East-Asian Alternatives to the Westphalian Order." *International Organization* 66(1): 1–25.

Rintala, M. (1988). "Made in Birmingham: Lloyd George, Chamberlain, and the Boer War." *Biography* 11(2): 124–139.

REFERENCES 247

Risse-Kappen, T. (1991). "Public Opinion, Domestic Structure, and Foreign Policy in Liberal Democracies." *World Politics* 43(4): 479–512.

Roberts, B. (1991). *Those Bloody Women: Three Heroines of the Boer War*. London: John Murray.

Rose, G. (1998). "Neoclassical Realism and Theories of Foreign Policy." *World Politics* 51(1): 144–172.

Rose, N. and Miller, P. (1992). "Political Power beyond the State: Problematics of Government." *British Journal of Sociology* 43(2): 173–205.

Rosen, S. (1973). "Testing the Theory of the Military-Industrial Complex. In Steven Rosen (Ed.), *Testing the Theory of the Military-Industrial Complex* (pp. 1–29.). Lanham, MD: Lexington Books.Rumelili, B. (2004). "Constructing Identity and Relating to Difference: Understanding the EU's Mode of Differentiation." *Review of International Studies* 30(1): 27–47.

Rumelili, B. and Towns, A. E. (2022). "Driving Liberal Change? Global Performance Indices as a System of Normative Stratification in Liberal International Order." *Cooperation and Conflict* 57(2): 152–170.

Røren, P. (2019). "Status Seeking in the Friendly Nordic Neighborhood." *Cooperation and Conflict* 54(4): 562–579.

Røren, P. (2020). "On the Social Status of the European Union." *Journal of Common Market Studies* 58(3): 706–722.

Røren, P. (2023). "The Belligerent Bear: Russia, Status Orders, and War." *International Security* 47(4): 7–49.

Røren, P. and Beaumont, P. (2019). "Grading Greatness: Evaluating the Status Performance of the BRICS." *Third World Quarterly* 40(3): 429–450.

Sagan, S. D. (1997). "Why Do States Build Nuclear Weapons? Three Models in Search of a Bomb." *International Security* 21(3): 54–86.

Sambanis, N., Skaperdas, S., and Wohlforth, W. C. (2015). "Nation-Building through War." *American Political Science Review* 109(2): 279–296.

Sandvik, H., Grønli, H., and Myklebust, B. (2016). "Sp vil melde Norge ut av Pisa." *NRK*, October 19. https://www.nrk.no/norge/sp-vil-melde-norge-ut-av-pisa-1.13185897.

Schelling, T. C. and Halperin, M. H. (1961). *Strategy and Arms Control*. New York: The Twentieth Century Fund.

Schueth, S. (2015). "Winning the Rankings Game: The Republic of Georgia, USAID, and the Doing Business Project." In A. Cooley and J. Snyder (Eds.), *Ranking the World: Grading States as a Tool of Global Governance* (pp. 151–177). Cambridge: Cambridge University Press.

Schulz, C. A. (2017). "Accidental Activists: Latin American Status-Seeking at the Hague." *International Studies Quarterly* 61(3): 612–622.

Schwartz-Shea, P. (2015). "Judging Quality Evaluative Criteria and Epistemic Communities." In D. Yanow and P. Schwartz-Shea (Eds.), *Interpretation and Method* (pp. 120–146). New York: Routledge.

Scott, J. C., and Light, M. A. (2004). "The Misuse of Numbers: Audits, Quantification, and the Obfuscation of Politics." In J. Purdy, A. Kronman, and C. Farrar (Eds.), Democratic Vistas: Reflections on the Life of American Democracy. New Haven: Yale University Press.

Scoville, H. J., Kulish, Y., Gallois, P., and Brennan, D. (1972). "Strategic Forum: The SALT Agreements." *Survival* 14(5): 210–219.

248 REFERENCES

Sending, O. J. (2002). "Constitution, Choice and Change: Problems with the Logic of Appropriateness and Its Use in Constructivist Theory." *European Journal of International Relations* 8(4): 443–470.

Shapiro, M. J. (2012). *Discourse, Culture, Violence*. London: Routledge.

Sharman, J. C. (2009). "The Bark Is the Bite: International Organizations and Blacklisting." *Review of International Political Economy* 16(4): 573–596.

Simola, H. (2005). "The Finnish Miracle of PISA: Historical and Sociological Remarks on Teaching and Teacher Education." *Comparative Education* 41(4): 455–470.

Sjoberg, L. (2013). *Gendering Global Conflict: Toward a Feminist Theory of War*. New York: Columbia University Press.

Sjøberg, S. (2007). "Hva tester Pisa?" *Aftenposten*, December 17. http://folk.uio.no/svei nsj/PISA-kronikker-Sjoberg-des2007.pdf.

Sjøberg, S. (2013). "Pisa trumfer alt." *Aftenposten*, September 5.

Sjøberg, S. (2014a). "Clemet og pisafisering av norsk skole." *Morgenbladet*, April 11. here:https://morgenbladet.no/debatt/2014/clemet_og_pisafiseringen_av_norsk_ skole.

Sjøberg, S. (2014b). "PISA-syndromet: Hvordan norsk skolepolitikk blir styrt av OECD." *Nytt norsk tidsskrift* 31(1): 30–43.

Sjøberg, S. (2019). "PISA: A Success Story? Global Educational Governance by Standardization, Rankings, Comparisons and 'Successful' Examples." In L. Langer and T. Brüsemeister (Eds.), *Handbuch Educational Governance- Theorien* (pp. 653–690). Heidelberg: Springer VS.

Skjeggestad, H. (2016). "15 år med testen som viser det du vil den skal vise." *Aftenposten*, December 4. https://www.aftenposten.no/meninger/kommentar/i/kVBmB/15-aar-med-testen-som-viser-det-du-vil-den-skal-vise-helene-skjeggestad.

Singer, J. D., and Braun, H. I. (2018). "Testing International Education Assessments." *Science* 360(6384): 38–40.

Socialist Left Party. (n.d.). "Oppvekst og kunnskap." Accessed April 26, 2020. https:// www.sv.no/arbeidsprogram/oppvekst-og-kunnskap/.

Solberg, Torstein Tvedt. (2020). "Testing er feil medisin." *Dagbladet*, January 23. https:// www.dagbladet.no/kultur/testing-er-feil-medisin/72055619.

Solveig, R. (2008). "Vi har mye å laere!" *Aftenposten*, January 16.

Steele, B. J. (2008). *Ontological Security in International Relations: Self-Identity and the IR State*. New York: Routledge.

Steele, D. (2000). "Salisbury and the Soldiers." In J. Gooch (Ed.), *The Boer War: Direction, Experience and Image* (pp. 3–20). London: Routledge.

Stokes, E. (1969). "Late Nineteenth-Century Colonial Expansion and the Attack on the Theory of Economic Imperialism: A Case of Mistaken Identity?" *Historical Journal* 12(2): 285–301.

Stolte, C. (2015). *Brazil's Africa Strategy: Role Conception and the Drive for International Status*. New York: Springer.

Subotić, J. (2016). "Narrative, Ontological Security, and Foreign Policy Change." *Foreign Policy Analysis* 12(4): 610–627.

Subotić, J. and Vucetic, S. (2019). "Performing Solidarity: Whiteness and Status-Seeking in the Non-aligned World." *Journal of International Relations and Development* 22(3): 722–743.

Surridge, K. (1997). " 'All You Soldiers Are What We Call Pro-Boer': The Military Critique of the South African War, 1899–1902." *History* 82(268): 582–600.

REFERENCES 249

Surridge, K. T. (1998). *Managing the South African War, 1899--1902: Politicians Vv. Generals.* Woodbridge, UK: Boydell Press.

Suzuki, S. (2009). *Civilization and Empire: China and Japan's Encounter with European International Society.* London: Routledge.

Svarstad, J. (2013). "Flere land har jukset i PISA-undersøkelsen." *Aftenposten,* November 8.

Svendsen, Ø. (2022). "Theorizing Public Performances for International Negotiations." *International Studies Quarterly.*

Snyder, R., Pelopidas, B., Lieber, K. A., and Press, D. G. (2018). "Correspondence: New Era or New Error? Technology and the Future of Deterrence." *International Security* 43(3): 190–193.

Tajfel, H. E. and Turner, J. (1979). "An Integrative Theory of Intergroup Conflict." In W. Austin and S. Worchel (Eds.), *The Social Psychology of Intergroup Relations* (pp. 33–47). Monterey, CA: Brooks/Cole.

Tal, D. (2017). *US Strategic Arms Policy in the Cold War: Negotiation and Confrontation over SALT, 1969-1979.* London: Routledge.

Tallis, B. (2016). "Living in Post-truth: Power/Knowledge/Responsibility." *New Perspectives* 24(1): 7–18.

Telhaug, A. O. and Aasen, P. (1999). "Både-og: 90-tallets Utdanningsreformer i Historisk Perspektiv. " *Oslo: Cappelen Akademisk Forlag.*

Tickner, J. A. and Sjoberg, L. (Eds.) (2013). *Feminism and International Relations: Conversations about the Past, Present and Future.* London: Routledge.

Timasheff, N. (1957). *Sociological Theory: Its Nature and Growth.* New York: Random House.

Towns, A. E. (2010). *Women and States: Norms and Hierarchies in International Society.* Cambridge: Cambridge University Press.

Towns, A. E. (2012). "Norms and Social Hierarchies: Understanding International Policy Diffusion 'from Below.'" *International Organization* 66(2): 179–209.

Towns, A. E. and Rumelili, B. (2017). "Taking the Pressure: Unpacking the Relation between Norms, Social Hierarchies, and Social Pressures on States." *European Journal of International Relations* 23(4): 756–779.

Treverton, G. F. (1989). "How Different Are Nuclear Weapons?" In P. Bobbitt, L. Freedman, and G. F. Treverton (Eds.), *US Nuclear Strategy* (pp. 112–121). London: Palgrave Macmillan.

Trimble, P. R. and Weiss, J. S. (1991). "The Role of the President, the Senate and Congress with Respect to Arms Control Treaties Concluded by the United States." *Chicago-Kent Law Review* 67(2): 645–704.

Tuchman, B. W. (1970). "Stilwell and the American Experience in China: 1911–1945." New York: Random House.

UFD. (2003). Gi rom for lesing! Strategi for stimulering av leselyst og leseferdighet 2003–2007. Utdannings- og forskningsdepartementet.

UFD. (2004). St.meld. nr. 30 (2003–2004) Kultur for laering Tilråding fra Utdannings- og forskningsdepartementet av 2. april 2004, godkjent i statsråd samme dag. (Regjeringen Bondevik II).

UFD. (2005). Realfag, naturligvis: Strategi for styrking av realfagene 2002–2007. Utdannings- og forskningsdepartementet.

U.S. Department of State, Office of the Historian. (2010). "SALT I, 1967–1972." In *Foreign Relations of the United States, 1969–1976.* Vol. 32.1-1016. Washington, DC: GPO.

U.S. Department of State, Office of the Historian. (2013). "SALT II, 1972–1980." In *Foreign Relations of the United States, 1969–1976.* Vol. 33.1-1020. Washington, DC: GPO.

250 REFERENCES

Van-Helten, J. J. (1982). "Empire and High Finance: South Africa and the International Gold Standard 1890–1914." *Journal of African History* 23(4): 529–548.

Van Munster, R. (2007). "Review Essay: Security on a Shoestring: A Hitchhiker's Guide to Critical Schools of Security in Europe." *Cooperation and Conflict* 42(2): 235–243.

Veblen, T. (1899). *Theory of the Leisure Class*. New York: Macmillan.

Volgy, T. J., Corbetta, R., Grant, K. A., and Baird, R. (2011). *Major Powers and the Quest for Status in International Politics: Global and Regional Perspectives*. New York: Palgrave Macmillan.

Volgy, T. J., Corbetta, R., Rhamey, P., Baird, J. P., and Grant, K. (2014). "Status Considerations in International Politics and the Rise of Regional Powers." In T. V. Paul, D. W. Larson, and W. C. Wohlforth (Eds.), *Status in World Politics* (pp. 58–84). New York: Cambridge University Press.

Volgy, T. J. and Mayhall, S. (1995). "Status Inconsistency and International War: Exploring the Effects of Systemic Change." *International Studies Quarterly* 39(1): 67–84.

Vucetic, S. (2011a). *The Anglosphere: A Genealogy of a Racialized Identity in International Relations*. Stanford: Stanford University Press.

Vucetic, S. (2011b). "Genealogy as a Research Tool in International Relations." *Review of International Studies* 37(3): 1295–1312.

Waever, O. (1995). "Securitization and Desecuritization." In R. Lipschutz (Ed.), *On Security* (pp. 46–86). New York: Columbia University Press.

Wallace, M. D. (1971). "Power, Status, and International War." *Journal of Peace Research* 8(1): 23–35.

Walt, S. M. (1990). *The Origins of Alliance*. Ithaca, NY: Cornell University Press.

Waltz, K. N. (1979). *Theory of International Politics*. Long Grove, IL: Waveland Press.

Waltz, K. N. (1981). "The Spread of Nuclear Weapons: More May Be Better." Adelphi Papers No. 171. London: International Institute for Strategic Studies.

Ward, S. (2013). "Race, Status, and Japanese Revisionism in the Early 1930s." *Security Studies* 22(4): 607–639.

Ward, S. (2017a). "Lost in Translation: Social Identity Theory and the Study of Status in World Politics." *International Studies Quarterly* 61(4): 821–834.

Ward, S. (2017b). *Status and the Challenge of Rising Powers*. Cambridge: Cambridge University Press.

Ward, S. (2020). "Status from Fighting? Reassessing the Relationship between Conflict Involvement and Diplomatic Rank. *International Interactions* 46(2): 274–290. https://doi.org/10.1080/03050629.2020.1708350.

Ward, S. (2022). "Decline and Disintegration: National Status Loss and Domestic Conflict in Post-disaster Spain." *International Security* 46(4): 91–129.

Wendt, A. (1992). "Anarchy Is What States Make of It: The Social Construction of Power Politics." *International Organization* 46(2): 391–425.

Wendt, A. (1999). *Social Theory of International Politics*. Cambridge: Cambridge University Press.

Width, H. (2002). "Finsk skole—best i klassen." *Aftenposten Morgen*, February 2.

Wilhelmsen, J. (2017). "How Does War Become a Legitimate Undertaking? Re-engaging the Post-structuralist Foundation of Securitization Theory." *Cooperation and Conflict* 52(2): 166–183.

Williams, C. (2013). "'Our War History in Cartoons Is Unique': J. M. Staniforth, British Public Opinion, and the South African War, 1899–1902." *War in History* 20(4): 491–525.

Wittgenstein, L. (1958). *Philosophical Investigations*. Trans. G. E. M. Anscombe. Oxford: Blackwell.

REFERENCES 251

Wohlforth, W. C. (1993). *The Elusive Balance: Power and Perceptions during the Cold War.* Ithaca, NY: Cornell University Press.

Wohlforth, W. C. (2009). "Unipolarity, Status Competition, and Great Power War." *World Politics* 61(1): 28–57.

Wohlforth, W. C. (2014). "Status Dilemmas and Interstate Conflict." In T. V. Paul, D. W. Larson, and W. C. Wohlforth (Eds.), *Status in World Politics* (pp. 115–140). Cambridge: Cambridge University Press.

Wohlforth, W. C. (2019). "Contribution to H-Diplo/ISSF Roundtable 10-27 on Steven Ward. Status and the Challenge of Rising Powers." Vol. 10, No. 27. https://networks.h-net.org/node/28443/discussions/4099020/h-diploissf-roundtable-10-27-steven-ward%C2%A0-status-and-challenge.

Wohlforth, W. C., de Carvalho, B., Leira, H., and Neumann, I. B. (2017). "Moral Authority and Status in International Relations: Good States and the Social Dimension of Status Seeking." *Review of International Studies* 44(3): 526–546.

Wohlstetter, A. (1959). "The Delicate Balance of Terror: Condensed from *Foreign Affairs* January, 1959." *Survival* 37(2): 8–17.

Wolf, R. (2011). "Respect and Disrespect in International Politics: The Significance of Status Recognition." *International Theory* 3(1): 105–142.

Wolf, R. (2019). "Taking Interaction Seriously: Asymmetrical Roles and the Behavioral Foundations of Status." *European Journal of International Relations* 25(4): 1186–1211.

Yanık, L. K. and Subotić, J. (2021). "Cultural Heritage as Status Seeking: The International Politics of Turkey's Restoration Wave." *Cooperation and Conflict* 56(3): 245–263.

Yanow, D. (2015a). "Neither Rigorous nor Objective? Interrogating Criteria for Knowledge Claims in Interpretive Science." In D. Yanow and P. Schwartz-Shea (Eds.), *Interpretation and Method* (pp. 152–178). New York: Routledge.

Yanow, D. (2015b). "Thinking Interpretively: Philosophical Presuppositions and the Human Sciences." In D. Yanow and P. Schwartz-Shea (Eds.), *Interpretation and Method* (pp. 5–26). New York: Routledge.

Yanow, D. (2009). "Ways of Knowing: Passionate Humility and Reflective Practice in Research and Management." *American Review of Public Administration* 39(6): 579–601.

Yanow, D. and Schwartz-Shea, P. (Eds.) (2015). *Interpretation and Method: Empirical Research Methods and the Interpretive Turn.* New York: Routledge.

Yunzhu, Y. (2008). "Chinese Nuclear Policy and the Future of Minimum Deterrence." In C. P. Twomey (Ed.), *Perspectives on Sino-American Strategic Nuclear Issues: Initiatives in Strategic Studies: Issues and Policies* (pp. 111–124). New York: Palgrave Macmillan.

Zala, B. (2017). "Great Power Management and Ambiguous Order in Nineteenth-Century International Society." *Review of International Studies* 43(2): 367–388.

Zalewski, M. (1996). "'All These Theories yet the Bodies Keep Piling Up': Theory, Theorists, Theorising." In K. Booth, S. Smith, and M. Zalewski (Eds.), *International Theory: Positivism and Beyond* (pp. 340–353). Cambridge: Cambridge University Press.

Zarakol, A. (2010a). *After Defeat: How the East Learned to Live with the West.* New York: Cambridge University Press.

Zarakol, A. (2010b). "Ontological (In)Security and State Denial of Historical Crimes: Turkey and Japan." *International Relations* 24(1): 3–23.

Zarakol, A. (2017). "Theorizing Hierarchies: An Introduction." In A. Zarakol (Ed.), *Hierarchies in World Politics* (pp. 1–15). London: Cambridge University Press.

Zhao, Y. (2020). "Two Decades of Havoc: A Synthesis of Criticism against PISA." *Journal of Educational Change* 2: 245–266.

Index

For the benefit of digital users, indexed terms that span two pages (e.g., 52–53) may, on occasion, appear on only one of those pages.

Tables and figures are indicated by *t* and *f* following the page number

Adler-Nissen, Rebecca, 206–7
Aftenposten, 151–52
Arbeiderpartiet (Norwegian Labour Party), 148, 153
arms. *See* nuclear arms

Baden-Powell, Robert, 102–3
barbarism. *See* methods of barbarism and barbarous
barbarous, 113–14, 210–11
Boer War, 15, 29–30, 33–34, 79–80, 83–84, 85–121, 205, 208–9, 211, 216–17, 223, 225–26, 230–31
Bull, Hedley, 75
Buzan, Barry, 22–23, 61–62, 69, 168

Canada, 100–1, 109–10
Carter, Jimmy, 159–60, 173–74, 177–78, 178nn.44–45, 179, 181, 194–97, 194n.94, 195n.99, 196nn.101–102, 198–99
Centre Party (Norway), 153
Chamberlain, Joseph, 89–90, 91, 94–95, 115–16, 210–11
China, 15, 167
Churchill, Winston, 157–58
civilization, 17, 91–92, 104–5
standard of, 84–85, 111, 113–15
Clemet, Kristin, 140–41, 142, 144–45, 146–47, 152. *See also* Olympic Games, Sports Metaphor and Programme for International Student Assessment (PISA)
club. *See* status clubs
Cold War, 157–59, 165n.15, 167, 168, 173–74, 200. *See also* nuclear arms

concentration camps, 30, 79–80, 86n.8, 105n.52, 110–12, 117–19, 119n.84, 120–21, 210–11, 225–26
Conservative Party (UK), 87, 91, 100–1, 107–8
constructivism, 17–18, 26–27, 62n.9, 67, 73–74, 74n.27, 206–7, 213–14
Copenhagen School of Security, 22–23

Dagbladet, 139–40, 141–42, 152
Daily Mail, 98
Darwinism. *See* neo-Darwinism
deterrence, 173–74, 186–87, 200–1
nuclear, 55, 162, 163, 164, 218–19
discourse, *14*, 18, 30–33, 56–57, 59, 63–66, 67, 69, 73–74, 75, 80–81, 101–2, 124, 135–36, 161–62, 205–7, 208
British, 29–30, 84–85, 88, 90–95, 96–97, 99, 100–1, 105, 109, 111, 114–17, 118–19, 217
domestic, 3–4, 8–9, 28–29, 66–67, 68–69, 119, 129, 215–16
and emotion, 78–80
gendered, 121, 199
Norwegian, 140–42, 145–47, 149–53, 212
US, 165–67, 176–79, 182–86, 188–91, 192–93, 194–95, 196–99, 201–2
Doyle, Arthur Conan, 100

Eurocentrism, 212

Ford, Gerald, 16–17, 159–60, 173–74, 173n.26, 175n.33, 179n.45, 181, 182, 184n.57, 186, 187–90, 188n.67, 188n.70, 190nn.77–78, 191–95, 195n.98

254 INDEX

game theory, 162, 199
gender, 118–19, 120–21
  equality, 122–23, 127–28, 131
  See also masculinity; women
Germany, 40–41, 72–73, 91–92, 92n.19,
  97–98, 139
Glaser, Charles, 157–58, 162, 164, 165,
  167, 168–69

Hansard, 73n.24, 87n.10, 90n.14, 91n.16,
  91n.17, 92nn.19–21, 93n.24, 93n.28,
  94nn.29–32, 98n.39, 110n.55,
  112n.61, 113n.63, 113n.64, 113n.66,
  114nn.67–69, 115n.72, 115n.74,
  116nn.75–77, 116n.79, 117n.80,
  117nn.81–82, 224t, 226
Hansen, Lene, 22, 73–74, 206–7
Hobhouse, Emily, 114–15, 115n.71,
  116n.77, 210–11
Hobson, John Atkison, 85–86
Høyre (Norwegian Conservative Party),
  148

ideal-type, 38–40, 56–57, 209
identity, 10, 13, 22, 26–27, 42–43, 49, 54–
  55, 67–68
  collective, 11–12
  formation; positional, 25–26, 26n.45,
  70–71, 73–75, 77, 204–5, 206–7
  See also intersubjectivity
ICBM. *See* intercontinental ballistic
  missile
interpretivism, 33–34, 221–22
intercontinental ballistic missile, 159–60,
  164, 175–76, 177, 193–94
intersubjectivity, 3–4, 8, 11–12, 15, 37,
  56–57, 60–61, 81, 127–28, 131–
  32, 134

Jackson Amendment, 179, 182,
  183–84. *See also* Strategic Arms
  Limitations Talks
Jackson, Henry M. 179–81, 182, 183–85,
  188–89, 201–2. *See also* Jackson
  Amendment
Jackson, Patrick, 25
Jervis, Robert, 157–58, 159–61, 166–
  67, 171–72
Joint Chiefs of Staff, 172, 176–77

Kissinger, Henry, 157–58, 171n.23, 173–
  74, 175–76, 177–78, 180, 184n.56,
  187–90, 192–93, 194–95, 198, 199,
  210–11, 216–17

Liberal Party (UK), 108–9, 110–11,
  112, 113
Lord Grandby, 80, 93n.25
Lord Landsdown, 89–90, 90n.13
Lord Salisbury, 92–93, 93n.24,
  101n.47, 108–9

McNamara, Robert, 165–66, 190–91
MAD. *See* mutual assured destruction
Mafeking, in Boer War, 77, 87–88, 95–96,
  102–3, 106–7, 118
masculinity, 36–37, 115, 121. *See*
  also gender
Mercer, Jonathan, 2–3, 6–7, 10, 15, 29–30,
  83–84, 88, 96–97, 105, 106–7, 108–
  10, 120, 217, 223–25
methodology, 1–2, 5, 7–8, 8n.17, 14n.28,
  18, 18n.37, 25, 32–34, 55–56, 60, 61,
  62–64, 65–66, 67–68, 78, 81, 159, 203,
  204–5, 221
methods of barbarism, 30, 84–85, 113
Milner, Sir Alfred, 87, 89–90
misrecognition, 28, 67
mutual assured
  destruction, 159–61, 162, 164–67,
  168–69, 200

neo-Darwinism, in British discourse, 44,
  91–92, 100, 115n.72
Neumann, Iver B. 18n.36, 75, 213–
  14, 231–32
New York Times, 177–78, 179, 224t
Nixon, Richard, 1, 1nn.1–2, 157, 165–66,
  173–75, 173n.27, 175nn.33–34, 177–
  78, 177n.41, 179–80, 181, 182, 186,
  187–88, 197–98, 197n.106, 198n.107,
  198n.108, 199n.112, 199
Non-Proliferation
  Treaty, 74–75
Norway. *See* discourse; Norwegian
nuclear arms
  control, 31–32, 33–34, 174–75
  race, 1, 55, 157–62, 165, 166–67, 168–
  69, 172, 174–75, 180–81, 200

nuclear revolution, 157–59, 164, 165–67, 170, 173–74, 200–1

OECD. *See* Organisation for Economic Development and Co-operation
Olympic Games, 15, 23–24, 36–37, 49–53, 69, 81, 84, 127, 168, 170–71, 200, 204–5
  in framing of PISA-ranking, 122, 135, 140–41, 152–53
  See also sports metaphor
Olympics. *See* Olympic Games
Onuf, Nicholas, 168, 197
Organisation for Economic Development and Co-operation (OECD), , 122, 124–25, 128–29, 134–35, 138–41, 140–41n.15, 142–43, 144–45, 146, 147, 148–49, 150–51, 224t, 226–27. *See also* Programme for International Student Assessment (PISA); sports methaphor

PISA. *See* Programme for International Student Assessment
positional identity. *See* identity
Pouliot, Vincent, 8n.17, 15
pride, 3–4, 13, 30, 36–37, 39, 52–55, 58–59, 69, 72, 77, 79–80, 84, 86–87, 94–95, 96–97, 100, 103–4, 105, 106, 109, 111, 115–16, 117–18, 119, 120–21, 127, 130, 135–36, 148, 208–9, 214–15, 217–18
prisoner's dilemma, 162, 167, 169
prizes, 39, 52–54, 55, 58–59, 69, 76, 94–95, 127, 130–31, 135–36, 162, 169–71, 183–84, 200, 201–2, 216–17. *See also* pride
Programme for International Student Assessment (PISA), 30–31, 44–45, 62–63, 77–78, 134–49, 209, 210–11, 212, 216–17, 226, 230–32
Putin, Vladimir, 158–59

race, 100–1, 126–27
  and civilization, 30, 91–92, 115n.72
  See also civilization and neo-Darwinism
rankings, 1–2, 6–7, 7n.15, 19–20, 42–43, 45–50, 53, 56–57, 67–68, 71, 124, 125, 127–28, 153–55, 212–13, 214–15
  international, 122–23, 132, 210, 227
  numerical, 123–24, 129

PISA, 30–31, 44–45, 62–63, 77–78, 122, 124–25, 128–29, 134, 139–40, 140–41n.15, 144, 147–48, 149, 150–51, 152, 210–11, 216–17, 226–27, 230–31
  relative, 126–27, 148, 149–50, 211–12
realism, 1, 10–11, 46–47
  defensive, 164–65, 167
  neorealist, 61
  philosophical, 64–65
  structural, 171–72
realists, 53, 94–95, 100–1, 163, 174, 218–19
  on nuclear arms, 31–32, 157–58
recognition, 57, 72, 75, 83–84, 112–13, 133, 206–7, 218–19
  international, 26–28, 29–30, 105, 119, 120–21, 208–9
  practices of, 26–27, 131–32
  See also misrecognition
reflexivity, 152, 153–54, 156, 231–32
refugee crisis, 72–73
Russia, 86, 91–92, 158–59, 160–61, 167, 187, 206n.4, 217. *See also* Soviet Union

SALT. *See* Strategic Arms Limitations Talks
securitization theory, 61–62, 68–69, 70, 78, 133
  and methodology, 32–34
security dilemma, 163–64, 165, 168, 200
Sjøberg, Svein, on PISA in Norway, 135, 137, 139–40, 143–44, 149–50, 152 n. 106. *See also* Olympic Games
Socialist Left Party Norway, 153
sociological, 14, 24, 29–30, 37–42, 43–44, 84–207
Solberg, Erna, 143–44
South Africa, 80, 86, 87, 91, 92–93, 94–95, 96–97, 100–1, 108, 111, 112, 113, 114, 117
Soviet Union, 157–58, 159, 164, 165–67, 168, 174–75, 177–78, 179, 191–92, 197–98, 200. *See also* nuclear arms; Russia; Strategic Arms Limitations Talks (SALT)
sports metaphor, 76–78, 103–4, 117–18, 197

INDEX

status clubs, 19–20, 24–25, 45, 46, 46n.12, 48f, 48–49, 205–6, 211–12

status hierarchy, 3–4, 7–8, 13–14, 15, 16, 18–19, 21–22, 24–26, 28, 30–31, 32, 34–35, 40–41, 42, 44, 46–47, 48f, 49, 53, 55–56, 57, 62–63, 65–66, 67, 68–69, 70–71, 72–74, 77, 80–81, 84, 88, 108–9, 123–24, 125–26, 129–30, 141–42, 148, 150, 155, 170–71, 180–81, 201–2, 203, 204, 205, 207–9, 211–12, 213–14, 216

status seeking, 2–4, 5–8, 10–12, 13–14, 15, 18–19, 20–21, 23n.42, 24–25, 37–38, 39, 43–44, 45, 46, 57, 83–84, 87–88, 105, 131–32, 155–56, 204–5, 206n.4, 211, 213–14, 216, 223

Stoltenberg, Jens, 143–44

Strategic Arms Limitations Talks, 1, 16–17, 31–32, 159–62, 168–97, 200–2, 205, 209, 212, 216–17, 228, 230–31

submarine-launched ballistic missile (SLBM), 159–60, 164–65, 175–76, 177

SV. *See* Socialist Left Party Norway

TIS. *See* theories of international status

The *Times*, 92n.19, 94–95, 97–98, 99, 104, 105n.52, 114–16

theories of status (TIS), 30–33, 55–56, 65–66, 67, 88, 90–91, 92–93, 95, 149–50, 208, 212
  competition, 18–19, 20–21, 26–27, 32, 33–34, 59–85, 121, 123–24, 128–29, 159
  international, 16–18, 26, 27–29, 80–81, 113, 118–20, 155, 205
  structural, 5–8, 15

Trump, Donald, 208–9

USSR. *See* Soviet Union

Walt, Stephen, 68–69

Waltz, Kenneth, 157–58, 163–64, 165, 218–19

Wohlforth, William C., 5, 6–7, 67–69, 189, 203, 217–18

women, in the Boer War, 111–13, 114, 115, 116–17, 120–21. *See also* Boer War; concentration camps; gender; masculinity